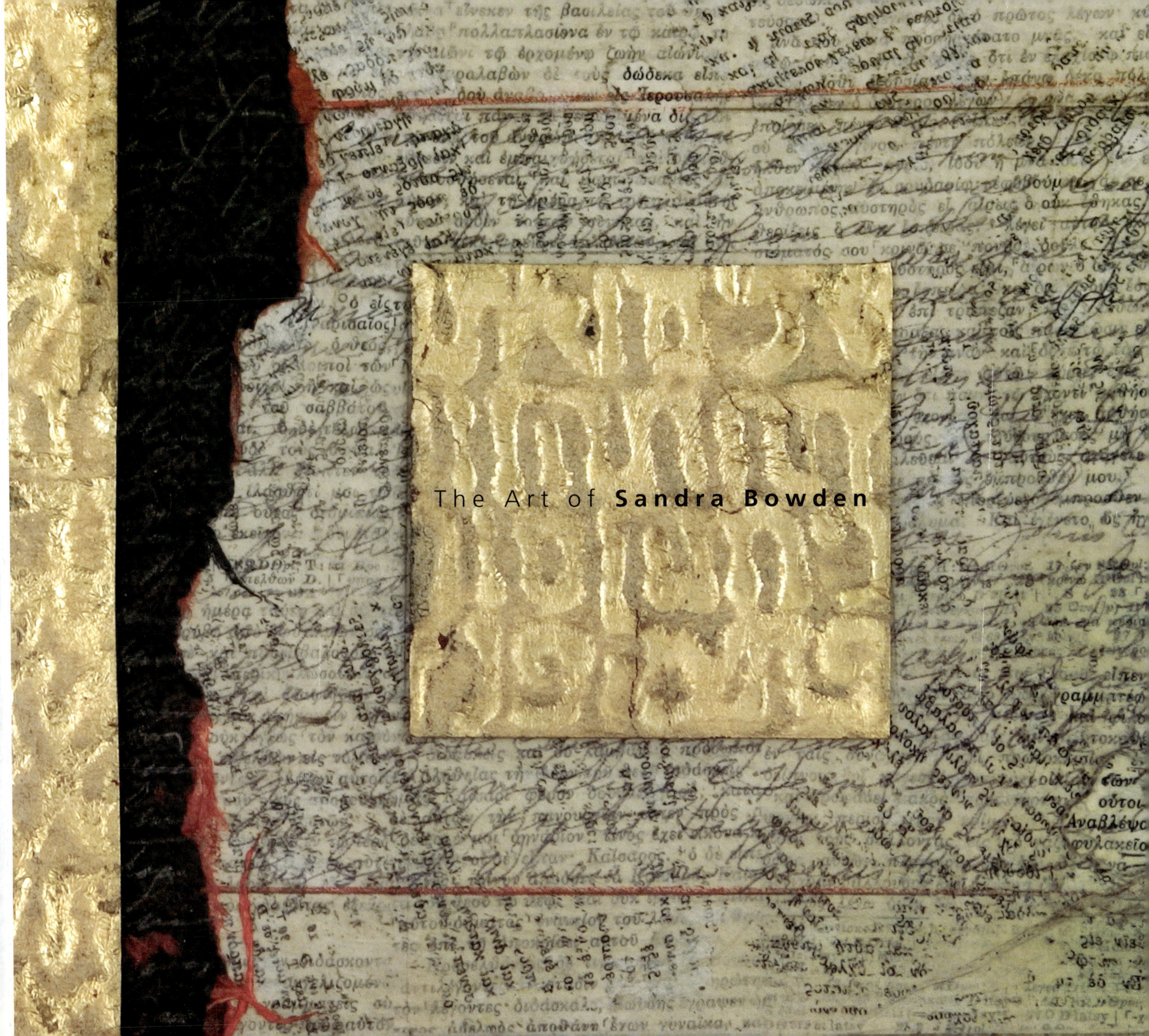
The Art of Sandra Bowden

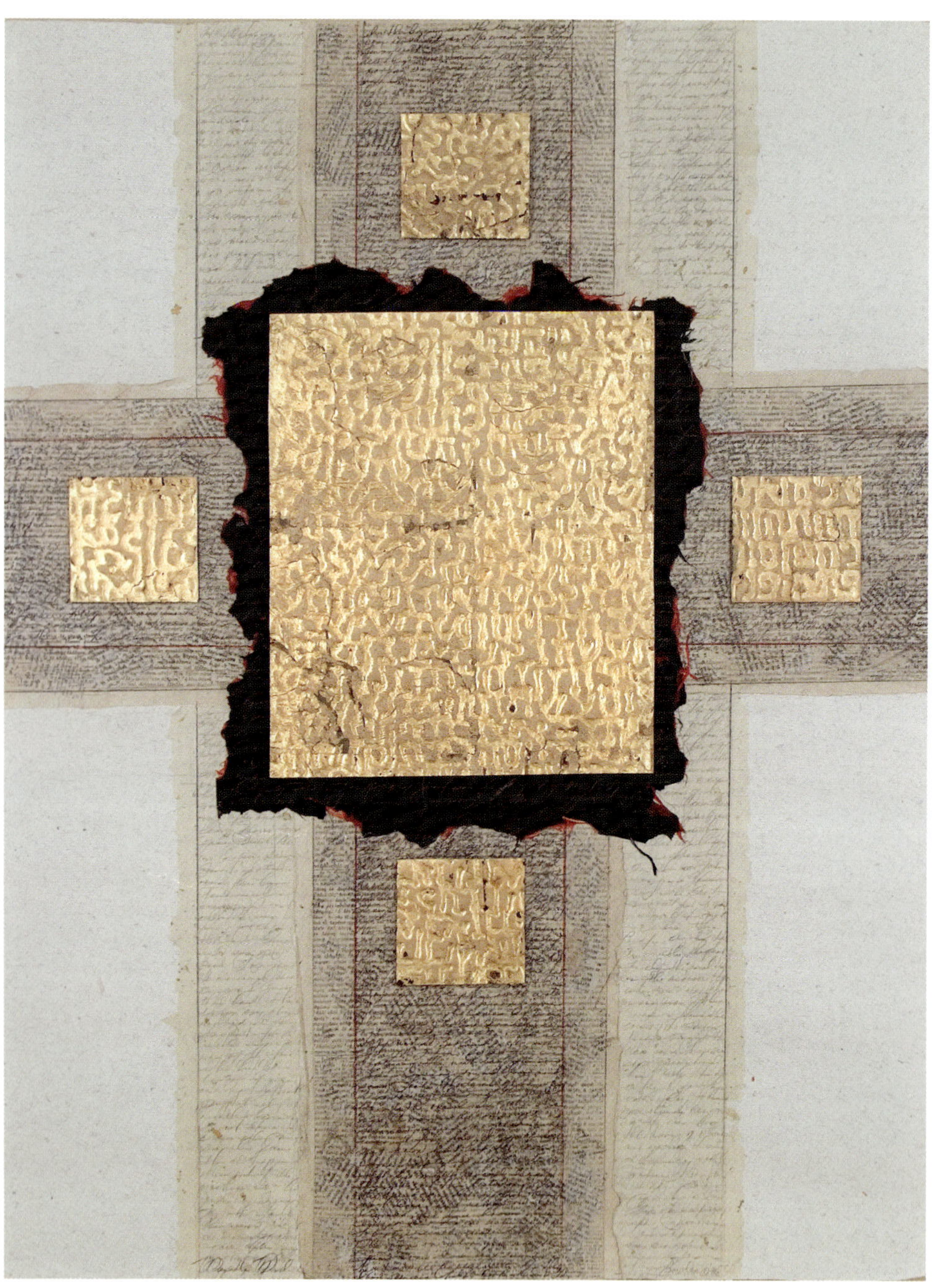

The Art of **Sandra Bowden**

JAMES ROMAINE

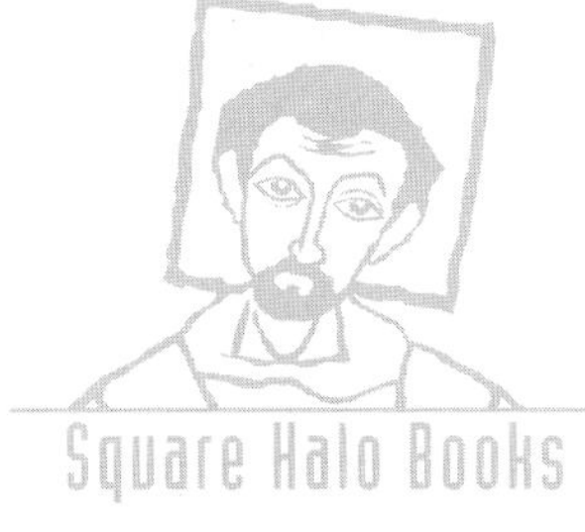

Go to www.SandraBowden.com to see more of the artist's work.

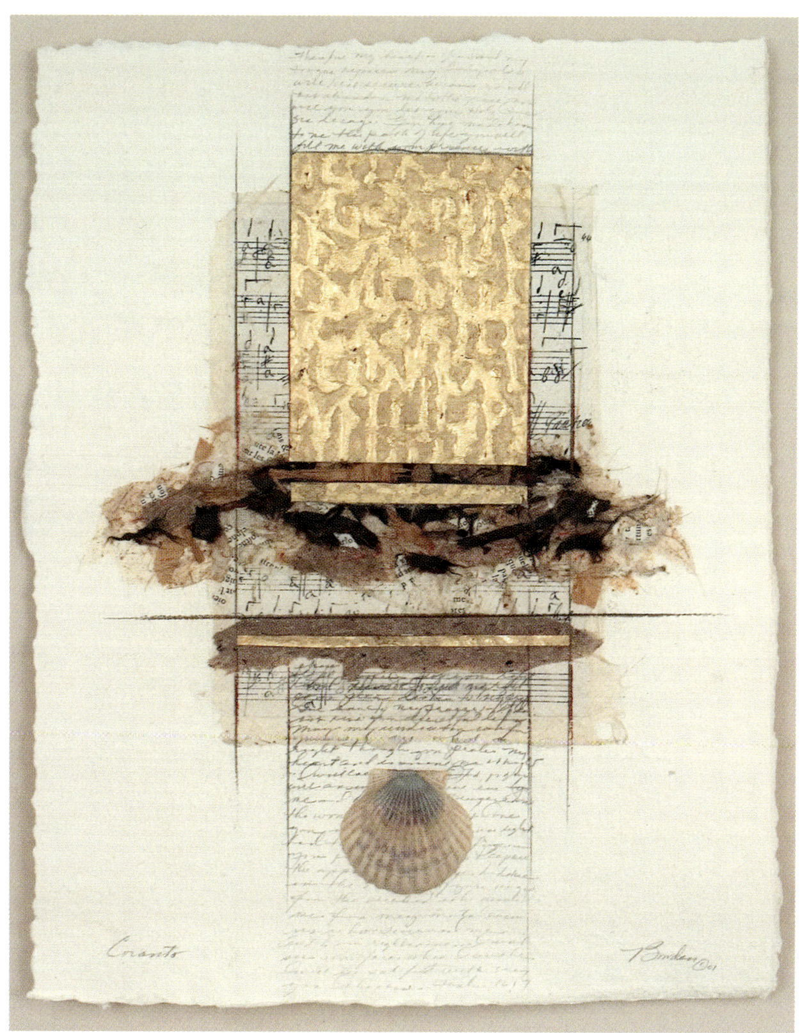

In Christian art, the square halo identified a living person presumed to be a saint. Square Halo Books is devoted to publishing works that present contextually sensitive biblical studies, and practical instruction consistent with the Doctrines of the Reformation. The goal of Square Halo Books is to provide materials useful for encouraging and equipping the saints.

Contents

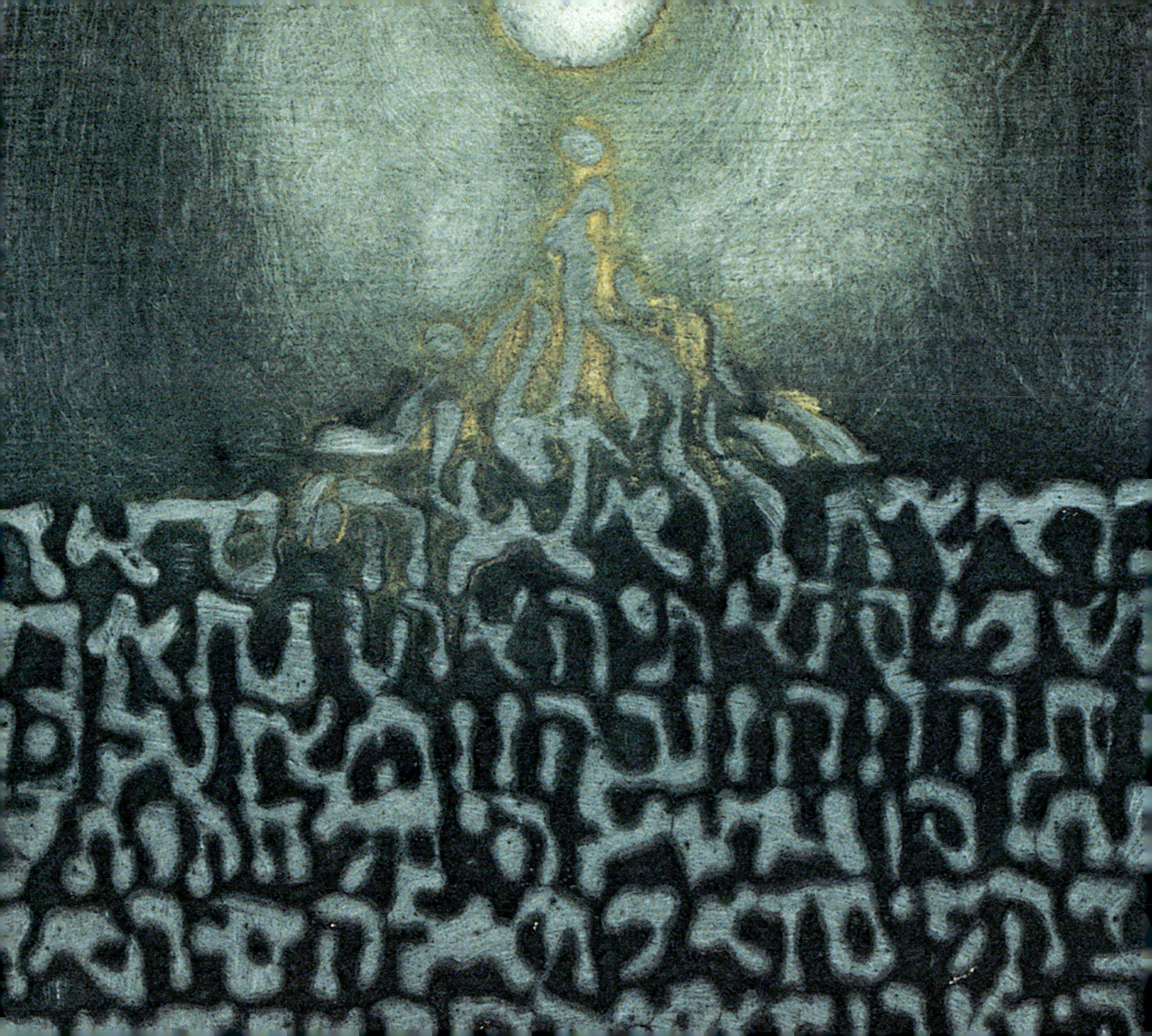

I have known Sandra Bowden and her work as artist and teacher for almost twenty years—only half of her active career. During this time I have been privileged to witness her impact on individuals, institutions, and whole systems of art and art patronage.

Simply put, Sandra Bowden is a *phenomenon.*

Though she has not, to my knowledge, held a formal teaching post at a college or university, she has infected countless people with a love of art and art discourse. As president of Christians in the Visual Arts (CIVA) she has acted as ambassador for the visual arts to hundreds of churches, colleges, and other institutions nationally and internationally.

As you will read in the eloquent essays within these pages, Bowden's work derives its inspiration and strength from a deep involvement in visual exegesis—that is, in a visual parsing of ancient biblical texts—forming an iconography that harkens back to the word and image of God in the Jewish and Christian scriptures.

Bowden's ministry—for that is what it must be called—is manifold.

As artist, she has birthed literally thousands of paintings, drawings, prints, collages, and artbooks which deeply engage the viewer in a response relationship with ancient tradition as well as contemporary artistic issues. As informal teacher and mentor, she has encouraged and inspired countless others to address the perennial hopes and problems of human community and its historic connections with language and image in the biblical tradition. As administrator and ambassador for CIVA, she has bequeathed a passionate visionary outreach with an immanently practical approach: she gets the job done whatever it may be, whether cultivating relationships with institutional leaders or stuffing envelopes to get the next brochure into the hands of CIVA's fifteen-hundred-plus membership (a phenomenon in itself, largely indebted to her efforts).

In the pages that follow, you will encounter representative images from each of Bowden's several themes, and you will read the careful interpretations of artist colleagues and historians. These critical texts are generated by the loving life work of this artist who is so deeply committed to the interrelationship of text and image. There is rich layering here—in both the secondary texts of critical appraisal and in the primary texts of Bowden's art.

Each of the essayists in this volume addresses a specific theme or genre of Bowden's *oeuvre.* Grouped according to either thematic foci or underlying inspiration, each chapter examines some important aspect of the artist's process—either from the standpoint of theory or of practice. For instance, in her essay on Bowden's sources, Jean Bloch Rosensaft, Exhibitions Director at Hebrew Union College–Jewish Institute of Religion, discusses the artist's *visual midrash*—visual interpretations of ancient "tels, texts, and time"—celebrating forty years of interaction with Jewish and Christian archeological relics.

Art historians Wayne Roosa and Karen

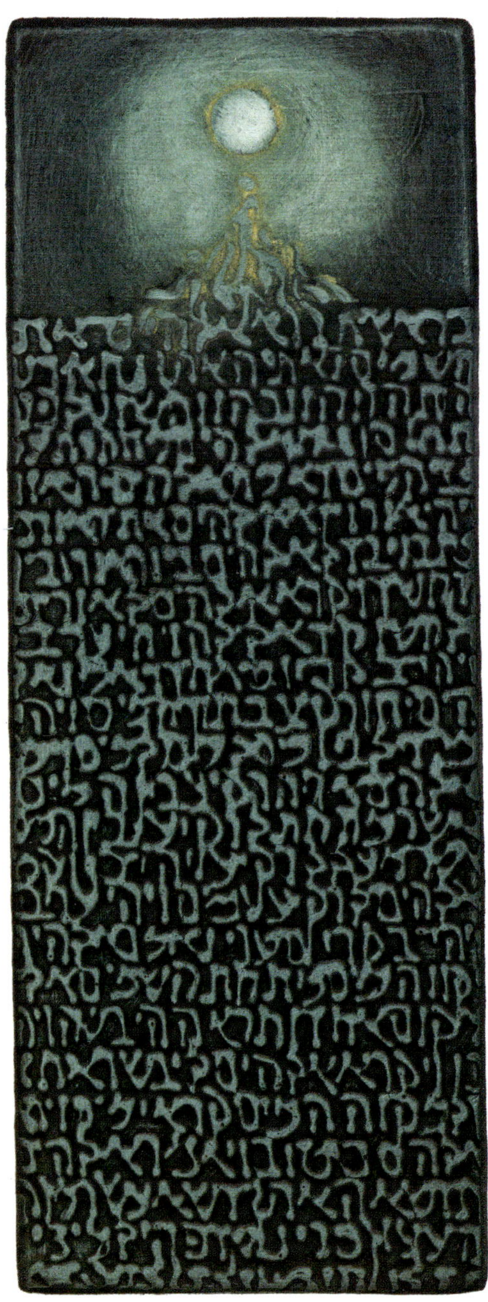

Mulder treat Bowden's use of language and materials respectively, giving an historical context to both crucial aspects of the artist's work. Professor Roosa offers a marvelous overview of the influence that both spoken and written language have had on Bowden—particularly the Bible, with its declaration of the Word as both incarnate God and as medium of creation. Roosa explores the mysteriously layered meanings of language—as speech-act giving form to the void, and as container of the world.

Mulder writes an ambitious context-setting essay on Bowden's use of symbolic materials, enabling the reader to grasp the complexity and richness of the historical and theological associations embedded in the work. Her careful examination of the various phases of the artist's evolving technique makes Mulder's essay invaluable to this volume.

Edward Knippers, long-time artist friend and co-conspirator in art collecting, comments on Sandra Bowden's use of the most compelling of visual metaphors: the cross of Christ. Knippers wonderfully describes and discusses how the cruciform shape is a constant across many phases of Bowden's artistic development. He shows how this central motif in Bowden's art employs theological, historical, and visual vocabulary to establish itself as the pivotal symbol of Bowden's artistic output: Word made Flesh and word made art.

Ena Giurescu Heller offers an essay that celebrates Bowden's "medievalism"—the artist's penchant for gilding textual fragments and paintings with beautiful texture and color over old Bible pages or manuscripts, harkening back to ancient medieval book illuminations. Heller,

who is director of the Museum of Biblical Art (MOBIA), knows her ancient books: her training as a medievalist at the Institute of Fine Arts gives her the expertise to comment meaningfully on the source of much of Bowden's inspiration.

Terrence Dempsey, director of the Museum of Contemporary Religious Art (MOCRA) in St. Louis, renders a fitting exposition of the precedents for Bowden's series of reliquary "art books"—using the Book of Kells as a paradigm for how the artist attempts to lend mystery and power to this contemporary art form. Book as object, book as container of precious secrets, book as metaphor for God's protective presence—these pivotal aspects of Bowden's work are unpacked beautifully by Dempsey.

Finally, James Romaine, art historian at the New York Center for Arts and Media Studies (NYCAMS) and editor of this volume, gives an introduction to Sandra Bowden's most typical stylistic and formal strategy: collage. He shows how Bowden has incorporated and commented upon this modern art form and lent it a certain dignity and transparency of meaning. Comparing and contrasting Bowden with contemporaries like Robert Rauschenberg, Romaine explicates the subtle difference that results from making collage which is influenced by a biblical worldview—coherence and understandability being the byproducts of a confident belief in God and God's authorial intent (as contrasted with the "absolute uncertainty" of deconstructionism).

All seven essays contained in this volume testify to the rich and varied aesthetic and theological texture of Sandra Bowden's art. In a sense, this book is an archeological site of sorts: dig deeply and you will find much to satisfy,

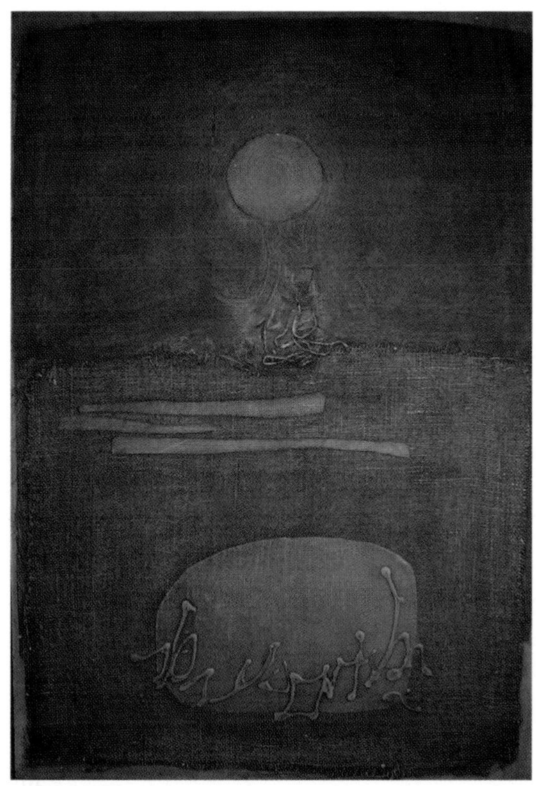

much to mystify, and much to draw you deeper into that central mystery of our existence—the human presence as speaker, writer, and iconographer. The artist herself becomes a medium through which a great tradition is reiterated in multiform expression. As Ed Knippers says in his essay on Bowden's use of the cross, the artist has answered the amnesia of our times with a "resurrection" of the robust tradition of meaningful iconic imagery—drawing from sources as diverse as Israeli archeological tels to Renaissance religious painting.

It is an honor to curate the retrospective exhibition representing forty years of artistic output by this wonderful artist—and a great pleasure to see this work and this book reach a wider audience still. It is my earnest desire to see Sandra Bowden's influence extended and established beyond its already considerable scope. And I see this influence as wholly life giving and richly meaningful in a time of scant hope.

Bowden's art points toward the possibility of reconciliation in the cultural traditions of Judaism and Christianity, the siblings of the biblical tradition that have historically acted as rivals rather than relatives. Her art reveals in celebratory manner the rich heritage these cultures share and the hope that the universal language of art can be a bridge of communion and community.

At Barrington Center for the Arts, Gordon College, we eagerly look forward to the power of this text and these images to bless and encourage and stretch the many people who will read this book and encounter the art of this extraordinary artist.

Bruce Herman
Gallery Director
Barrington Center for the Arts
Gordon College

Sandra Bowden may be one of the boldest artists of her generation. Her *oeuvre,* a record of an artistic and spiritual journey of more than forty years, tests the boundaries that define artistic expression. Most professional artists find their voice, some sooner than others, some stronger than others, and settle into a comfortable production of work based on a predictable set of visual vocabulary. We call this a "signature style," and, for many artists, their style sets certain parameters on what their art can be, a Faustian exchange for the safety and marketability that such limits bring. Sandra Bowden never made that deal. Instead, she has plunged herself into exploring the systems and limits of vocabulary and language itself.

The central concern of Bowden's art has been the intersections, correspondences and distinctions of textual and visual language. The viewer is meant to "read" her works, like *Ancient Writings* (Figure 21), in multiple ways at once, with each informing our understanding of the other, creating a textual layering of meaning. The exploration of language as a vehicle for communication and meaning is not particular to her art. Indeed, it has recently become fashionable for artists, especially painters, to critique their own vocabulary. The question of meaning, whether it exists at all or can be communicated through art, remains a contentiously fought battleground for various camps of art and literary critics. Bowden's interest in language and meaning not only predates these trends but shares little in common with them.

Many of the artists and theorists engaged in deconstructing language have originated from an opinion that there are no absolutes, that the critique of language undermines communication itself. Their work, often a reflection of artistic "avant-garde" mannerism and religious relativism, becomes a vacant, unintelligible muttering. As doubt turns to despair, many artists have simply given up, concluding that meaning is a myth and that the author is dead.

Bowden's interest in language is rooted in her faith in a living, personal, and creative God we can know, in part, through the veiled mysteries of the lingual systems, textual and visual, with which He has endowed us. She believes not only that communication is possible but also that it is vital, that we were created with a need for expression which is manifested in our urge to create. Her work is rooted in a history that extends to the beginning of time and space itself, to the Genesis event in which God revealed his creative nature. If being created in the image of God is the origin of human creativity, what could be more natural than becoming an artist?

If Bowden's art commences from a sense of certainty regarding the origin of her creativity, it quickly moves into the realm of mystery. Through her innovative uses of languages, written and visual, she opens up possibilities and challenges that no single reading could fatigue. Although she often utilizes written text, a media that in the Protestant tradition has been associated with revealed and infallible truth, she has constantly

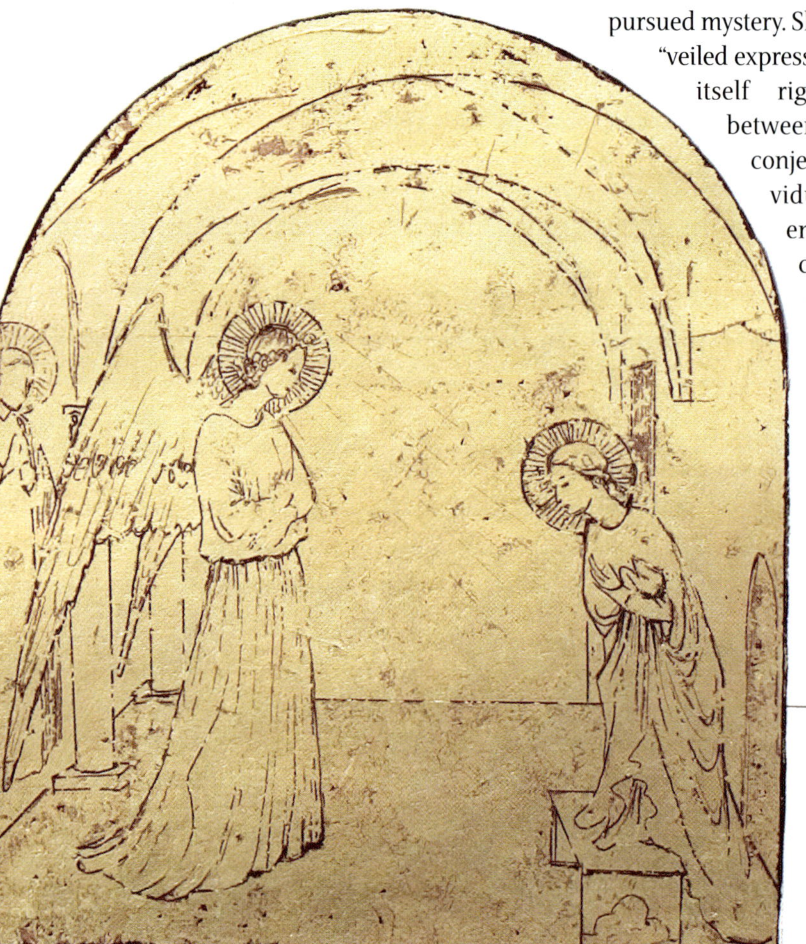

pursued mystery. She describes her art as a "veiled expression that doesn't explain itself right .away." Balanced between decipherability and conjecture, her art, both individual works and her entire *oeuvre*, is about connections between seemingly disparate elements that connect or cross for fleeting moments in which we catch a glimpse of something, something true, that draws us deeper into complex narrative beyond cognitive logic into faith.

Sandra Bowden approaches her creativity as a natural extension of her faith, but this important fact does not make her unique in the history of art. Any study of art, visual and otherwise, from across time and world cultures would find that a vast majority of it has very close connections with religious practice. In the Western tradition to which Bowden is an heir, Christianity has played a leading role in the development of the visual arts over the past two thousand years as one of its most prolific patrons. Indeed, it would be impossible, and certainly misleading, to discuss the history of the visual arts without includ-ing the role the Church has played in providing financial, intellectual, and spiritual resources. As a result of its active support of the arts over two millennia, many of the most important artists, at least in the West, have been Christians or have worked in the service of the Church.

In *Art History 101: Icons of Western Art,* Bowden explores how artists from different historical periods and faith positions have continued to search for forms that make the invisible visible. She tests our recognition of such diverse works as Fra Angelico's *Annunciation* (Figure 6), Rogier van der Weyden's *Deposition* (Figure 91), and Claude Monet's *Rouen Cathedral* (Figure 93). These pieces' gilded surfaces remind one of ancient icons, windows into the immaterial, while their roughly sketched forms alert us to the tactility of their material surface. She appropriates these forms from the past in order to explore their qualities of design that transcend the barriers of time; they challenge her to reinterpret them in ways that make them resonate in the present.

We live in an image-driven and multicultural context where the arts are one of the principal forums in which the values of a society are contested and promoted. Believing that as a Christian she has something unique and critical to contribute to the current dialogue, Bowden proposes what seems strikingly original, even controversial: that we can make sense of our present moment by seeing it rooted in history. Her art addresses issues that are both timeless and current; it calls us out of our daily routines to meditate on eternal things. Ancient forms of civilization are reflected in contemporary visual vocabulary. In *Walls of Stone* (Figure 31),

Midnight Wall (Figure 32), and *Night Wall* (Figure 5), she bridges the divide between the ancient world and contemporary art. These pieces at once reference pre-historic structures and the post-modern minimalist language. Their subtleties create beautiful spaces for meditation. The works stretch our sensitivity and attentiveness to spiritual richness of material that surrounds us. We need voices like Bowden's now more than ever.

Most recently, Bowden has devoted herself to her artist's books series. Some of these, like *Abyss* (Figure 127) or *Aureola I & II* (Figures 7 and 8), have wonderfully painted surfaces. Others, like *And Even the Stones* (Figure 135), are containers for objects, reliquaries for everyday items. Special among these book-as-container works is *Book of Nails* (Figure 124). This book, first a container of words, now a container of nails, continues Bowden's long pursuit of new strategies of evoking the mystery of Christ as incarnation of the word. All of these artist's books are part of her ongoing engagement with word-image structures that allow us to imagine the possibilities of an increasingly dynamic interrelationship between the Christian faith and the visual arts.

What is, in some ways, most impressive about Sandra Bowden's art is not its conceptual or technical qualities but the fact that it *is* at all. She brazenly answered a calling to be an artist in a religious culture that elevated the word above all forms of communication, where the term "Christian artist" was considered by many to be either an oxymoron or an illustrator of Bible stories, and many churches had completely abandoned the visual arts. Her art directly challenged these presuppositions. By incorporating texts into her art, she not only affirms the viability of the image as an appropriate means of communicating but shows that the opposition between image and text is false. Nevertheless, as a young Christian interested in the visual arts, she had few, if any, contemporary models to follow. There were no organizations of Christian artists to which she could join or plethora of publications and exhibition venues sympathetic to her faith. Through her extravagant selflessness, such as her service as president of Christians in the Visual Arts (CIVA), Bowden has played an enormously important role in forging new links between the Christian faith and the visual arts, a solid foundation from which generations of Christians will flourish as artists. Her example has given numerous Christians permission to shamelessly pursue their artistic vocation to the glory of God and helped to precipitate a quiet renaissance of a clear and culturally relevant Christian presence in the visual arts unseen in a century or more.

Although Sandra Bowden can rightly say that her art and efforts have helped to breathe new life into one of the richest traditions within the history of the visual arts, she is less concerned with her own personal legacy and place in the history of art than with the impact that her work can have on others. A letter from Cindy Myers is a testimony to the power of Bowden's art that surpasses any praise that an art critic could lavish on it. Myers described how *It Is Finished* (Figure 47) sustained her faith through a difficult time:

It reminds me of the summer and fall of 1980 . . . . My brother Warren was killed

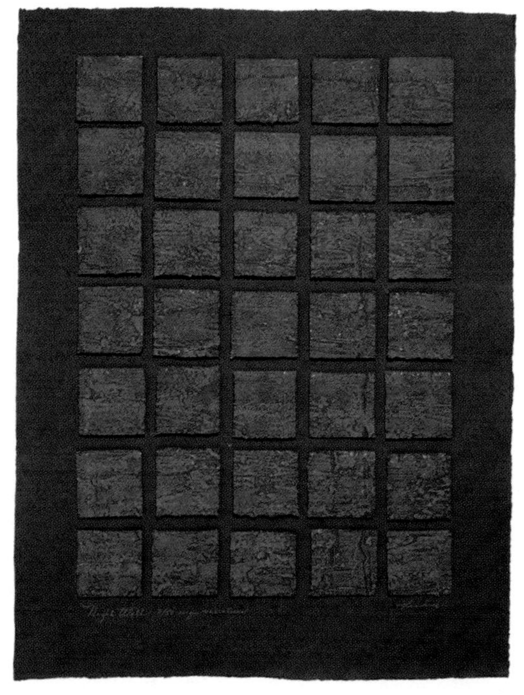

suddenly in a car accident in early July. It seems so trite to say my world collapsed. But it's the bald truth. I had cared for him as more of a mother than a sister since the first month he was in kinder-garten. Keeping him alive, healthy, happy, educated—this was my personal mission on the planet. Virtually every-thing in my life from fourth grade through high school and beyond had been focused on him. Suddenly, he was gone, and in a moment my whole cognitive-relational structure dismantled.

I hung *It Is Finished* in my living room, and for the next several months I sat and stared at Christ crucified hour after hour. It was common for me to spend entire evenings and many weekend hours as well staring at that picture. I didn't read the Bible; I couldn't study. I couldn't pray—certainly not aloud or even in coherent thought.

I just sat and stared.

It was the only act of faith I could manage. I could hang on to Christ. Even though nothing else made sense, I knew that if ever there was any hope, any possibility that this depression and sense of loss would ever go away, it would center in Him and come to me as His gift. Actually, I felt numb and wondered if I had any faith at all. I just sat and stared . . . .

Sandra, I want to express to you how much God has used your art to bring me through "dark nights of my soul," recur-ring nights that for me have lasted months and years. God has used your work to focus my attention on Him when nothing else could even get my attention. Meditating on Christ crucified and on the implications of His grace has brought me through to a place of stronger faith and renewed joy. I must say there's a lot less of intellectual interest in theology for me, but much more draws my heart and soul toward the Lord.

Sandra Bowden is a very special artist. This book is more than a survey of one artist's career; it is, as she has described it, "visual evidence that faith was alive in our time."

This book would not have been possible without the vision and aid of a great many people. I would like to thank Sandra Bowden for her openness, creative diligence, and personal generosity throughout the process of this book, not only cataloging all of the work and archives associated with it, but also for reviewing all the essays and participating in every aspect of this book. I would also like to thank Bob Bowden for his support of Sandra's art over many years and throughout this project.

I am grateful to Ned Bustard and everyone at Square Halo Books for passionately pursuing this project. Ned brought an amazing enthusiasm to every step of the process, from conceiving the organization of the book, to selecting works and designing the layout. Terrence Dempsey, Ena Giurescu Heller, Edward Knippers, Karen L. Mulder, Jean Bloch Rosensaft, and Wayne Roosa each contributed brilliant essays to this text that exhume the wide-ranging riches of Bowden's art.

This book was published in conjunction with a retrospective of Bowden's art at the Barrington Center for the Arts at Gordon College in Wenham, Massachusetts; gallery director Bruce Herman has contributed an insightful forward for this text.

We would also like to thank Jennifer Disney, Elizabeth Douglas, and Stephanie Gordon, who have each lent their expertise to this book. I could not have undertaken this project without the support and aid of my wife, Susan Cottenden, and I thank her for everything she has done to make it possible for me to do this work.

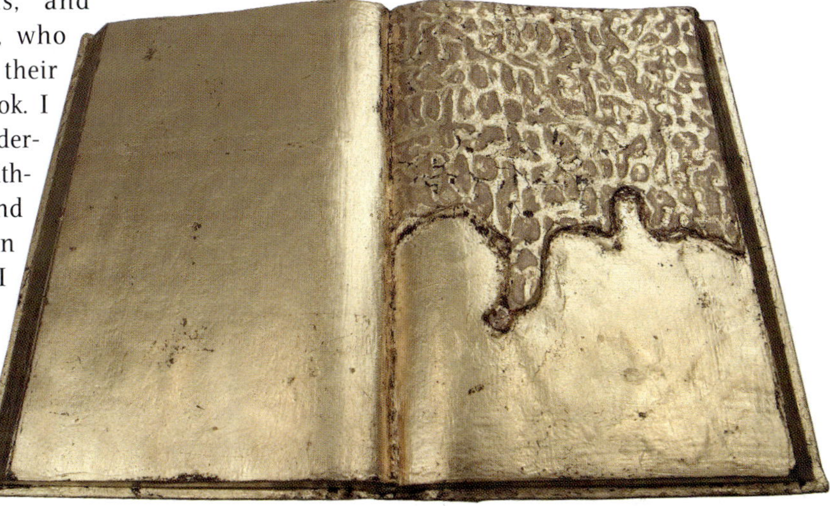

FIGURE 7
(OPPOSITE)
AUREOLA I
Mixed media
2004
11 1/2 x 9 1/2 x 1

FIGURE 8
AUREOLA II
Mixed media
2004
11 1/2 x 9 1/2 x 1

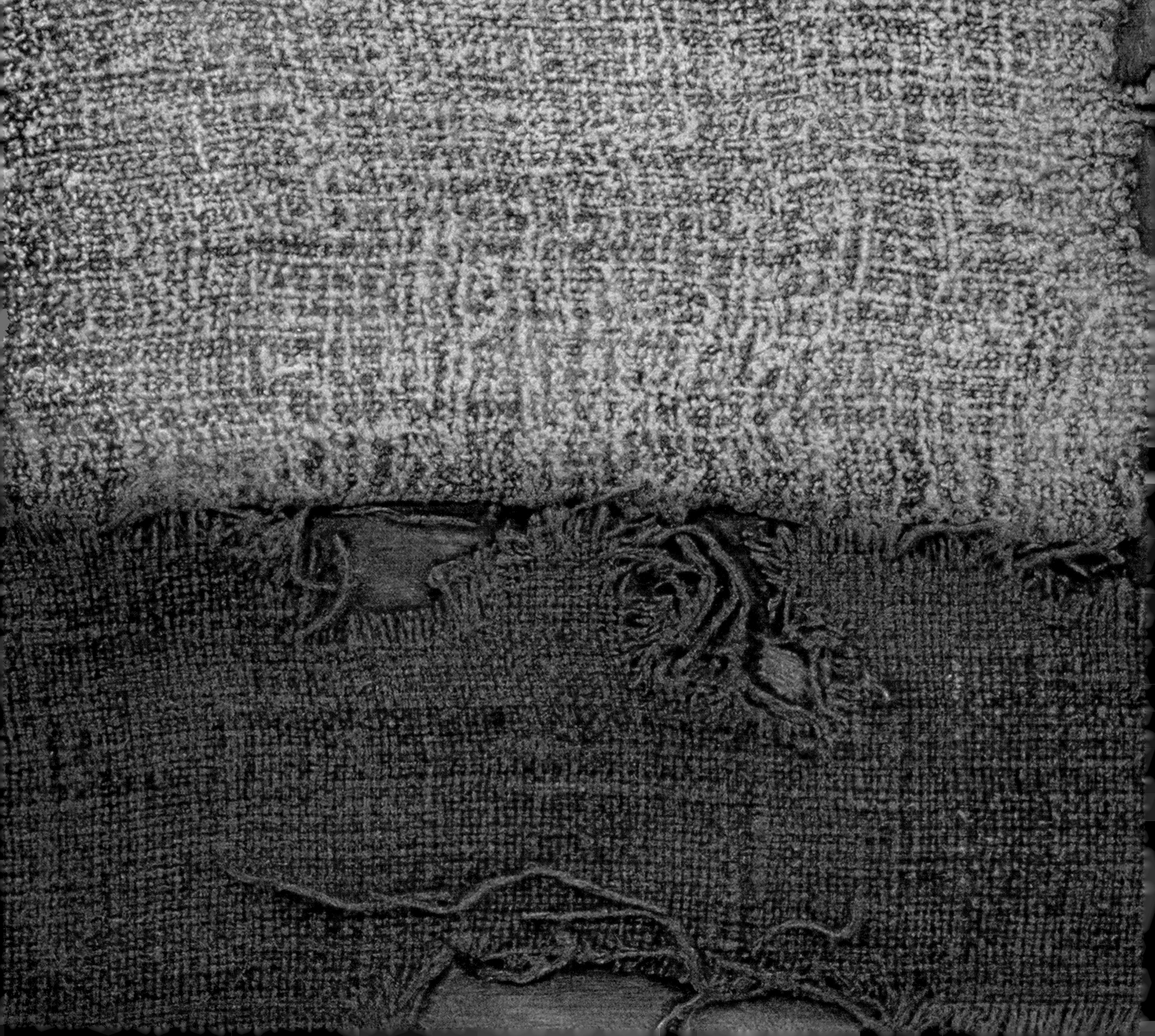

MAY 3, 1943

Born in Manchester, NH, to Barbara M. (Moore) and Owen G. Burtt

JUNE 1961

Graduated from Lee High School, Lee, MA

Won Berkshire Art Association 1st Prize for High School Art

1961-2

Berkshire Christian College, Lenox, MA

Painting course at Berkshire Art Museum

1962-3

Massachusetts College of Art, Boston, MA

AUGUST 31, 1963

Married Robert W. Bowden, Lenox, MA, and moved to Beverly, MA

SEPTEMBER 1964

Birth of first child, Jennifer Bowden, Beverly, MA

MAY 1965

First religious art show at Beverly Baptist Church, Beverly, MA

SPRING 1966

First solo exhibition, Gordon College, Wenham, MA

Birth of second child, Bert Bowden, Beverly, MA

OCTOBER 1966

Moved to Syracuse, NY

OCTOBER 1967

Moved to Clifton Park, NY

1969

Art instructor at Loudonville Christian School for twelve years

1972

Began studying Hebrew

Oak Room Artists Solo Show, Schenectady, NY

First crucifixion painting

First cuneiform text in paintings: *Deluge*

1973

Mohawk-Hudson Regional Exhibition, Albany Institute of Art and History, Albany, NY

Patmos Gallery, solo show, Toronto

1974

Mohawk-Hudson Regional Exhibition, Schenectady Museum, Schenectady, NY

1976

Several new large crucifixion paintings created

Private Gallery, solo show, Kensington, MD

1977

Course at College of Saint Rose in intaglio printmaking—first collagraph

Studied Geology, Hebrew, and Biblical Archaeology at SUNY-Albany

1978

Received BA Degree in Art from State University of New York, Empire State College, Albany, NY

First collagraph with Hebrew text

1979

Mohawk-Hudson Regional Exhibition, Albany Institute of Art and History

Attended first CIVA (Christians in Visual Arts) conference in St. Paul, MN, when the organization adopted its bylaws

1980

First trip to Israel

Exhibited at Art Expo New York and gained national and international exposure

1982

Second trip to Israel with husband and children

1983

Tel Suite and *Color Series* completed

1984

Taught collagraph printmaking at Calvin

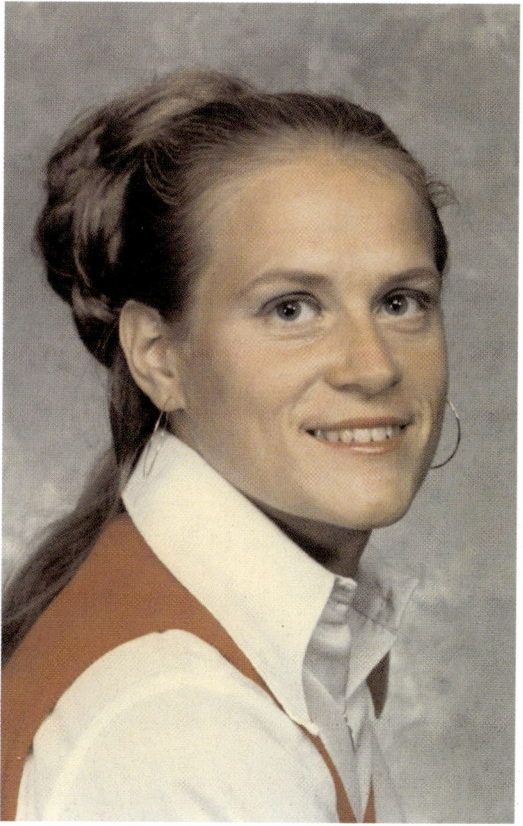

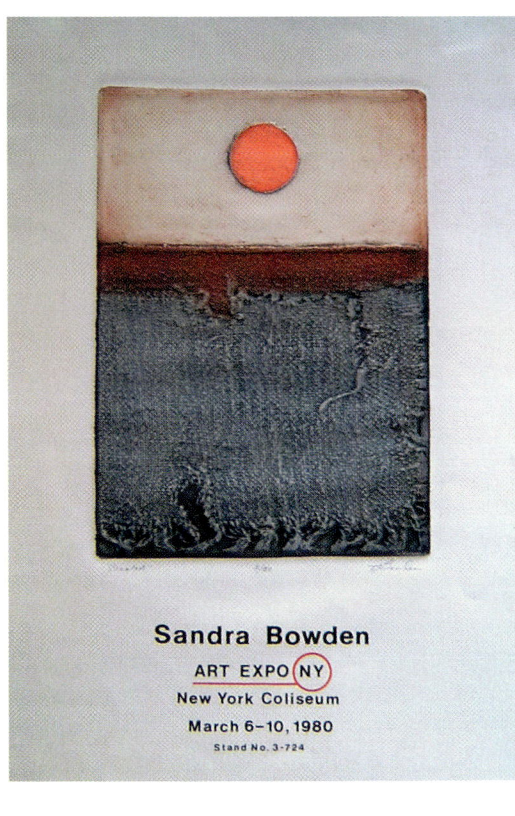

College during winter semester two consecutive years

Purchased first Rouault piece from the *Miserère* Series

1985

Taught collagraph printmaking at College of Saint Rose, Albany, NY

1987

First piece from *Music* Series completed

1988

Images of the Holy Land, invitational, Calvin College, Grand Rapids, MI

1989

It Is Finished chosen for ELCA's *Art For Faith's Sake* collection and traveling exhibition resource

Honorable Mention: *Sacred Arts X,* Billy Graham Museum, Wheaton, IL

Word as Image, solo show at Kolbo, Boston, MA

Albany Catholic Diocese, bishop's chasuble commission, Albany, NY

1990

Illumination series initiated by an invitational called *4 x 12 x 12* at Emma Willard School in Troy, NY

Episcopal Diocese of Albany, bishop's chasuble commission, Albany, NY

St. Sophia's Greek Orthodox Church, painting commission, Albany, NY

1991

Segment on Bowden's art in the book, *State of the Art: Bezalel to Mapplethorpe,* by Edward Gene Veith, Crossways Books

Knesseth Israel Synagogue, commission to design stained glass windows, menorah, eternal light, and ark doors, Gloversville, NY

1992

First artist's books were created

1993

Elected President of Christians in Visual Arts (CIVA)

Church of the Holy Cross, commission for Stations of the Cross, Warrensburg, NY

1994

Back surgery in January

Beginning of *Collage* series

Law and Gospel was created as a progression of gilding the collagraph text panels

Testament in Art, two-person show, Hampton College, Amherst, MA

1995

Purchase Award, *Contemporary Works of Faith,* Liturgical Guild of Ohio

1996

Solo exhibition at Bible Lands Museum in Jerusalem

Illuminations, solo show, Center Galleries, Albany, NY

1997

First gilded cross was created

Mosaic, a video segment on Bowden, published by Evangelical Lutheran Church of America

Artists Books, invitational, Oculus Gallery, Seattle, WA

Second Annual Small Works Exhibition, invitational, The Art Place Gallery, Chicago, IL

1998

Taught collage course at United Theological Seminary, New Brighton, MN

The Word Became Art, article on Bowden's art by Karen Mulder in *Christianity Today*

Good Friday bulletin cover published by ELCA using *It Is Finished,* 1,000,000 copies distributed

Arte Sagrado, juried exhibition, Concordia University, Austin, TX

Purchase Award, Creation: *Contemporary Christian Art and Artists,* Rall Gallery, Crete, Nebraska

Paper in Particular, juried show, Columbia College, Columbia, MO

Paper Plus, invitational, Arts Center Gallery, Saratoga, NY
Meditations Across Time, solo show, Visions Gallery, Albany, NY
Artist As Collector, invitational, Messiah College, Grantham, PA
First showing of *Art History 101: Icons of Western Art,* Wheaton College, Wheaton, IL

1999

Christian Artist Steeped in Hebraic Aesthetics, article on Bowden's work, written by Edward Gene Veith for *Christianity and the Arts*
It Is Finished selected to be in an exhibition called *Behold the Wood of the Cross,* Georgetown University, Washington, DC
Juror's Award, *Visions V,* Cathedral Basilica of the Assumption, Covington, KY
Women of Vision, invitational, Foxhall Gallery, Washington, DC

2000

Three artist's books in national exhibition, *Like A Prayer,* curator Ted Prescott, at the Tryon Center for Visual Art, Charlotte, NC
Law and Gospel selected to be in *Anno Domini: Jesus Through the Centuries* at the Provincial Museum of Alberta, Edmonton, Alberta, curated by David Goa
Two crucifixion pieces included in *Word as Art: Contemporary Renderings,* invitational, The Gallery at the American Bible Society, New York
Abstraction: The Power of Memory, CIVA traveling show
Reproduction and preface in *It Was Good: Making Art to the Glory of God,* Square Halo Books
Spirit Infused, invitational, Salisbury State University, Salisbury, MD

2001

2001 calendar (month of August), Aid Association for Lutherans with a reproduction of *It Is Finished*

2002

Opening of *Collector's Items: Biblical Art and Private Devotion,* 75 pieces from the Bowden Collection at The Gallery of the American Bible Society, NYC
Via Crucis: The Way of the Cross, solo show, Instituto San Lodovico, Orvieto, Italy
Object of Grace: Conversations on Creativity and Faith, Bowden interview by James Romaine, and several reproductions
Best of Show, *VI Annual Sacred Art Exhibition,* Golden Isles Arts and Humanities Association, Brunswick, GA

2003

Advent Book exhibited in *Under Cover Arts,* Saint Louis Arts Guild National Juried Exhibition, Saint Louis, MO
Bread Upon the Waters, CIVA Traveling show, *Martini's Annunciation* chosen for this show
Cross Country III, juried show, Weaver Gallery, Bethel College, Mishawaka, IN
Gave plenary lectures on *Importance of Creativity* and *Art in the Life of a Christian,* Concordia University Faculty Retreat, Mequon, WI

2004

Cape Cod Printmakers Juried Exhibition, Cape Museum of Fine Arts, Brewster, MA

2005

Publication of book *The Art of Sandra Bowden,* Square Halo Books
Word as Image: A Retrospective of Sandra Bowden's Art, Gordon College, Wenham, MA
Co-editor of *Faith and Vision: Twenty Five Years of Christians in the Visual Arts,* a book documenting the history of CIVA
Book of Nails chosen to be in *Art and Faith in the Modern World,* Museum of Biblical Art (MOBIA), New York

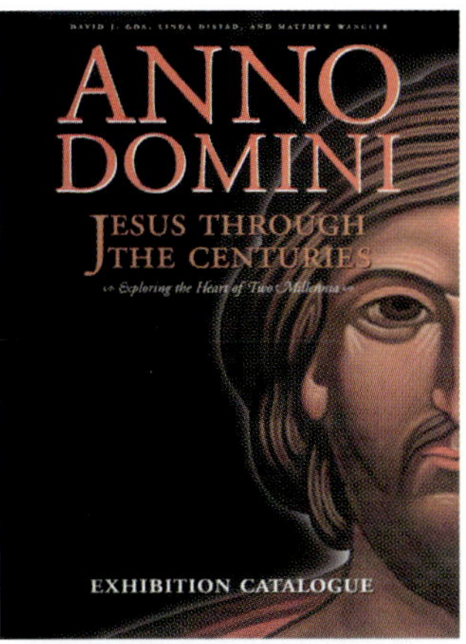

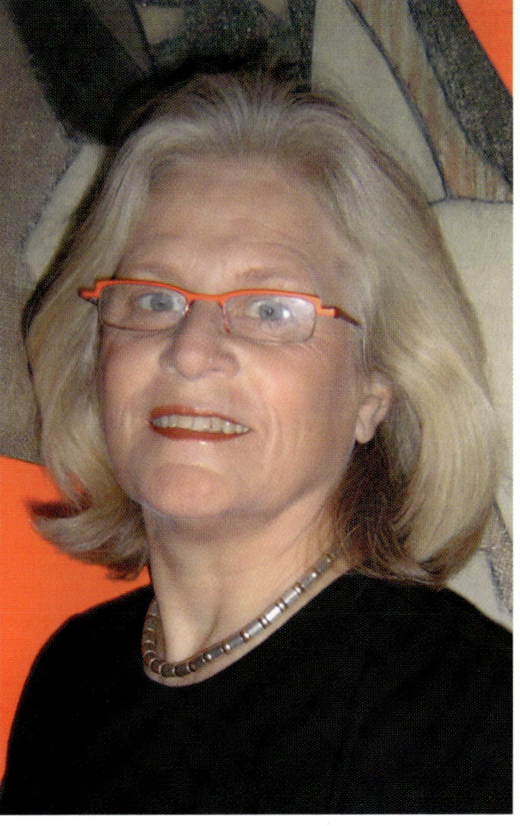

Early Explorations

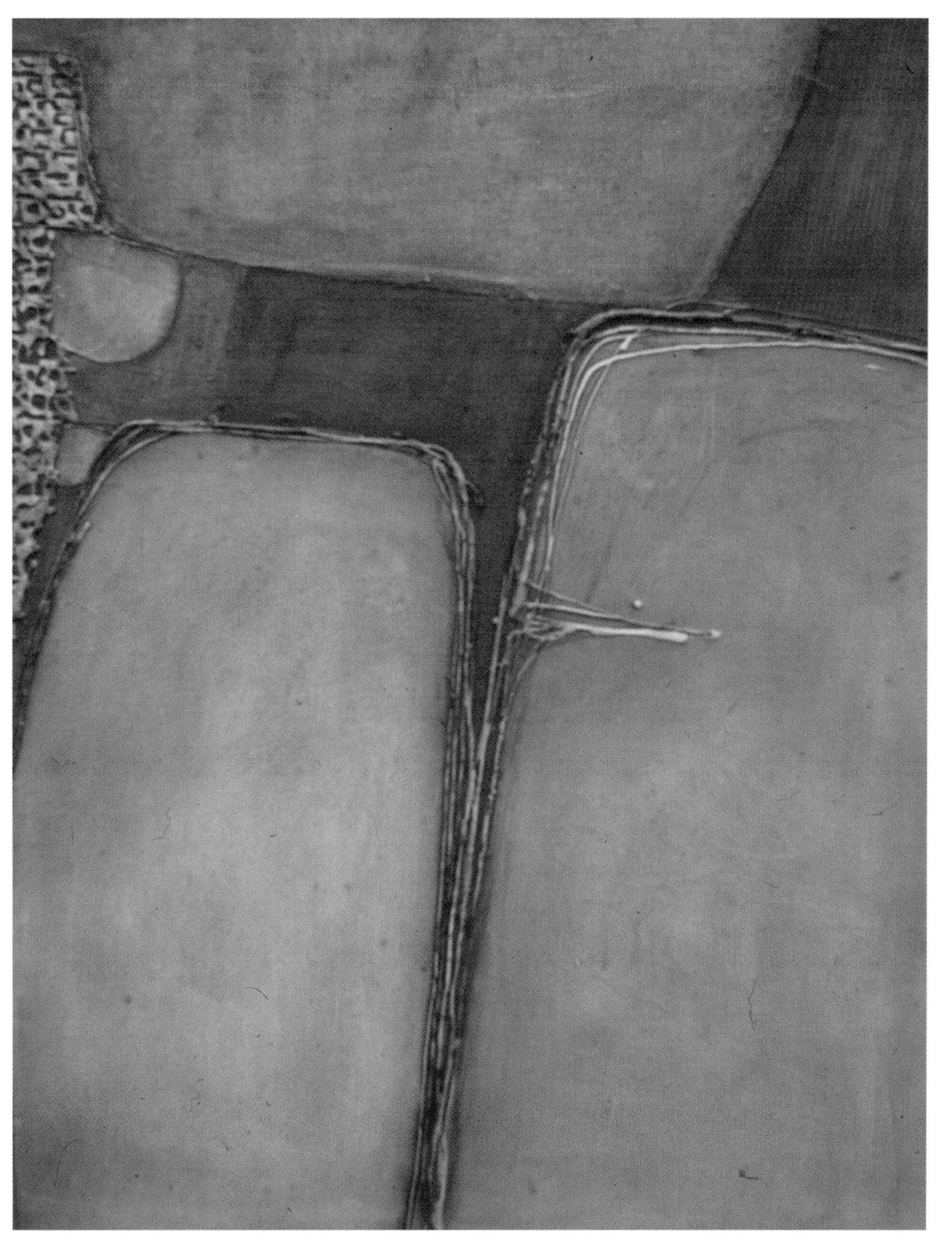

FIGURE 9
EMPTY TOMB
Oil collage
1970
48 x 36

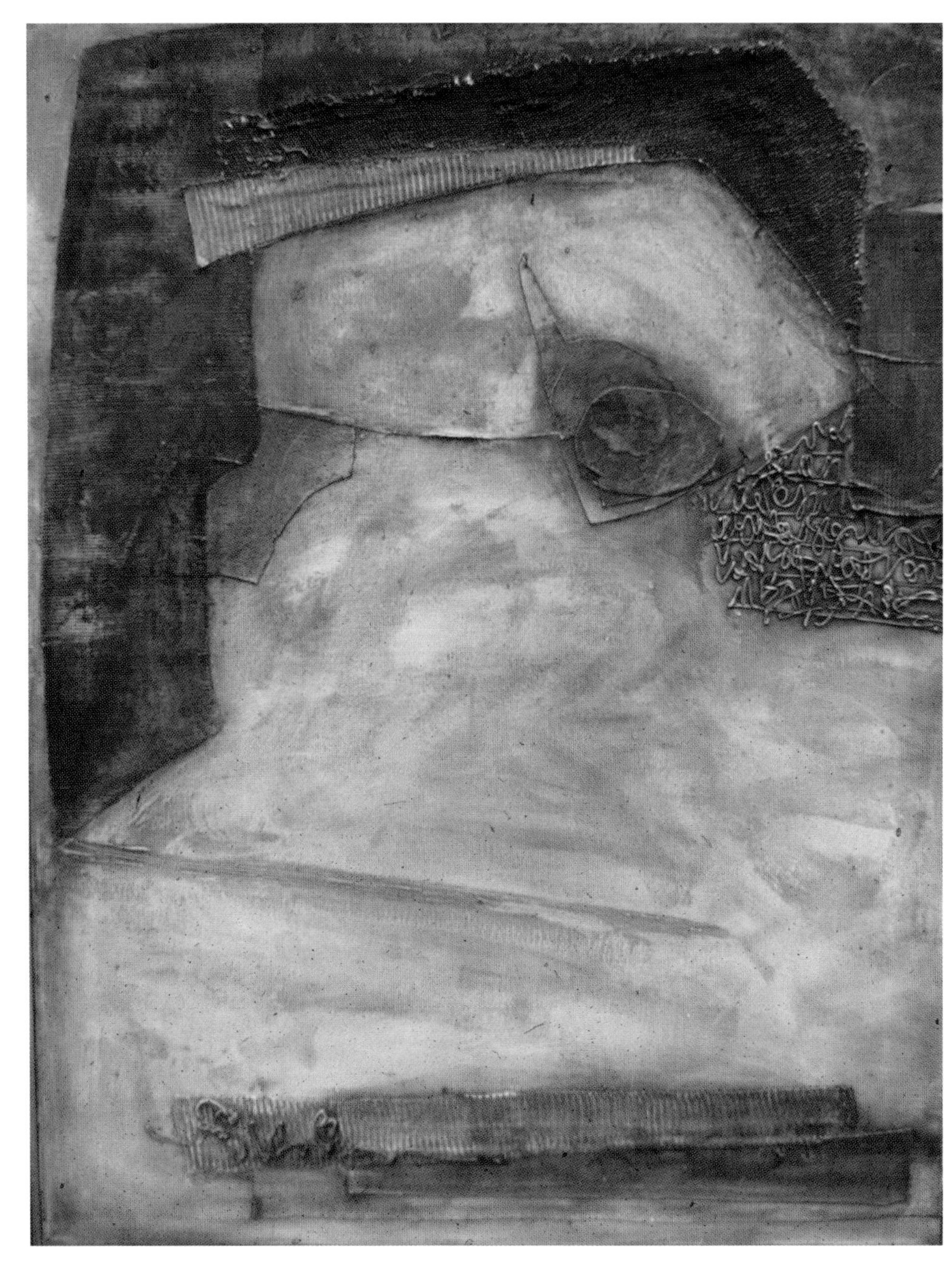

The Art of **Sandra Bowden**

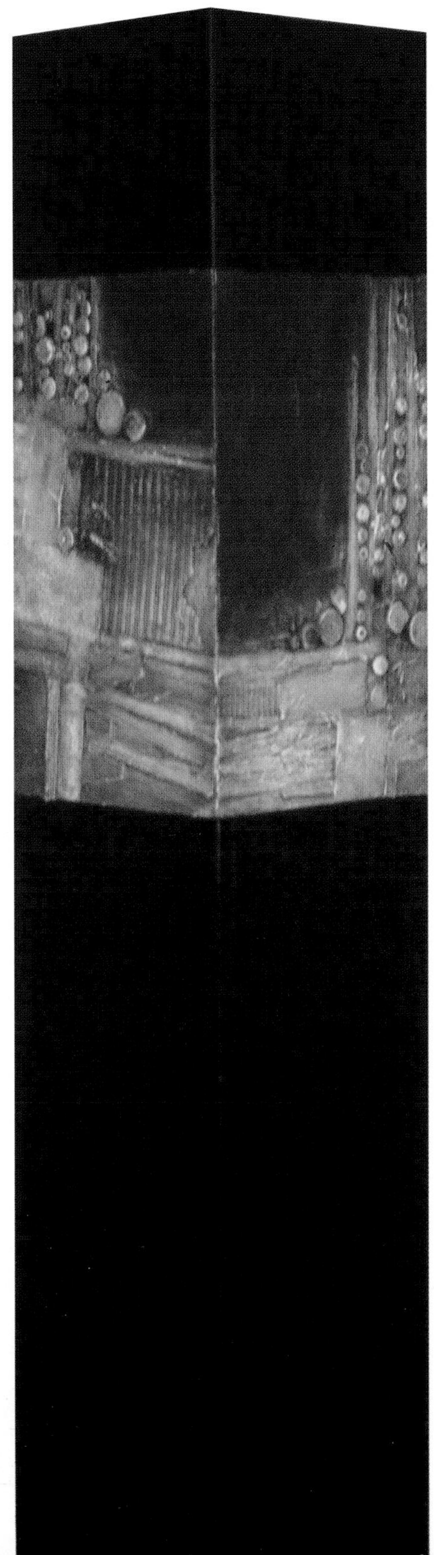

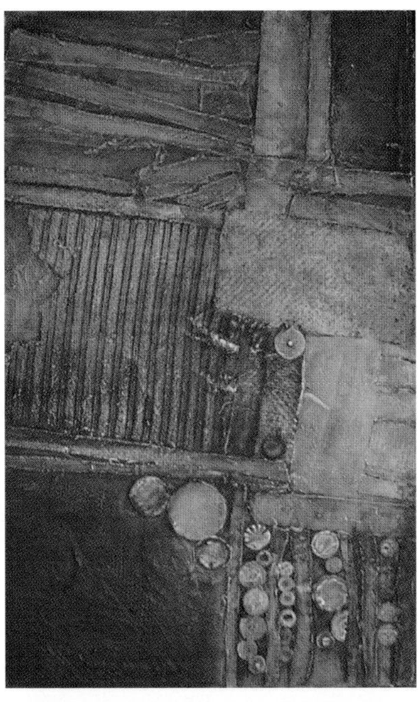

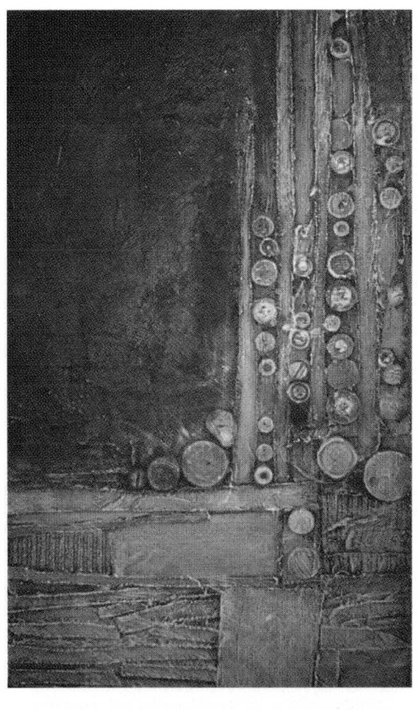

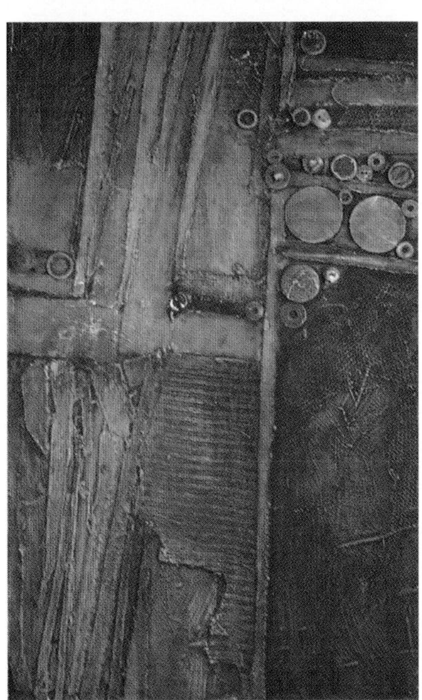

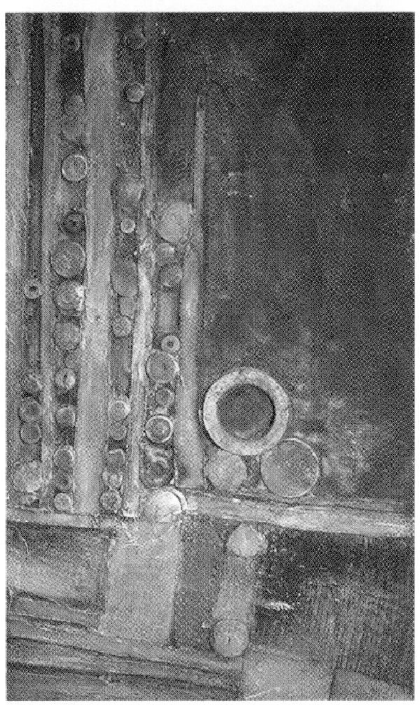

MOABITE STONE
Oil collage
1970
48 x 36

FOUND PIECES
Oil collage
1971
12 x 12 x 24 box on
pedestal with cap

Texts

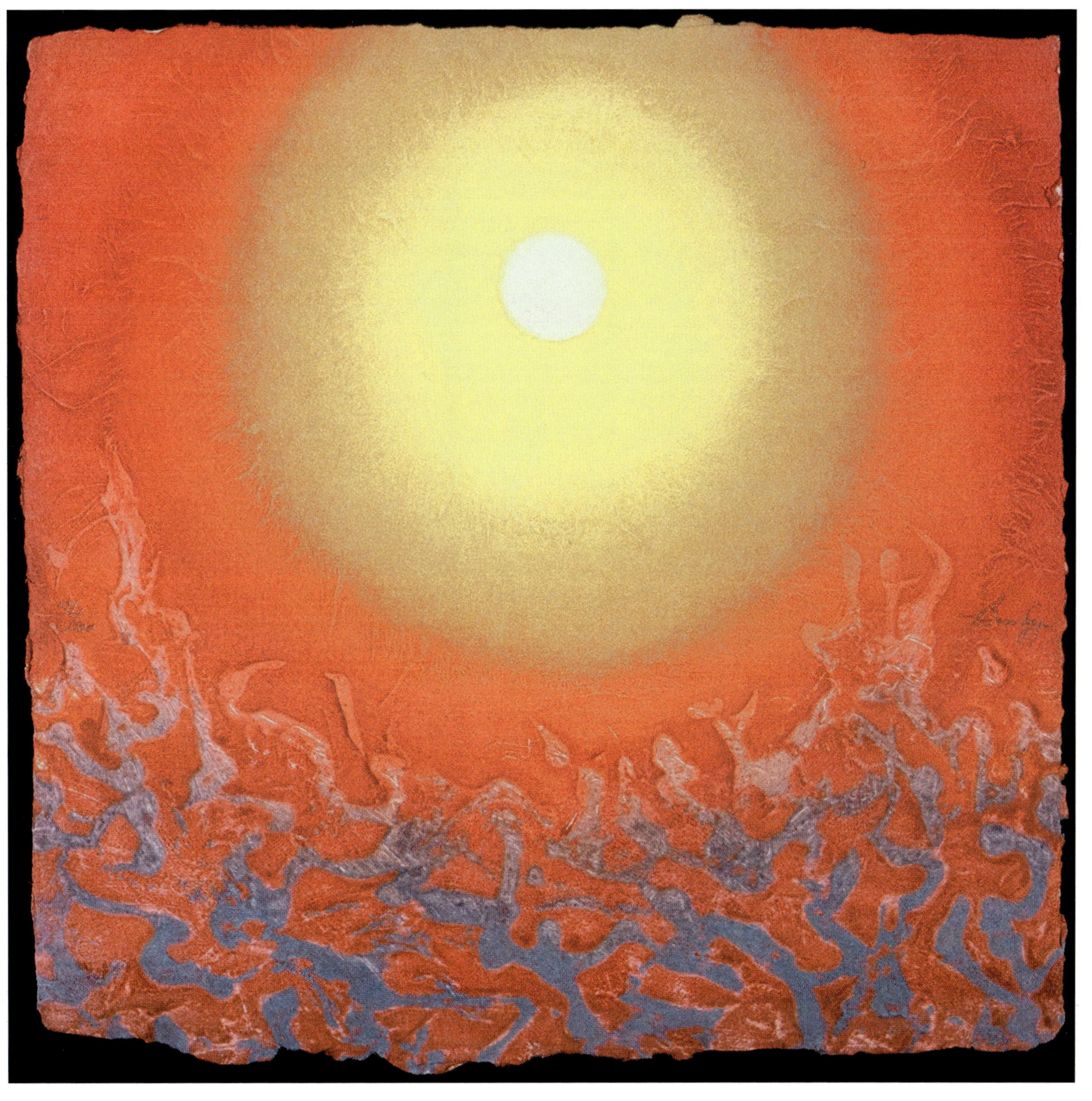

FIGURE 12
LIGHT
Collagraph
1982
10 x 10

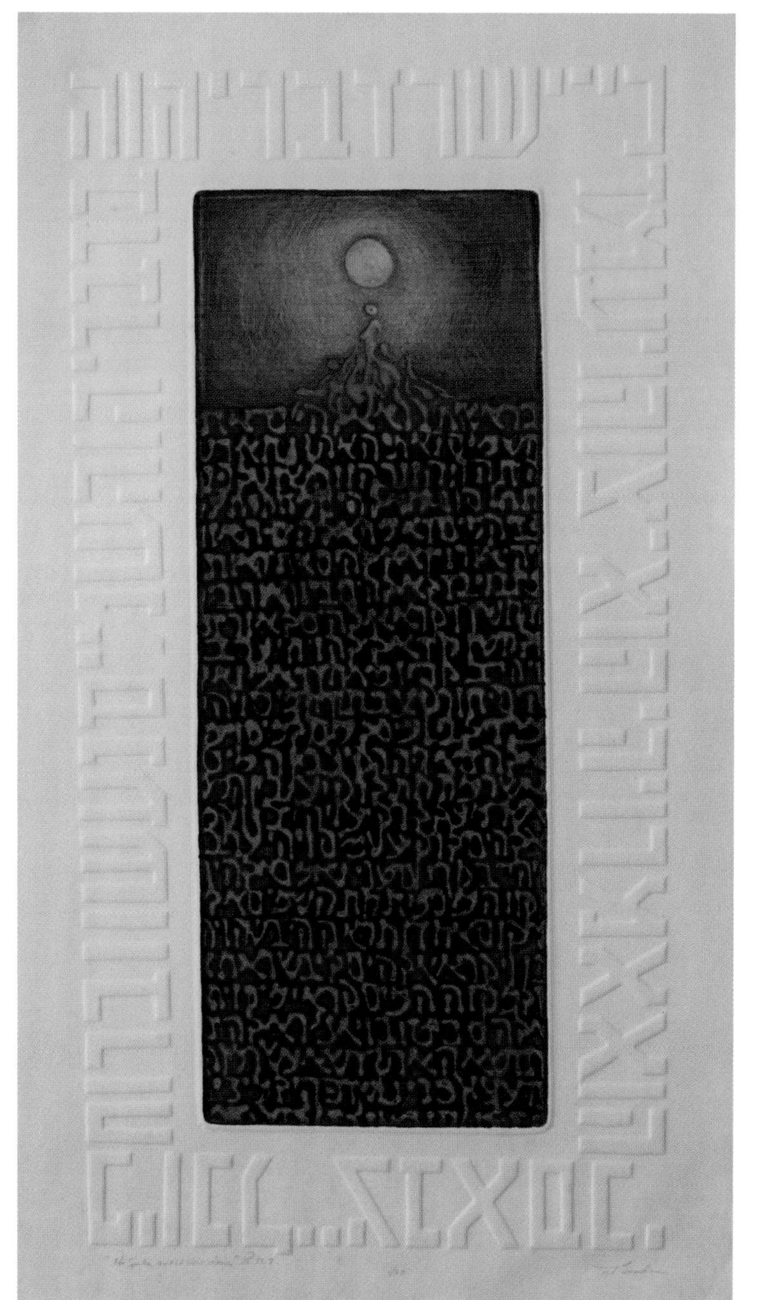 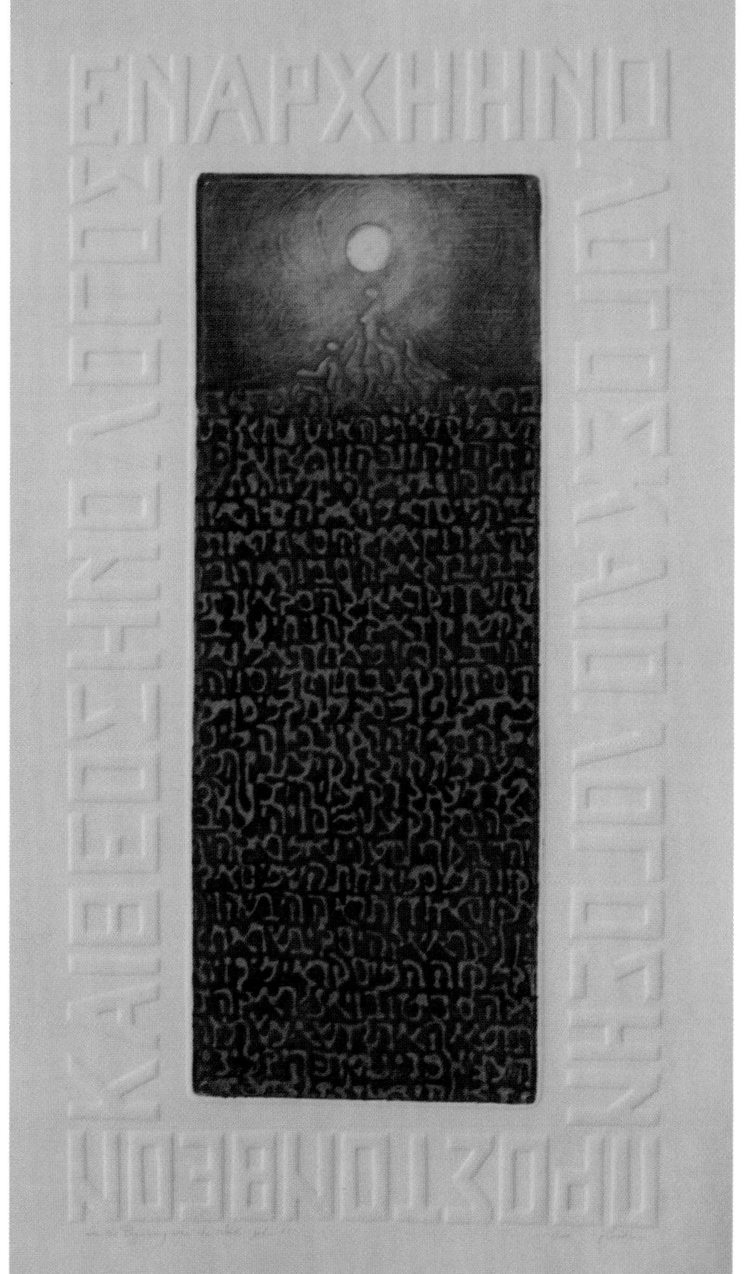

The Art of **Sandra Bowden**

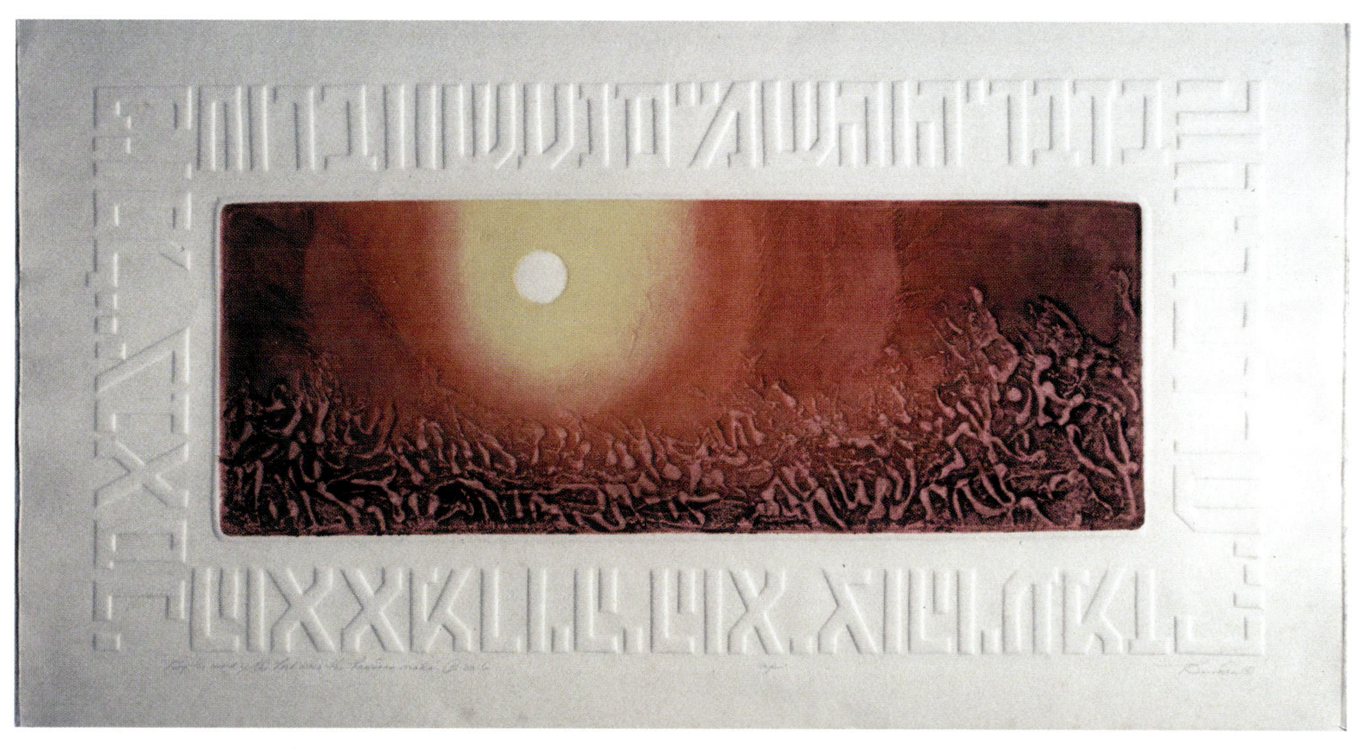

FIGURE 13
(OPPOSITE LEFT)
**HE SPAKE AND IT
WAS DONE**
Collagraph with
embossing
1979
30 x 18

FIGURE 14
(OPPOSITE RIGHT)
**IN THE BEGINNING
WAS THE WORD**
Collagraph with
embossing
1982
30 x 18

FIGURE 15
(TOP)
**BY THE WORD OF
THE LORD WERE
THE HEAVENS MADE**
Collagraph with
embossing
1980
17 x 30

FIGURE 16
(BOTTOM)
GOD CREATED
Collagraph
1980
7 3/4 x 21

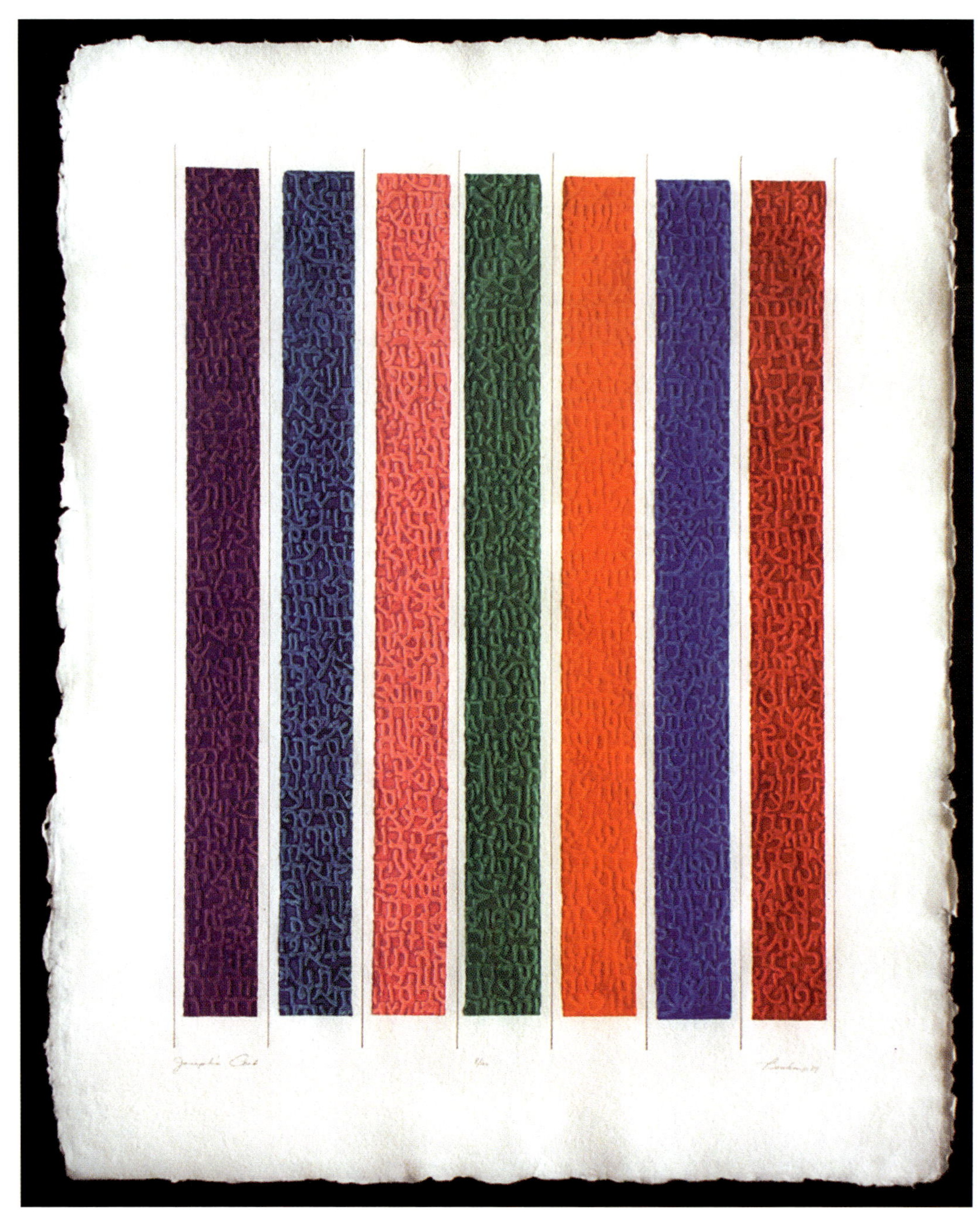

The Art of **Sandra Bowden**

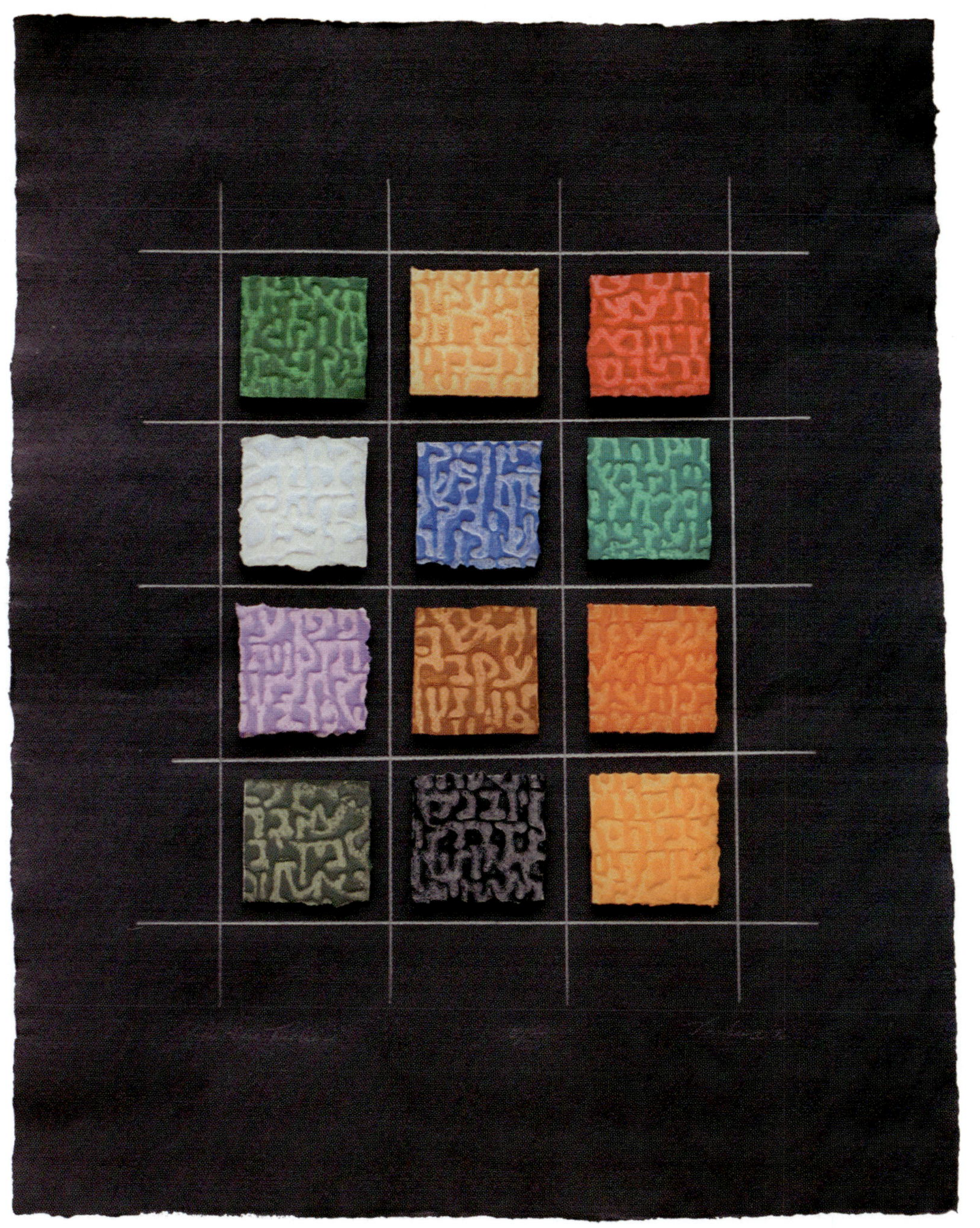

FIGURE 17
(OPPOSITE)
JOSEPH'S COAT
Collagraph
assemblage
1984
40 x 30

FIGURE 18
TWELVE TRIBES
Collagraph
assemblage
1987
19 x 13

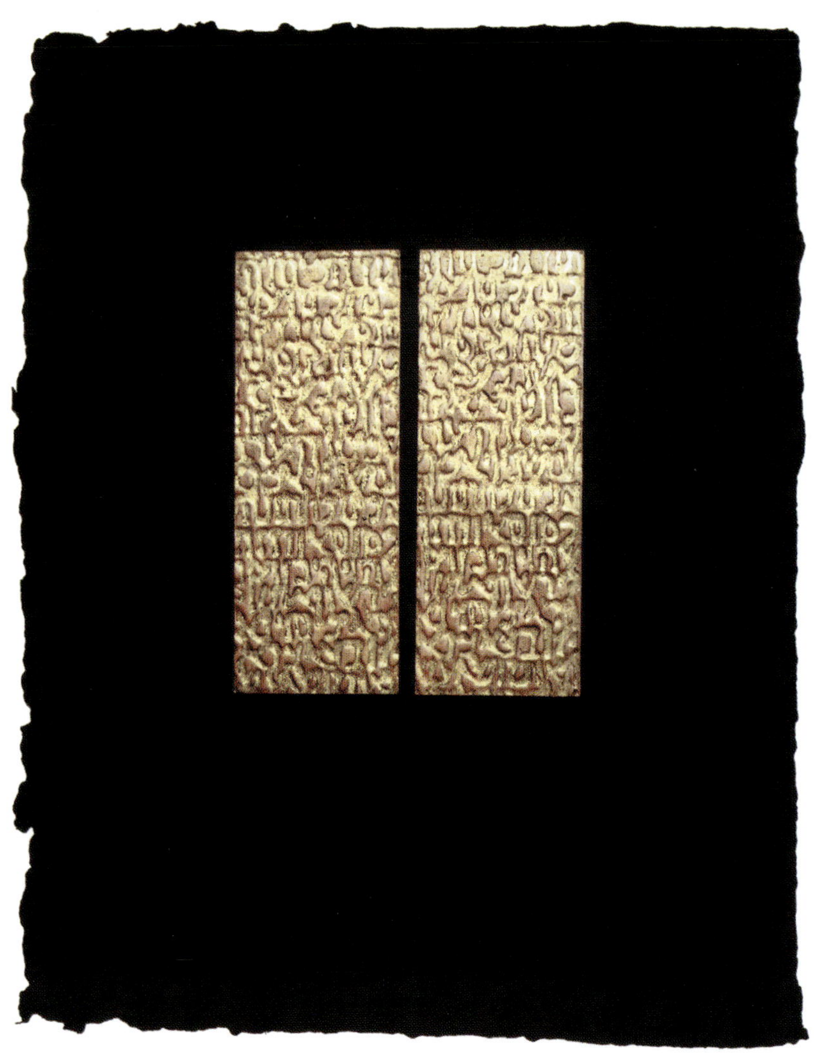 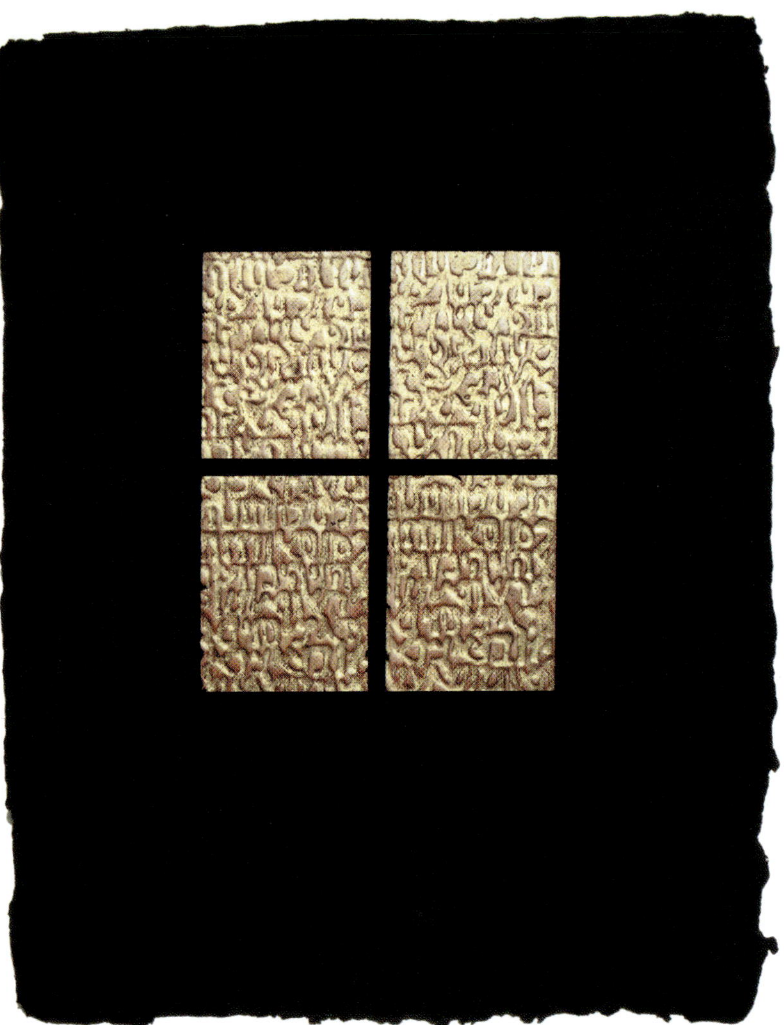

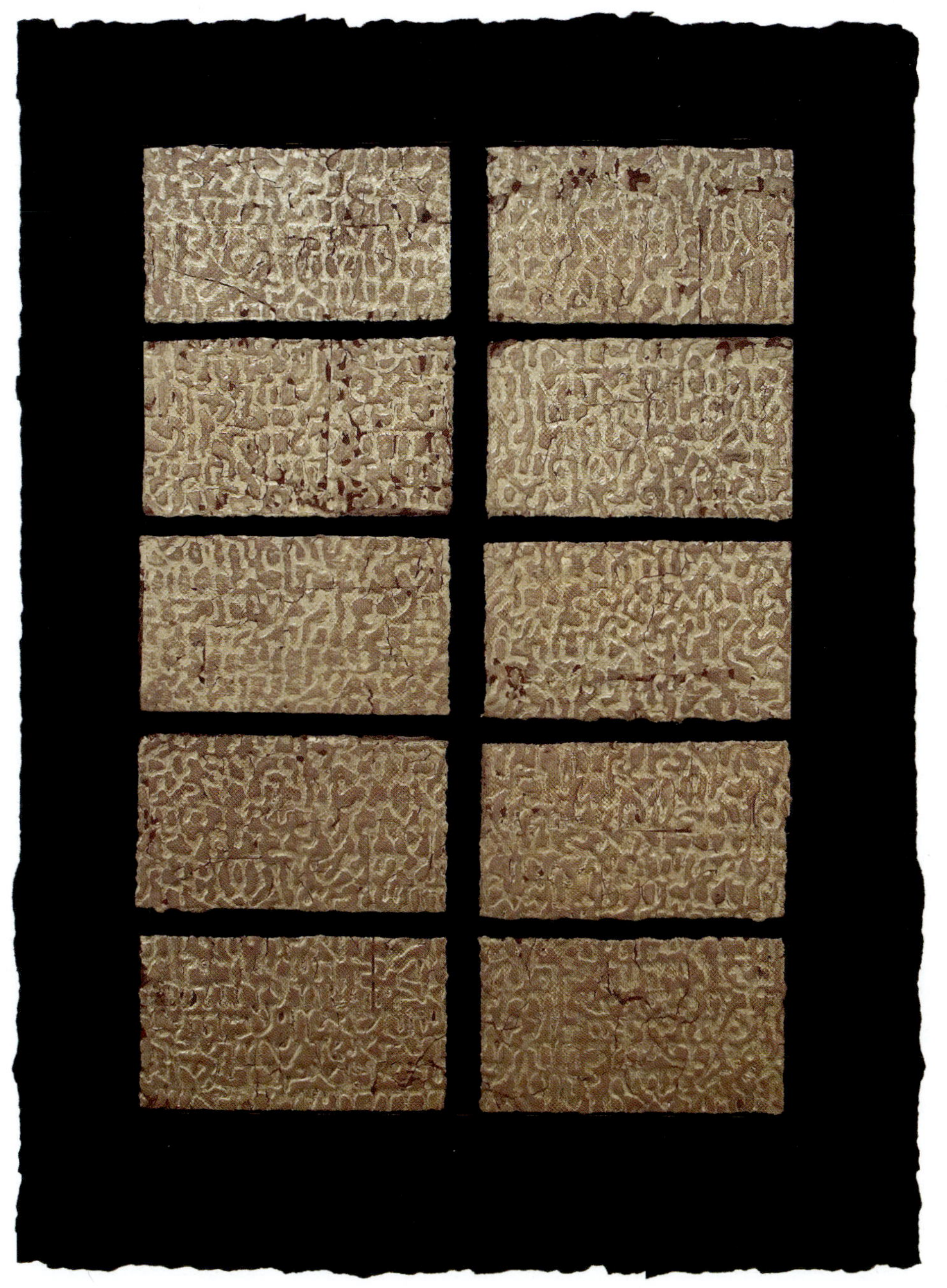

FIGURE 19
(OPPOSITE)
**LAW AND
GOSPEL (on Black)**
Collagraph
mixed media
1994
Two 26 x 18 panels

FIGURE 20
**TEN
COMMANDMENTS
(on Black)**
Collagraph
mixed media
2003
30 x 22

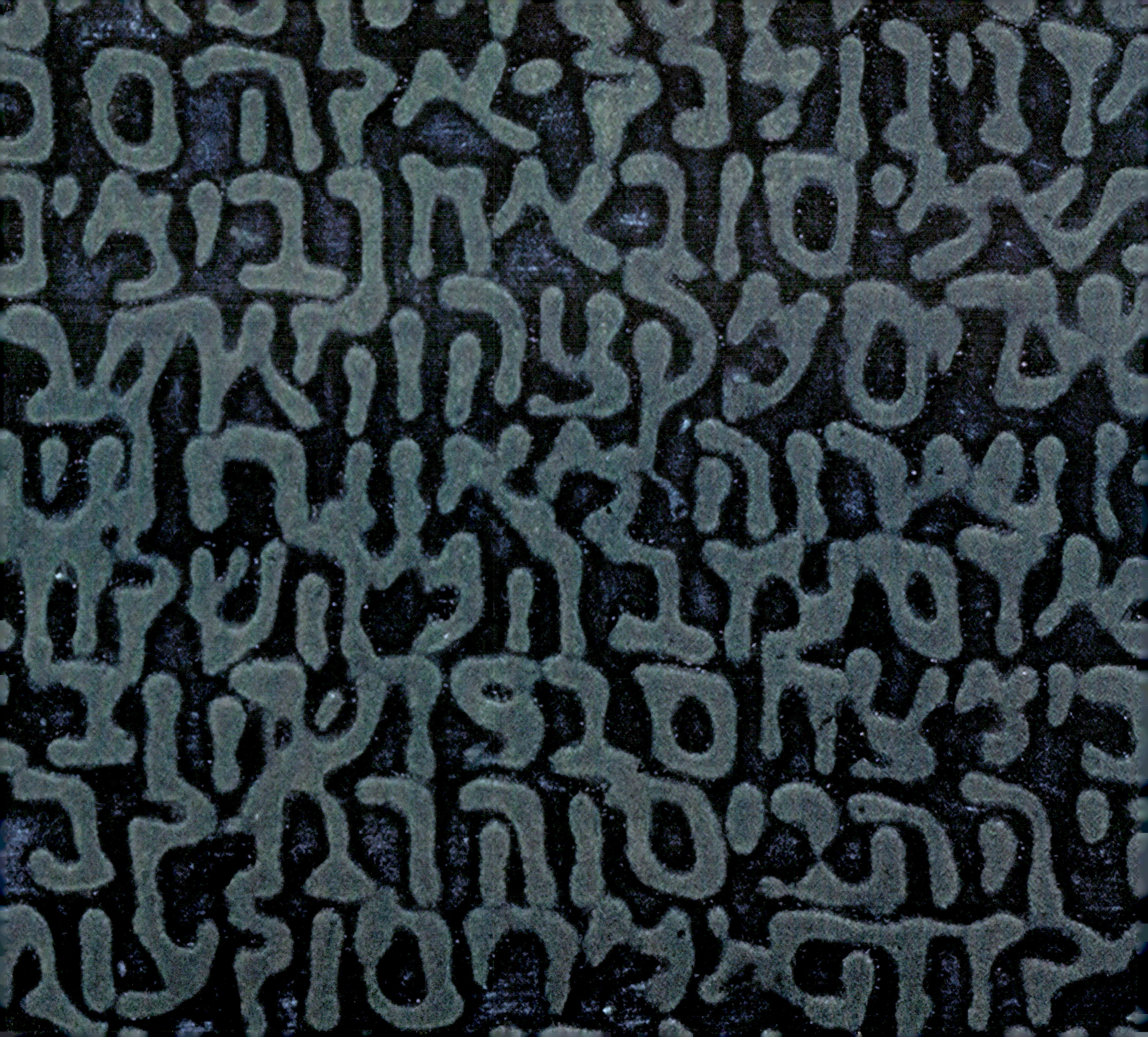

WAYNE ROOSA

Exploring the role of language in Sandra Bowden's art is a bit like exploring the role of DNA in human biology and personality—language is a generative force in her art. She uses language in a double sense, as both structural form and subject matter. Structurally, in its visual character as registers of alphabetic signs and symbols, and blocks of written text, language serves as strata of abstract forms within her compositions. But language also operates in Bowden's art as a central element of her subject matter, as the content of her interests. Semioticians speak of language in two aspects: one being the broadest conception, as *langue*—a system of signs or a set of semiotic codes common to a community of speakers; the other being in a narrower conception, as *parole*—specific acts of speech, printed words, or images. If *langue* is pervasive, then *parole* is particular. As such, language operates intrinsically and extrinsically in human efforts to articulate experience and express its meanings. This two-tiered, or dual-natured, quality of language saturates Bowden's art. Put another way, her art looks as it does because it is both *of* language and *about* language. In this, language is her *logos,* her ordering principle, as well as her *Logos,* her informing wisdom.

Because Bowden's art is so deeply informed by Jewish and Christian understandings of *Logos,* of *The Word,* her interest in language's intrinsic and extrinsic shaping force bears a rich correspondence to the Hebrew and Christian traditions. For the Hebrew scriptures, "In the beginning . . . *God said,*" is the creative word of God, which is to say, it is the medium by which God created the world.[1] Christians built upon this tradition, most notably in the Prologue of John's Gospel, which opens with, "In the beginning was the *Word* . . . and the Word became flesh."[2]

Indeed, as one examines the development of Bowden's art over a forty-year period, one finds an increasing ability to make language simultaneously more immanent as generative structure and more provocative as overt subject. One senses in this an artist's desire to partake somehow in reality by discovering ways that the use of language can resonate with John's claim of *The Word* as the internal life and light of the world by which everything was formed, and as that specific act of speech by which *The Word* became flesh in a particular subject, as a particular man in the Incarnation.

In the light of all of this, there is a fittingness between Sandra Bowden's interest in language and her preferred physical processes and media. For in her *practice* as an artist, Bowden is strongly drawn to those processes related to the "press" and to "printing." After all, the processes of printing belong as much to the visual art of printmaking and collagraphs as to the verbal arts of bookmaking. It makes sense that, in forty years of work, Bowden will shift between prints using visual images, prints using words, prints combining the two, collages using pages of books merged with fragments of visual prints (and vice versa), until, finally, she is now making

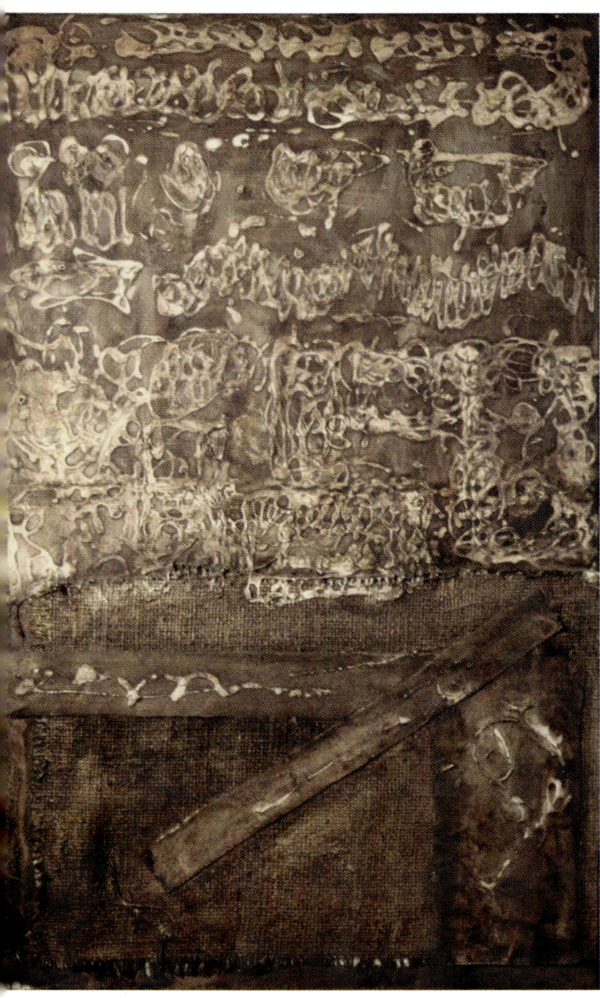

artist's books that are equal parts object, image, print and page.

By letting her work be an exploration of the interfaces between visual and verbal, images and texts, print-collages and book-objects, Bowden teases out the wonderful "mental tactility" by which language-cum-art operates. In short, what she explores is the arena of "translations." Not, certainly, as in translating French to English, but as in translating from one *langue* (words) to a different *langue* (images). What I mean is that Bowden's interest is not solely in words *or* images, as it is in the mysterious realm of both, or to use Martin Buber's term, the realm of "between."[3] For what she explores is really a kind of "translation" or "transferring" between a linguistic way of signifying and a plastic way of signifying. Indeed, in Latin, *translatus* is the past participle of *transferre,* to "transfer" or "translate." It is to "ferry across" or bear something from one state or form to another state or form. But it is also more. For her work is about the "ferrying" itself. It is about where word and image meet, coexist, engage each other in dialogue. It is about how word and image fully collaborate and mutually inform in *relationship* to each other.

For a fuller understanding of the role of language in Sandra Bowden's art—one that is more interesting and rewarding because it allows us to engage and dwell within Bowden's works one at a time—we must really look at her works, taking pleasure in their sensuous character while thinking about how language bodies forth meaning precisely by way of donning that sensuous character. First observations quickly reveal the consistent presence of language as an element of Bowden's imagery throughout all phases of her last forty years of work. Or, perhaps more accurately, first observations underscore the presence of *written text,* which by measure of its being written (not spoken) becomes equal parts linguistic content and physical, visual object. Bowden best exploits the rich play between language as narrative or religious content and language as physical text or sensuous texture and patterned form. Fragments of ancient cuneiform, Hebrew, and Greek appear as archaeological remnants of ancient cultures, but also as fragments of the religious and mythical stories on which ancient cultures were founded. Some recall primeval events of creation and flood, while others reference cultural life, such as a cuneiformic calendar record listing the months of planting and harvest. This is especially typical of the earlier works such as *In the Beginning* (Figure 22), *Deluge* (Figure 23), and *Gezer* (Figure 42).

In these works, textual fragments serve a narrative and cultural meaning even as they also serve a geological function as calligraphic strata in the landscape's geography. Although the texts actually remain faithful to their original content, Bowden has compressed the typography and removed spaces between characters to ensure this double visual role. Such a coupling of function—as nature and narrative—relates to the issue of language's role in reality. Such doubling of function as human writing (typo-*graphy*) and earth's writing (geo-*graphy*) recalls that there are, traditionally, two sources of revelation, the "Book of Scripture" and "Book of Nature." But in this tradition, a "double" role does not simply mean a "stacking" but rather an intertwining, a reciprocity. For in the Judeo-

Christian tradition, the function of "word" runs beyond language, as a phenomenon wherein divine wisdom (*Logos/Sophia*) is both immanent and other to the world. "In the beginning, *God said,*" speaking, as it were, the world into being. Or again, in the Prologue of John's Gospel, "In the beginning was the Word . . . ."

Thus, it is not only in the mysterious generative sense that "under the rocks are the words" (to borrow Norman Maclean's phrase),[4] as in *And All the Deep Places* (Figure 25); it is also that specific acts of speech can be uncovered in the ancient Tels of human history, as in works from the Archaeological series, such as *Fortress Finds* (Figure 28) and *Gezer* (Figure 42), of 1983. Here the earth's sedimentary layers resonate with the geographical layers of human cultures. Earth's geography and humanity's written language both have their own structure, syntax, and grammar of forms. The plasticity of rows of Hebrew calligraphy and the plasticity of earth's sedimentary strata join into a fuller notion of "language."

In a second series of works, *Texts,* from the late 1970s and early 1980s, Bowden invented another visual strategy for relating text to word to nature to history. In *In the Beginning Was the Word* (Figure 14), and *He Spake and It Was Done* (Figure 13), she uses a kind of visual conceit wherein the Hebrew text of the Genesis creation story is placed at the image's center. As text, this block of Hebrew typography stands for itself, for the Genesis narrative. As image, with its spaces removed and its type compressed into near-abstract registers of rhythmic pattern, it stands for the nature that those words created. Together, it stands for the mystical belief that

God said and it was done. This core collagraph, brooding in dark ink at creation's center, is then surrounded by another layer of words as a border of embossed typography raised in the white of the paper. In *In the Beginning . . .,* the embossed text coming from John 1, is in Greek. In *He Spake . . .,* the white embossing is the Hebrew text of David's Psalm 33. This visual conceit of nesting one ancient text inside another becomes its own kind of "linguistic tel." As such, the whole image stands for how each generation inherits formative language then builds upon, but also alters or covers over, that origin through interpretation. For Bowden, this nesting of ancient texts creates a kind of visual Midrash, with David or John commenting upon and interpreting Moses. Such layers suggest more complex theological ideas, particularly in, *In the Beginning . . .,* where the Hebrew Word of Creation forming the world becomes the Greek Logos of Incarnation, and the Word that was always immanent in the earth's ordered strata now becomes flesh and walks upon that earth's surface. And so the complete visual conceit of this series stands for a history of language, from the inciting incident of its early speaking through its generations (in both senses of "generations") as religious tradition.

The development of Bowden's manner of handling passages of text in her works from the 1970's and '80's should be stressed. It matters to her that the integrity of the passage's content remains intact. Her interest in ancient religious texts is not a generic or broadly universalized interest. Though she loves the general look of ancient writing and the abstract notion of "language" and "writing," the content of the writing

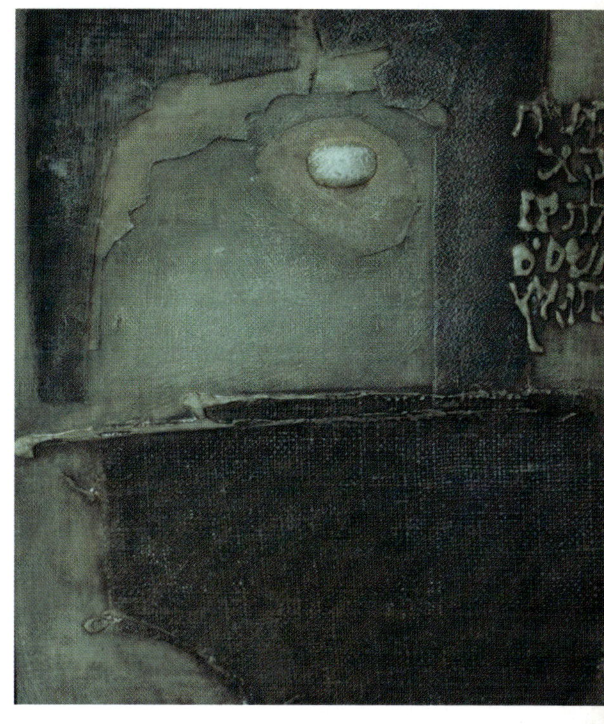

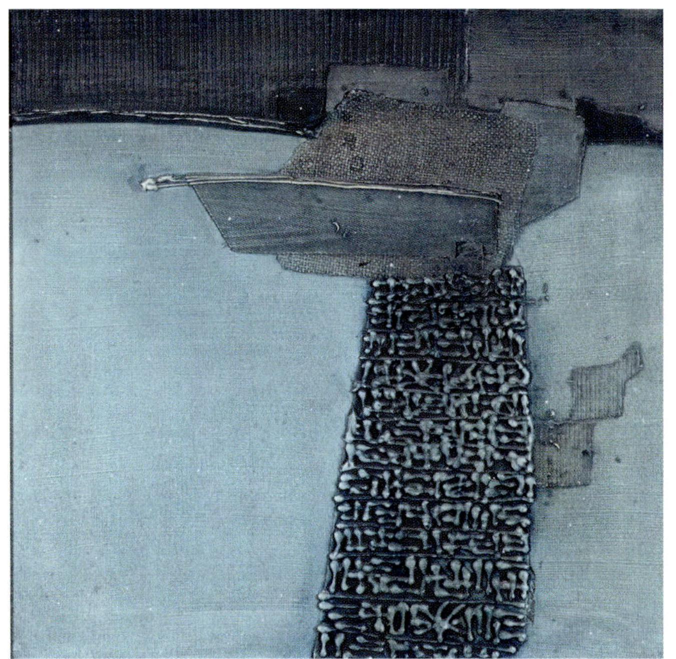

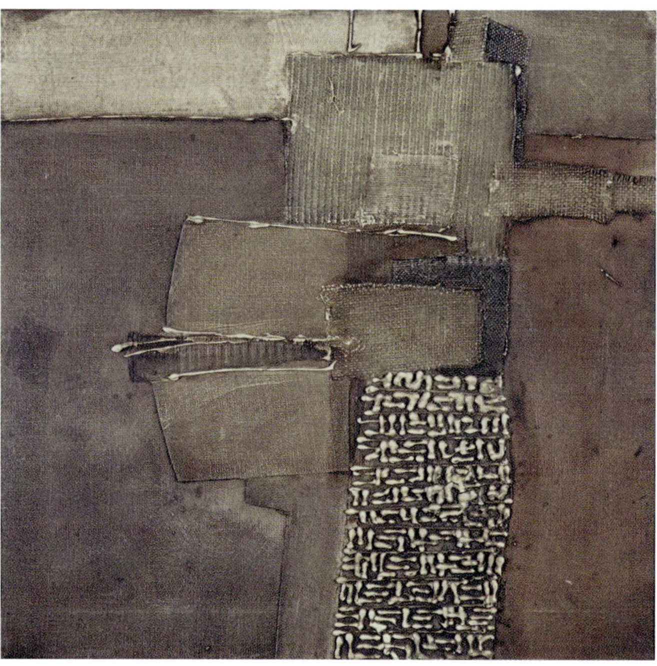

doctrine is what language and meaning should be reduced to.

She maintains enough of the original sense as to ground "writing" or language, but then abstracts it enough from a literal reading to evoke the deeper truth of the Jewish and Christian faiths, namely that despite the weight given to The Book, it is really about the Mystery to which The Book points. Indeed, Bowden's exploration of language within

as grounded in a real belief system also matters. Thus, instead of generalizing calligraphic gestures into a generic or highly personal set of markings (as the Abstract Expressionists did, for example), she has kept the specific content of each passage, and discovered its universality by removing the spaces between the words and lines to make a compacted text that appears first of all as an abstract pattern. In this, Bowden seeks to resolve a central question debated today, about whether language has any transcendent meaning that matters or whether language is an arbitrary system limited in significance to local conventions of social construction. Is language arbitrary and generic, or is it grounded in revelation? Bowden sides with the latter, but, crucially, she avoids such literalism as to suggest that dogmatic

her art touches upon one of the important struggles for people of biblical faith. Her comments about her own pilgrimage in these issues are relevant here to her work as an artist, for it affects how her imagery evolves over a forty-year period. As she put it in a letter to me,

"Because of my early childhood training, like many of us, the Bible was placed above everything (sometimes, I fear, above Jesus). Yet there was a real reverence for the Word. I shared that love, [but] have come over the span of years to realize that we do not find all the answers in words. I have come to distrust the dogma, the systematic theology and the judgmental attitudes that result from too high a regard for 'words.' But those words engage us in a conversation, even across time and place, that [do] help us plumb the depths of the Mystery, God with us."[5]

Late in the 1980s and early 1990s, Bowden's pieces began to show the influence of other antique texts, but in a different way. She began to use pages of facsimiles as collage elements, worked over with gestural layers of acrylic, gold gild, and fragments of the intaglio Hebrew passages cut from earlier collagraphs. Works such as *Illumination XVI* (Figure 109), *Illumination XXV* (Figure 108), and *Passage* (Figure 106) present a rich, even luxurious surface, increasingly fecund in their multiple layers of text, texture, and gestural markings. In these works of the early 1990s, Bowden's art suddenly attains a freedom of expression not felt in the previous work. These new pieces are more passionate, personal, abandoned. They bear a kind of expressive density and intensity in their layers that speaks of greater artistic depth emerging with power and joy. Perhaps this indicates a deepening of life experience in the artist; perhaps it indicates a new freedom in realizing that one's faith need not rest on systematic rows of literalisms, but can plunge with deep abandon into "the Mystery, God with us."

Whatever the explanation, Bowden's *Illuminations* gathers up her earlier uses of language, image, and layering into a new and rich integrity of media, feeling, and text. Whereas the earlier work developed her ideas and interests in an aesthetic conception that was, so to speak, an "edge-to-edge," or additive approach to organizing forms and layers, the *Illuminations*

now take on a more organic aesthetic. These pieces achieve greater seemlessness of integration through an interweaving and overlapping of forms and layers. Here, one layer is placed *over* a previous layer, such that the under-layments bleed through and inform what is over them. Bowden's works shift from being a kind of assembling of puzzle parts to becoming a kind of palimpsest.

A palimpsest is an ancient parchment written upon twice, the original writing having been rubbed out or effaced to make place for the second, but such that the original writing still shows through. The effect is an enormously rich, but evocative, surface that allows the parchment to bear within itself its own dialectical history. In Bowden's *Illuminations,* as well as concurrent works from her *Collage* series such as *Passage* (Figure 106), one senses the deep physical and emotional processes by which the work was made as becoming essential to the

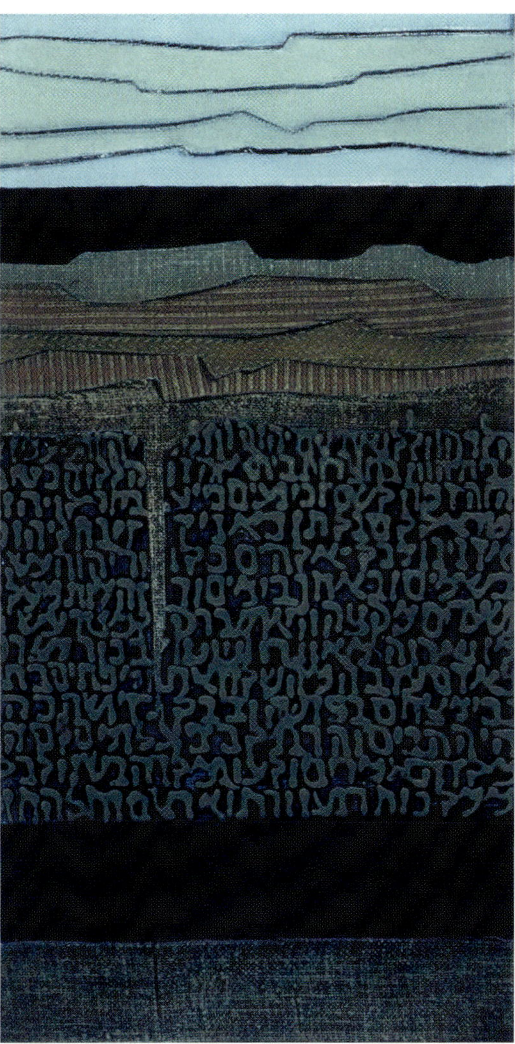

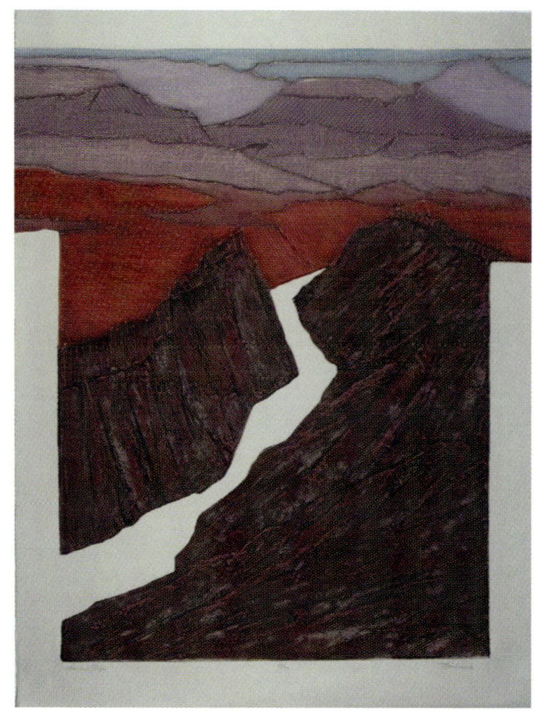

work's total appearance. Bowden has interwoven in collage layers of gold leaf, pages of medieval manuscripts, Psalms, and so on, combined with her own personal, calligraphic mark-makings in metallic acrylic paints, oil crayons, and pencil. The cumulative result is a work that bears witness not only to the grounded texts of religious faith and scriptures, but equally to the passionate engagement of the hand and eye as it traversed these layers of language, interpreting them until they become one's own.

The historian accounts for such breakthroughs at great risk. But it is interesting that *Passage* of 1994 leads into *Logos* (Figure 105) of 1995 with what seems to be a powerful momentum of ever-freer expression. In her own notations about *Passage,* Bowden speaks of its being made "during a time when I was recovering from back surgery and could not really work in the studio. So in desperation I began to cut apart portions of previous work, applied them to the surface of beautiful paper. So this little experiment launched another six or seven years of work." What fascinates is how often the encountering of severe limitations, and being forced to find new ways of working, can cause an artist to literally cannibalize earlier work and push it in new directions. With works such as *Passage* and *Logos,* Bowden has taken the accumulations and compressions of formal and linguistic fragments—which had by 1994 become her language—and used them as a new starting point, as a new and very personal kind of "language fragment" signifying her own relationship to these questions of meaning, belief, text, image, and creative process.

She now uses such fragments in the *Collage* series of the mid-'90s. As *Logos* reveals, the root of Word, of page, of text, felt both as content and abstract form, still unite. But now the gold gilded calligraphic rhythms of Hebrew text float before the collaged page of a Greek passage from John. The mysterious relationship between these texts, written centuries apart but joined within the Christian faith and its art, is evoked. Both Hebrew and Greek passages are about origin and Word as creative force. But in this extremely expressive piece, Bowden's earlier idea of visual Midrash is now raised to a far greater—far more *visually* expressive—level. The Mystery of "In the beginning God created," and of "darkness was upon the face of the deep; and the Spirit of God was moving over the face of the waters;" the mystery of the Word as being "In the beginning," as being with God and being God; and the mystery of these as textual revelations in The Book: these mysteries are here evoked as an abstract, gold Hebraic fragment hovering, in a division of three, above the face of the Greek text on the page, a text mostly effaced by darkness. One feels here how our language is, at best, a series of signs, indeed, generations of signs, which seek to mediate the gap between Mystery and our own consciousness.

At this point it becomes clear how generative language, word, and image are for Bowden's art. And, given all this, it makes sense that her next body of works takes a leap into three-dimensional objects in her most recent pieces, artist's books. Perhaps in the context of thinking about the role of language for Bowden, the richest example is her *Icon Book* (Figure 27) of 1993. Here the book itself stands in for language, both

     The Art of **Sandra Bowden**

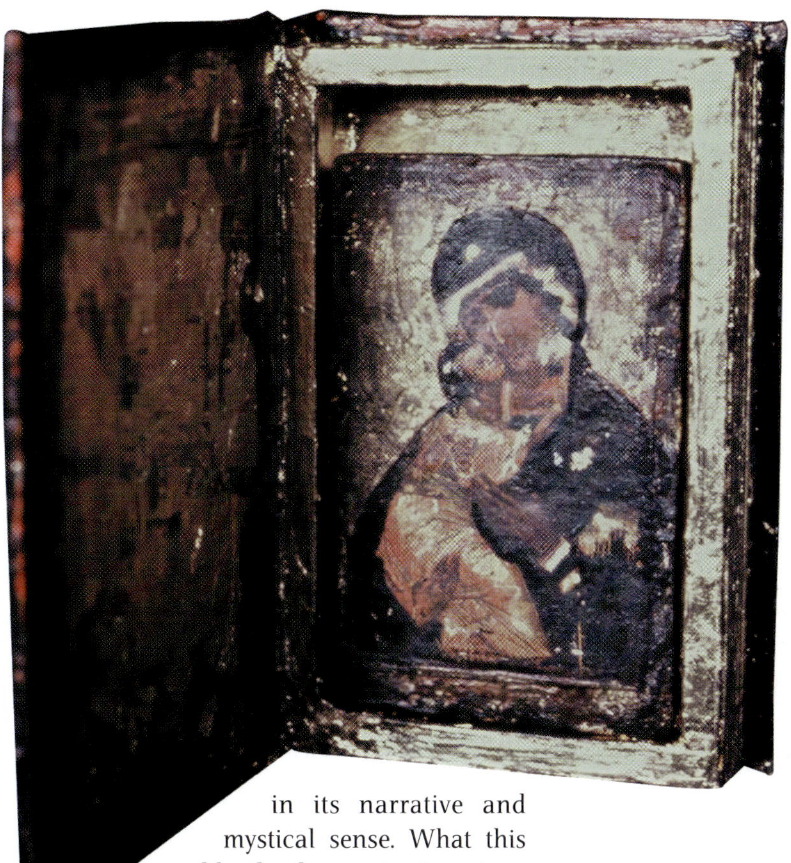

holds Mary, the vessel of the Christ Child's revelation to the world. With great finesse, Bowden's "Icon Book" is wonderfully both an oxymoron and a tautology; that is, it is a paradox. The full answer to the question of language's role in Sandra Bowden's art is that the language and image it contains and implies, the idea of God become human as the God-Man; the idea of Word as personal, and language as incarnate; all this is scooped up into paradox and, as Bowden acknowledges, into "Mystery, God with us."

in its narrative and mystical sense. What this golden book contains is an icon of Mary and the Christ Child. For Christians, The Book is God's Word, but the Christ is the Word incarnate. In the beginning it was the Word that underwrote the world in creation; and in the Incar-nation, the Word becomes flesh and lives now as God's image, God's *Eikon,* inside of the very world it had previously spoken into being. The Word contains the world, which now contains the Word. The vehicle of the book, as a vessel of revelation now

1   Genesis 1:1–3.

2   John 1:1–14.

3   Martin Buber. "Distance and Relationship," (1950), reprinted in *The Martin Buber Reader, Essential Writings.* ed. By Asher D. Biemann (New York: Palgrave, Macmillan, 2002), p. 210.

4   Norman Maclean. "A River Runs through It," in *A River Runs through It and Other Stories.* (Chicago: University of Chicago Press, 1976), p. 93.

5   Letter dated c. August 1, 2003.

Archaeological Findings

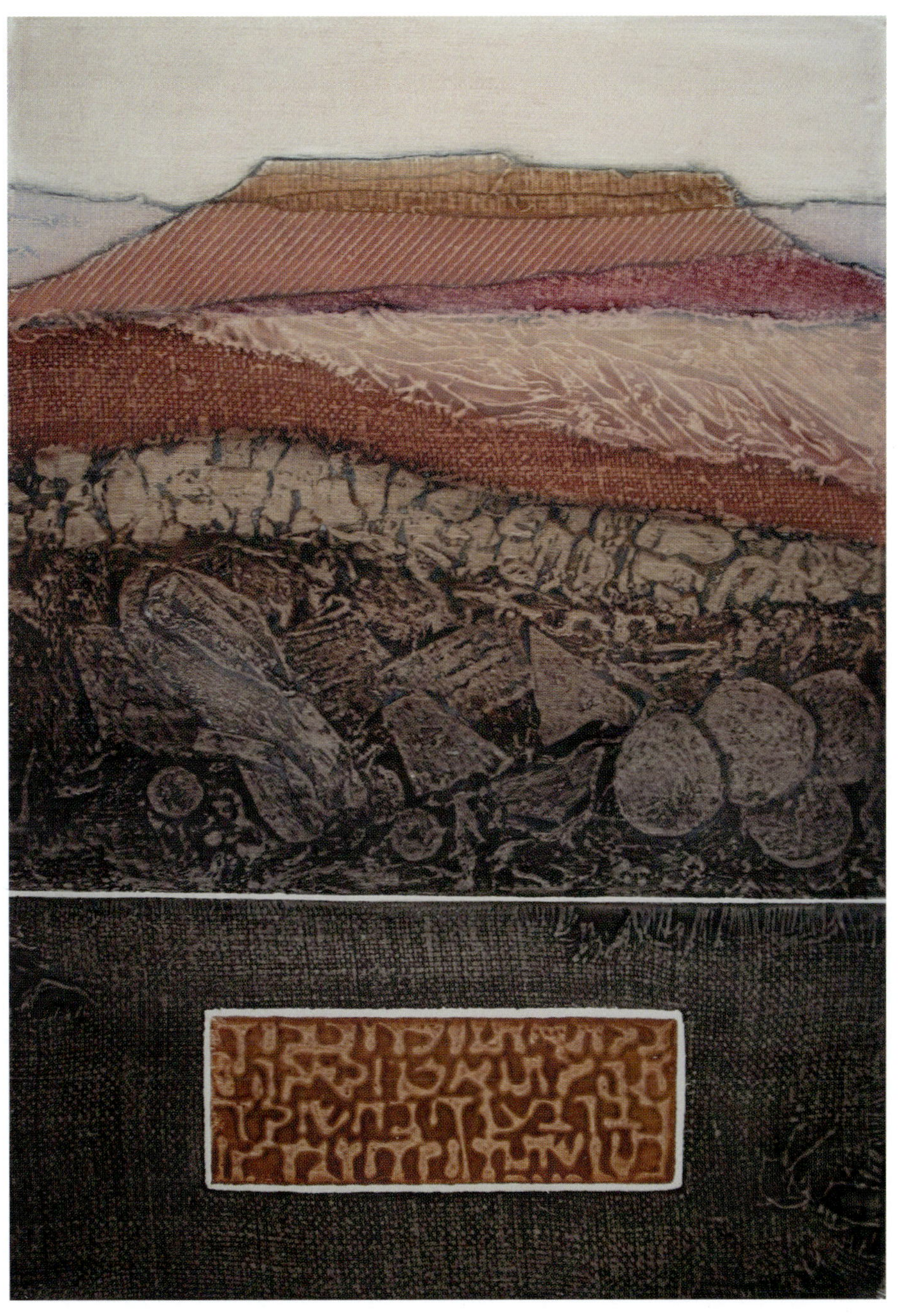

FIGURE 28
FORTRESS FINDS
Collagraph
1983
30 x 22

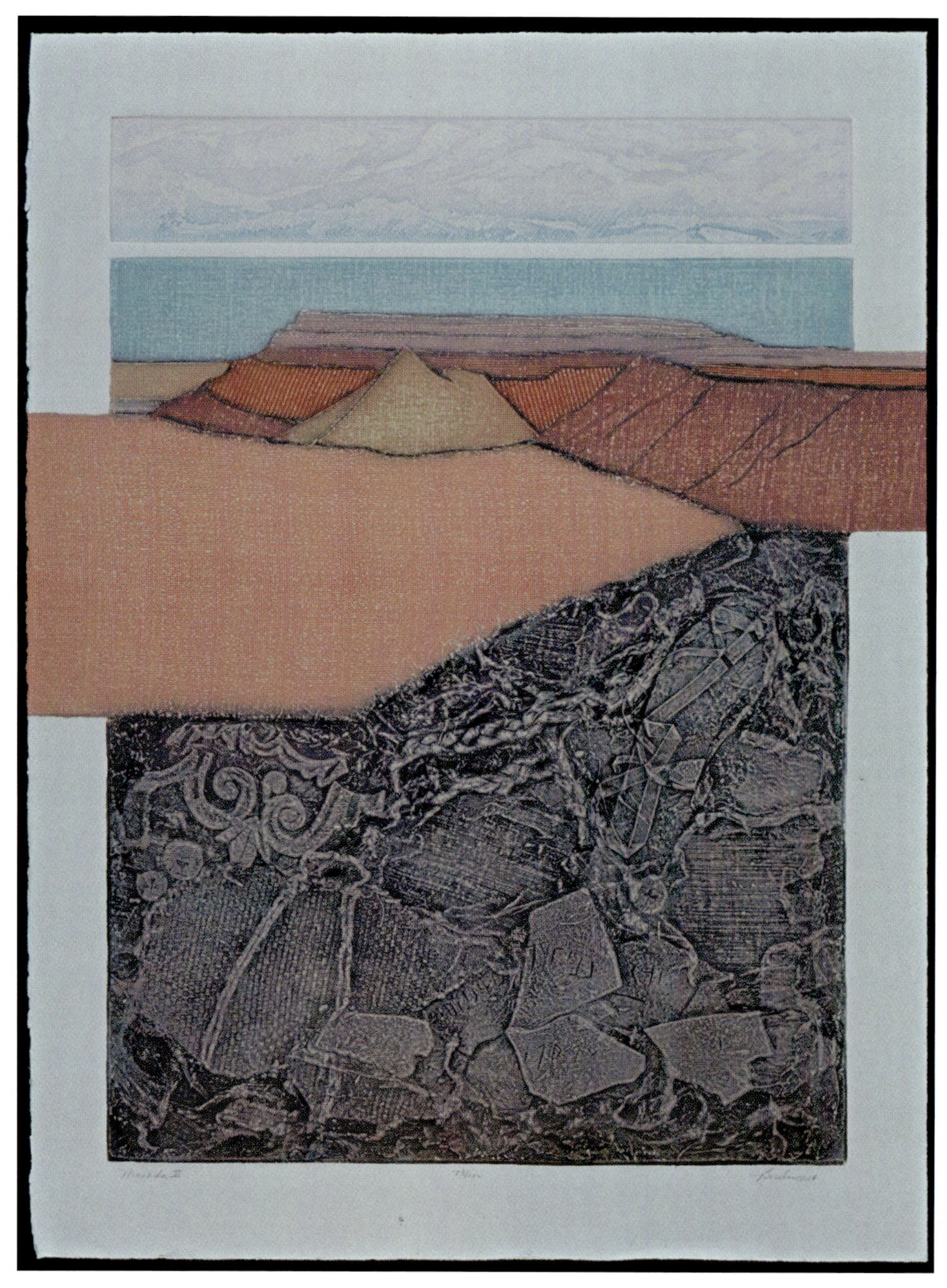

The Art of **Sandra Bowden**

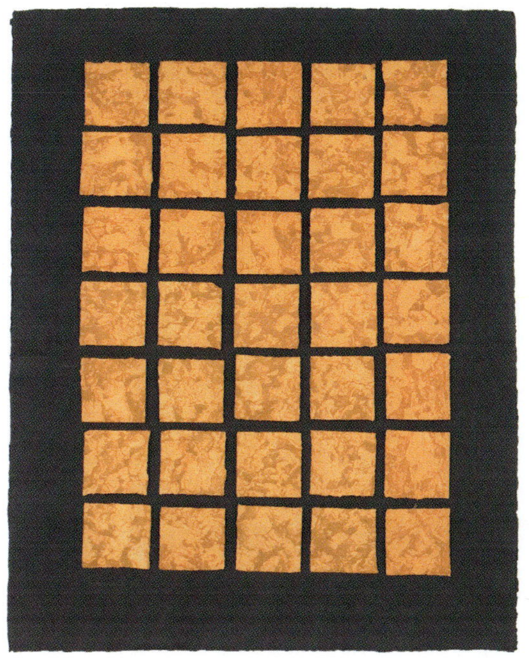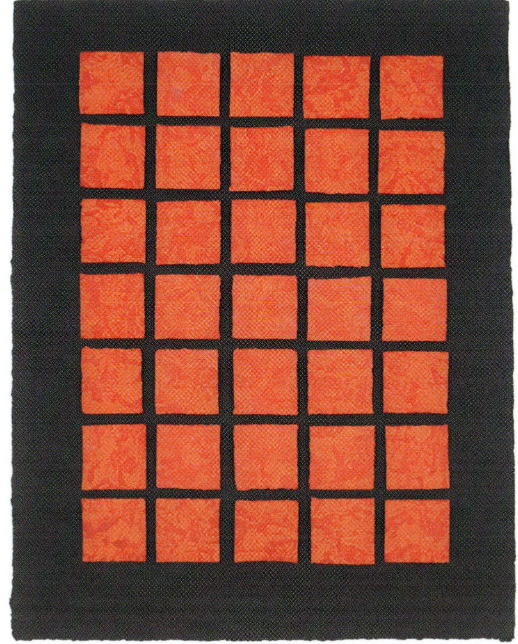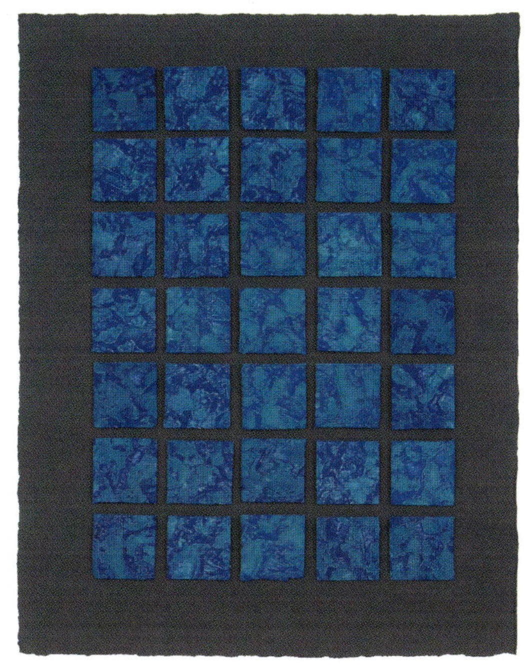

FIGURE 29
(OPPOSITE)
MASADA II
Collagraph
1984
30 x 22

FIGURE 30
**THREE PROPHETS:
ISAIAH, JEREMIAH,
EZEKIEL**
Collagraph
1984
26 x 20 each

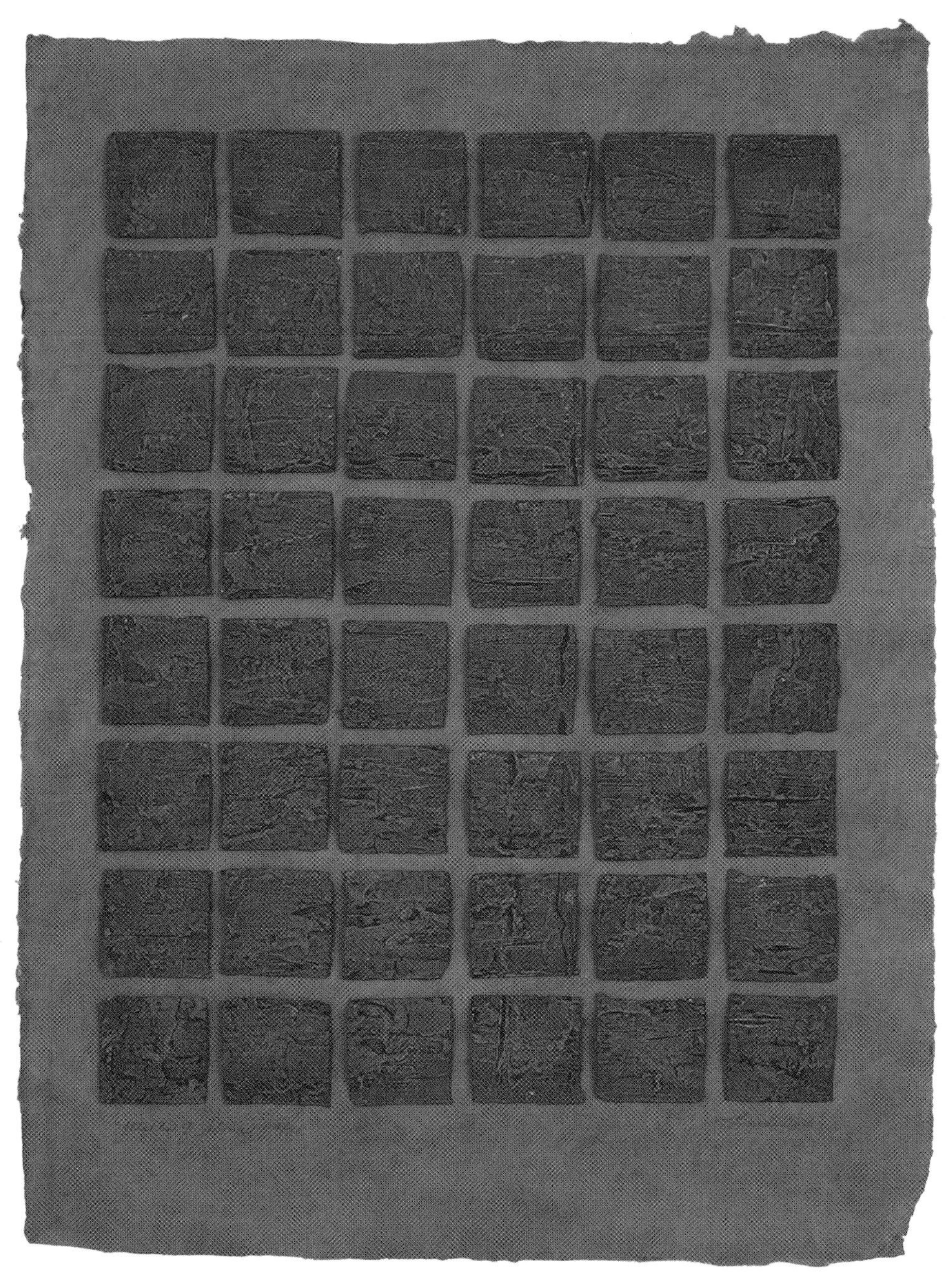

44   The Art of **Sandra Bowden**

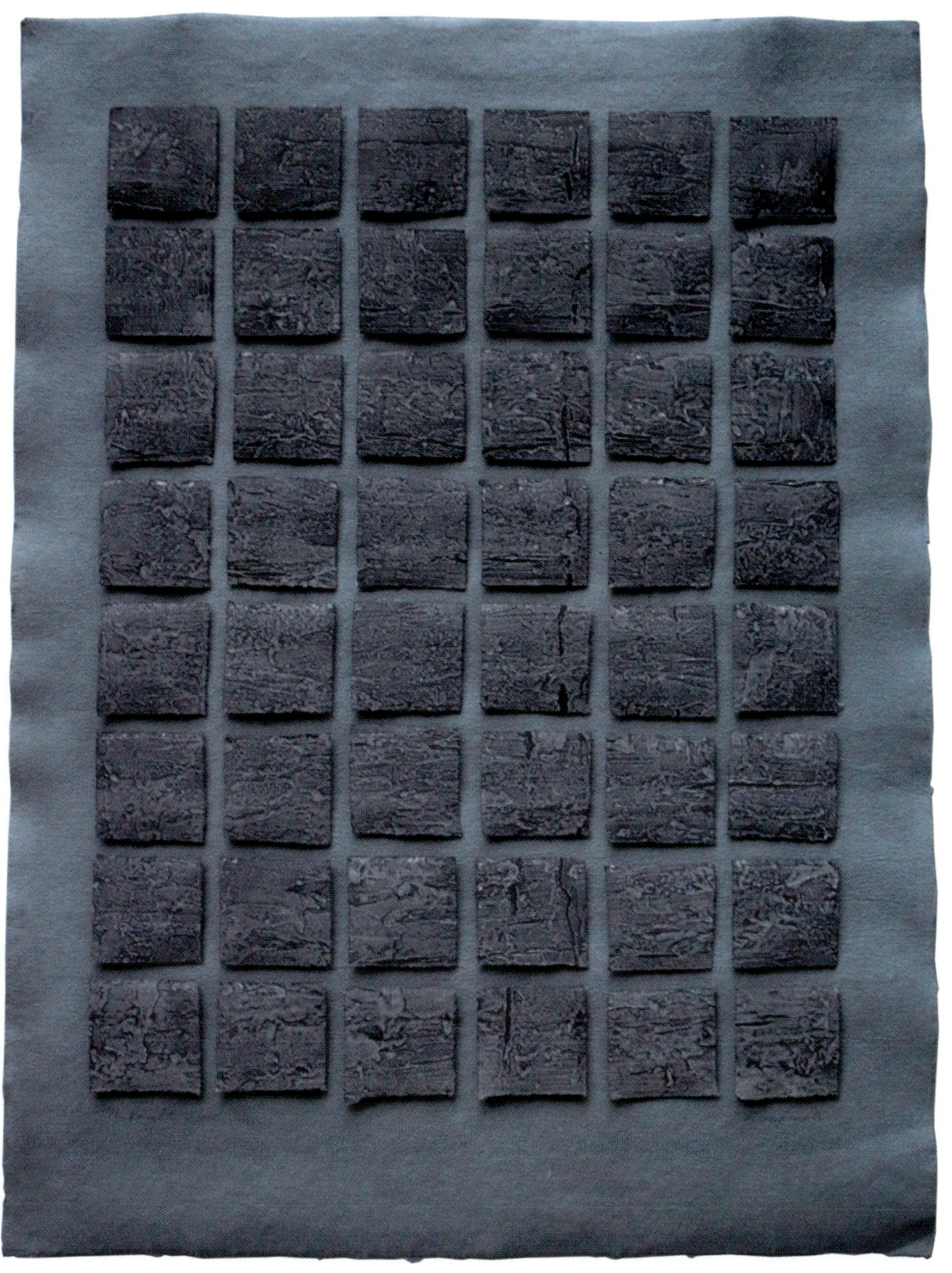

Geological Forms

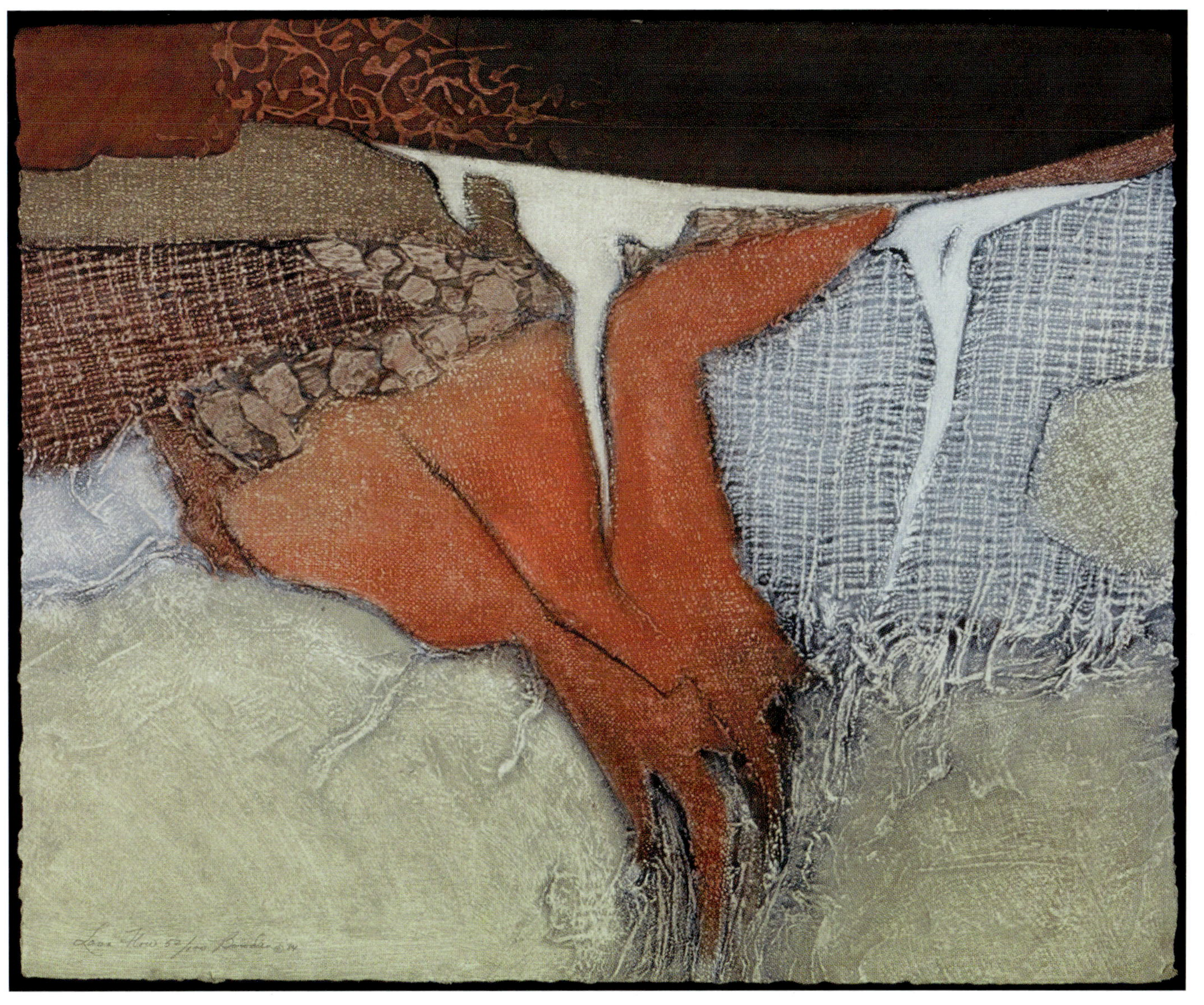

FIGURE 33
LAVA FLOW
Collagraph
1981
20 x 26

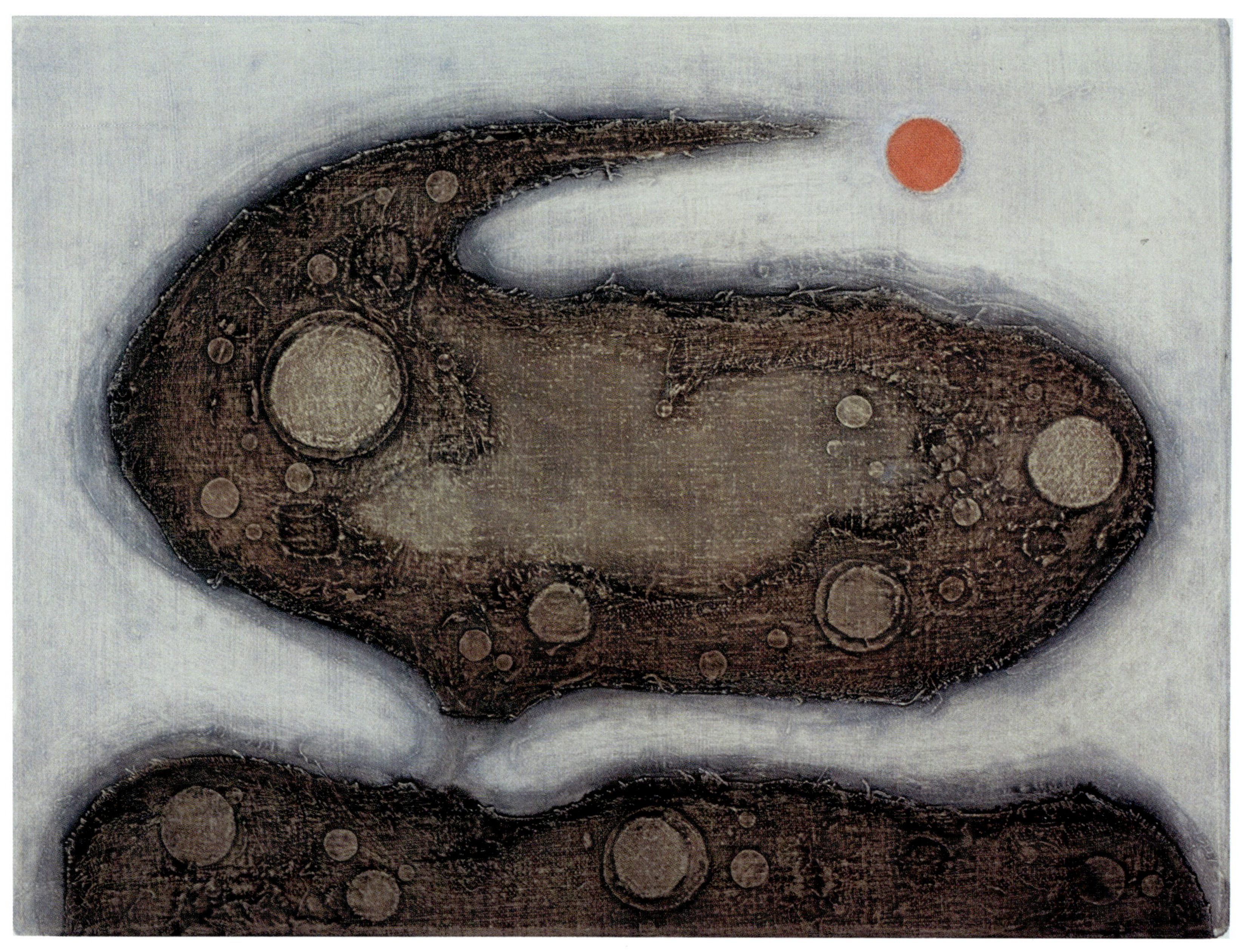

The Art of **Sandra Bowden**

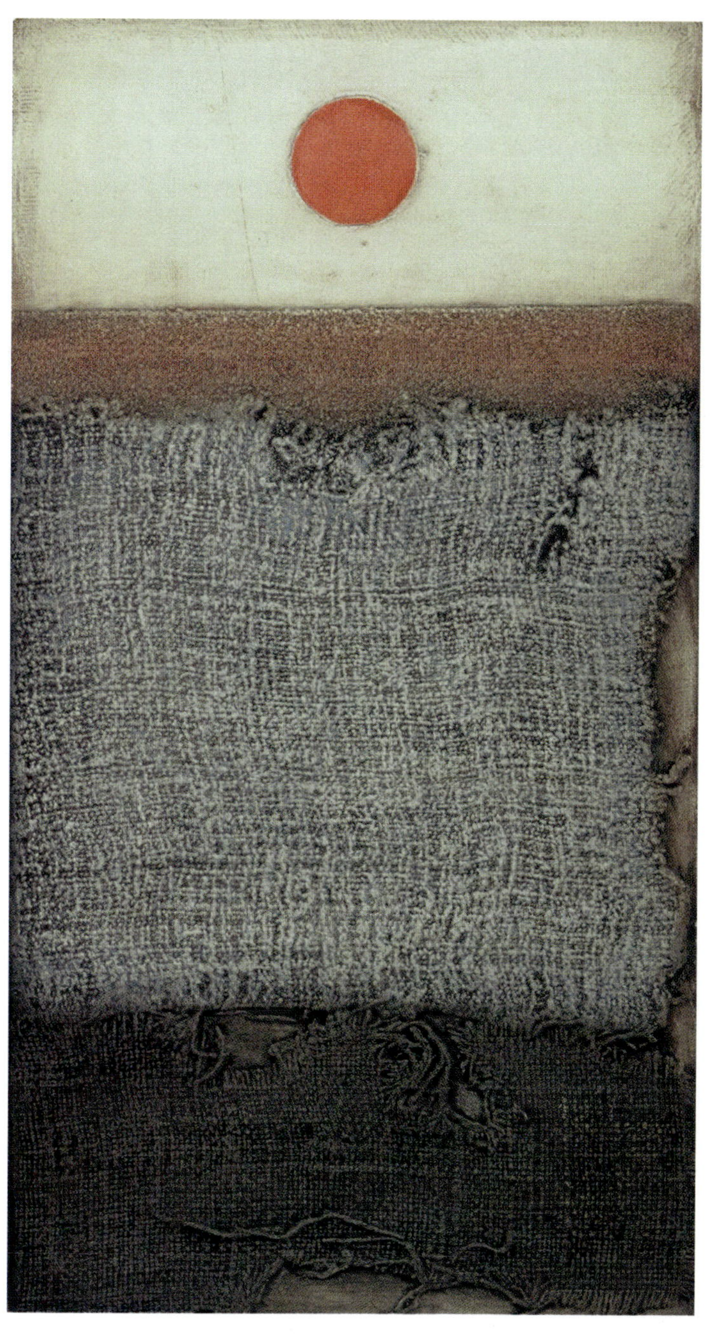

Geological Forms

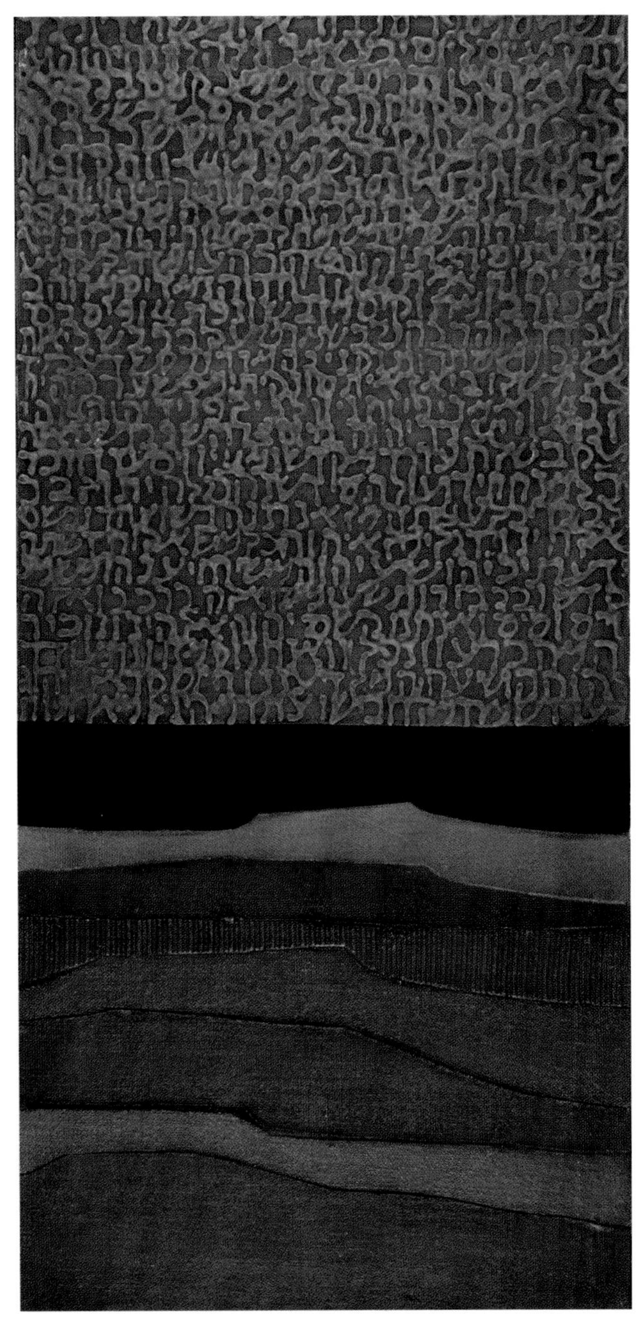

The Art of **Sandra Bowden**

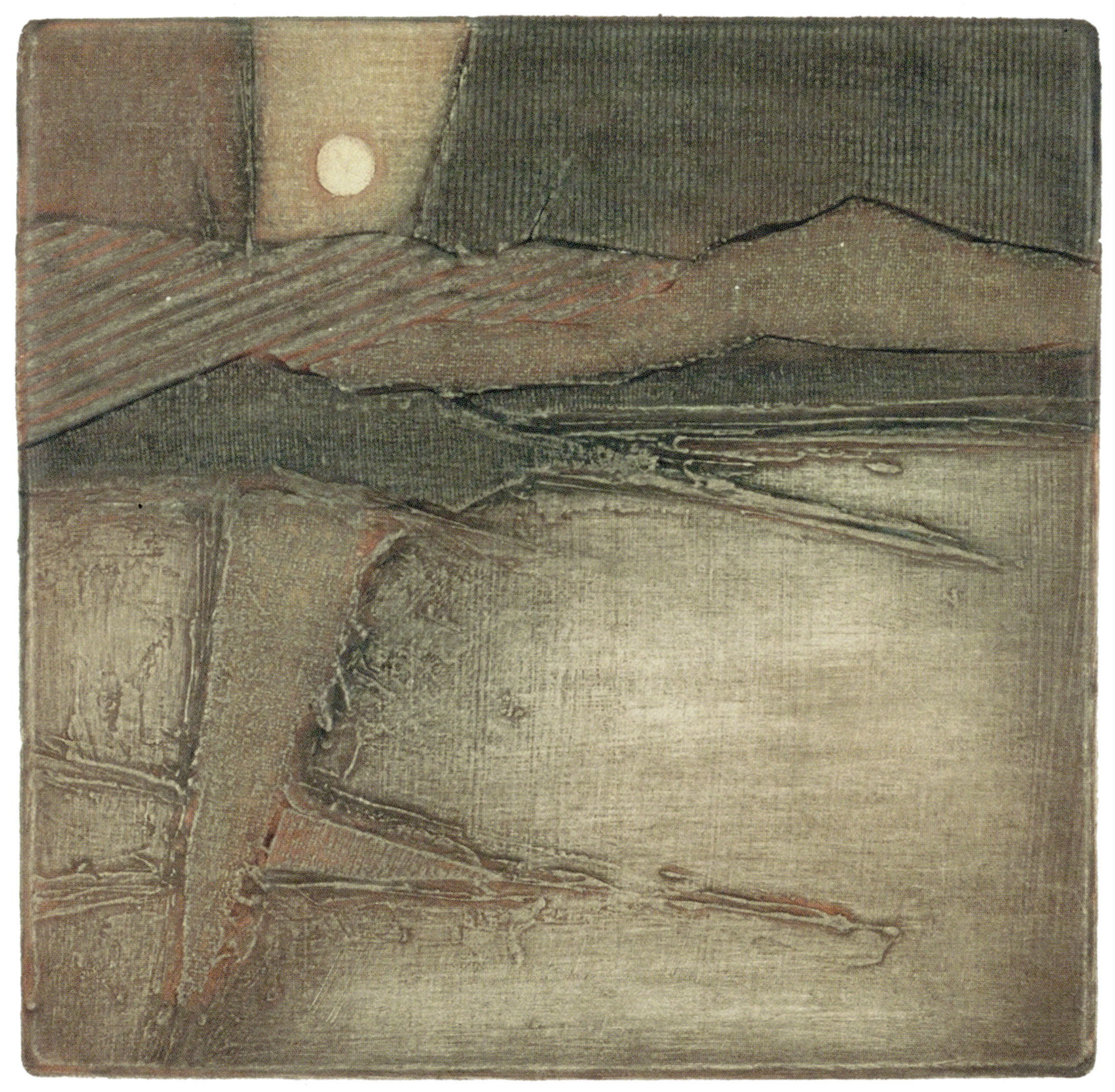

FIGURE 36
(OPPOSITE LEFT)
HEAVENS DECLARE
THE GLORY OF GOD
Oil painting
1975
34 x 16

FIGURE 37
MOON RISING
Collagraph
1980
16 x 16

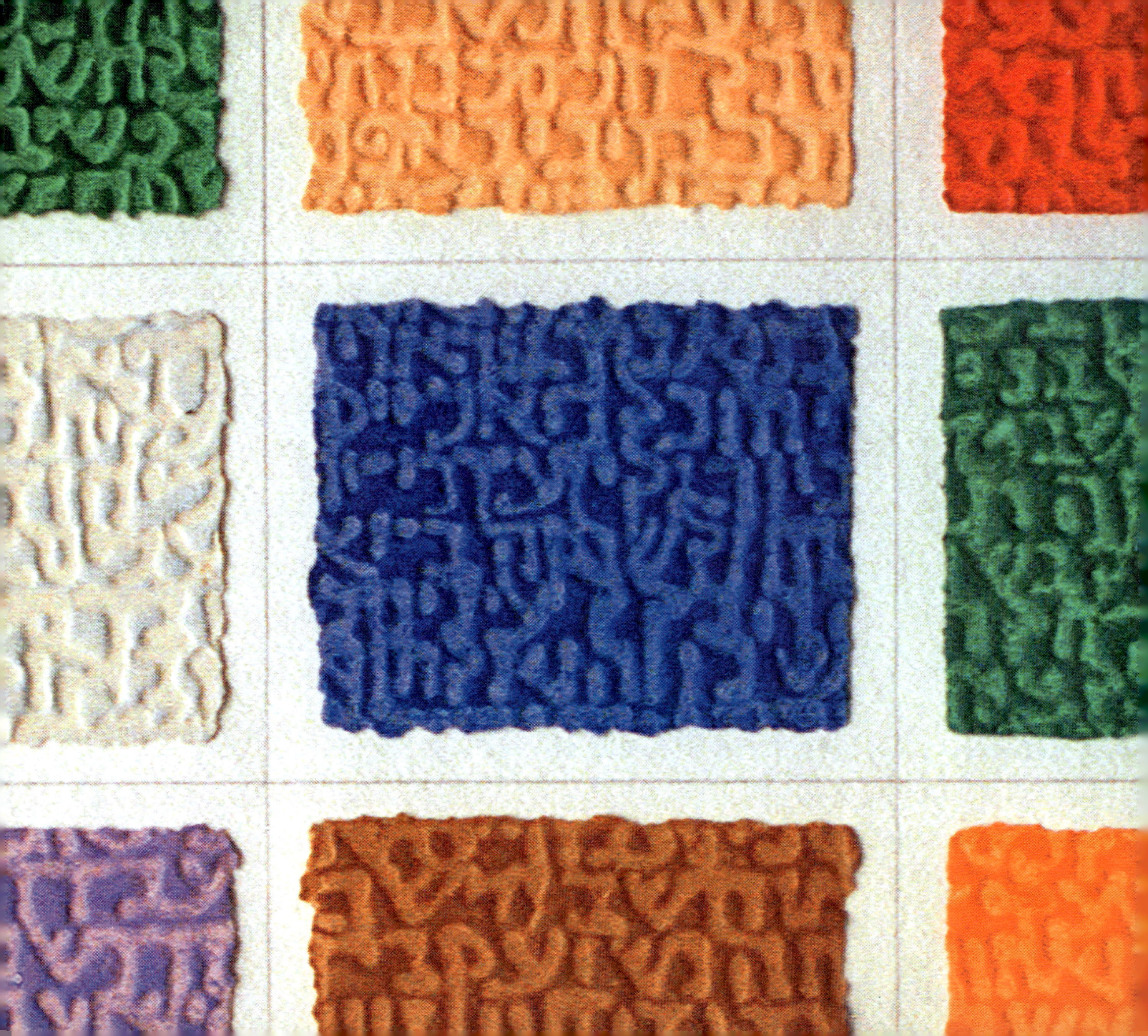

JEAN BLOCH ROSENSAFT

The Lord spoke to Moses: See, I have singled out by name Bezalel, son of Uri son of Hur, of the tribe of Judah. I have endowed him with a divine spirit of skill, ability and knowledge in every kind of craft: to make designs for work in gold, silver, and copper, to cut stones for setting and to carve wood—to work in every kind of craft. *Exodus 31:1-5*

The creation of art is first depicted in the Bible when God describes to Moses, in exquisite detail, all the fittings for the sanctuary—the Tabernacle, ark and its curtain, table and lampstand, the menorah, altars, entrance screen, laver, hangings, and vestments for Aaron, his sons, and others officiating in the sanctuary. Bezalel and his assistant, Oholiab, of the tribe of Dan, are identified as "endowed" with the "divine spirit of skill" of the carver, the designer, the embroiderer, and the weaver.[1] They are specifically instructed to create the beautiful ritual objects and fittings which will enhance the People of Israel's spirituality—their worship of God.

Throughout history, this "divine spirit of skill" has produced art and artifacts that have sustained worship and perpetuated faith-based identity from generation to generation. Such artistry has reinforced spirituality and continuity, from antiquity to the present day.

Sandra Bowden situates herself within this artistic and biblical heritage. Seeking the origins of Judeo-Christian civilization, for forty years she has embarked upon an intellectual and personal journey of discovery that has served as the wellspring of her imagination. In 1972, she began her study of biblical and modern Hebrew, later going on to study archaeology and to explore the excavated ancient sites in Israel in the early 1980s. Going back to these sources, in which text and artifact attest to biblical history, she has discovered the subject matter of her *oeuvre* and produced work transmitting the seamless continuum of antiquity and modernity, immediacy and eternity.

Bowden's earliest work, *Ancient Writings* (Figure 21), forecasts her artistic directions, with its calligraphic, collage, and reduced palette elements. In *Unearthed* (Figure 24) she expresses the hidden treasures of the ancient past, embedded in layers of earth and stones, waiting to be revealed. The encoded stone, buried beneath the undulating desert sand and weighty, layered rubble awaits discovery when, Bowden explains, "it will serve to help reconstruct the past and offer insight for the future."[2]

Deluge (Figure 23) evokes the biblical flood story, with Noah's ark pitched precariously between the torrent, conveyed by corduroy fabric, and the striated blue waters. Cuneiform writing provides the support for the ark, adrift in the open sea, suggesting divine guidance and the promise of redemption.

Hebrew text enters into Bowden's works with *In the Beginning* (Figure 22) of 1972, and the tentative inclusion of the Genesis text. The textured letters, "In the beginning God created heaven and earth," move gently into the canvas

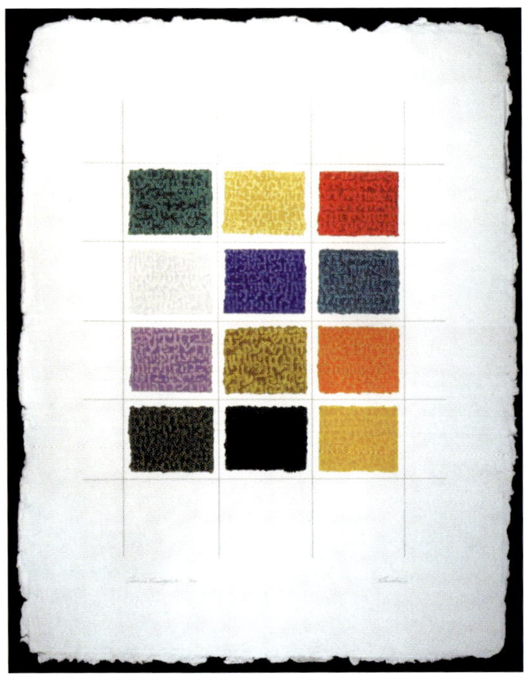

on the right edge of the canvas; their right-to-left movement reinforces the direction of the Hebrew language.[3] These first words, only the beginning of the biblical verse, evoke the first moments of creation: "In the beginning God created heaven and earth—the earth being unformed and void, with darkness over the surface of the deep and a wind from God sweeping over the water—God said, 'Let there be light;' and there was light."[4] The canvas echoes these words, with its horizontal division between the lower formless earth and the arc-like opening of the heavens above. The orb of light, conveying God's presence, bursts through the space, bringing illumination and suggesting an *ovum,* the beginning of life.

The *Earth Was Without Form and Void* (Figure 40) expresses the roiling chaos before creation, while the amoebic forms taking shape forecast the potentiality of fertility. *Lava Flow* (Figure 33) erupts with an explosive force, as the earth, sea, and sky convulse with the force of creation. The rent forms and apertures suggest birthing. Through these works, Bowden acknowledges the divine source of all new life.

The presence of archaeological study can be felt immediately upon viewing Bowden's works. The striations of the *tel,* indicating layers of time, are intrinsic to her compositions. The textures of her collagraphy, the earth, sea, and sky-toned palette, and the accretion of signs, symbols, and elements, many of which are drawn directly from excavated biblical sites, attest to the inspiration drawn from biblical archaeology.

Bowden's 1983 series, the *Israelite Tel Suite* (*Megiddo, Gezer, Hazor,* and *Lachish*), employs a horizontally layered composition, suggesting a movement through time, from the sky-filled

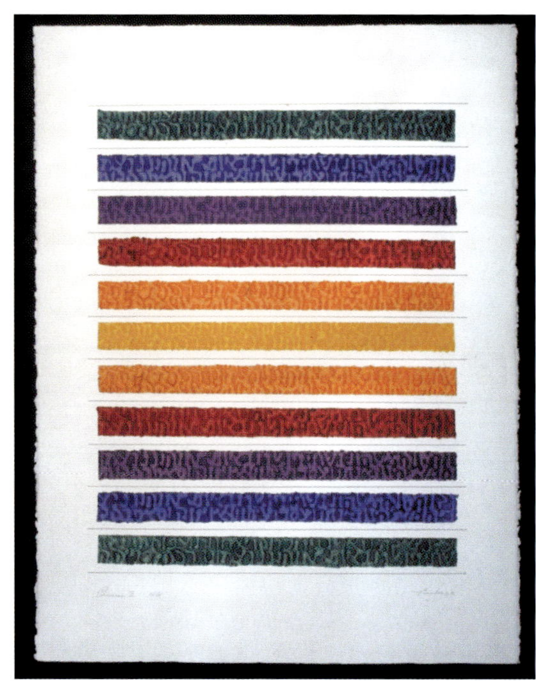

arid landscape at the top we encounter today, through the sedimentary accretions in the middle ground, and the archaeological artifacts laying at the historical source. *Megiddo* (Figure 41), for example, features a section of the Solomonic gate of this ancient Israelite city as well as its famed lion seal, with its inscription, "Belonging to Shema, servant of Jeroboam."[5] *Gezer* (Figure 42), inspired by excavations of the Canaanite city included in the dowry King Solomon received from one of his wives, includes a burial site and the Gezer calendar, dating from 950 B.C., an agricultural calendar listing the months of harvest, gathering, and planting. *Hazor* (Figure 43) recalls the ancient city in the Northern Galilee where archaeologists unearthed a Canaanite

The Art of **Sandra Bowden**

sanctuary containing basalt steles, one etched with two hands raised toward a lunar symbol. *Lachish* (Figure 44) evokes the Israelite city southwest of Jerusalem which yielded stones etched with cursive Paleo-Hebrew; the figurative frieze at the base of the work depicts a portion of a mural found at Nineveh depicting the Israelites being marched into captivity by King Sennacherib.

Isaiah, Jeremiah, Ezekiel (Figure 30) develops Bowden's archaeological interests further by focusing on the masonry of ancient stone walls, irregularly shaped, roughly mortared, and casting shadows as they jut into space. Here, the raised and roughly surfaced fragments of textured paper construct walls symbolic of each Old Testament prophet's era: Isaiah's golden Jerusalem, Jeremiah's Jerusalem aflame, and Ezekiel's entry wall into Babylon, whose walls were adorned with intense ceramic blue.

Enriching these works is the pervasive presence of Hebrew text, reinforcing the antiquity that is at the heart of the artist's imagination. Indeed, Bowden stands among a number of twenty-first century artists who are committed to the vitality of biblical text and its enduring meaning for our own time. In her case, it is the written word that is of paramount importance. Appropriating the role of the scribe, who throughout the millennia has copied the Hebrew Bible, Bowden embeds her work with excerpts of Hebrew text, ranging from Genesis to the prophets. Her calligraphy is rooted in ancient letterforms, thick, textured, and graced by her unique hand. Her interest, however, is not just to reproduce this text, but to somehow extend its meaning. Therefore, she omits the spacing between these words so that the letters

become an open-ended, continuous element which constructs her compositions.

Bowden inscribes the complete Hebrew text of Psalm 19 in *Heavens Declare the Glory of God* (Figure 36): "The heavens declare the glory of God, the sky proclaims his handiwork . . .. His rising-place is at one end of heaven, and his circuit reaches the other, nothing escapes his heat . . .. The teaching of the Lord is perfect, renewing life . . .."[6] The horizontal striations of the hilly landscape lead the viewer's eyes upward, where God's omnipresence is expressed through the dominant upper half of this painting. The words of the psalm fill the visual field and seem to extend beyond the limits of the canvas itself.

Bowden's scribing expresses her love for the sacred. Text becomes interpretation and, in doing so, Bowden's art becomes *Midrash*. *Midrash* is the discovery of meanings other than literal in the Bible and denotes literature that interprets scripture to extract its full implication and meaning. Throughout the ages, these interpretations were formed as a response to the needs of a particular age or environment. Such commentaries, particularly of the Hebrew

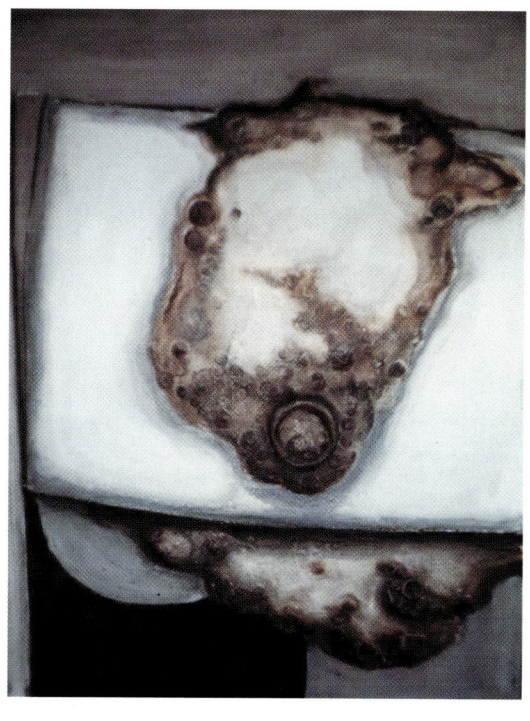

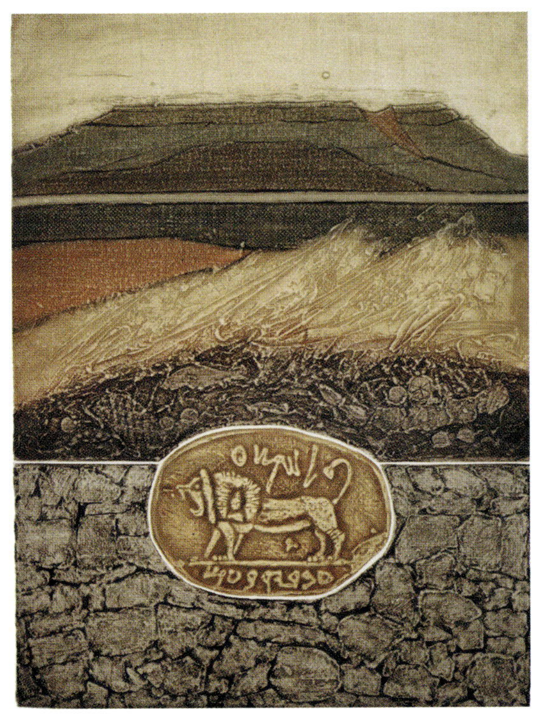

Bible's legal portions, go back to very early origins, with scribes and scholars studying the traditional interpretation of the written law and applying it to the everyday needs of the community. These early *halakhic midrashim,* originating with the teachers whose sayings are preserved in the Mishnah, dealt for the most part with Mosaic law.

The aggadic *Midrash,* on the other hand, expounded on the nonlegal parts of scripture and tackled subject matter encompassing theology, ethical teaching, exhortation, popular philosophy, legend, allegory, and fables. Midrashic literature offered a way of delving more deeply than the literal meaning of the word as scripture and served as a method of linking the various parts of the Bible together by the discovery of typological patterns, verbal echoes, and rhythms of repetition. Aggadic *Midrashim,* in particular, were instruments for imparting contemporary relevance to biblical events. Midrashic literature transcends time, as scholars throughout the centuries engaged in layers of interpretation and references in a dynamic exchange between past and present.

Bowden's series of Hebrew text-works exude many of these qualities of patterning, repetition, and reinterpretation. A 1978 version of *In the Beginning* employs a Dead Sea Scroll script, and the first chapter of Genesis comprises the image of this collagraph. Her compacted writing creates an overall patterning, legible but not easily read. In the first line of the first verse of Genesis, the words "God created" rise from the center toward a celestial body.

In *He Spake and It Was Done* (Figure 13), she further develops this imagery. The same Genesis

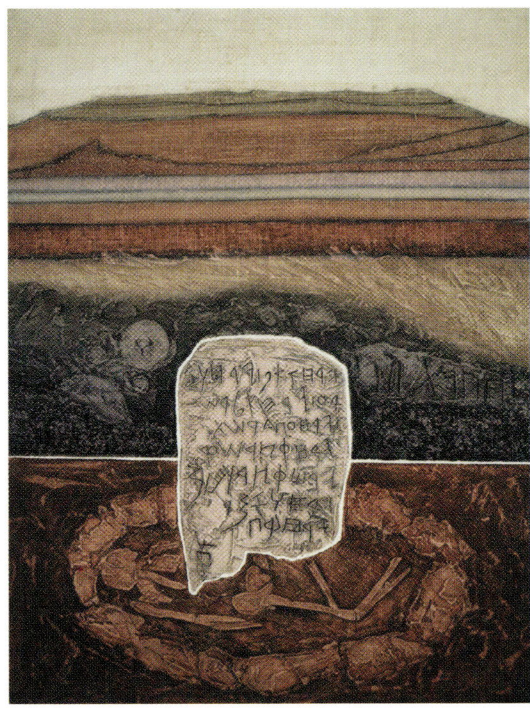

text appears in the center of the work, but embossed around it are the words of David: "By the word of the Lord the heavens were made.... For he spoke, and it was; He commanded and it endured."[7] As in rabbinic commentaries, multiple texts appear on the same page; the core, central text is elaborated, dissected, and contemporanized by surrounding texts dating centuries apart. As Bowden explains, "From these markings we are able to share thoughts and ideas across the barriers of time and place. We are privileged to continue a conversation or story with those from thousands of years ago . . . adding our voice to ideas that resonated with thinkers from another time."[8]

Aaron's Breastplate (Figure 38) is Bowden's

    The Art of **Sandra Bowden**

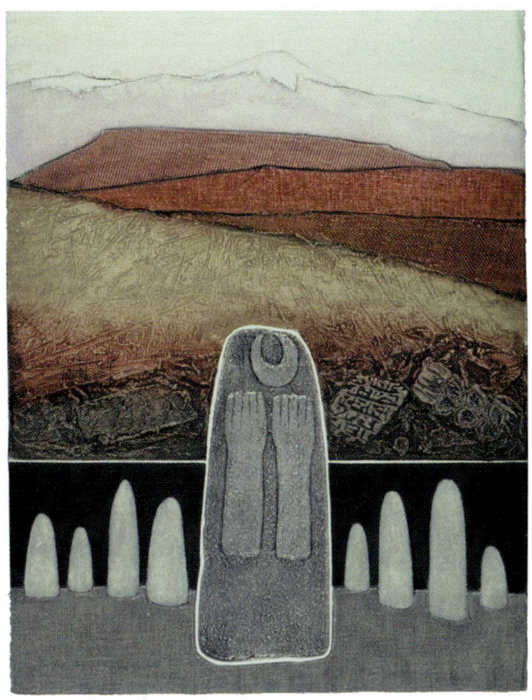

interpretation of the High Priest's vestments for officiating in the Tabernacle, described in detail in Exodus 39:8–14. Aaron's breastplate, made of gold, blue, purple, and crimson yarns, and of fine twisted linen, was square and inset with four rows of stones engraved like seals with the names of the twelve tribes of Israel and encircled with frames of gold. The dimensionality of Bowden's assemblage simulates the biblical sacral garb. Her palette reflects the semi-precious stones detailed in the Bible: The first row was carnelian, chrysolite, and emerald; the second row was turquoise, sapphire, and amethyst; the third row was jacinth, agate, and crystal; and the fourth row was beryl, lapis lazuli, and jasper. In Bowden's assemblage, she not only inscribes the names of each of the twelve tribes but also includes the Genesis 49 text of Jacob's blessing for each of his twelve sons.

The preciousness inferred in this work is further elaborated in Bowden's *Illuminations*. Bowden sees herself as a successor to the scribes of centuries past who embellished sacred texts with illuminations, gilding, and imagination. In *And There Was Light* (Figure 114), Bowden describes, "I have used iridescent paint and oil crayons, as well as a variety of leafing . . . gold, silver, and multicolored foils, to give these pieces a richness and precious quality. The Genesis text 'and there was light' is inscribed into the surface of the gold leafing as if onto the illuminated page."[9]

She extends these techniques in her artist's books, as in *Book for Remembrance* (Figure 121), in which the inner and outer surfaces are textured with gold leaf and inscribed thoughts and treasured memories construct a precious, personal object for meditation and delight.

Her *Collage* series provided Bowden with a new direction for working in a smaller scale, particularly during the period when she was recovering from back surgery in 1994 and unable to paint or work her etching press. These works were created by recycling older works by cutting them up and reassembling them into new formats on handmade papers, and incorporating appropriated materials such as old printed Bibles in multiple languages from around the world, musical scores, dictionaries, and other tactile materials.

Psalm 150 (Figure 141) is the artist's expression of joy. The gilded central Hebrew text is superimposed onto "Hallelujah," a French

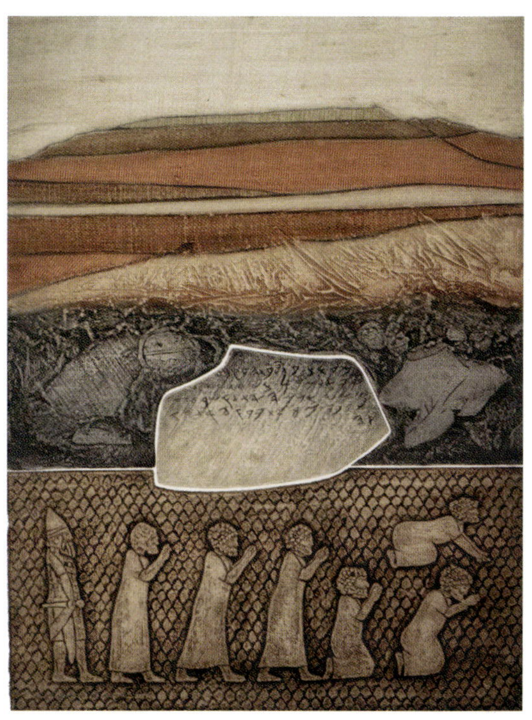

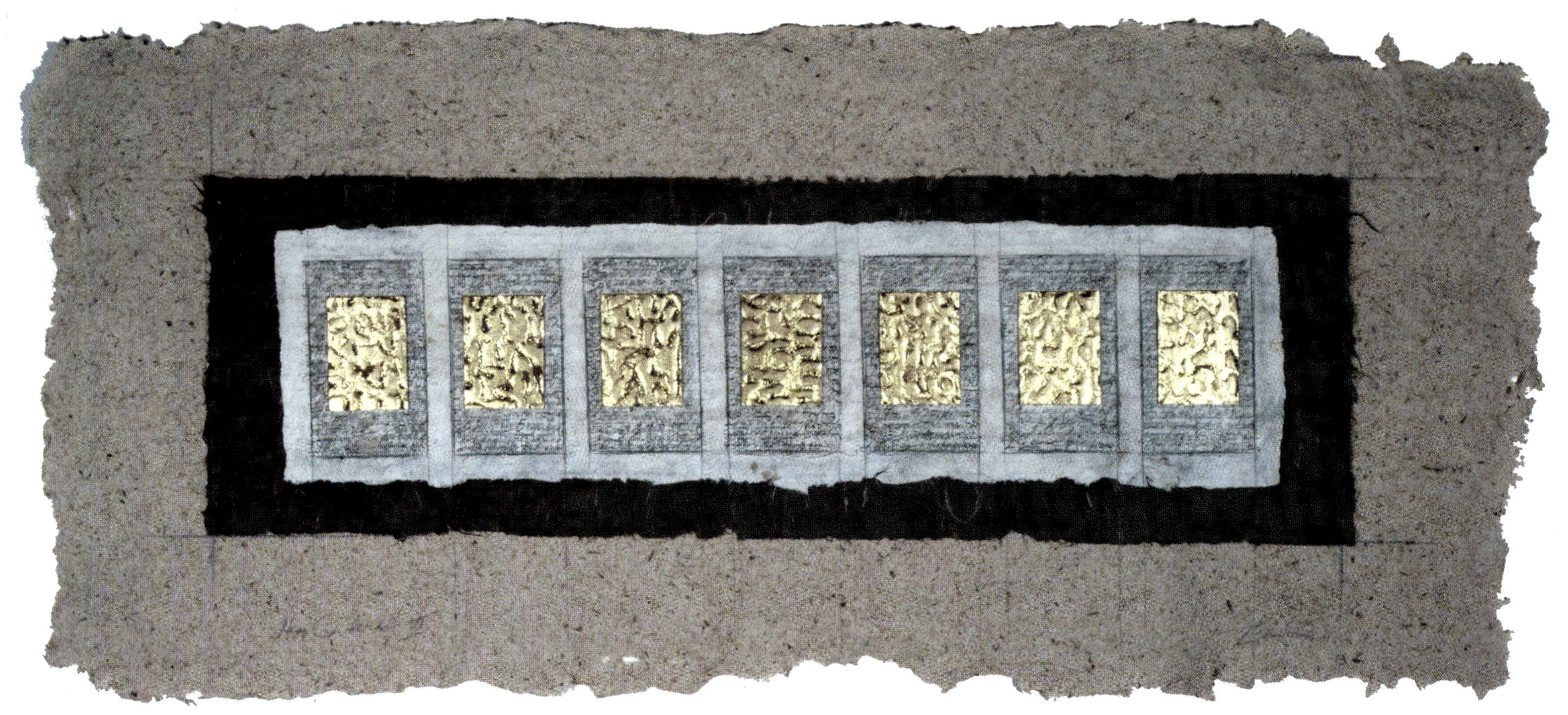

hymn setting of this text dating from 1568. As throughout her *oeuvre,* Bowden compresses time, so that biblical text traverses the millennia in an encounter with European sacred music and a contemporary artist's sensibility and imagination.

Hear, O Israel (Figure 45) culminates Bowden's forty years of creativity. Here, the sacred affirmation of the Jewish faith, the *Shema,* inspires an exultant work. In Judaism, this text of Deuteronomy 6:4-9 and 11:13–21 is inscribed on parchment and tightly rolled into a small case.

The *mezuzah,* which is affixed to doorposts in Jewish homes in accordance with the prescription in Deuteronomy 6, represents the sanctification of the home and a reminder of God's omnipresence. Bowden follows in the tradition of Jewish ritual art, in which the *mezuzah* case itself has been one of the objects of artistic expression, particularly since the eighteenth century. Her collage on richly textured banana paper supports a central field made of white vellum, the parchment material traditionally used for the *mezuzah* scroll, upon which she has transferred portions of the

    The Art of **Sandra Bowden**

Deuteronomy text. Over this transfer she has inscribed the same text in English. Surrounding the central panels are the words, "Hear, O Israel," written numerous times. The gilding of the seven vertical elements, symbolizing the seven days of creation, reinforces the beauty and precious nature of this sacred instruction:

> "Hear, O Israel! The Lord is our God, the Lord alone. You shall love the Lord your God with all your heart and with all your soul and with all your might. Take to heart these instructions with which I charge you this day. Impress them upon your children. Recite them when you stay at home and when you are away, when you lie down and when you get up. Bind them as a sign on your hand and let them serve as a symbol on your forehead; inscribe them on the doorposts of your house and on your gates."[10]

Here, Bowden affirms the continuity of universal values and spirituality in a work of powerful beauty.

The text, the *tel*, and time remain at the core of Bowden's art. The words of the Hebrew Bible are the physical, emotional, and spiritual substance of her works. Again and again, Bowden returns to the beginning, to Genesis. In her depictions of the heavens and the earth, she celebrates God's creation. Moreover, she reflects on the artist's role as a creator and the divine inspiration that sustains creativity.

With archaeology as the partner to biblical text, she demonstrates that digging through the *tel* is like digging into the text to find multiple meanings relevant to contemporary life and experience. As a contemporary midrashist, her rhythmic juxtaposition of the hidden and the revealed; texture, pattern and repetition; and core text and interpretation convey the permeability of time, where the past, present, and future communicate across the millennia, expressing the enduring vitality of Torah as a tree of life to those who uphold it. For Sandra Bowden, the markings of antiquity take root in a contemporary artist's creativity, providing the language, both visually and metaphorically, for expressing faith.

1   Exodus 31:3.

2   Conversation with the artist, August 2003.

3   Genesis 1:1.

4   Genesis 1:1–3.

5   Conversation with the artist, 2003.

6   Psalm 19.

7   Psalm 33:6 and 9.

8   Artist's statement, 2003.

9   Ibid.

10 Deuteronomy 6:4–9.

FIGURE 45
(OPPOSITE)
HEAR, O ISRAEL
Collage mixed media
2001
16 x 33

Crucifixions

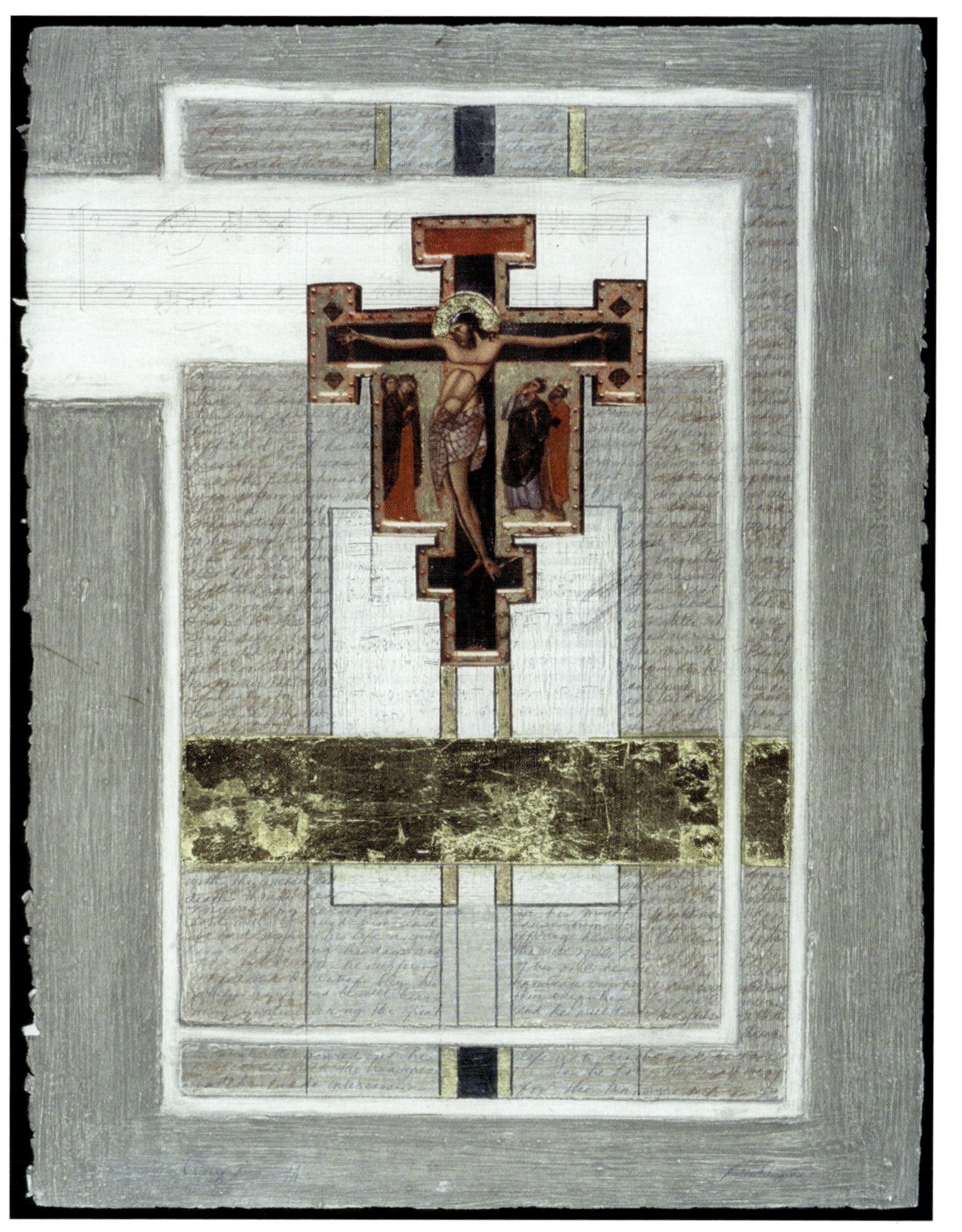

FIGURE 46
**HE WAS WOUNDED
FOR OUR
TRANSGRESSIONS**
Collagraph
mixed media
1992
30 x 22

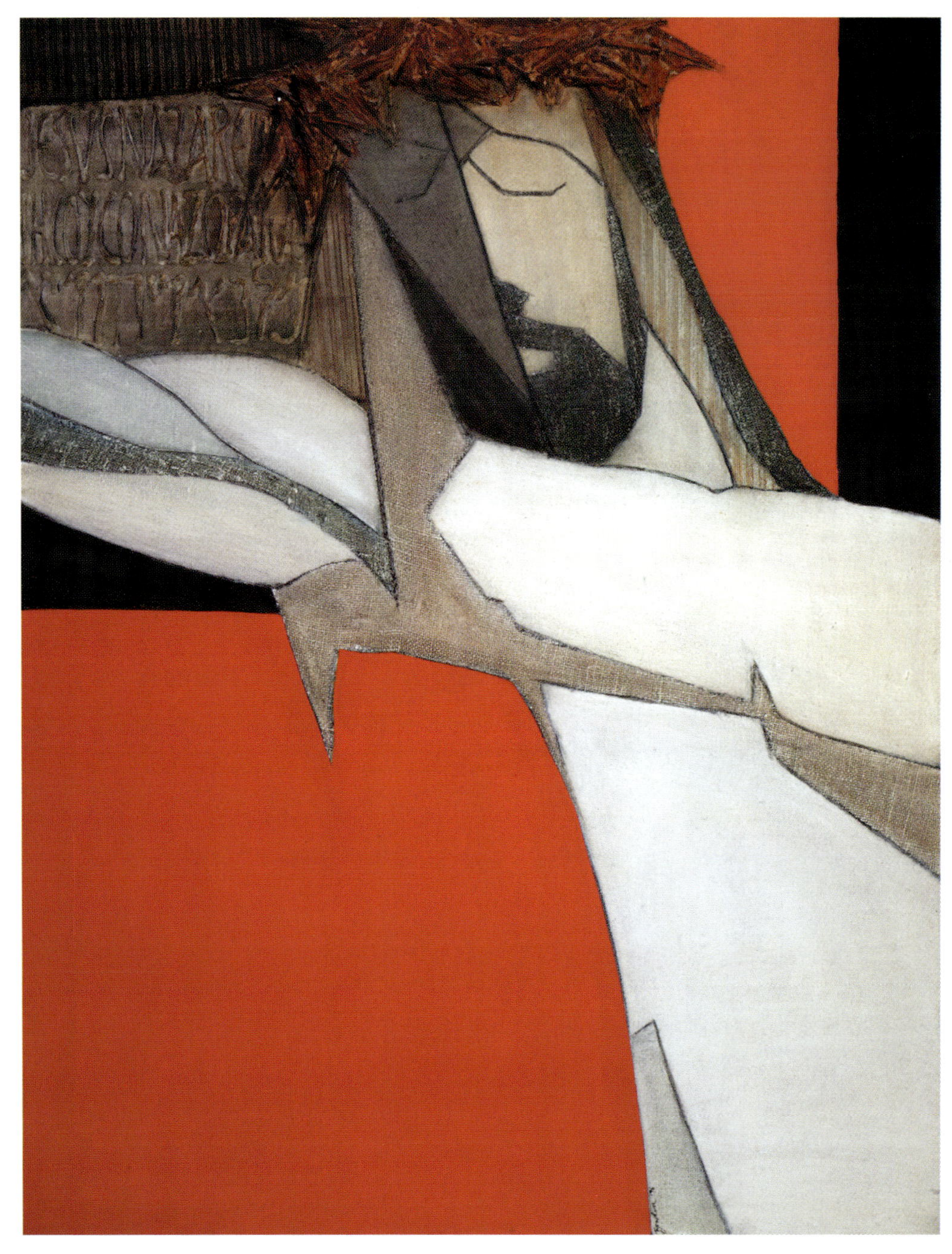

The Art of **Sandra Bowden**

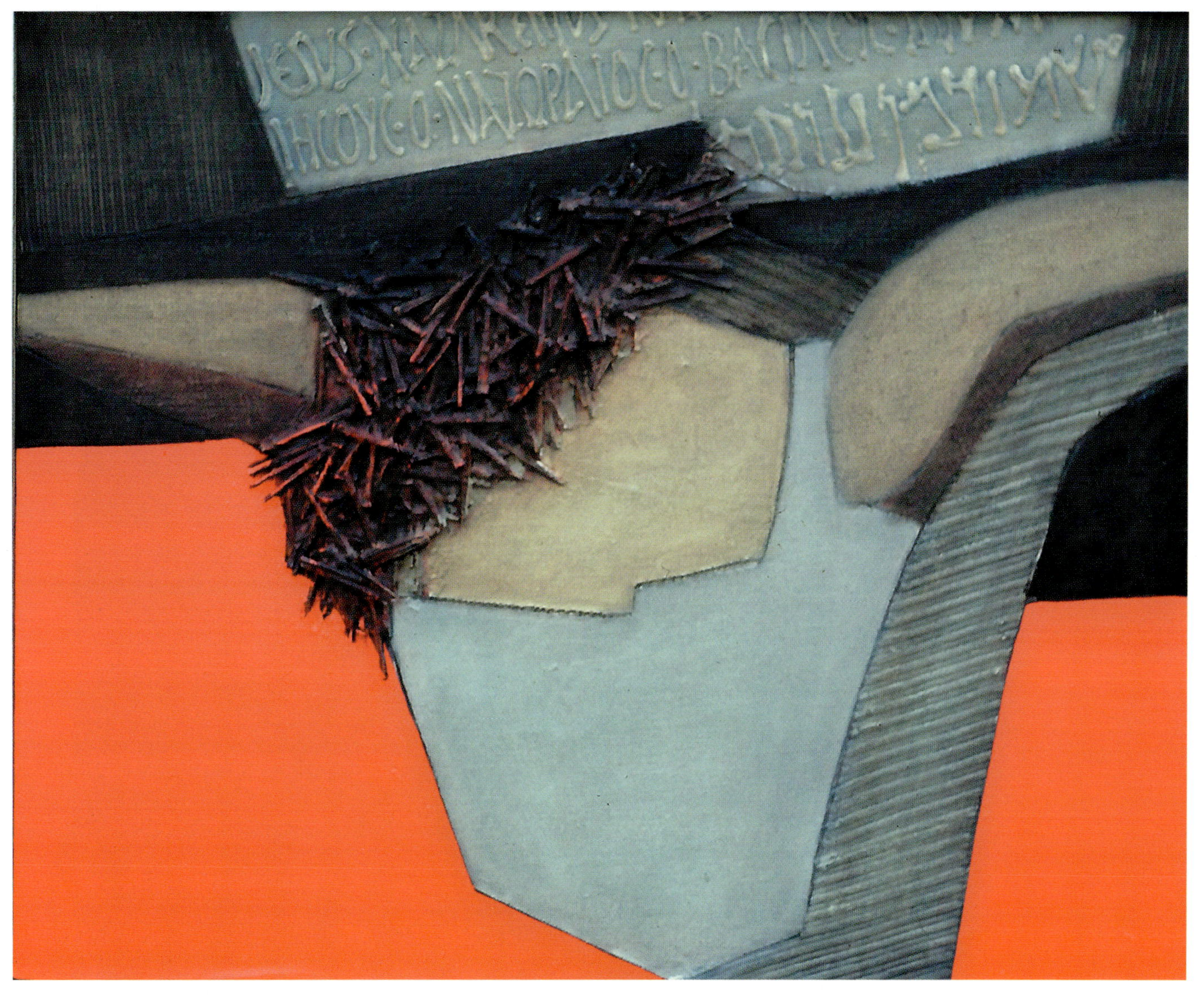

FIGURE 47
(OPPOSITE)
IT IS FINISHED
Oil collage
1976
48 x 36

FIGURE 48
HEAD OF CHRIST
Oil collage
1976
30 x 36

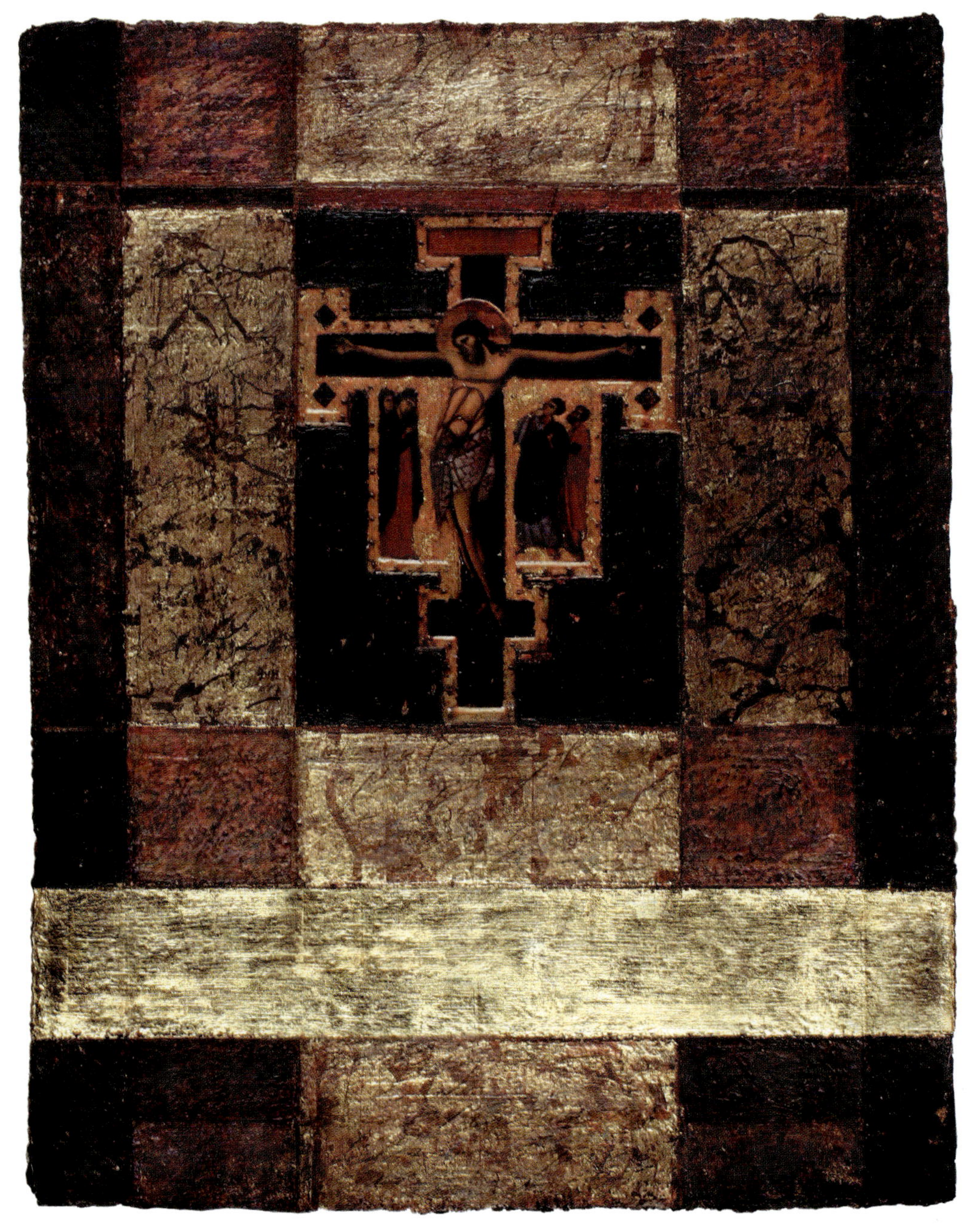

  The Art of **Sandra Bowden**

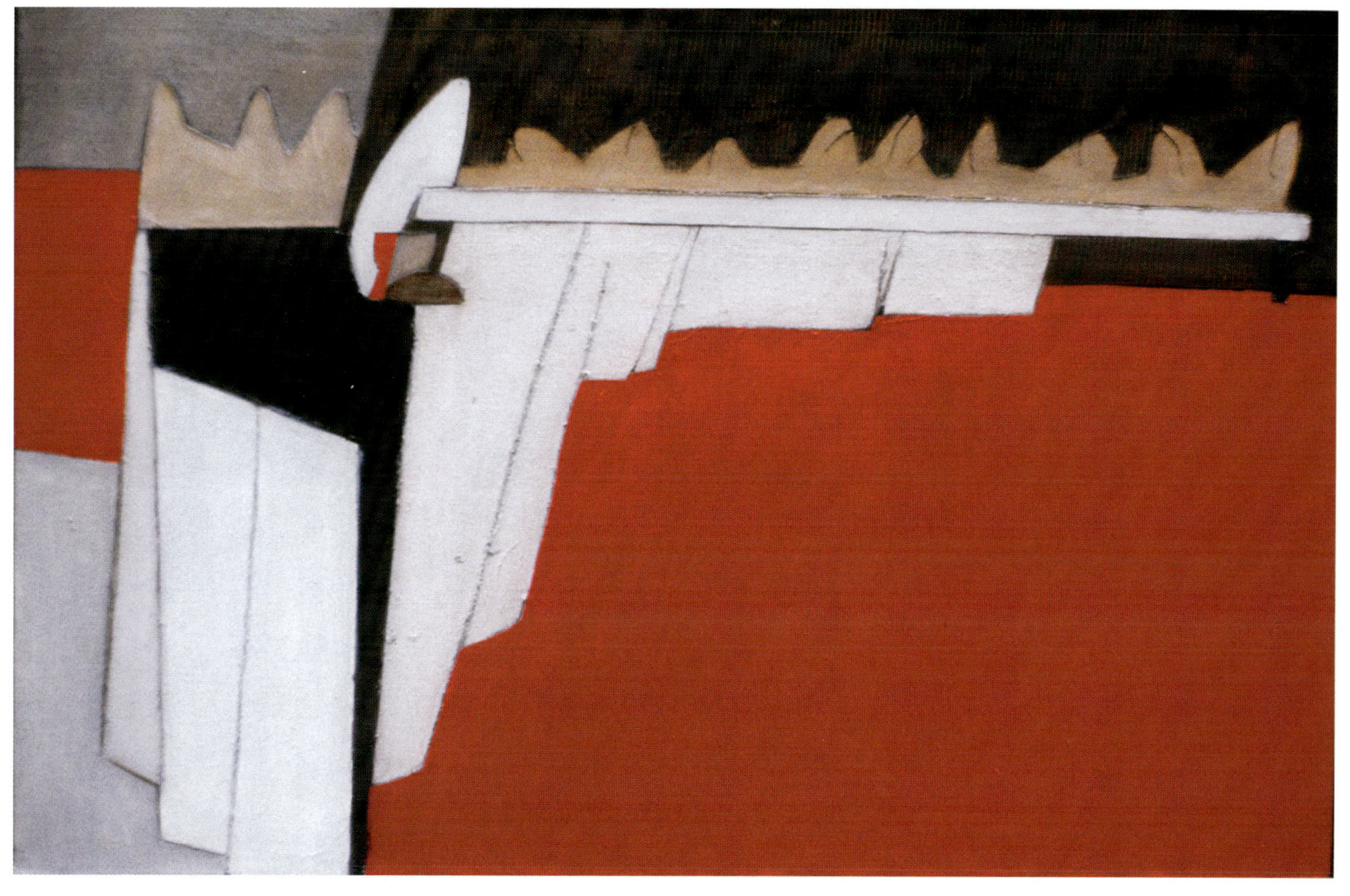

FIGURE 49
(OPPOSITE)
**CRUCIFIXION WITH
CROSS OF MAITREDE
SAN FRANCESCO
[AFTER UNKNOWN
ARTIST?]**
Acrylic mixed media
1992
24 x 18

FIGURE 50
LAST SUPPER
Oil collage
1976
40 x 60

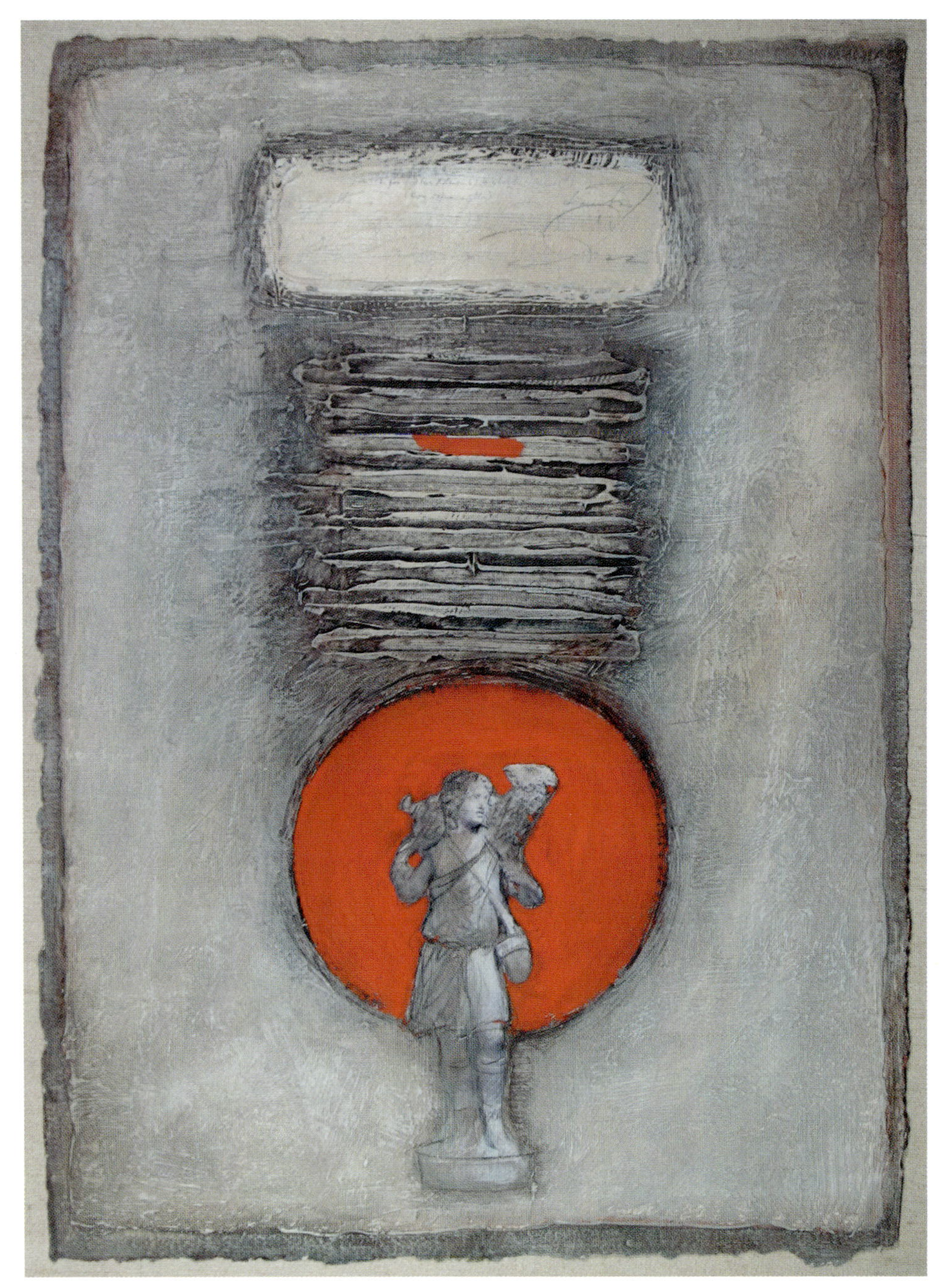

The Art of **Sandra Bowden**

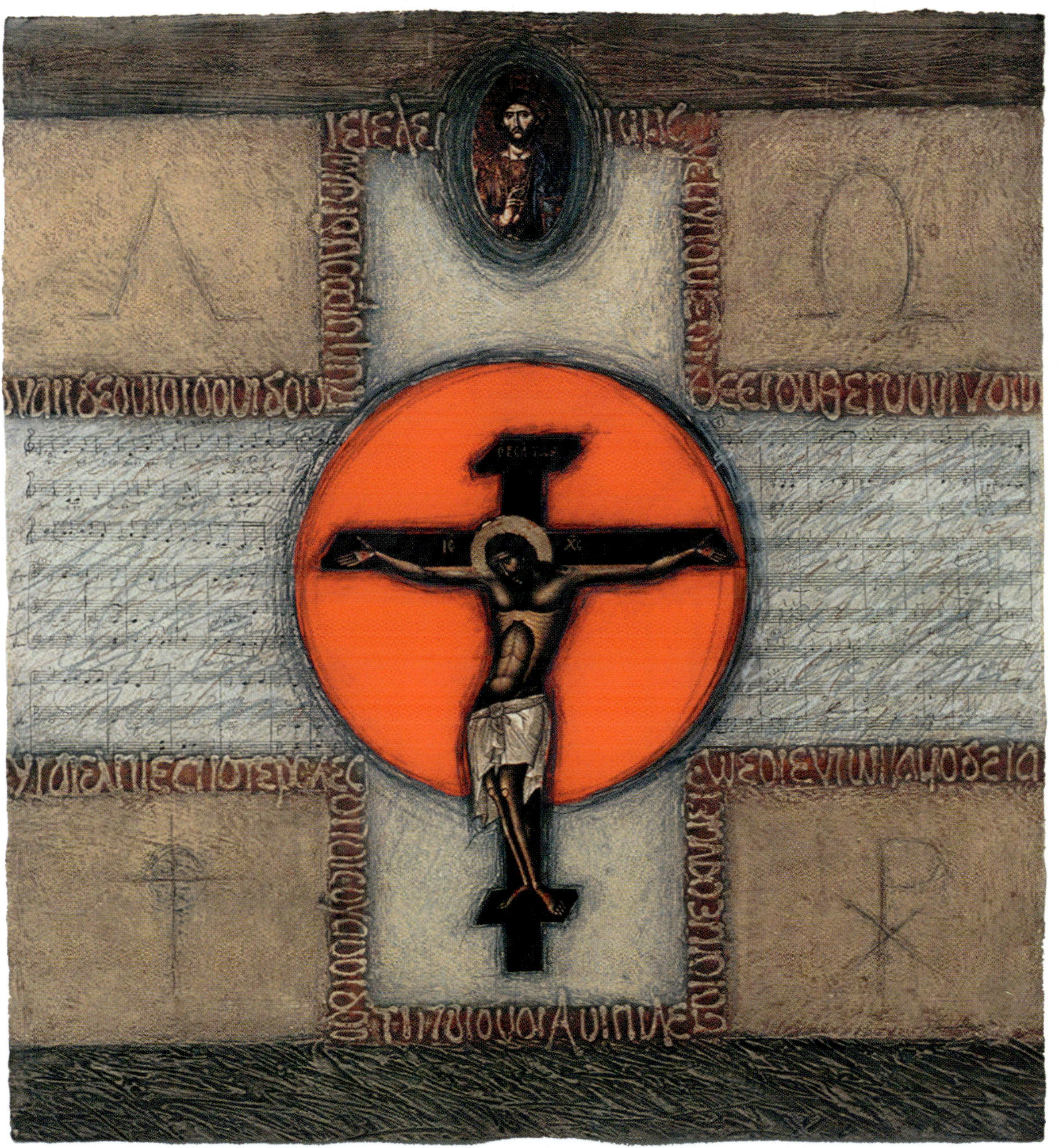

FIGURE 51
(OPPOSITE)
PSALM XXIII
Acrylic mixed media
1988
26 x 18

FIGURE 52
SEVEN LAST WORDS
Collagraph
mixed media
1990
20 x 20

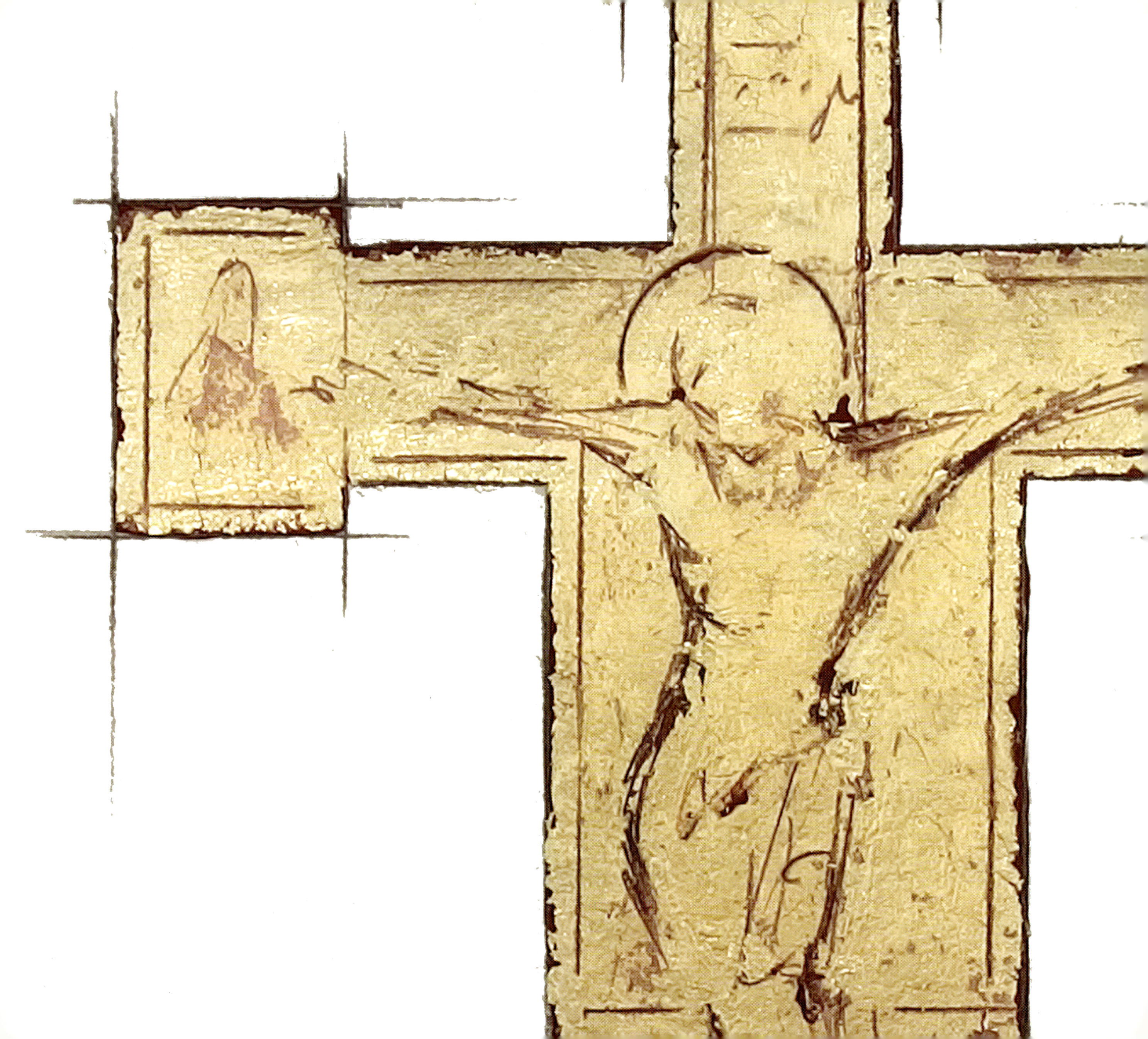

The theme of Christ's Crucifixion is elemental to Sandra Bowden's art both in form and in substance. It is recurrent in her artistic endeavors because, as she has said, "The Crucifixion is central to Christianity, a crossroad of history."[1] Being an artist of the word in whose work text is central, Bowden embraces the Christian orthodox view that in the flesh of the Christ is the Word of God—"The Word was made Flesh." In Sandra Bowden's early *Crucifixions* we find this truth distilled into the symbolic abstract shapes that have been the visual thread throughout much of her production. In more recent years the Crucifixion has been a major thematic bridge for her to the great artistic forms of the past found in the altars and paintings of Giotto (Figure 88), Cimabue (Figure 89), the Master of San Francesco (Figure 53), and many others. In both cases her intent has been the same—to probe the ancient mystery of the Incarnation in order to make it alive today.

Even in an early work on another theme, in retrospect, allusion to the Crucifixion can be seen. The piece is an oil collage from 1969 entitled *Desert Dig* (Figure 54). About this assemblage she has written, "Amazing how bones of dinosaurs in the desert have been found, unlocking for us mysteries to the past."[2] The composition is cruciform in nature and the reference to bones as a way to unlocking past mysteries becomes almost a talisman-like idea within the context of our current considerations. It is as though aspects of the Crucifixion of our Lord were lying dormant within the crafting of this work. The cruciform composition is also unmistakably present in other works like *Deluge* (Figure 23).

It is in the works of the 1970s that these cruciform compositions become overtly corporal in speaking of Christ's Incarnation. *Crucifixion* (Figure 140) was one of the first of these. In this 40" x 48" oil collage the bowel area of the corpus is cut away, carved out, as Bowden searches for a visual metaphor to express the theological understanding that Christ emptied Himself on the cross. Bowden quotes her New England grandmother's saying, "I am starved. I can feel my stomach touching my backbone."[3] She felt that this was a fitting and descriptive way of visualizing this *kenosis* or emptying Himself. This maw shape carved from Christ's torso

FIGURE 53 from **NAME THE ARTIST AND CHURCH CROSS AFTER MASTER OF SAN FRANCESCO**

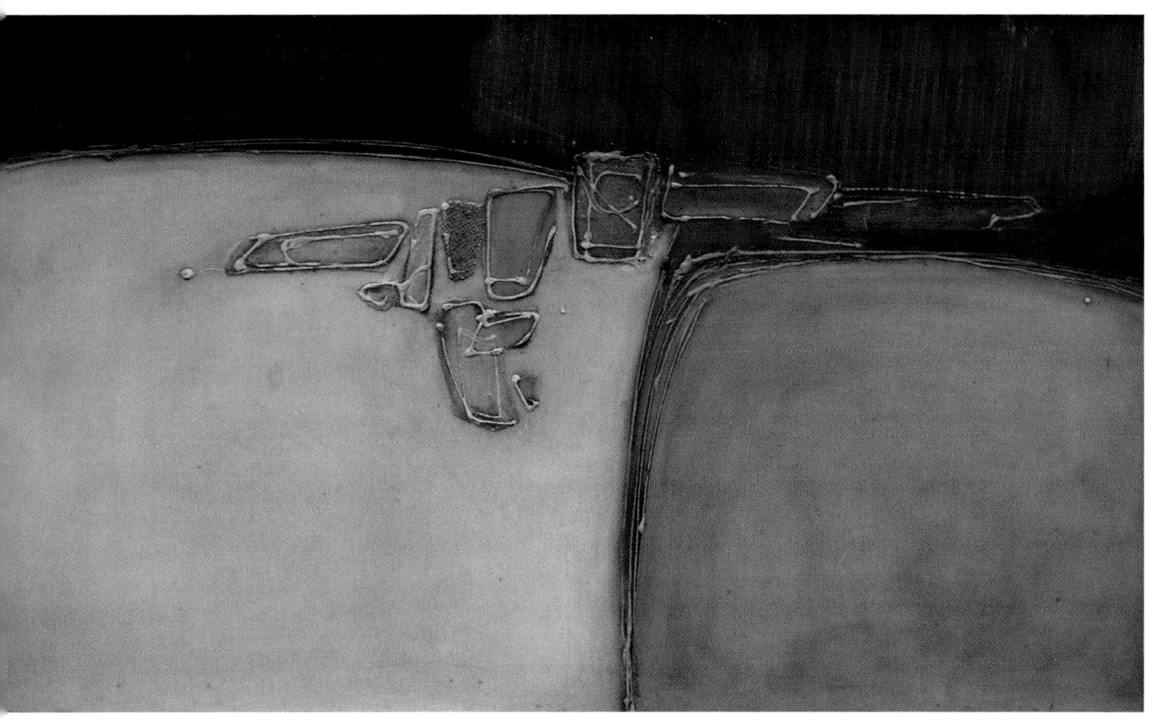

with its saving grace.[5] In this visual ambiguity, Bowden embodies the basic Biblical doctrine of the death of Christ: that as we killed Him, Jesus poured out His life-giving blood upon us. Also, she suggests that His death is our life as we continually eat His flesh and drink His blood in our celebration of the Eucharist.

Jesus of Nazareth (Figure 55) does much of the same thing but in a more simplified form. The increased simplification of form is continued in *Head of Christ* (Figure 48). The symbolic nature of the shapes that form the body in these pieces makes the corpus more akin to the embossed lettering proclaiming "Jesus of Nazareth, King of the Jews," written in Hebrew, Greek and Latin in each piece, than it is to visual reality. This allows the text to be read, as abstraction does, in a more poetically ambiguous and general way than a physically present Christ might be read. But it also removes us from the immediate horror of the physical reality of the event at the same time. Albert Gleizes deals with the subject of the Crucifixion with much the same remove, catching in a skein of shapes and colors the idea and symbols of this ancient event. There is a neo-Platonist element in the artistic vision of both Gleizes and Bowden at this point in her work. One suspects that the philosophical stance of Bowden's art is simply derived from the pictorial language in which she has chosen to work rather than a conscious belief. Her search for the past through the physical presence of the found objects and the bones of archeological digs, instead of through some imaginary construct of a virtual reality, is clear evidence that her feet are firmly planted on terra firma.

is filled with the continuation of the red shape that is adjacent it. At first glance the red seems to be consuming His flesh. This is a rich visual metaphor for Christ's statement, "Whoso eateth my flesh, and drinketh my blood, hath eternal life; and I will raise him up at the last day."[4] In this way, *Crucifixion* becomes a meditation on the Eucharist. If we follow Bowden's line of thought about Christ emptying Himself on the cross, though, we must read this visual metaphor in reverse. It will then suggest the crowds before Pilate saying, "His blood be on us, and on our children," as they unwittingly proclaim, in their admission and careless acceptance of guilt, the theological truth that His blood did in reality flow over all of humanity

The Art of **Sandra Bowden**

Further, it is not a surprise that Bowden "speaks" artistically with a cubist accent. Cubist-type modernism was at the basis of the treatment of religious subjects in post-WWII Europe, especially in France. There, the Sacred Arts Movement was in full force under the guidance of the Dominican Marie-Alain Couturier. This visionary was able to bring together such world-known artists as Henri Matisse, Fernand Leger, Marc Chagall, Georges Braque, Pierre Bonnard, and Georges Rouault, as well as Albert Gleizes, to work on his projects. There were many other artists, too, such as Jean Lurcat, Paul Bony, Paul Bercot, Germaine Richier and Jean Bazaine. He looked for the best artists he could find to serve the Church whether or not they were Christians, a cause for much controversy. The ravages of war, both physically and emotionally, and this stirring of art patronage in religious circles could not help but radiate a reconsideration of faith subjects within the larger arts community. It was very important that, if the ancient subjects were to be revisited by these moderns, the results must be new, not a rehash of the past. The Church at midcentury, in many quarters, also felt the same need for modernity.

Although Bowden's work does not have the ponderous weight of pictorial theory that often burdens Gleizes and his followers, she nonetheless has absorbed something of the Cubist method of abstraction. As with much twentieth century religious painting, we instinctively know that her paintings are to be more contemplated than viscerally experienced. The relationship of this visual vocabulary to her abstracted script from ancient languages brings

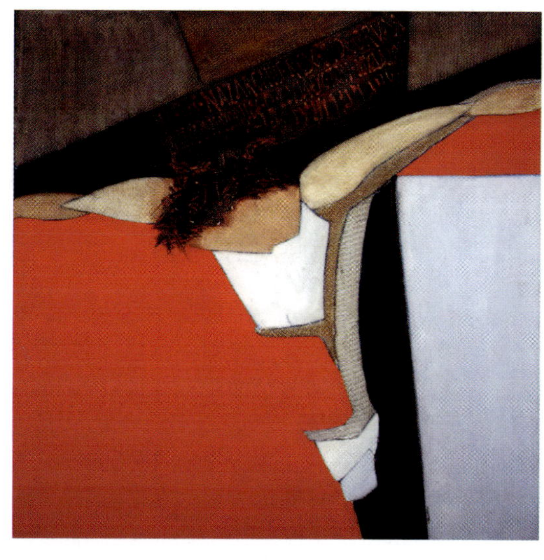

to mind the work of the icon painter who is said to write an icon, not paint one. And in reality these are as much icons as are the later crosses based on the work of the old masters, which she explicitly calls "a kind of contemporary icon."[6]

Sandra Bowden's best-known image of the Crucifixion, *It Is Finished* (Figure 47), is more fully developed than the previous works. There is still the ambiguity of the Cubist mode and the symbolic use of color (particularly the brilliant red) but the frontal facial view engages the emotions. Whereas the other works we have discussed tend to give us an idea of human suffering because of the subject matter, this painting shows us suffering in a way that the heart can understand. Not that it "wears its heart on its sleeve," nor is it in any way maudlin. In fact, there is distance here but not aloofness. The painting is much more stoic than was the preparatory drawing on the canvas (Figure 57). In the drawing, the head was larger and more centered and depicted that pain caught on the face as if in a momentarily off-handed glance.

The head for *It Is Finished,* as drawn, has much to do with the heads of Alex Jawlensky, the great master of the abstract face. It is probably not a coincidence that Sandra Bowden would be drawn to the paintings of Jawlensky

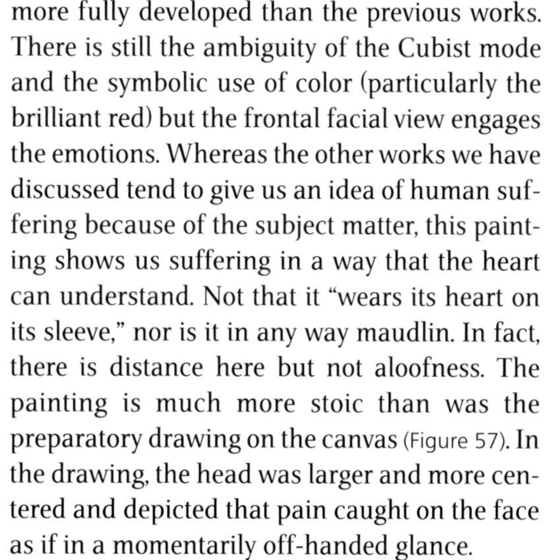

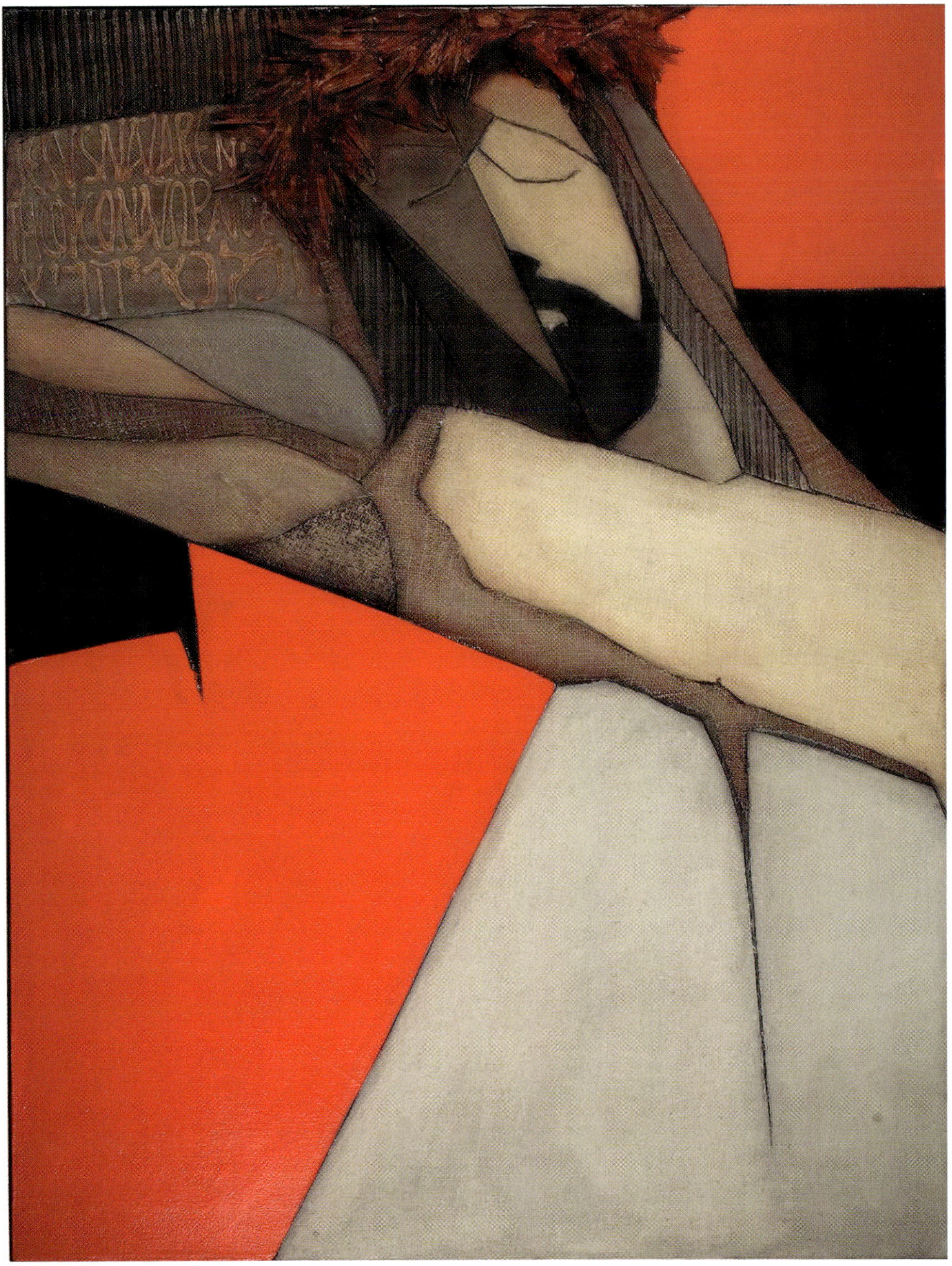

who, being Russian, was steeped in the icon tradition. Yet, living in Germany, he absorbed much from the modernist vocabulary. His poignant explorations on the theme of the head moved inexorably toward his last small paintings, which were called Meditations, in which he had found the cross of Christ embedded in the human countenance. As with Bowden, these too are modern icons. His life's motto was, "*Kunst ist Sehnsucht zu Gott* (Art is a longing for God)."[7] Bowden being influenced by Jawlensky would not be a surprise, but she does not remember that she was aware of this Expressionist master at the time she completed this work. It is evident, though, that they were both working from the same pool of images and spiritual inspiration.

As *It Is Finished* was developed from the drawing to the painting with many collage elements, the proportions changed and the emotional content solidified. It became more formal, more iconic. The crown of thorns has been constructed using old floor nails and fabric and other materials have been layered on the surface. (Bowden's use of nails to reference Christ's Passion continues in her recent work *Book of Nails* [Figure 124 and 134]). The abstracted forms of *It Is Finished* suggest "the brokenness Christ endured, distorted by our sin in order to restore our relationship to God."[8] In notes on the work, she calls attention to the large arrow shape that makes up the majority of the torso, "thrusting itself into a flat broad area of red."[9] At first, this is hard for the viewer to see because its light value as seen against the darker red makes it readable as a somewhat negative space, which acts as a slight echo of the compositional

The Art of **Sandra Bowden**

symbolism of the *kenosis* of *Crucifixion.* The thrust of the arrow shape carries us to the inscription at the side of Christ's head proclaiming him to be "Jesus of Nazareth, King of the Jews." The red shape, instead of penetrating the figure as in the 1972 painting, gently nudges Christ's body with the elegance of an Ellsworth Kelly form in space while the cross is implied rather than stated.

This work merges the presence of a public work with the intimacy of a portable icon. In the mind's eye, one can't help but see *It Is Finished* as an altar painting for one of the many small stone chapels that dot the countryside of France and Spain's El Camino. As one enters such spaces on a hot day, the coolness inside calms and refreshes one. Such a painting as this

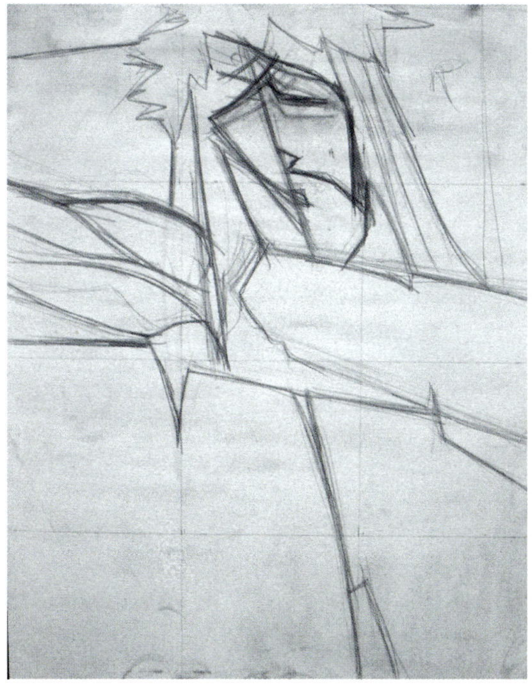

would be quite at home in one of those ancient sacred places. Here we begin to have the synthesis of new form and old beliefs. In this painting the bones of the modernist pictorial vocabulary begin to allow us to unlock the mysteries of our salvation history.

A series of collagraphs beginning in 1988 recasts Bowden's images of the Crucifixion. In works such as *Sanctus* (Figure 58), *Sanctus* (Figure 61), *Seven Last Words* (Figure 52) and *He Was Wounded for Our Transgressions* (Figure 46), she juxtaposes text with photo images lifted from masterpieces of the Middle Ages. One text that is recurrent in these works is Benjamin Britten's *War Requiem,* written for the dedication of the new Cathedral at Coventry which was resurrected in a new incarnation on a site beside the ruins of the bombed-out Gothic church. The rebuilding of Coventry Cathedral served to aid the healing process of war-ravaged England. Its glorious resurrection as it rose phoenix-like from the rubble of hostility served as a defiant witness to the world that war was not to be the last word—that all was not lost.

There is a restoration of sorts also in this

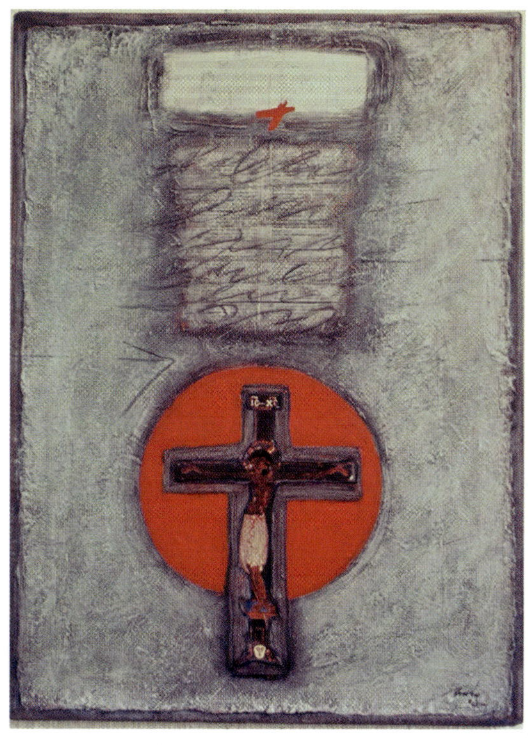

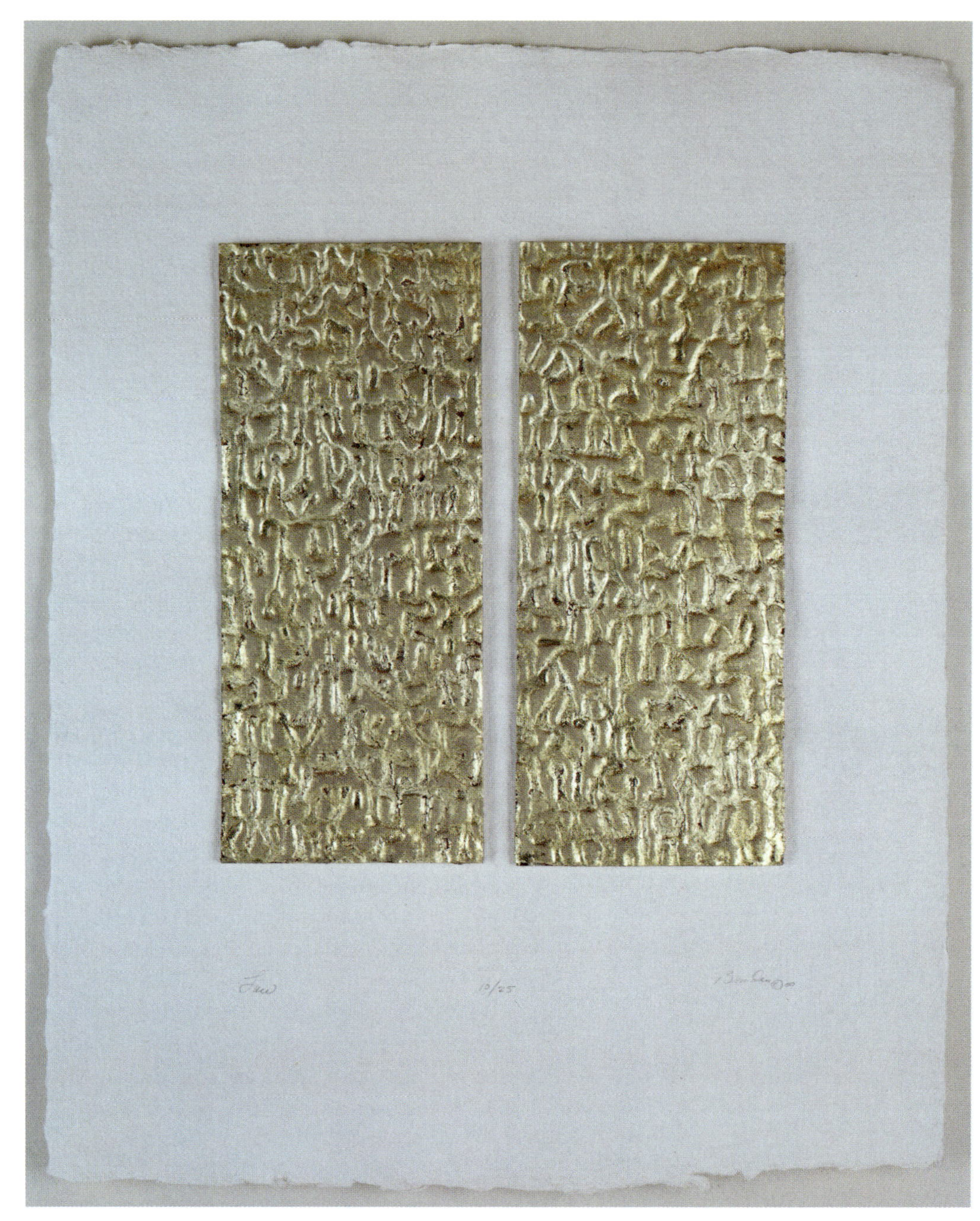

The Art of **Sandra Bowden**

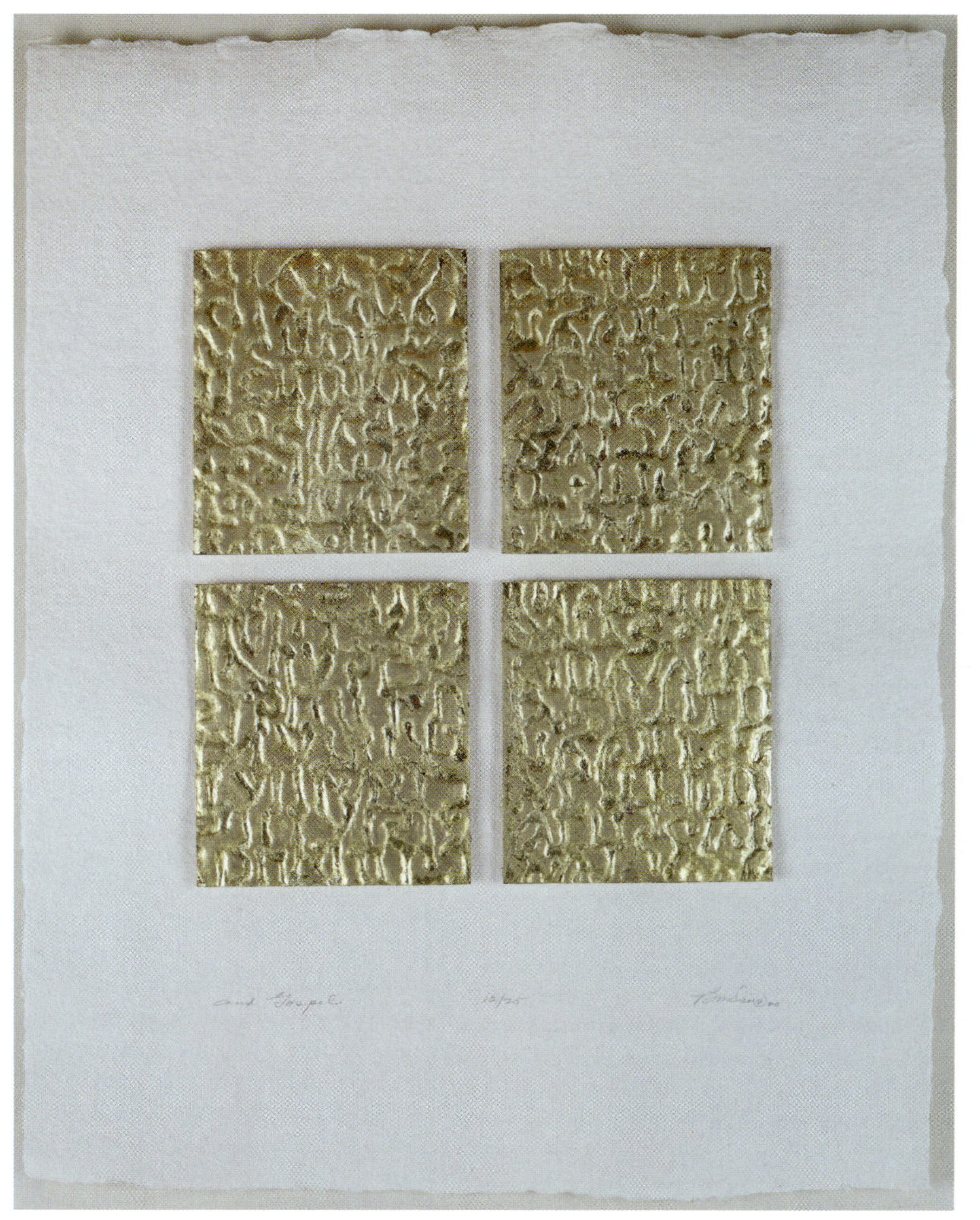

and Gospel   10/25   Knippers 00

FIGURE 59
(BOTH PAGES)
LAW AND GOSPEL
Collagraph
mixed media
1994
Two 18 x 14 panels

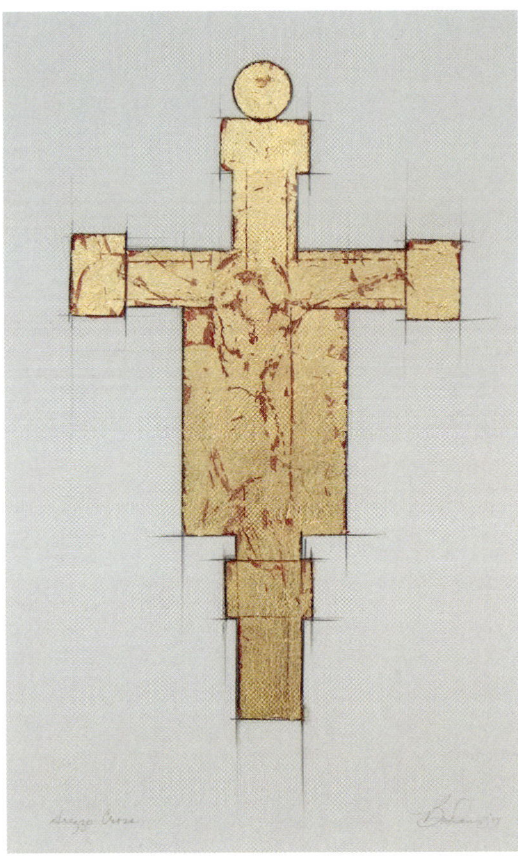

artifacts of the twentieth century an art of forgetting. Amnesia of all things prior to 1850 was praised as anything new was embraced. Even the non-art of Dadaism was preferred to the high art of Michelangelo. In this *Collage* series, Bowden's "resurrection" of a twelfth-century German crucifixion, and a fourteenth-century crucifixion by the Italian Maitrede San Francisco, signaled a break in her work from this tyranny of the new. The art establishment's unquestioned need to be modern at all cost, even as the thinness of the modernist artistic vocabulary had become rote and shopworn, was beginning to tire. In this series, just as with the building of the Cathedral, the lost was being found.

Law and Gospel (Figure 59), formerly titled *Law and Grace,* is a brilliant summation of much before it and a foretaste of what is to come in the work of Sandra Bowden. The corpus is gone once again and the symbols of both word and form are presented with a seemingly straightforward simplicity. The work consists of four panels of raised letters, compressed Hebrew from the Ten Commandments that is gold leafed with added color achieved through iridescent craypas over the raised areas. The two panels to the left have been left intact. The two to the right have been cut across the middle. "When we have finished an item on our 'to do' list, we put a line through it, marking it done. Christ came to 'fulfill' the Law and, when He declared 'It is finished,' He was marking it as 'done.' This is what I was thinking as I took the Law, marked it *done,* with a horizontal line, only to see a cross appear," explains Bowden.[10] There is Grace in the completion of the Law as suggested by the earlier title but there is also sug-

series of Bowden's work. But whereas the builders of Coventry Cathedral replaced the old with the new, Bowden replaced the new with the old, yet to the same ends. In the early part of the twentieth century, modernity had declared war on the past. The Futurists (a telling name) had called for the burning of the museums and had suggested that Rembrandt's canvases should be used for ironing board covers. This prevailing attitude produced throughout much of the century's cultural elite a pseudo-sophistication of forgetting. Some have even dubbed the gested the tablets of the four Gospel writers as stated in the current title. The arrangement stays the same, however, with the vertical tablets of the Law on the left and the Cross on the right. This is the way the English reader would naturally approach the work—Law and Gospel. The Hebrew reader might well see it in reverse, from right to left, as the text reads making it Gospel and Law. Either order adds layers of theologically correct insight, however. Grace was to be had in the giving of the Law as much as the Law was fulfilled with the Good News of Christ's Crucifixion and Resurrection. For God, it is of a piece—He is simply letting us know that He can be trusted as He reaches out to us with His love. This cyclical reading from English to Hebrew and back again sets up an intellectually satisfying presence in a visually pleasing work, one of Bowden's most successful.

In her more recent works on the Crucifixion, Bowden has combined the gold of *Law and Gospel* with the historic cross images of the *Collage* series from the late eighties and early nineties. There is no text, only the distinctive elegant complicated shape of the individual altars (Figure 60). The shape is laid down in gold leaf hiding a red ground. The gold is then scraped away to the undercolor to reveal the corpus of the Christ in outline. Instead of a collage (a modern invention) with a photo image of the older art superimposed, here the modernist language gives way completely to the older forms. We see the ancient compositions encased in gold as if to exalt them and to make them permanent. In this series the ancient images of our Christian past have become a memory kept alive through the meditative

process of their making.

It is interesting to note that the progression of Sandra Bowden's work from modernist forms to appropriation of ancient images mirrors a similar progression in the contemporary Church. By the mid-twentieth century, much of the Church sought to embrace the modern—in architecture, liturgy, and even theology (and other parts of the Church were similarly captive to modernism by being consumed with the effort to counter it). The ancient was dismissed as irrelevant to current needs and challenges. But as the Church has moved into the twenty-first century, there are multiple movements to rediscover earlier form and content to the faith. Two thousand years worth of music, liturgy, art and architecture—not to mention books and essays—are newly available for use in worship and study. Sandra Bowden—through her important interactions with ecclesiastical leaders, through her passion for helping the Church recover its role as a patron of the arts, and, of course, through her own work—is more than an example of this recovery; she is one of its leaders.

1 Artist statement, 2003.

2 Ibid.

3 Ibid.

4 John 6:54.

5 Matthew 27:25.

6 Artist statement, 2003.

7 Clemens Weiler. *Jawlensky Heads Faces Meditations,* (New York: Praeger Publishers, 1971). p 19.

8 Artist statement, 2003.

9 Ibid.

10 Conversation with the artist.

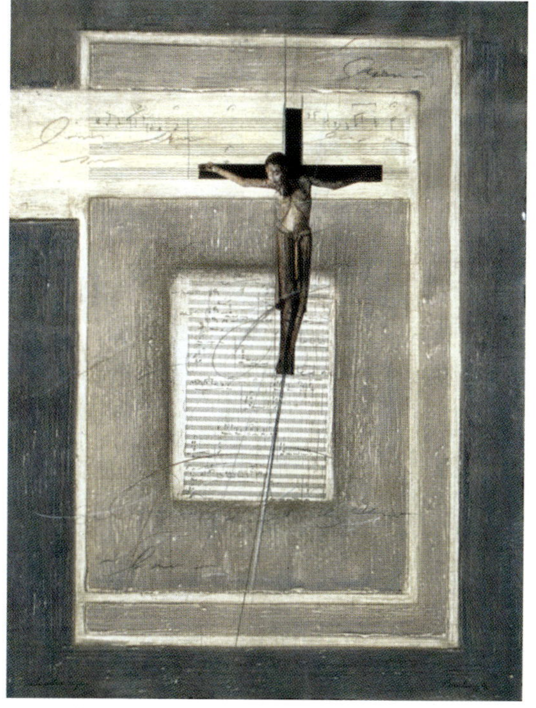

FIGURE 60
(OPPOSITE)
AREZZO CROSS
Mixed media
drawing with
22-carat gold leaf
1997
14 x 11

FIGURE 61
SANCTUS
Collagraph
mixed media
1990
30 x 22

Collection

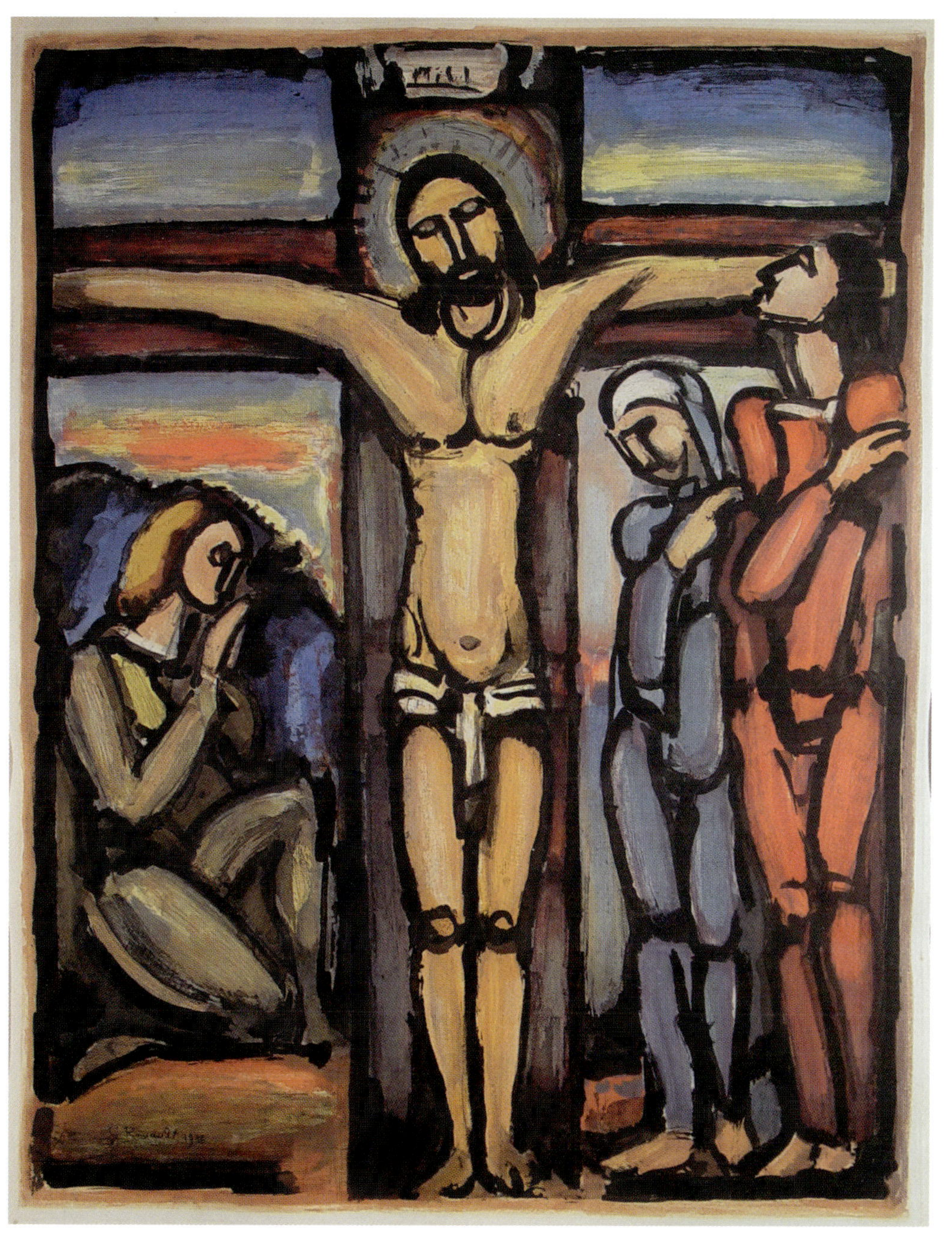

The Bowden Collection

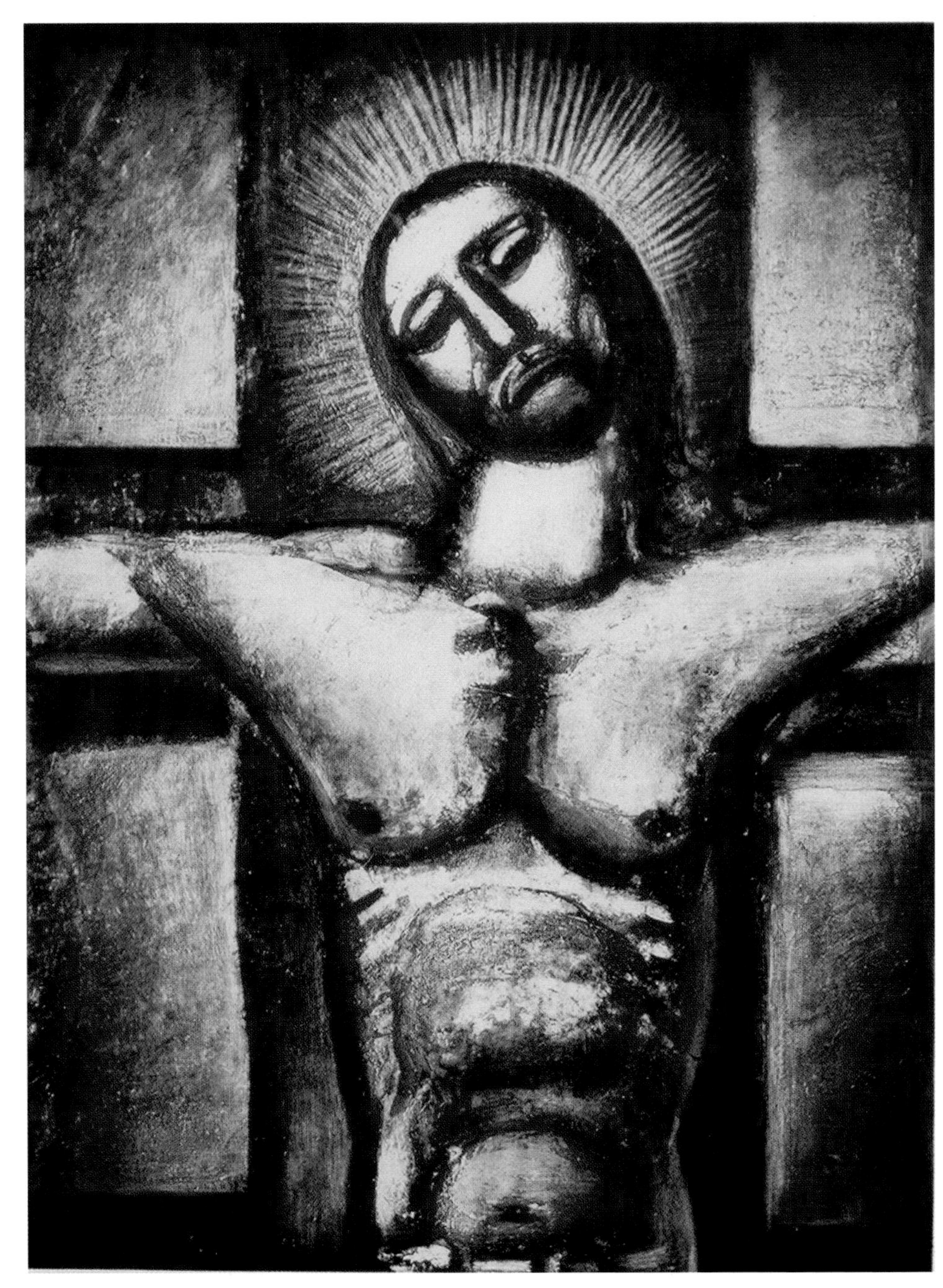

The Art of **Sandra Bowden**

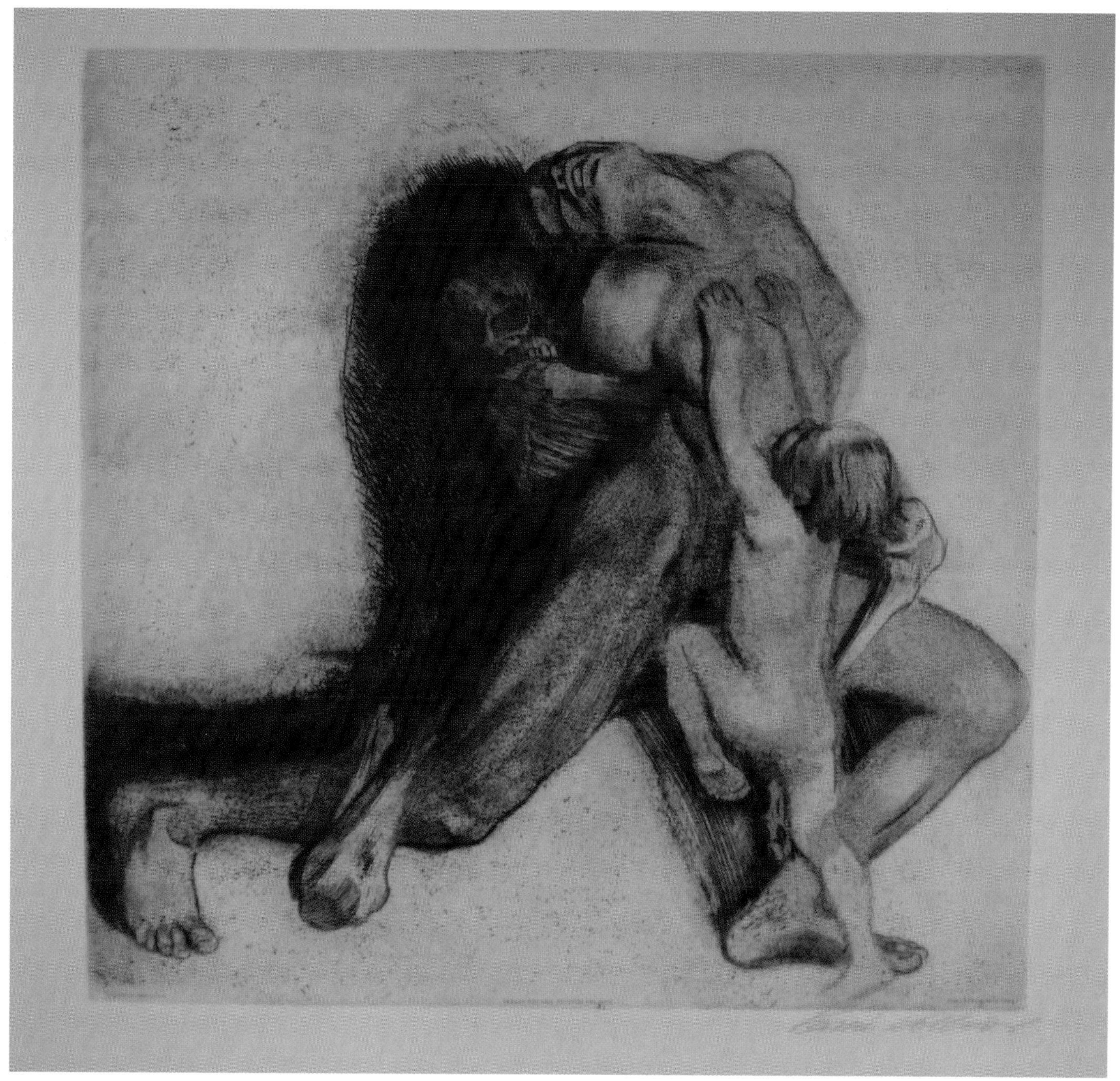

FIGURE 63
(OPPOSITE)
Georges Rouault
**HE WAS OBEDIENT
UNTO DEATH,
EVEN DEATH
ON THE CROSS**
Intaglio with photo-
gravure #17 from
Miserère Series
1926
22 7/8 x 16 5/8

FIGURE 64
Kathe Kollwitz
TOD UND FRAU
(Death and Woman)
Etching
1910
17 5/8 x 17 1/2

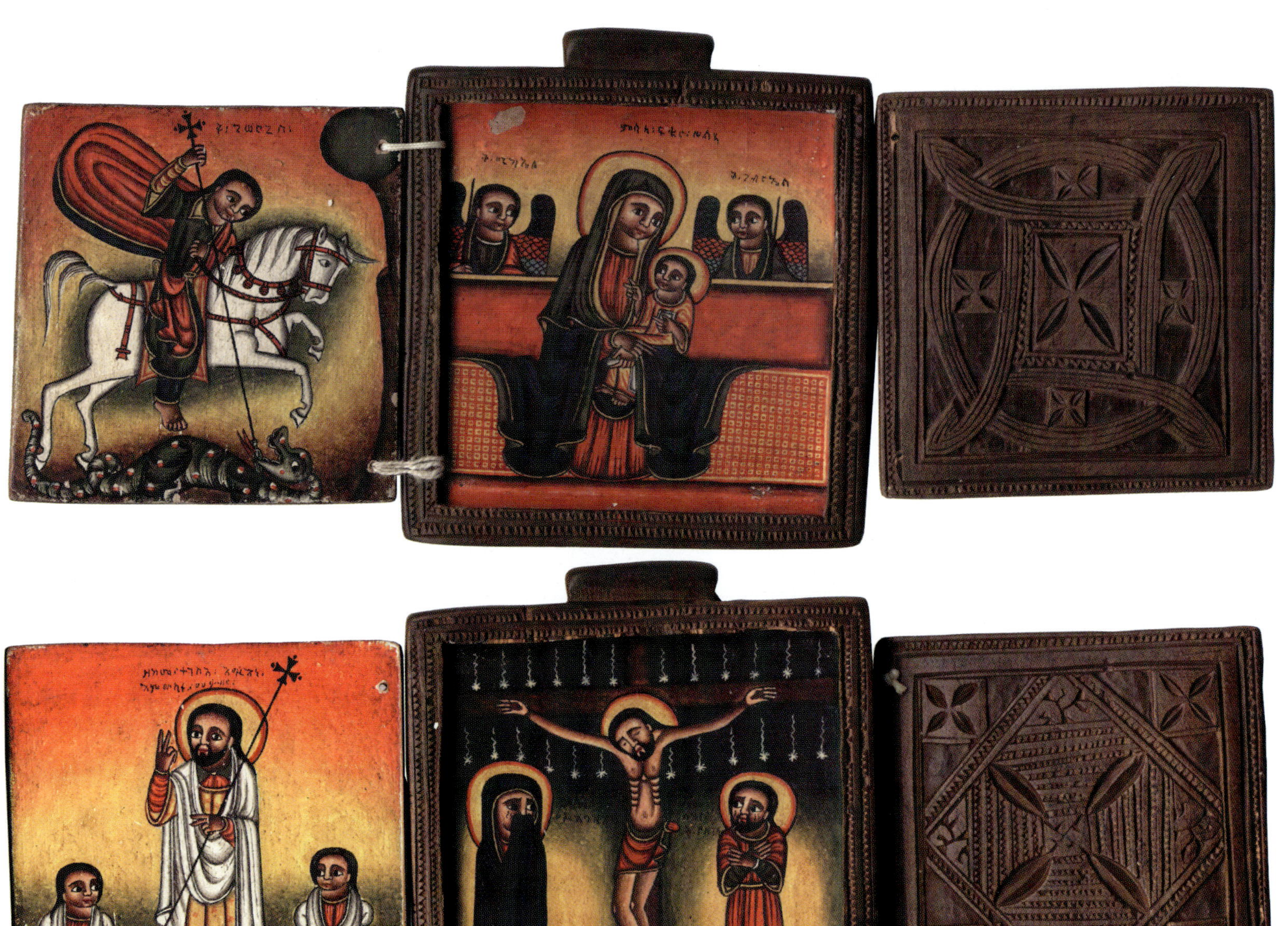

The Art of **Sandra Bowden**

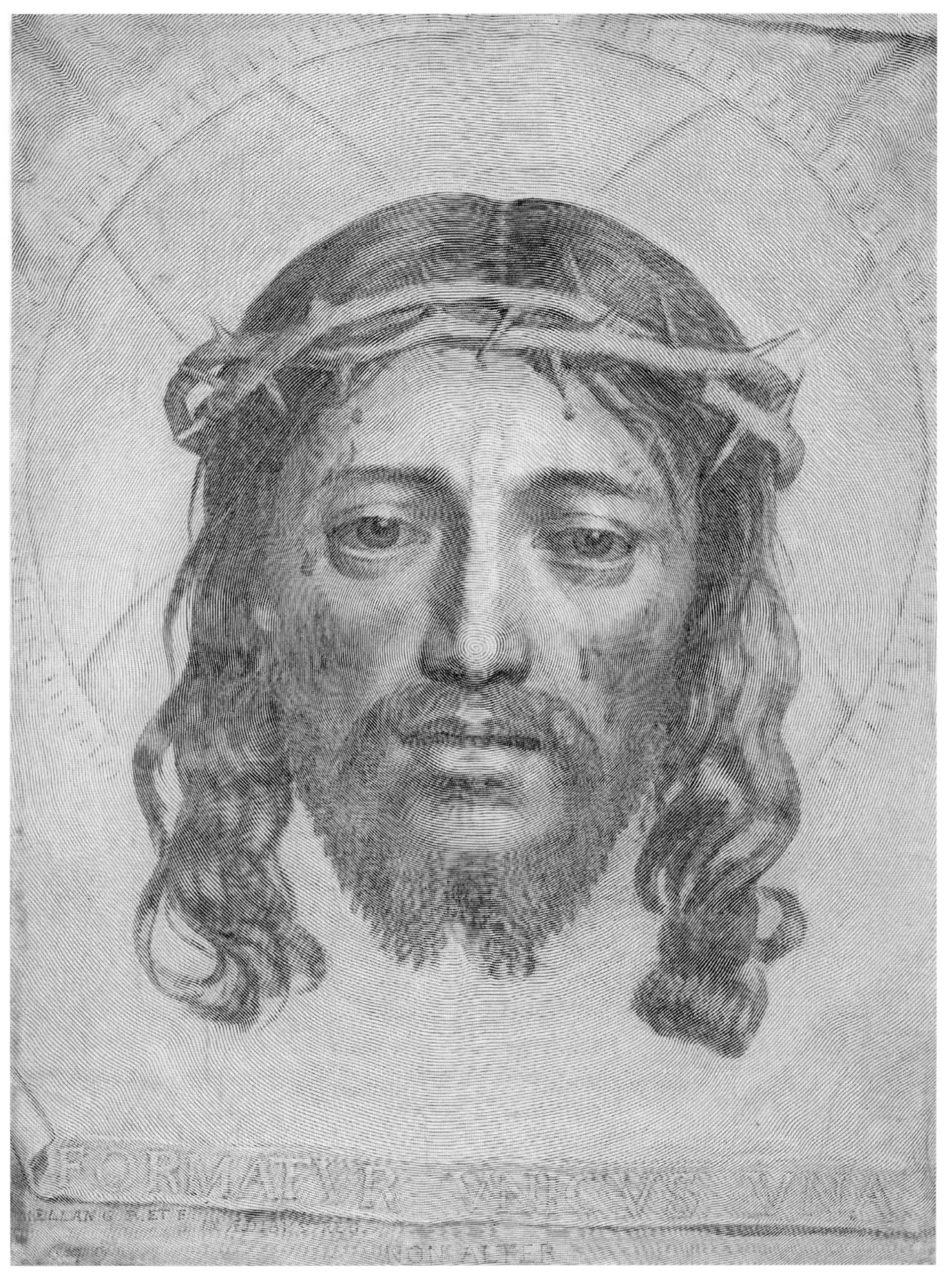

The Bowden Collection

Music Notations

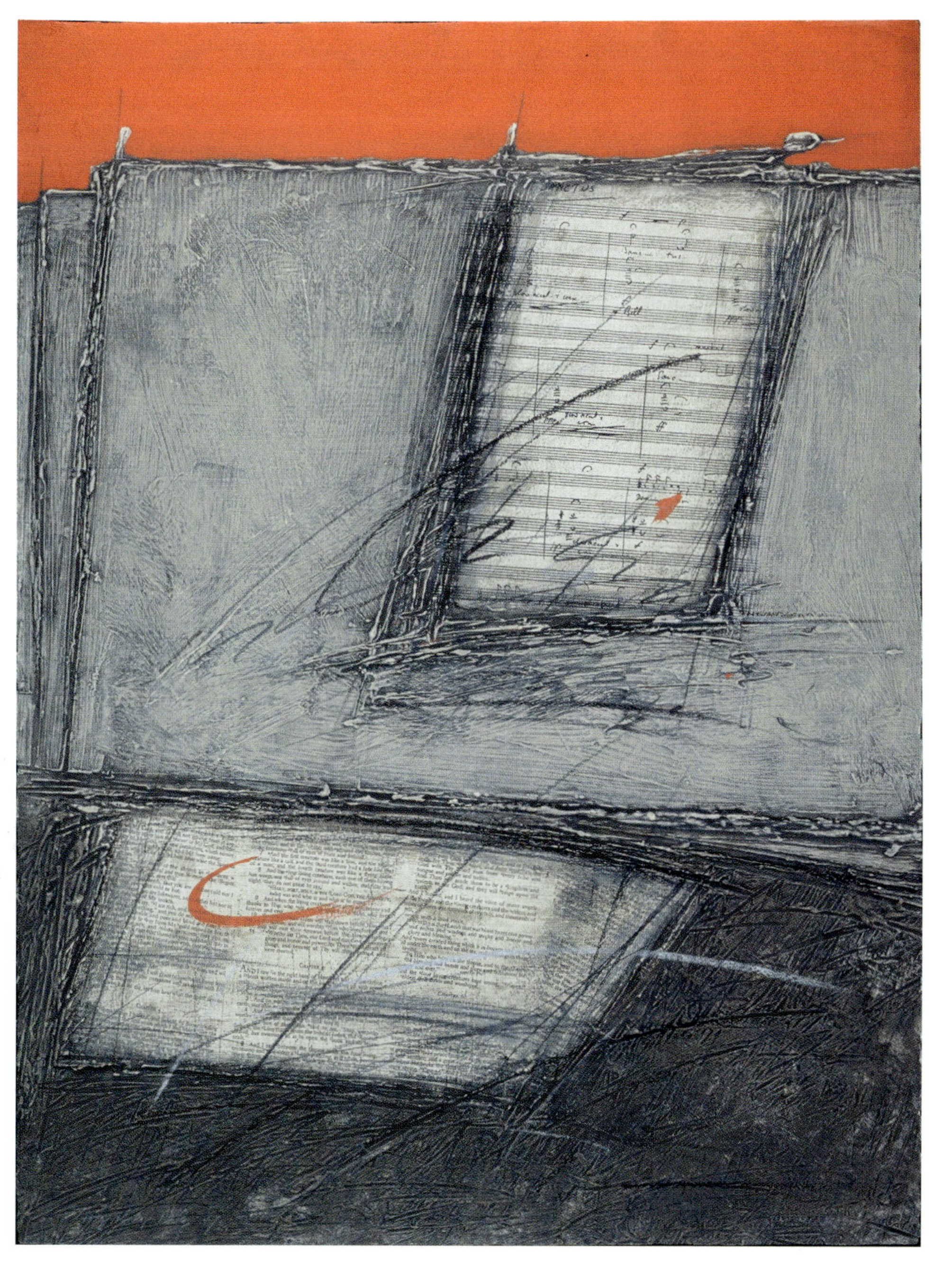

FIGURE 67
**HOLY, HOLY, HOLY
(SANCTUS)**
Collagraph
mixed media
1990
30 x 22

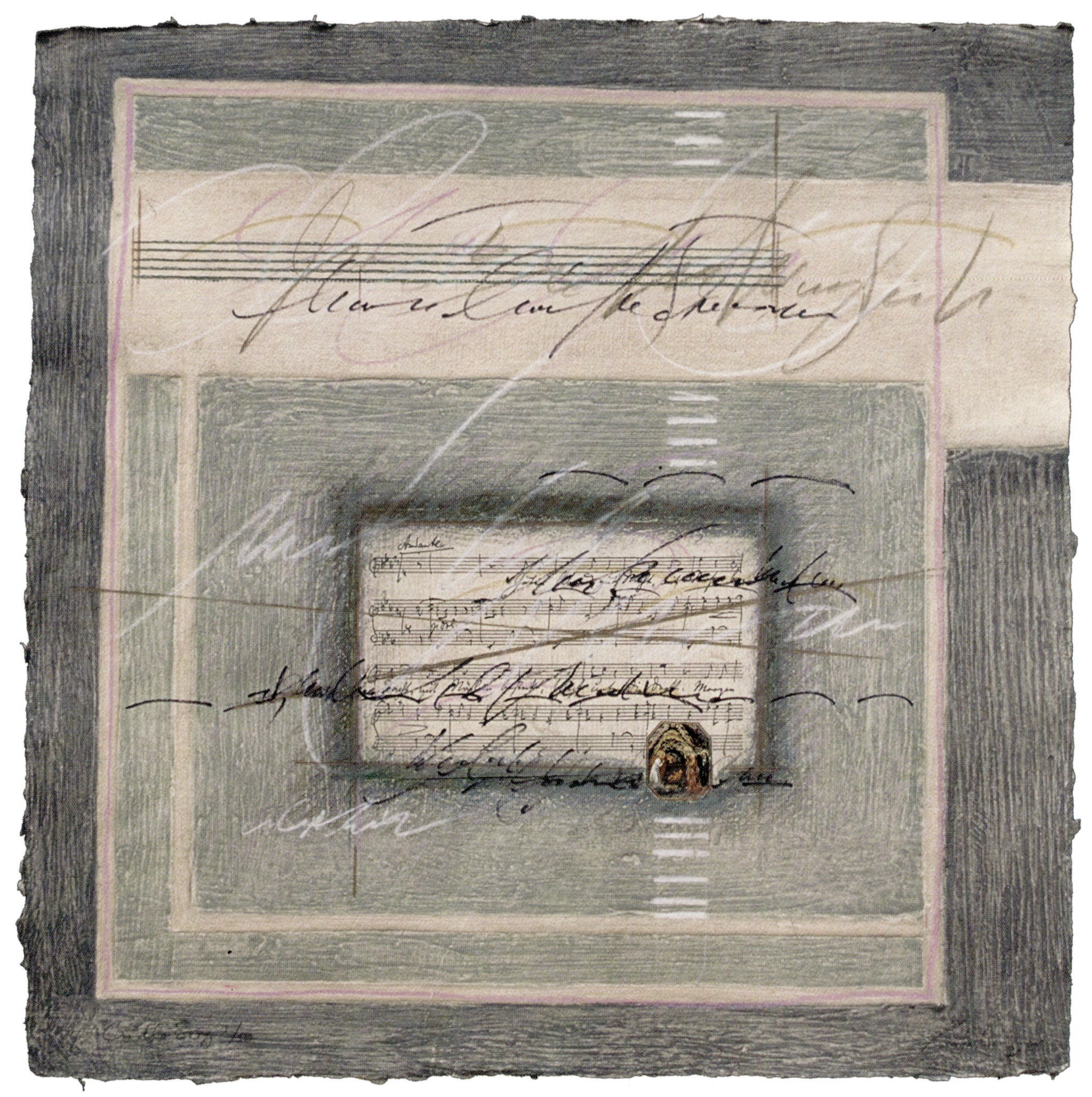

The Art of **Sandra Bowden**

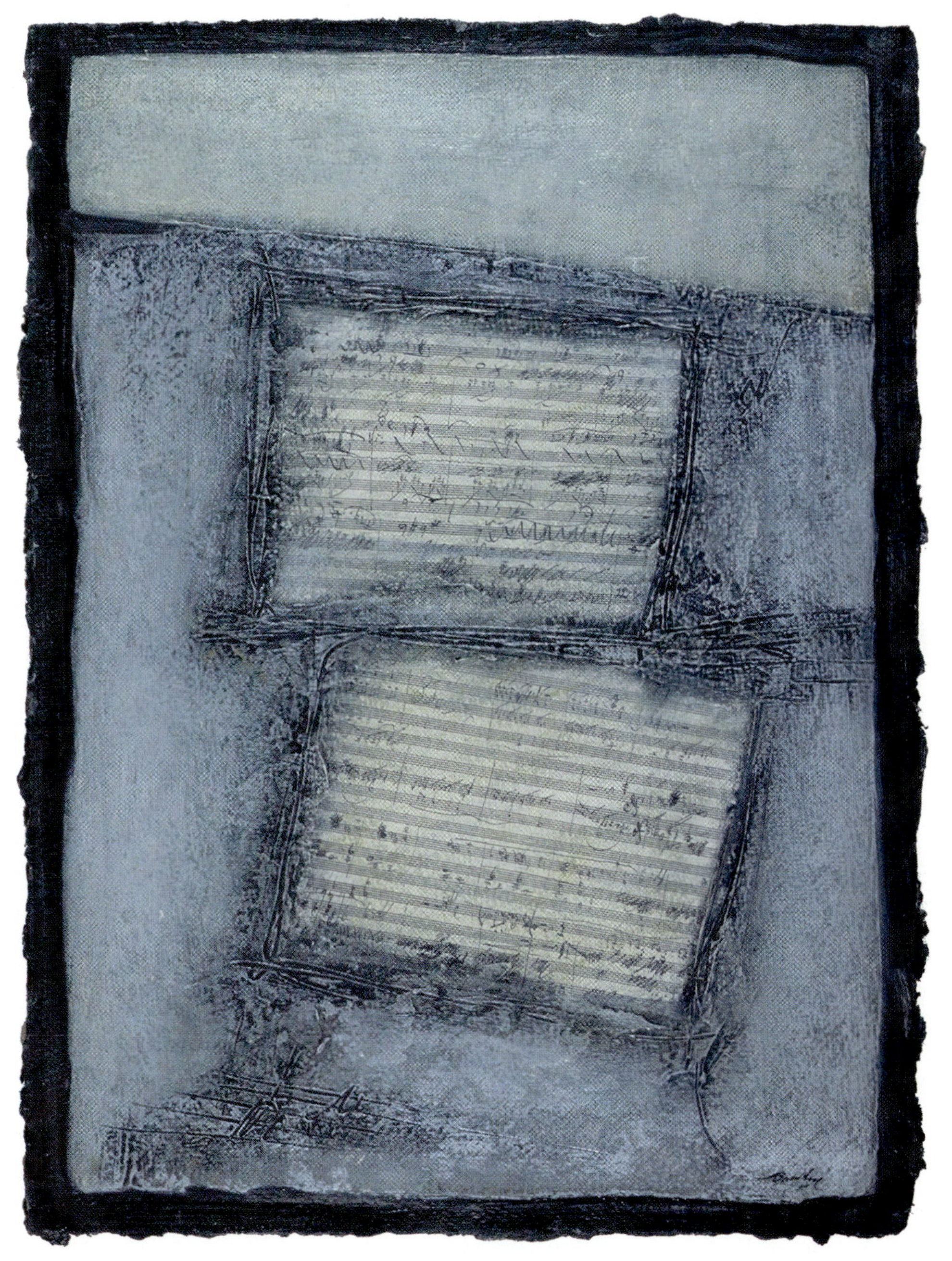

FIGURE 68
(OPPOSITE)
CRADLE SONG
Collagraph
mixed media
1988
20 x 20

FIGURE 69
SONATA
Oil Collage
1987
30 x 22

Music Notations

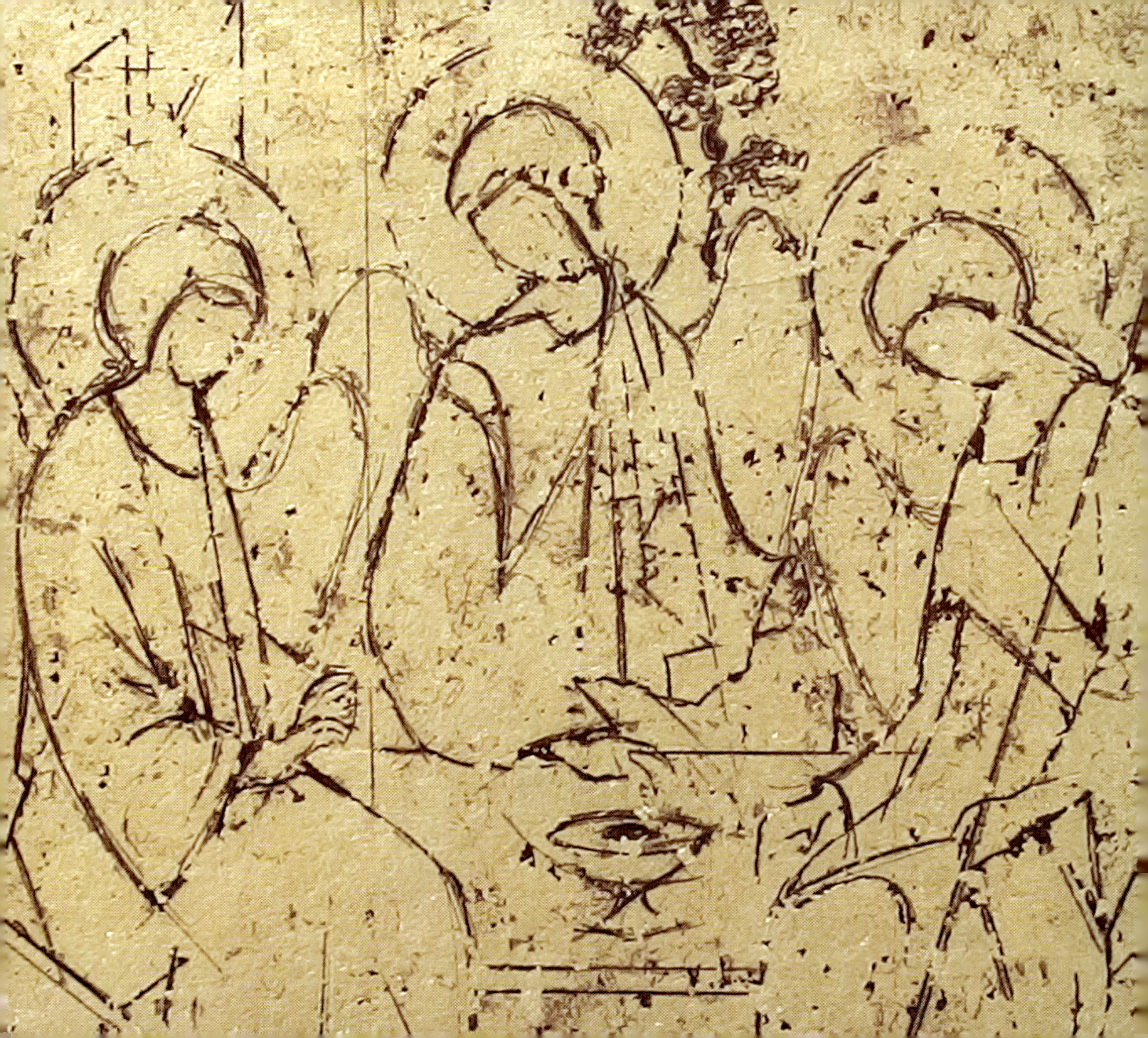

The inescapable paradox of "religious art," in all its guises, involves a troublesome exchange between earthly material means and elevated spiritual ends—in essence, the use of raw and perishable objects as foils for the immaterial and numinous. During the medieval era, theologians like Abbot Suger searched for the glimmer of divine light in precious metals, sparkling gems and scintillating colored windows. Conversely, Sandra Bowden uses a bounded set of material elements to signify divine presence in human history. She places the roughest materials—such as graphite or wax crayon—next to the most fragile materials, such as delicate Japanese art papers or the timeworn folios of eighteenth- and nineteenth-century books. She punctuates flat, layered topographies with the suggestion of precious things, like gossamer-thin leaves of 22-carat gold, ancient fragments excavated from biblical sites, or gilded ciphers from scriptural texts.

Bowden's collages enact this paradox of the material and immaterial by attempting to project the timeless and infinite stability of Jehovah through obviously perishable and inherently finite matter. Her calligraphic lines, overlapped texts, and heavily worked surfaces are supposed to clarify and expand rather than obscure the ultimate mysteries of existence. Excerpts of Hebrew or unspecified scripts intimate a visual *glossolalia* that opens a symbolic portal, through the veil of material layers, to the spiritual realm. This spiritual language, tacitly exchanged between the artist and God at the moment of its inception, implies a sacred fount of knowledge. Between the artist and the viewer, inscrutable fragments of information become figures of speech. These fold a hidden dialogue between complicated layers of meaning and history into a solitary, purposively ambiguous statement of fact.

Virtually all the Abstract Expressionists that Bowden mentions as formative influences toyed with material paradoxes in the collage genre, contrasting delicate gold flecks against roughly textured burlap and canvas surfaces, or smothering varnished snippets of newsprint in thick gesso impastos. When the Guggenheim Museum held the first American retrospective dedicated to twentieth-century collage, assemblage, and found objects in 1988, curator Diane Waldman described these art forms as "significant achievements" that "revolutionized our ideas about the nature of art, influenced virtually every major movement of our time ... and ... expanded the language of art."[1] For Robert Motherwell, one of Bowden's inspirations, collage presented a "modern equivalent to still life," stimulated by the "love of paper, love of edge, love of giving shape to the simplest of means," as well as a sensual fascination with "physically operating on the world."[2]

In addition to the materiality of the Abstract Expressionists, Bowden also absorbed the tactile menace of Antoni Tàpies' heavy hung canvases encrusted with pigment and found objects. Although his paper collages receive less critical attention, Tàpies flirted at length with

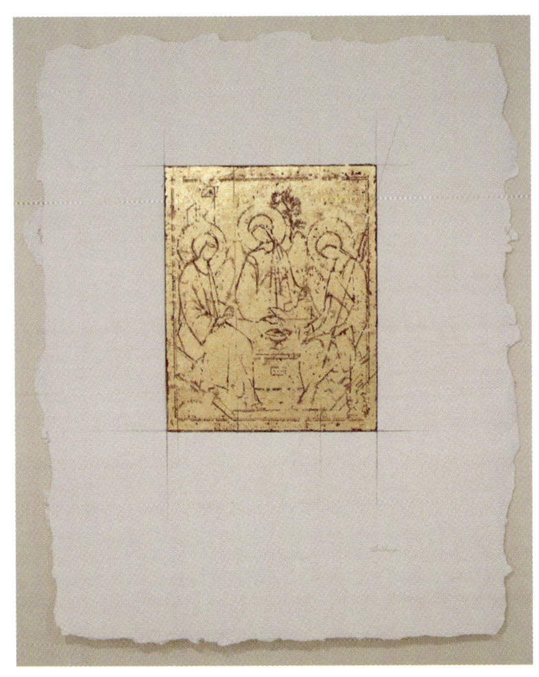

the medium's fragility and ephemerality.[3] Additionally, Bowden vividly remembers the formative impact of Ad Reinhardt's black-on-black series, which convinced her that monumental presence was attainable in small as well as large compositions.[4]

Collage particularly suits Bowden because it operates on an intimate, personal scale that simultaneously accommodates grand statements, as well as fine details and poetically delicate associations. The format provides endless opportunity for that virtually alchemical interaction between the material and spiritual. It involves tearing objects out of their original context, only to reconfigure and reconcile them within a coherent compositional framework of meaning. The process of excerpting and reconciling, however, merely provided the carrier for Bowden's systematic visual grammar. The calligraphic scrawl, blocked-out compositional grid, confined palette, and textural surfacing that brand her works emerge as early as 1965, in *Ancient Writings* (Figure 21) and other oil collages.

Bowden's geological landscapes from the early 1970s provide a prime example of her uncomplicated exegetical logic, which literally embeds spiritual meaning into material reality. These early compositions demonstrated the "earth giving proof" for the word of Yahweh, supported by scientific evidence from archaeological, paleontological and geological explorations. Bowden's collages literally grounded scriptural truth in the rocks and soil of geological strata, interlaced with enigmatic Hebrew scripts. In some compositions, the texts began to stretch, contorted by the implied gravitational strength of an energy source representing the Prime Mover, such as the hot starlike element in *God Created* (Figure 16).

No longer satisfied with merely imitating the visuality of Hebrew script, Bowden decided to learn Hebrew in earnest. By 1975, she studied regularly with an Israeli rabbi who also encouraged her study of the mysticism of kabbalistic Judaism. Although she claims that her fluency in Hebrew peaked in 1982, fellow artist and collector Edward Knippers recalls that Bowden amazed Jewish dealers at Black Sun Prints in New York City only a few years ago by effortlessly deciphering Psalm canticles in Ben Shahn's lithographic collection *Hallelujah*.[5] Further studies in Hebrew and biblical archaeology at SUNY-Albany led Bowden to Harry Orlinsky's *Understanding the Bible through History and Archaeology* (1972) and Kathleen Kenyon's accounts from excavations at Jericho, Jordan, Palestine and Jerusalem between 1952 and 1967.[6] After years of vicarious travel through books and museum exhibits, Bowden chose to make her first overseas trip to Israel in 1980.

Finally in the Holy Land, reading the actual Dead Sea Scrolls, touching the stone circle of the altar at Megiddo where Canaanites sacrificed infants, or walking through the water tunnel that afforded escape to Jews besieged by Roman legions, Bowden absorbed permanent personal epiphanies. At the time, potsherds strewn randomly throughout Megiddo presented a profound paradox to her; plain utility vessels attained an elevated status, as material witnesses to a specific and brutal historical event, fully corroborated in Joshua and Judges. "Masada was the finale of my 1980 trip," Bowden recalls. "I could imagine the horrible suffering of being expelled, being invaded—it added depth and

     The Art of **Sandra Bowden**

richness to everything that I believed—but you believe it blind until you see it."[7]

Bowden's respect for the Mishnah, an authoritative rabbinical commentary comprising the Talmud, probably arises from her fascination with the dialogue of ancient inquiries, arguments and rationales on the deeper meanings of scripture that embroider the Mishnah's margins. Her compositions invoke this record of vivid, timelessly relevant conversation, particularly in her use of wide margins around columns of text and overlapping or juxtaposed blocks of Greek and Hebrew verse.

Continuing to be that rare liaison between the active contemporary spheres of Hebrew and Christian tradition, Bowden's rapport within Jewish communities and a wider circle of acquaintances sharpened her ability to dialogue, frankly and respectfully, between two faiths distinctly divided by their histories. Gene Edward Veith, who has written several times on Sandra Bowden's art, surmises that her assimilation of Judaica nurtured a "hebraic aesthetic."[8] Appealing to Thorlief Boman's *Hebrew Thought Compared with Greek* (1960), Veith emphasizes several key distinctions that, he argues, inform Bowden's compositions.[9] For example, hebraic accounts provide straightforward descriptions of construction methods or functional items (i.e., the Tabernacle measurements) without attempting to *re-present* the object in the mimetic sense suggested by Plato and Plotinus. Bowden's collages are associative, rather than descriptive or representative. Hebrew tradition specifies no set of rules for representation, and certainly none of the formulaic paradigms that attempt to reflect ideal

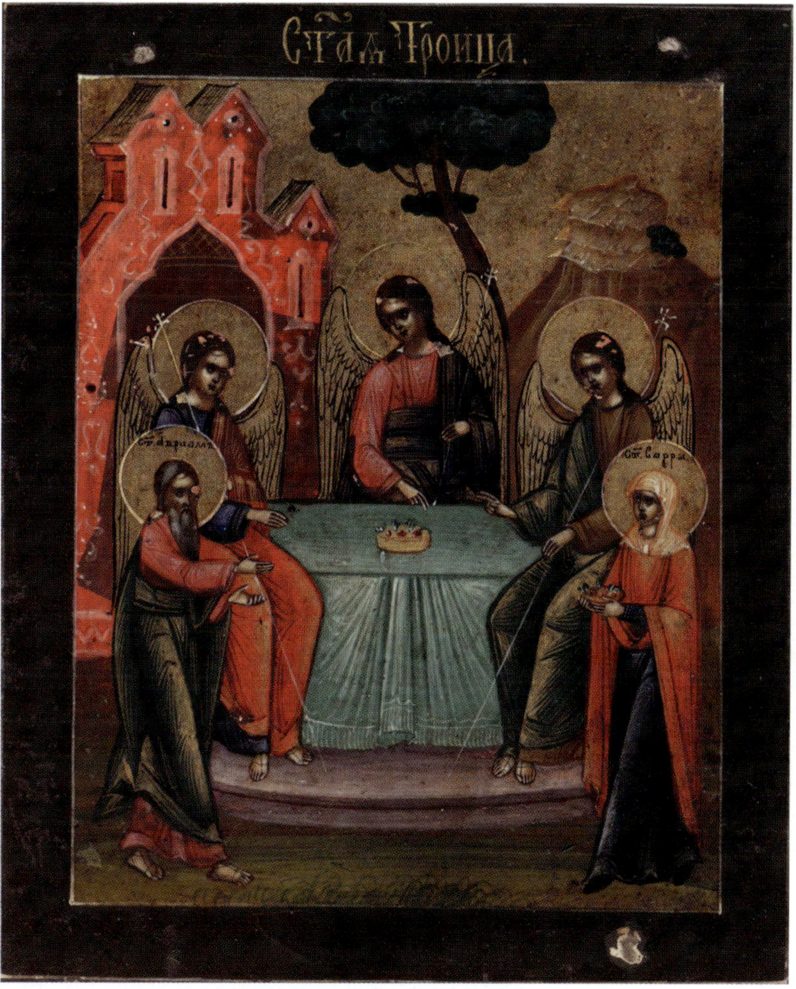

FIGURE 70
(OPPOSITE and PREVIOUS)
**TRINITY AFTER
ANDREI RUBLEV
(C. 1360–1430)**
Mixed media
drawing with
22-carat gold leaf
1998
21 x 16

FIGURE 71
Unknown
iconographer
TRINITY
Russian Icon
1890
7 x 5 1/2

platonic forms. Whereas the Hellenic approach seeks universal and eternal expression, Hebrew literature anchors itself to specific places, histories, and chronologies with definite beginnings and endings—certainly characteristic of Bowden's Geological and Archaeological series. Moreover, as Veith argues, the emphasis on text as a descriptor for

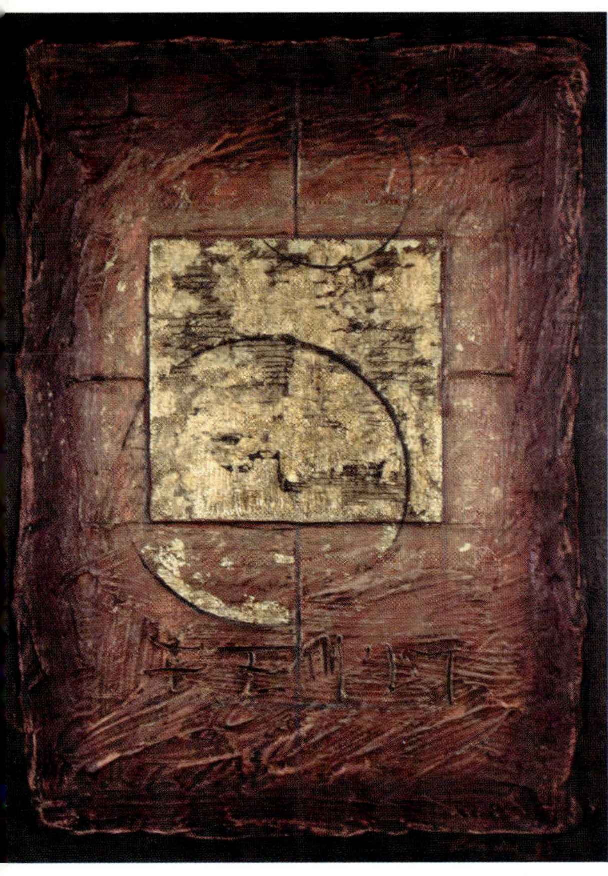

presence and materiality engenders an abstract quality in the Torah, tempered by the fact that it always corresponds to a fixed code of meaning.

As Veith suggests, Bowden's use of Hebrew literally *enscripturates* biblical information; the Hebrew code she presents incorporates the real "stuff" of transcendent, God-given meaning without giving it a mimetic visual form in the traditional Western sense. Bowden's Hebrew texts accurately emulate the nonpunctuated script of the Dead Sea Scrolls. Their implied authority and authenticity as visual ciphers arise from their formal accuracy—not their legibility as discrete scriptural legends. The textural physicality of Bowden's lettering translates the active word of Jehovah directly into the limited physical form of a "spiritual" alphabet. In embossed collagraphs—like *He Spake and It Was Done* (Figure 13) or *In the Beginning Was the Word* (Figure 14)—this spiritual alphabet enables Bowden to propose transgenerational dialogues. She particularly prizes exegetical links between God's word and created reality, between Moses (or the Genesis author) and David (i.e., Psalm 33:6), and between the "word" as God's creative act in Genesis and the Word as Jesus Christ (*Logos*) in the Gospels. She describes such conversations between scriptural excerpts as a Protestant *Midrash,* or commentary, which affirms the enduring connection between the Hebraic and Christian faiths.

One byproduct of her passionate interaction in the sphere of Hebrew is Bowden's tendency to view herself in terms of a set of binaries, held together by an overarching faith of the Judeo-Christian tradition. In fact, she relishes her ostensible self-descriptions as a Protestant Hassidic, a Lutheran Kabalist, an Anglican protagonist in a Chaim Potok novel, a medieval modernist, or a pragmatic mystic. In addition to Bowden's rabbinical sense of inquiry through dialogue and binary logic, which drive her practice of faith as strongly as her art praxis, she constantly explores the esoteric aspect of spiritual experience. "I haven't really put this into words before," she muses, "but maybe coming from a conservative Protestant background, everything I learned was so cognitive—there was little place for mystery. Early on, perhaps what I was really fishing for in Jewish thought and Jewish mysticism was something that was a little veiled, something ancient."[10]

On the other side of Bowden's Hebraic *ethos*, she often describes herself as "going medieval" after her first trip to Europe in 1986. Nothing quite prepared her for the visual impact of seeing, firsthand, the golden altarpieces and glittering icons. The overall luminosity of gilded surfaces and the alternatively intimate or colossal scale of many familiar art objects seen in reality rather than print struck her to the core. Gold, broadly considered the "most spiritual color," is the ultimate analog for holy entities or zones.[11] Mixtures of other colors never produce *true* gold; only its own mineral essence colors *true* gold. This condition of fact provides an excellent synecdoche for the indivisibility and inestimable worth of the Godhead, as well as a visual approximation of pure light in the age before electricity and neon.

When Orthodox iconographers create sacramental icons, they initiate a devotional ritual that produces a physical object of a greatly

    The Art of **Sandra Bowden**

elevated spiritual status. As the iconographer coats non-resinous wood panels with three to thirty layers of sanded gesso or chalk paste on a binder of woven linen, each layer and each action, accompanied by prayer, prepares the ground for gold leaf or gold paint, representing the numinous realm. In this context, gold transcends any superficial role as an art supply, becoming a literal metaphor for transfiguration, divine light, inner radiance, or more cryptically, the illumination of God's "uncreated"—hence, uncorrupted—light.[12]

During the fifth century, liturgical murals in Rome, Milan and Ravenna shifted from the Roman preference for scenic partitions to large undifferentiated wall spaces solidly surfaced in gold mosaic, designed to scintillate by daylight as well as candlelight.[13] Perhaps this change corresponded to Augustine's complicated teaching on divine light, which describes intellectual illumination as an aid to perception, "[irradiating] into the soul the immaterial intelligible objects—forms, ideas, reasons, rules."[14] The use of uninterrupted zones of glittering gold in rounded apses further emphasized the metaphysical reality of an otherworldly realm, suggesting a three-dimensional trope for eternity in the implied form of a never ending circle. Gold surfacing exaggerated the sense of visual endlessness in these curved forms, presenting a continuous space without depth, shadow, or often any focal point other than iconic images of Jesus Christ *Pantocrator* or *Majestus.*

Although architectonic uses of gold profoundly affected her, when Bowden refers to illumination she primarily alludes to medieval manuscripts, an artform that she has avidly researched. After the tenth century, Charlemagne and his Ottonian successors sponsored books that featured entire pages of burnished gold backgrounds—the only material deemed suitable enough to portray the heavenly zone.[15] By the thirteenth century, royal patrons preferred folios with solid gold backgrounds built up on gesso forms, which parallel the sculptural quality of Bowden's heavily textured grounds and scored mixed-media pieces from the *Illuminations* series, such as *Hidden Worlds I* (Figure 72).

Whereas gold theoretically functioned as a light container in medieval applications, Bowden's use of gilding symbolizes inestimable worth in material as well as spiritual terms. This is apparent in Bowden's only interactive installation, *Art History 101: Icons of Western Art,* which began as an experiment in a hotel room during a stay in Florence, Italy. These works evoke the untarnished gold highlighting and exquisite craftsmanship of certain late thirteenth-century masterpieces—particularly, the remarkable painted cross of the thirteenth century by the Master of San Francesco that hangs in the Basilica of San Francesco in Arezzo (Figure 138).

The crucifix at the famous basilica of San Francesco in Arezzo led her to translate the basic composition of these works into flattened contours. Even though the silhouette reduced the actual artwork's visual information, Bowden became fascinated by the wealth of information that her minimalistic renderings still man-

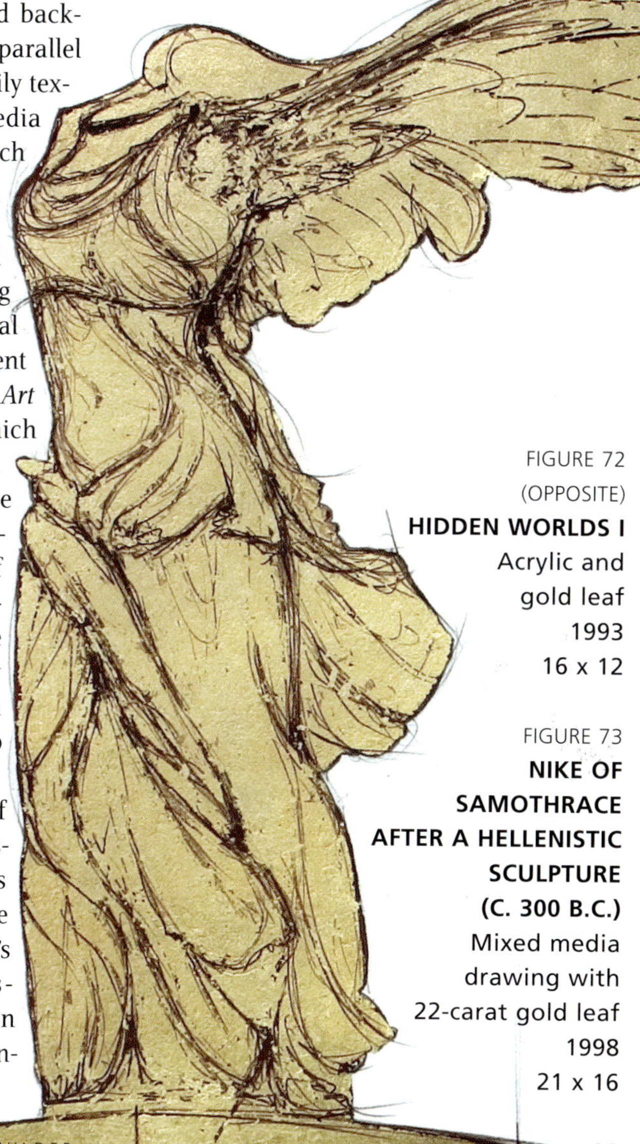

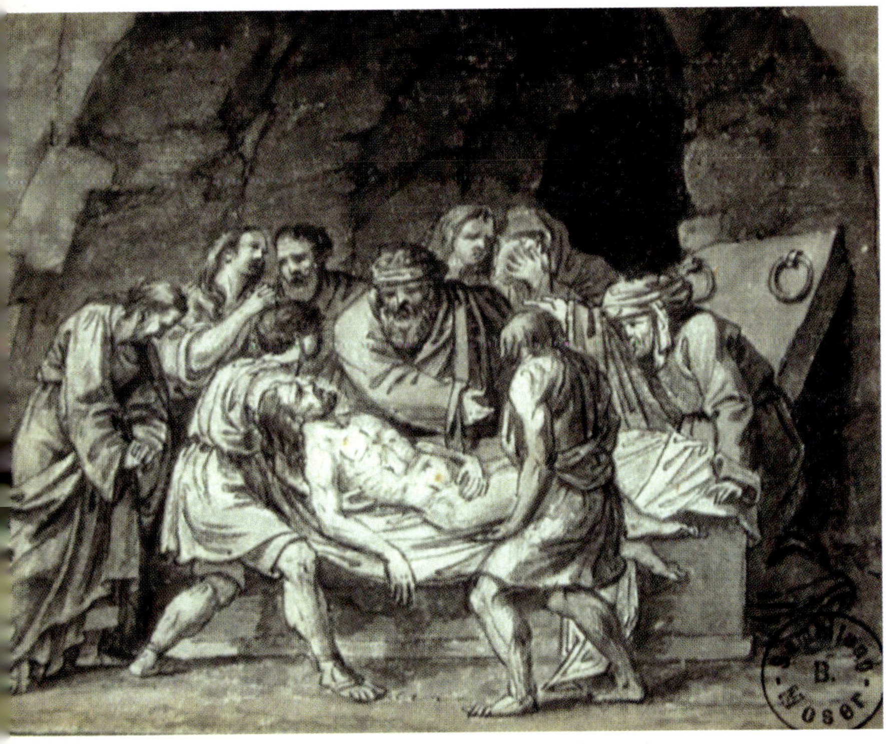

aged to communicate to anyone relatively familiar with the artwork. Eventually, Bowden created visual ciphers for thirty-six untitled images, gilded in 22-carat German gold, on a ground of richly finished, feather-deckled handmade paper. Realizing that the identity of certain works would be more or less familiar to a random variety of viewers, Bowden provided a set of illustrated art history books for reference with the exhibit. Anyone who took the time could locate, for example, the *Nike of Samothrace* (also known as *Winged Victory*) (Figure 73), Rublev's *Trinity* (Figure 70), Vincent van Gogh's *Starry Night* (Figure 94), or Christo's *Running Fence* project (Figure 96). Handouts on clipboards invited participants to test their knowledge with a friendly "quiz" sheet, also providing a key to the answers.

Bowden's symbolic preservation of each of the chosen works in a precious coating of gold leaf implies a heightened sense of value and respect, in essence, for major works from the Western canon. As an exhibit, *Art History 101* represents a perfect pedagogical scenario for Bowden—a self-professing teacher who prefers no classroom, and a perpetual student who never claims to be a scholar. As a collection of visual ideas, *Art History 101* represents a grouping of iconic images that engages the viewer in a dialogue with a history spanning twenty-three centuries.

This approach underscores Bowden's perennial role as a caretaker of the past, clearly represented by her continued use of fragmented excerpts from history in her own artworks. In recent decades, Bowden has translated her curatorial motivation into the practice of preserving religious imagery, in particular, for future generations. Since the early 1990s, she added the role of collector to her endeavors as artist, arts administrator, teacher, and student. In 2002, at the New York opening for *Collector's Items: Biblical Art and Private Devotion* (*A Selection from the Collection of Sandra and Robert Bowden*), Bowden explained that her focus on religious art gives the collection a concerted direction, creating a stronger ensemble.[16] The Bowdens are convinced that exhibiting twenty- and twenty-first-century religious art next to historical examples will contest the prevailing academic implication that this era was devoid of competent, religiously themed imagery.

Sandra Bowden and Edward Knippers persistently encourage others to collect, especially at a time when Christian themes are largely ignored on the market, and therefore currently more affordable and accessible than other genres. The two friends sieve through bins at Parisian flea markets, search through galleries in New York and London, and surf Internet auction sites while praying to be led to some new and amazing discovery.

Although Bowden claims that her first col-

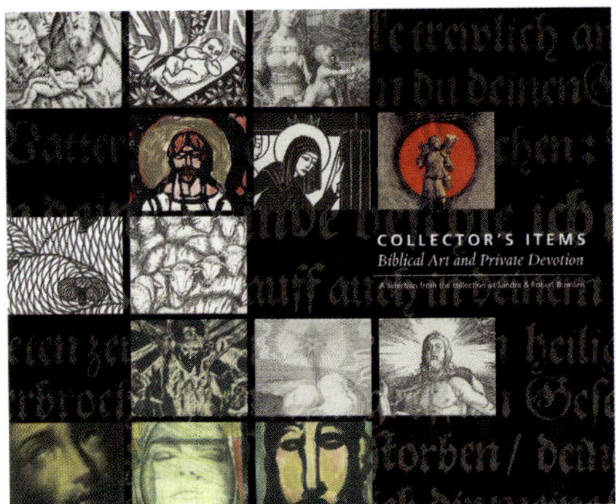

The Art of **Sandra Bowden**

lection began in childhood, with buttons and fabric swatches saved from household sewing projects, artist Donald Forsythe recalls an important milestone in Bowden's development as a serious collector. During an art and architecture tour to Budapest in 1992, he and Bowden happened upon a government-controlled sale of religious artifacts featuring stoles, vestments and altar cloths, all thickly embroidered in gold thread.[17] Unable to let this opportunity pass them by, both artists intuitively realized that collecting items considered useless by a secularized state would preserve them, in effect, for others in the future—a motivation that still dominates Bowden's rationale for collecting.

Bowden relishes the history behind her acquisitions almost as much as their possession. Always an intuitively astute "acquirer," Bowden is equally satisfied with overlooked "finds" by unknown artists, such as the modest nativity piece she bought for $3.50 at Paris's Port de Clignancourt flea market. "I still don't know who did the woodcut," she explains. "It only came with a signature of 'P.B.', but it is *loaded* with narrative information."[18] Another time, while "stuck" in Wiesbaden, she recalls, "I found a little bookstore, and I looked, and there was this wonderful gouache of Christ being laid in the tomb (Figure 74), with several collectors' stamps, and when I got home, I realized that it was by Barent Fabritius— a student of Rembrandt. Since we already had a work by Rembrandt, this addition was very exciting." Friends and dealers often alert Bowden of new discoveries, which is how Kathe Kollwitz's valuable woodcut, *Tod und Frau* (Figure 64), came into the Bowdens' collection. The Bowdens gratefully accepted another masterwork when a deal-

er successfully bid in their place at a Parisian auction for Claude Mellan's 1694 etching of the face of Christ. The most astonishing aspect of *La Sainte Face* (Figure 66) is that Mellan, one of the leading engravers of his time, meticulously modeled the features of Christ's face on Veronica's veil through the gradual thickening and thinning of a *single* line, which spirals outwards from the composition's center.

The narrative behind each work often captivates Bowden's interest. She experiences similar delight when she discovers collectors' stamps, signatures, scrawled inscriptions and marginalia generally hidden from public view by matting and framing. Of Ernst Barlach's *Group in the Storm* (Figure 75), Bowden says,

> The image was in perfect condition, but out on the edges there was every imaginable kind of tape, rips at the corners, smudged ink—basically, it's a history of where the work has been. I immediately have any new pieces matted and get them into safe environments—I don't let them deteriorate any further. My job is to leave them in better condition than when I bought them.[19]

Ownership represents far more than holding the physical acquisition in hand, although that is satisfying enough. Bowden describes her cataloguing process as a discipline, if not a devotional practice. Each piece receives an exhaustive examination. She records its condition, wear, and age as well as its subject matter, iconographical approach, method of production, and relation to other precedents or artists.

In the early 1990s, Bowden discovered eight

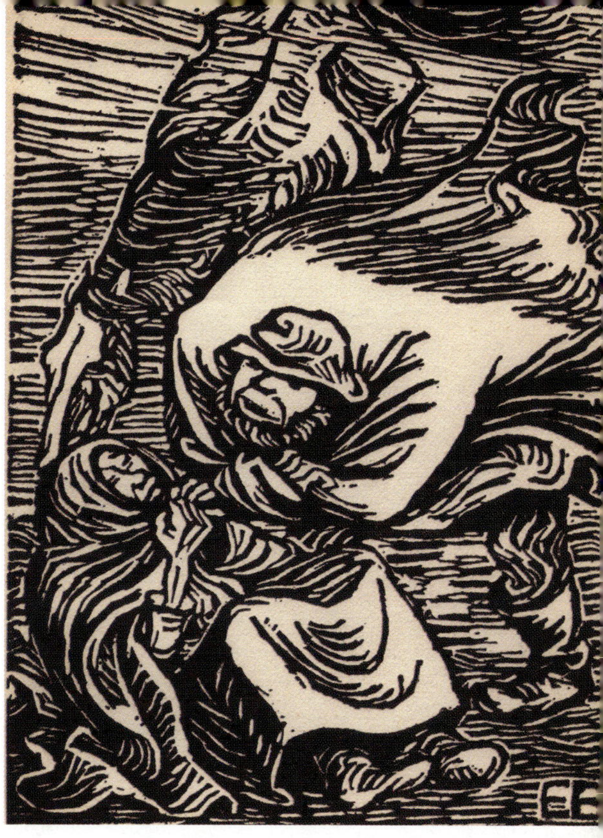

FIGURE 74
(OPPOSITE)
Barent Fabritius
BURIAL OF CHRIST
Gouache
1624–1672
3 3/4 x 4 3/4

FIGURE 75
Ernst Barlach
**GRUPPE IN STURM/
GROUP IN A STORM**
Woodcut
1920
4 3/4 x 6 3/4

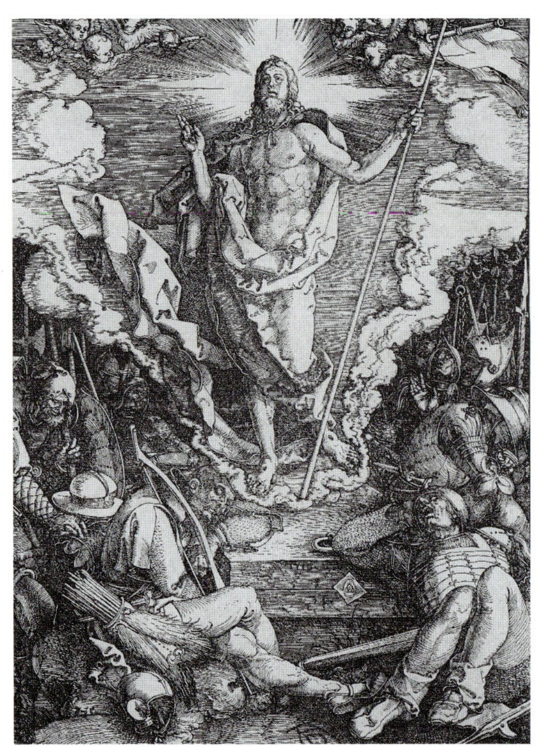

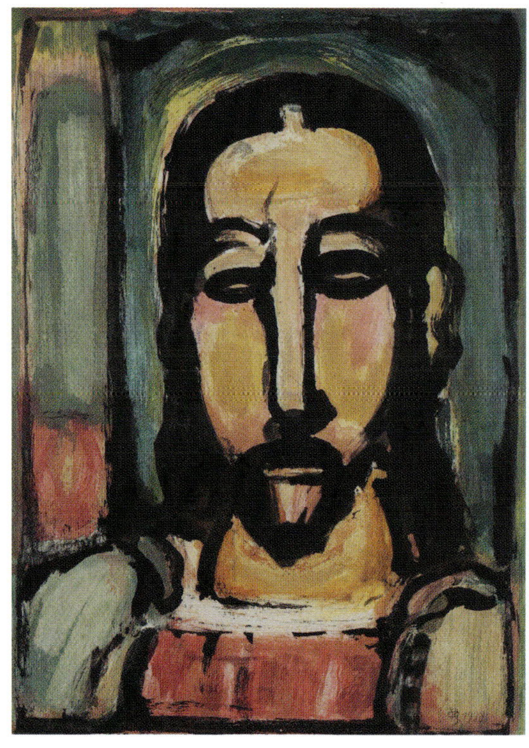

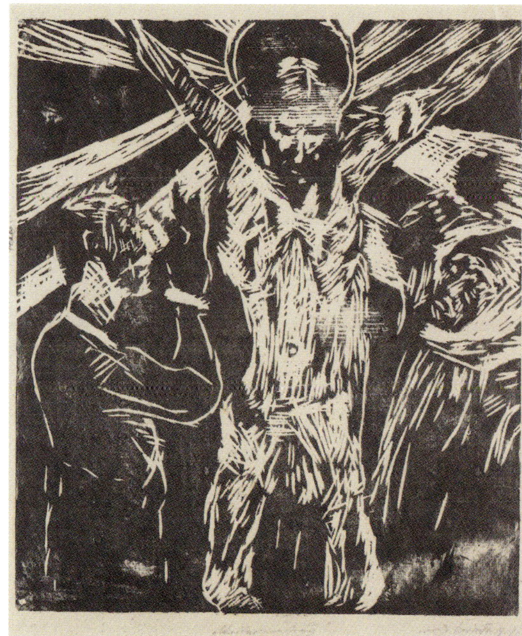

Georges Rouault intaglios for sale. When she told the dealer that she not only planned to take excellent care of the works, but to curate them as a traveling exhibit, he affably dropped the price of each significantly. In 2003, a Parisian dealer invited Bowden to review a rare, unopened *Miserère* set in its original case. The significance of this experience, and the Bowdens' eventual acquisition of the full set, can only partly be appreciated by some understanding of its origination, which also explains its allure as a collector's item.

Rouault's dealer, Ambroise Vollard, supported Rouault on a stipend, and summarily presumed that anything the artist signed belonged to him. Vollard photo-gravured the *Miserère* series, which Rouault meticulously reworked with unparalleled depth and texture between 1913 and 1927. When a freak accident involving a car and a soup-pot lid killed Vollard in 1939, Rouault feared that Vollard's greedy relatives would abscond with his entire life's work, and indiscriminately put his unfinished pieces on the market. After a series of bitter lawsuits enabled him to regain the rights to some of his own works, Rouault was finally able to recover the prints from a warehouse and publish the *Miserère* in 1948.[20]

A specially designed exhibition niche in the Bowdens' home creates a space to meditate, in passing, on themes that preoccupied at least five centuries of artists. Icons from Ethiopia (Figure 65) and Russia (Figure 71) complement

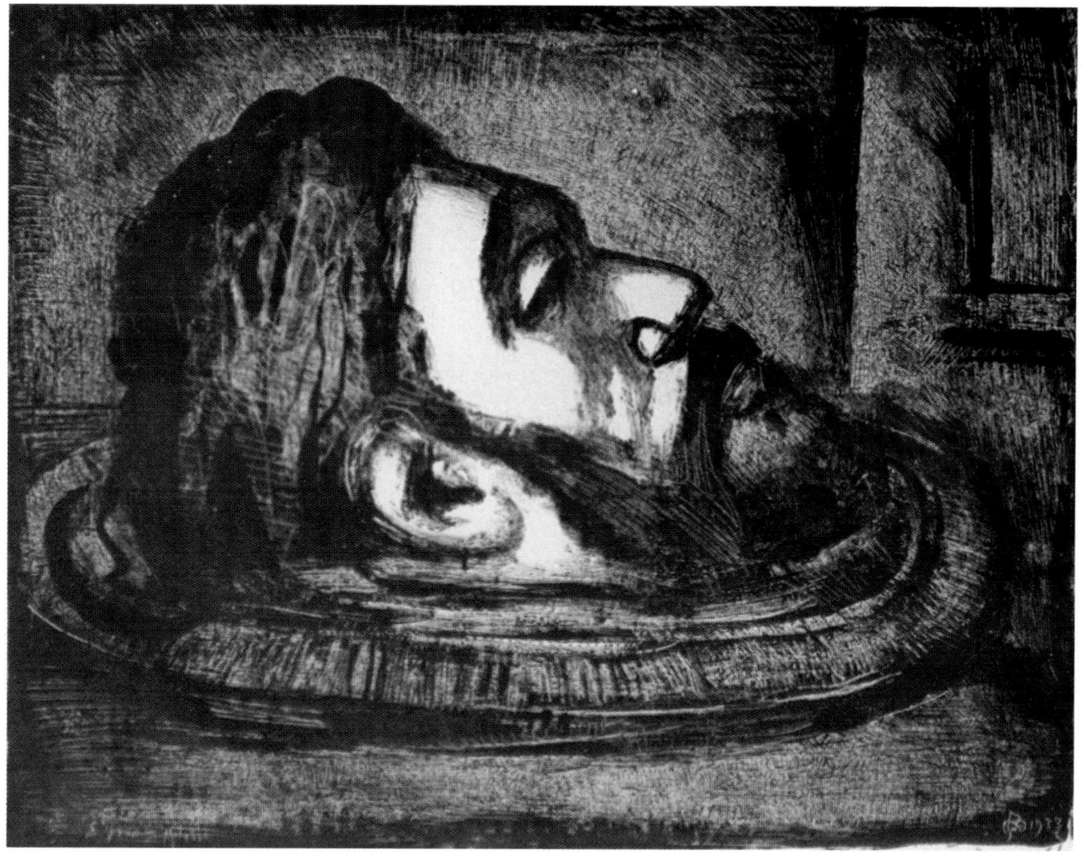

Albrecht Dürer's *Resurrection* (Figure 76), Georges Rouault's sugar-lift aquatint of Christ's face (Figure 77), and Lovis Corinth's *Christ on the Cross* (Figure 78). In essence, Bowden's penchant for dialogue receives satisfaction in her daily interaction with the collection, which enables her to transcend time and place by "dialoguing" with fellow artists, past or present, as she reviews their work. Hoping eventually to endow these fruits of labor to a public exhibition space, Bowden eagerly anticipates her part in bringing the conversation into the future.

Every phase of Bowden's formation involves material as well as intellectual absorption, assimilation, or acquisition. Kernels of the concepts that intrigue her eventually germinate into a series of visual propositions. New materials also inspire new series, and often enter her creative sphere serendipitously, through the inspired donations of acquaintances. For example, a collection of old Bibles with slightly singed edges corresponds to Bowden's increasing use of Bible page fragments. It also fostered her international campaign, over the years, to

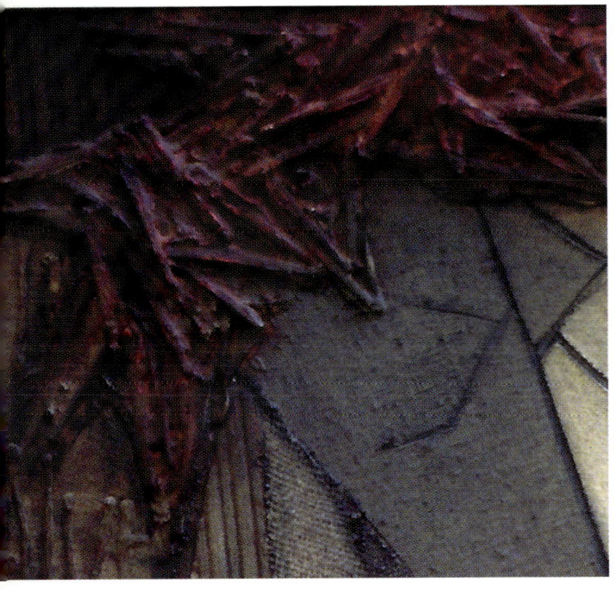

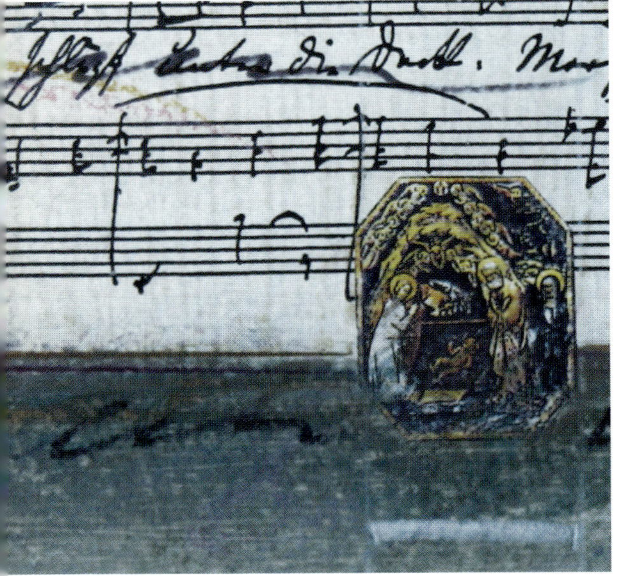

accumulate a large archive of liturgical texts in dozens of languages, including old Vietnamese and Cambodian Bibles. Old floor nails proved useful in a series of expressionist crucifixions, including *It Is Finished* (Figures 47, 80), featuring a crown of thorns created by nails embedded in gesso. Nails reappear in Bowden's latest artist's books. For instance, *Book of Nails* (Figure 124), which Bowden considers an important new departure for her, is gilded in pure 22-carat gold but filled with a clump of old rough-edged nails. Together, gilded planes and rusty nails create a succinct visual and textural contrast between two metaphorically loaded symbols.

Dozens of musical facsimiles occasioned a musical series between 1987 and 1994. These copies of scores, notated in the hands of famous composers, "triggered my imagination," Bowden explains, "so I studied actual scores at Yale and other libraries, and now I can identify which scores are Stravinsky, Beethoven, or Bach just by the personalities of their handwriting."[21] Intrigued by the concept that music is even more of an abstract universal language than Hebrew scripture or visual expression, Bowden began adding or scratching texture and line into the music collages to emphasize their handcrafted genesis as a metaphor for creation-at-large. The first musical *chine collé*, *Sonata* (Figure 69), featured a Beethoven piano sonata set within a textured oil ground of layers of gesso and molding paste on paper. By the 1990s, Bowden chose to emphasize how music and art dialogue with a series of visual counterpoints. For example, *Cradle Song* (Figures 68, 81) juxtaposes Brahms's *Lullaby and Good Night* with a copy of the Renaissance nativity fresco

from Santa Maria Novella in Florence. *Holy, Holy, Holy* (Figure 67) contrasts an excerpt from the *Sanctus* of Benjamin Britten's dignified *War Requiem* with a passage from Revelations 4, on the Almighty Lord "who is and who is to come."

Working on a smaller and less demanding scale after back surgery in 1994, Bowden began a series literally appropriated from her own flat files, recycling excerpts of gilded Hebrew texts and early collagraphs. The resulting collages culminate in one elegant idea that, in typical fashion, Bowden has worked and reworked. While the concept is not necessarily original, Bowden beautifully expresses it through her highly disciplined handling of materials. *Law and Gospel* (Figure 59), which had previously been titled *Law and Grace*, presents the form of the "law" columns on the left in a stylized quotation of the two tablets of the Decalogue. A clearcut gap on the "Gospel" or "Grace" form to the right signifies, as Bowden explains, Christ's radical, redeeming entry into the "Law." In its subtractive process, this gap generates a cross. The void evokes the ripping of the veil at the moment of Jesus' death. More generally, it implies a sense of separation between life and death or the divide between humanity and divinity that Jesus pulls together in one being on the cross; it might even pose the complicated presupposition that Jesus' act of negation, in death, created a new condition of resurrected life, symbolized by the cross.

Through her art, Bowden has wrestled with a troublesome internal conflict, prompted by her mandate as a visual artist focused on texts. At first, her natural inclination towards excerpting texts seemed to perpetuate a Protestant partiality for word over image. Eventually, Bowden realized that dialogue could keep such disparate binaries (such as "text" and "image") in conversation or creative collaboration—just as dialectical logic holds the spiritual and material together in the fruitful collaboration known as religious art.

Dialectical logic, which carries two distinct values together in a peaceable tension, originated with the nineteenth-century German Idealists, and is often linked to philosophers Kant and Hegel. Some postmodern commentators, like British-based literary critic Michael Edwards, argue that the dialectic and its corollary notion of "paradox" riddle ancient biblical literature.[21] However, while Hegelian dialectic doggedly aims toward an immediate "synthetic" resolution or union (synthesis) between two oppositions (thesis and antithesis), theological oppositions—such as "good" and "evil" or "flesh" and "spirit"—receive their actual resolution through eventual redemption in the hereafter. This grants a sense of paradox to the entire Christian experience, since Christians live between unresolved realities in the present and the future hope of resolution.

In the end, everyone tolerates a certain degree of unresolved tension, which Edwards describes as the "incongruous texture" of life. "We arrive after generations of shady complicity between language and the world," Edwards explains, "to find ourselves in an inextricable yet incongruous texture of words, self, things."[22] One could concede that faith, characterized in Hebrews as the province "of things unseen," accepts the possibility of restoration without the luxury of demanding its

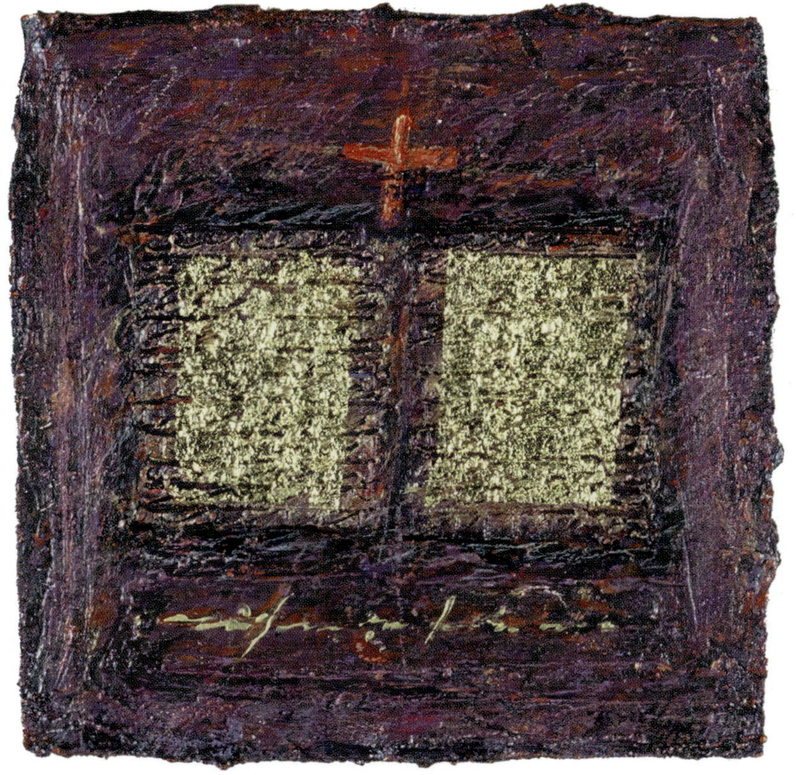

material proof. Since the Christian exegesis presents the final stage as a veiled truth claim, always delivered in the future tense (i.e., "will come," "is to come," "will be seen"), accepting the promise of full restoration is truly an act of faith rather than an exchange of material verities. And yet, the widespread evidence of material analogs as pointers to the spiritual seems to affirm a driving human need for them. As Edwards says, observant visitors from outer space could not fail to be amazed by the sheer volume of human attempts to reproduce, or even improve upon the world, as evidenced by art, literature and music.[23]

FIGURE 80
(OPPOSITE TOP)
IT IS FINISHED (detail)
Oil collage
1976
48 x 36

FIGURE 81
(OPPOSITE BOTTOM)
CRADLE SONG (detail)
Collagraph
mixed media
1988
20 X 20

FIGURE 82
ILLUMINATION III
Acrylic mixed media
1990
10 x 10

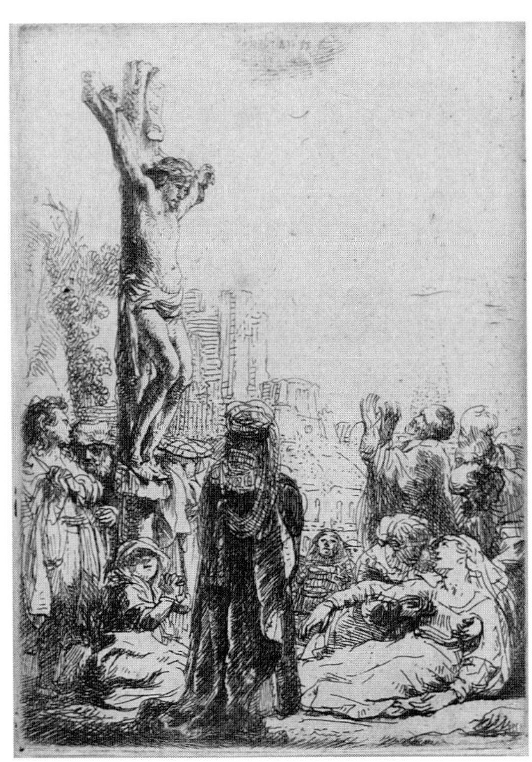

Edwards insists, "The incongruity of language . . . is precisely our chance. Explored, language becomes a domain of suggestions, fragments of a novel reality re-emerging with fragments of a novel speech."[24] The apparently unresolved status of this suggestive, fragmental language inspires the best art, in Edwards's view. More pertinently, Bowden's primary trope works this unresolved/ resolved binary out with a fragmented visual language. Bowden's "fragments of a novel speech" suggest the presence of this completed picture, but never illustrate its entirety. She intentionally leaves such resolutions to the viewer. Veiling her own personal expectation for a future distinguished by completion, transformation, and restoration, Bowden's juxtapositions provide space for free association. Her dialogues mine the paradox of our existence, as creatures with one foot on the earth and one in heaven, or beings that are incomplete at present, yet fully completed in the future tense. She avidly acquires things and ideas that she knows will not matter in the same way during a future that promises total redemption. She fully accepts the fact that the value we currently assign to "material" or "spiritual" things in this realm will fade away in the light of God's "true image."

On the other hand, rather than celebrating ambiguity that arises from a lack of resolution—which typifies generically "spiritual" postmodern art—Bowden's willingness to court the unresolved or the "'apparently ambiguous'" rests firmly on her lifelong expectation of God's final redeeming act. At that juncture, she anticipates the "final answer" to all questions. In this present context, she frequently refers to her process as one of simply following the questions that her art poses to their logical ends, as far as she can go with artistic expression. "My work is a record of my intellectual and spiritual journey—a process of personal inquiry," she often explains. "The work continually raises new ideas, and I chase those questions."[25] Bowden's uncomplicated expressive logic is as pragmatic, industrious, and persistent as the faith of her New England forebears. Her dialogues range between different epochs, art forms, and denominational biases. She proposes veiled material analogues that reflect, "through a glass darkly," deeper spiritual verities.

As the eleventh-century monk Theophilus wrote in *De Diversis Artibus*, "Anything [the artist] can invent or learn or understand about art is the fruit of the Seven Gifts of the Holy Spirit."[26] Sandra Bowden's investment in the process of invention, learning, and understanding directly transforms a physical analog into a spiritual analog for the true and total subject—the living God. Inasmuch as it can be done in this life, Bowden's work attempts to reconcile the inescapable paradox between material means and spiritual ends—an endeavor that will surely constitute part of her legacy.

1   Diane Waldman. *Collage, Assemblage, and the Found Object.* (New York: Harry N. Abrams, Inc., 1992). p.8.

2   Waldman, p. 221; Robert Motherwell in "Beyond the Aesthetic," *Design* 47. (April 1946). p.15.

3   Waldman, p. 241.

4   Interview with Sandra Bowden, June 5, 2003. Ad Reinhardt (1913–1967) is most widely known for monochromatic abstract expressionist paintings from the 1950s, which contributed to the

   The Art of **Sandra Bowden**

emerging canon of Minimalism.

5   This and other Edward Knippers' statements are from an interview on September 27, 2003.

6   Harry M. Orlinsky, *Understanding the Bible through History and Archaeology* (New York: Ktav Publishing House, 1972). Some of Dame Kathleen Kenyon's books include *Royal Cities of the Old Testament* (New York: Schocken Books, c.1971); *Archaeology in the Holy Land* (New York: Praeger and W.W. Norton, 1970, 1979); and *The Bible and Recent Archaeology* (Atlanta: John Knox, 1978).

7   Interview, April 13, 1996.

8   Gene Edward Veith, "A Christian Steeped in the Hebraic Aesthetic: Sandra Bowden," in *Christianity and the Arts.* (Winter 1999). p.18-22.

9   Thorlief Boman. *Hebrew Thought Compared with Greek.* (New York: W.W. Norton and Sons, 1960, 1970).

10 Interview, June 5, 2003.

11 Thomas F. Mathews. *The Clash of Gods: A Reinterpretation of Early Christian Art.* (Princeton: Princeton University Press, 1993). p.95.

12 Leonid Ouspensky and Vladimir Lossky, *The Meaning of Icons* (St. Vladimirís Press, 1989) p. 40, 53, and Brother Aidan Hart's *Sacred Icons: Paradise Regained,* Oriel 31; (Newtown, Powys, Wales: Davies Memorial Gallery, 1991) pp.9-10.

13 Mathews. p. 95.

14 David Knowles. *The Evolution of Medieval Thought,* second edition. (Harlow, Essex, England: Longman Group Limited, 1988). p.40.

15 Christopher de Hamel. *A History of Illustrated Manuscripts.* (London: Phaidon Press, 1986/1994). p.124 ff.

16 Featured in the exhibit booklet *Collector's Items: Biblical Art and Private Devotion (A Selection from the Collection of Sandra and Robert Bowden).* (New York: The Gallery at the American Bible Society, 2000).

17 Interview with Don Forsythe, September 26, 2003.

18 Interview, June 5, 2003.

19 Interview, June 5, 2003.

20 As a devout Catholic, Rouault was one of the few believers to reach the upper tiers of acclaim in modern expressionism. A recent revival in interest, spurred in part by Bowden's campaign with the *Miserère* series, may result in a future Rouault retrospective in New York. Although currently out of print, another good source is William Dyrness' *Rouault: A Vision of Suffering and Salvation* (Grand Rapids, MI: Eerdmans, 1971).

21 Interview, June 5, 2003.

22 Michael Edwards. *Towards A Christian Poetics.* (Grand Rapids, MI: Eerdmans, 1984).

23 Edwards, p.11.

24 Edwards, p.201.

25 Interview, April 13, 1996.

26 Theophilus, *De Diversis Artibus.* translated by C.R. Dodwell. (London, 1961), also quoted in Umberto Eco.

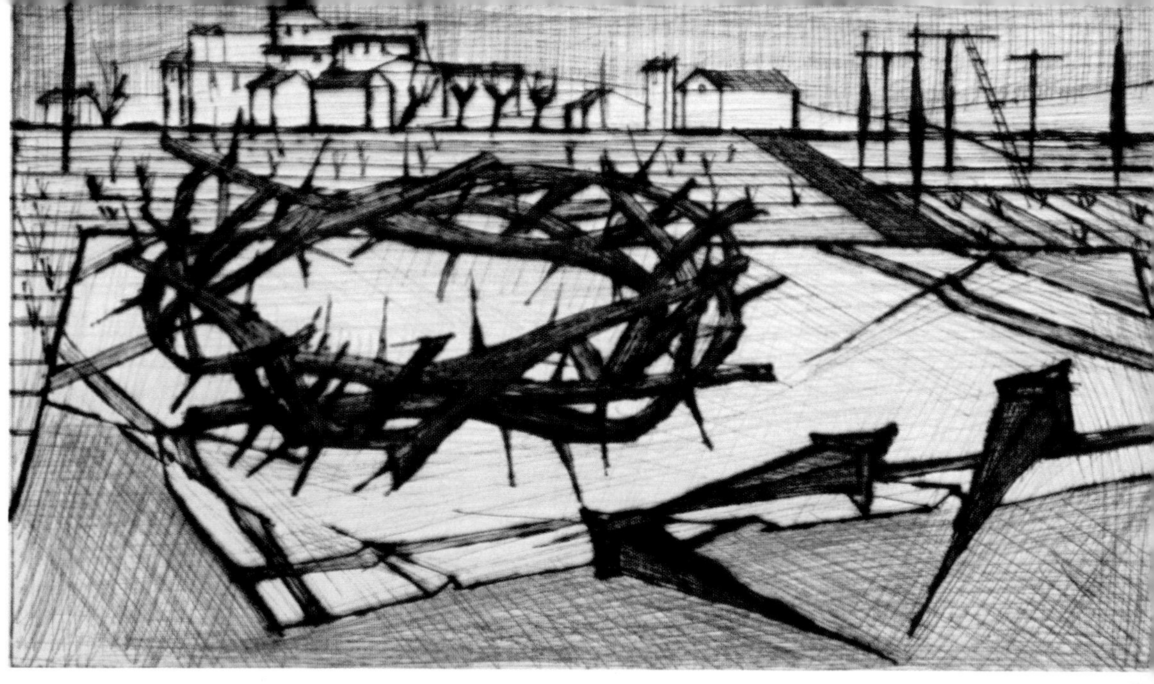

FIGURE 83
(OPPOSITE)
Rembrandt van Rijn
THE CRUCIFIXION: SMALL PLATE
Etching
1635
3 3/4 x 2 1/8

FIGURE 84
Bernard Buffet
CROWN OF THORNS,
from *Images from the Passion*
Etching
5 1/2 x 9 1/2

Art History Interpretations

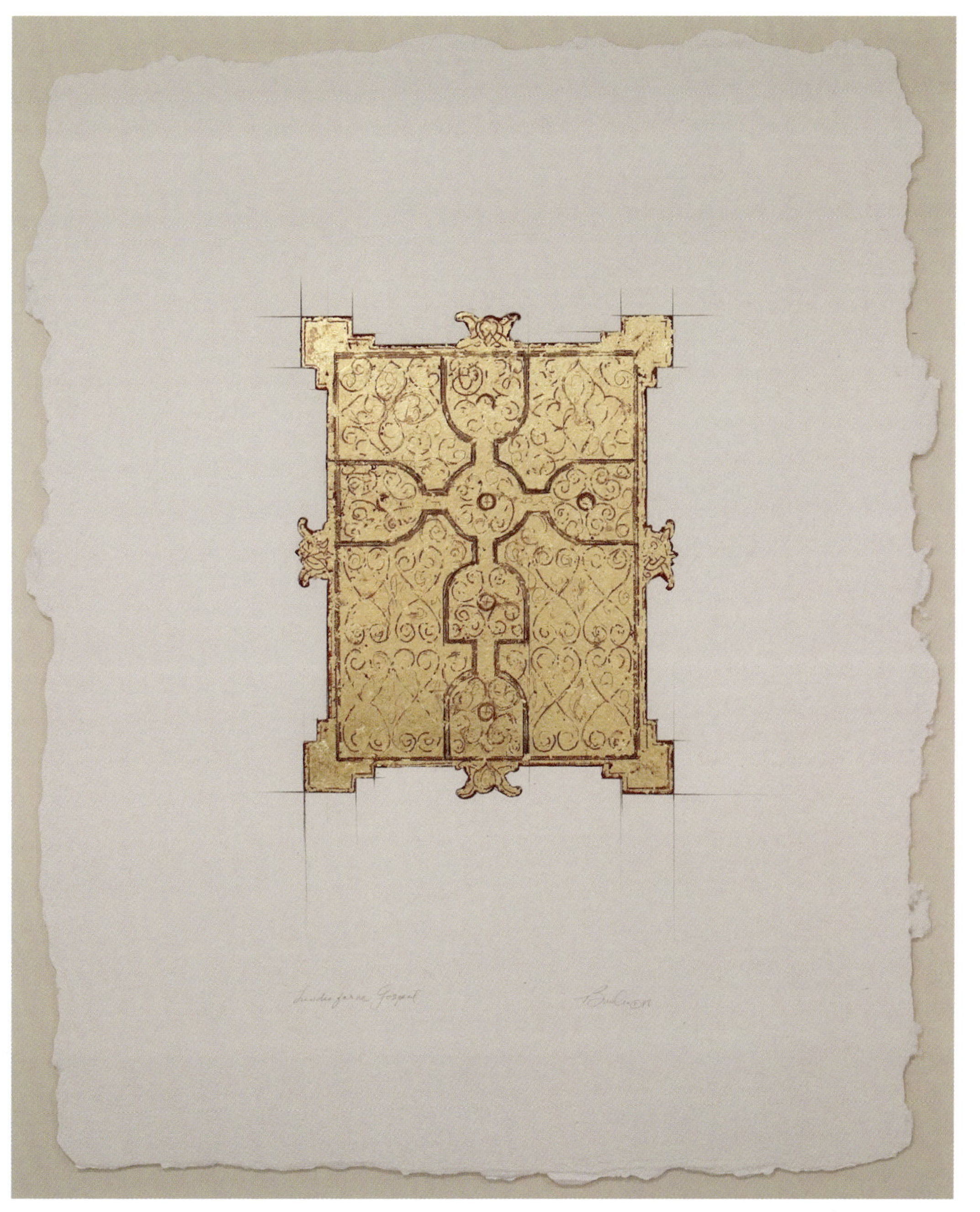

FIGURE 85
**CROSS PAGE FROM
LINDISFARNE
GOSPELS AFTER
UNKNOWN ARTIST
(C. 700 A.D.)**
Mixed media
drawing with
22-carat gold leaf
1998
21 x 16

Kneeling before this crucifix which
inspired his conversion in 1205ad
St. Francis wrote this prayer.

"All Highest, Glorious God
Cast your light into the darkness
of my heart.
Give me right faith,
firm hope
perfect charity,
and profound humility,
with wisdom and perception
O Lord. So that I may do
what is truly your most holy will.
Amen "

St. Francis

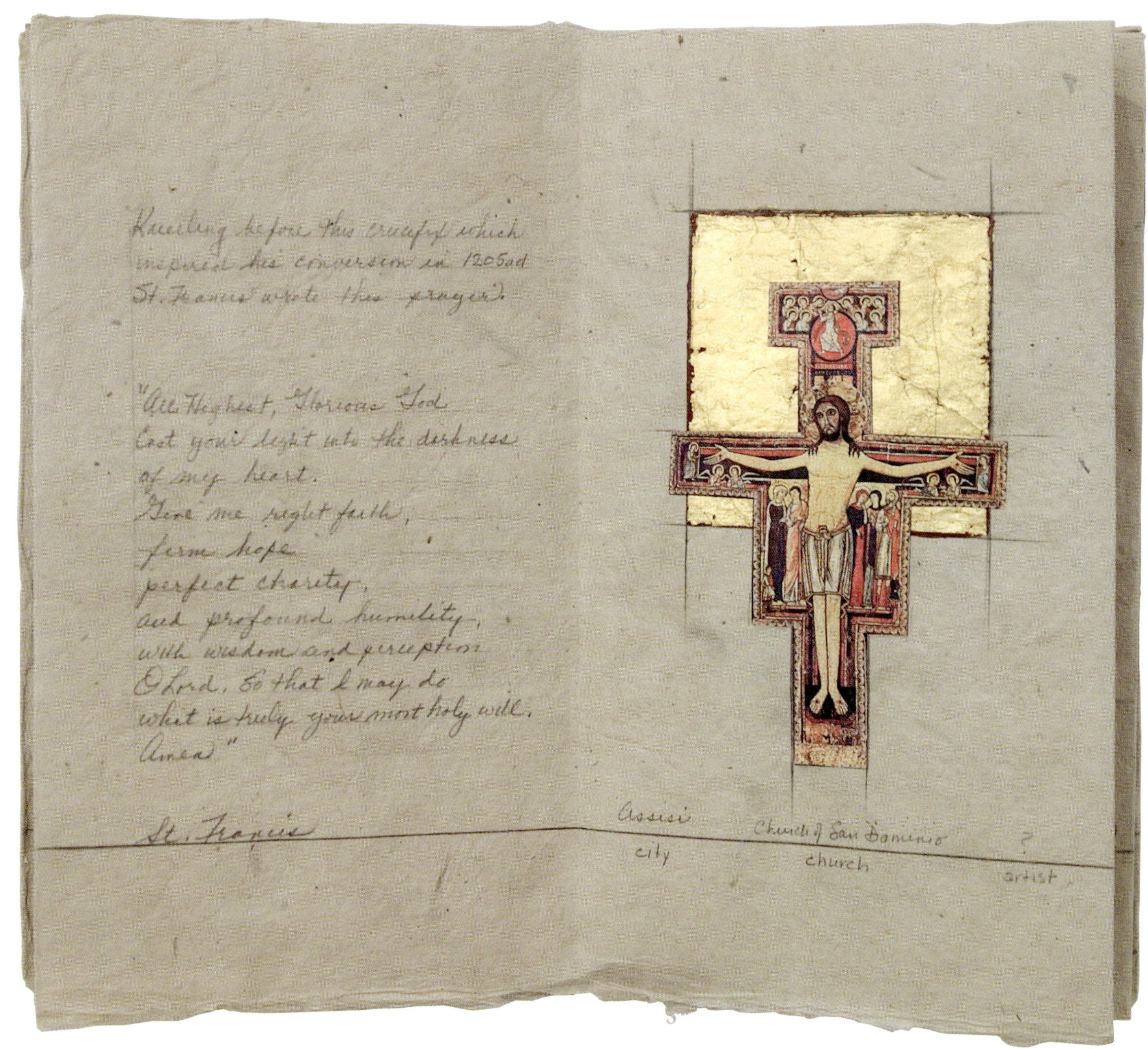

The Art of **Sandra Bowden**

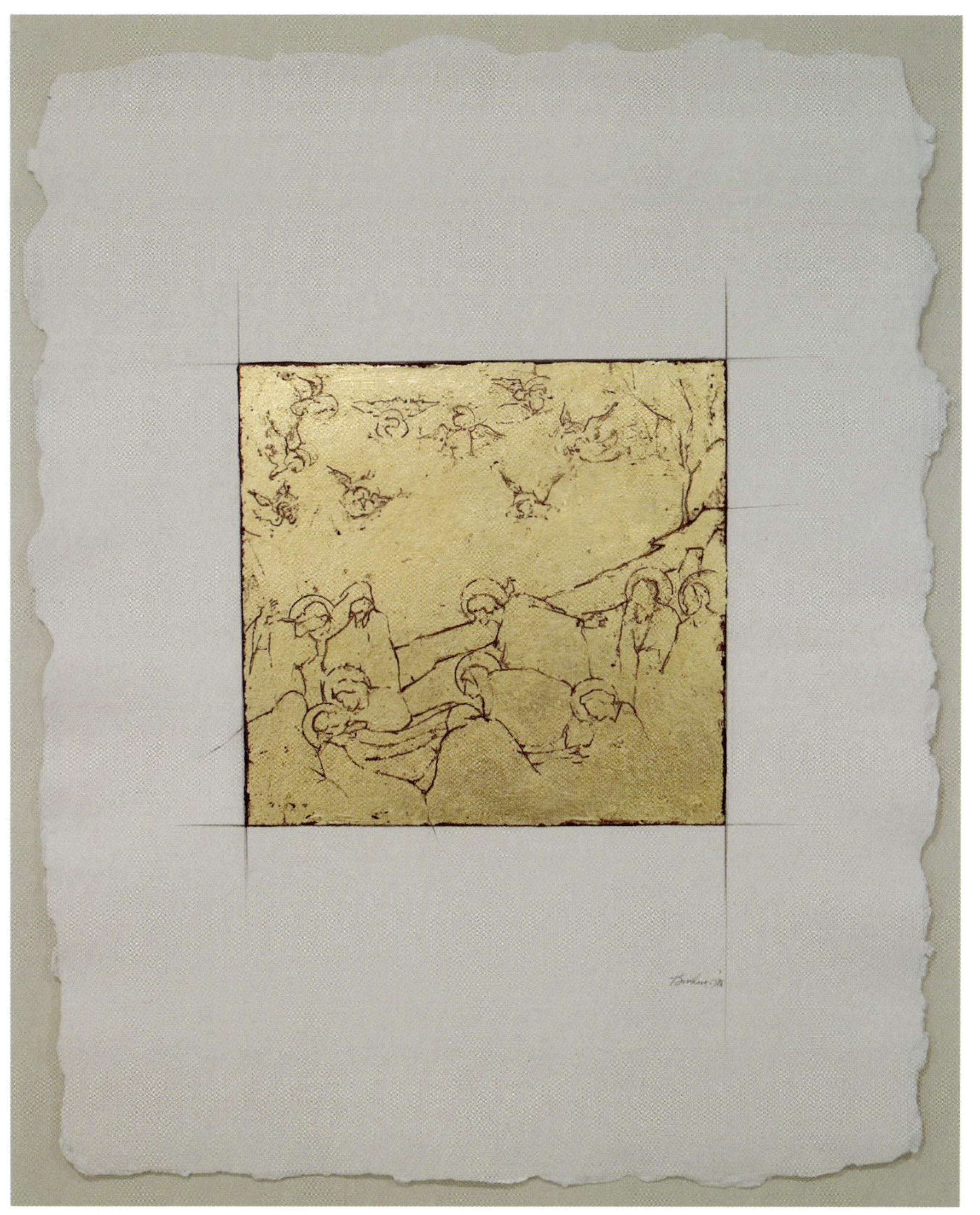

FIGURE 86
**NAME THE CITY,
CHURCH AND ARTIST**
Mixed media
drawing with
22-carat gold leaf
1997
Four 18 x 14
gilded crosses with
an accordion book
measuring 12 x 54

FIGURE 87
**LAMENTATION AFTER
GIOTTO DI BONDONE
(1266–1337)**
Mixed media
drawing with
22-carat gold leaf
1997
21 x 16

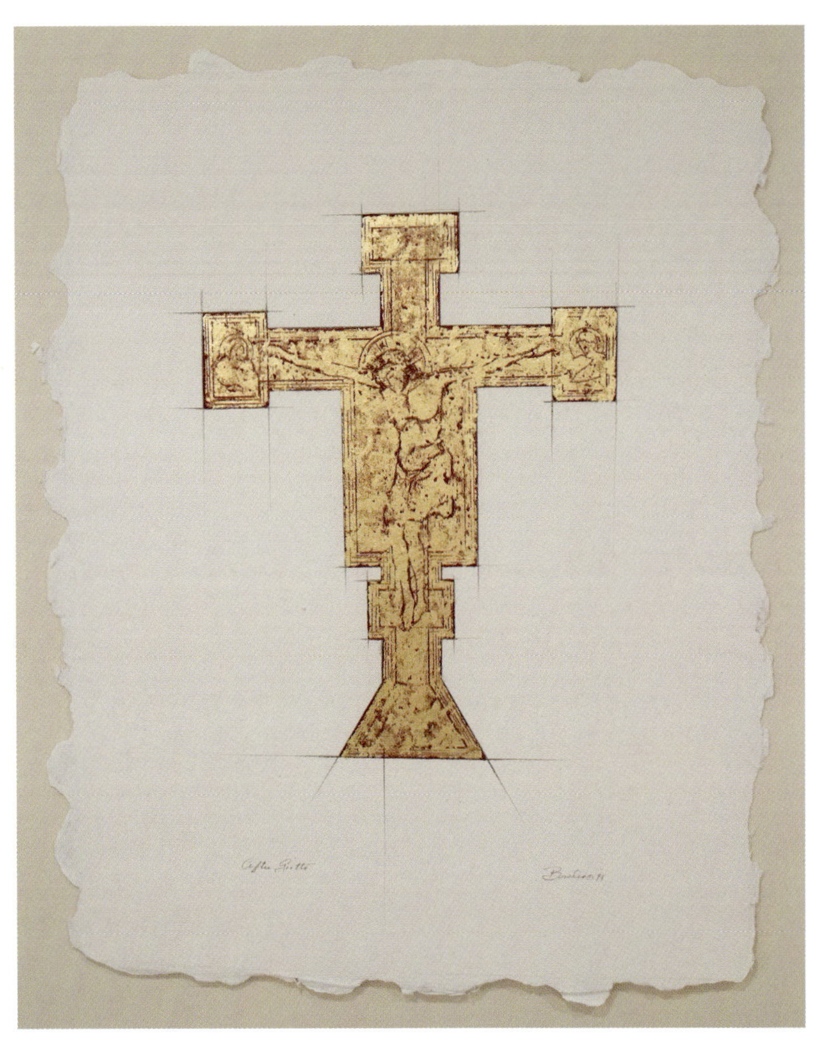

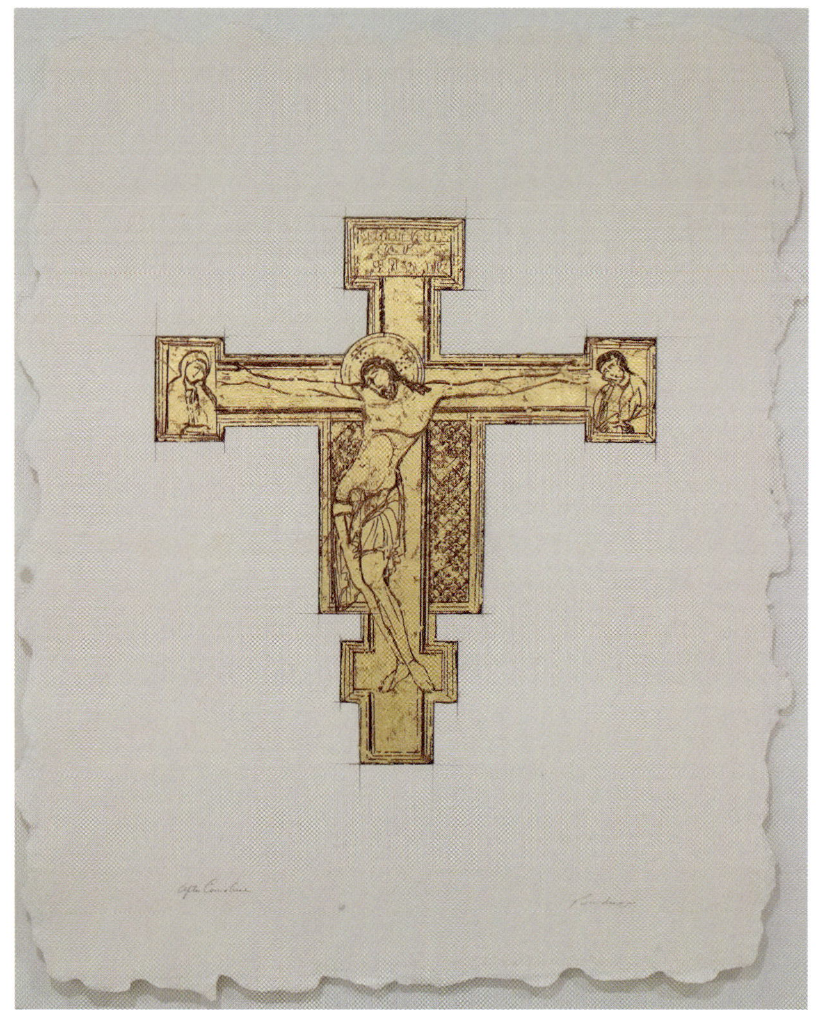

The Art of **Sandra Bowden

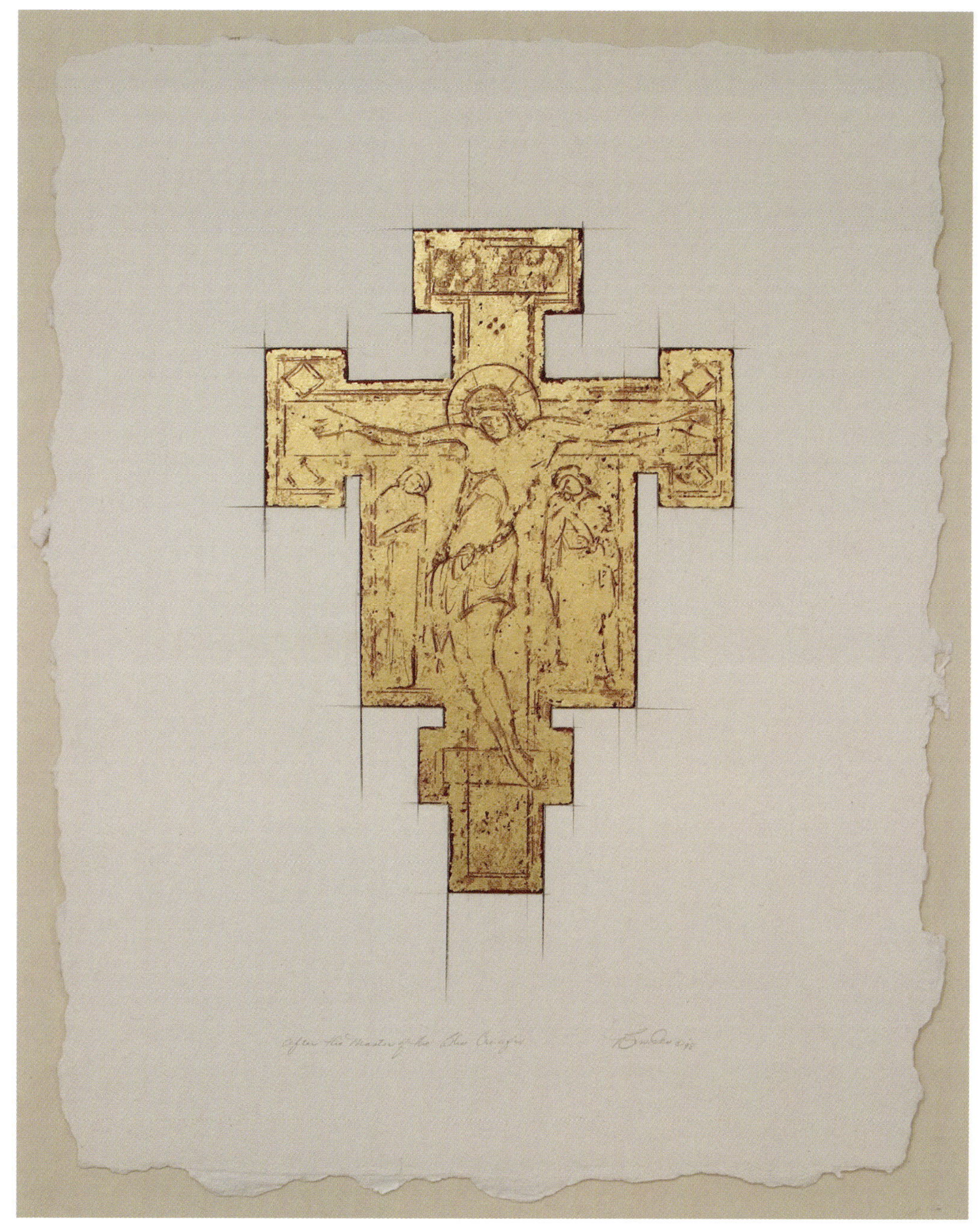

FIGURE 88
(OPPOSITE LEFT)
**CRUCIFIX AFTER
GIOTTO DI BONDONE
(1266–1337)**
Mixed media
drawing with
22-carat gold leaf
1997
21 x 16

FIGURE 89
(OPPOSITE RIGHT)
**CRUCIFIX AFTER
CIMABUE
(1240–1302)**
Mixed media
drawing with
22-carat gold leaf
1997
21 x 16

FIGURE 90
**CRUCIFIX AFTER THE
MASTER OF THE
BLUE CRUCIFIX
(13TH CENTURY)**
Mixed media
drawing with
22-carat gold leaf
1997
21 x 16

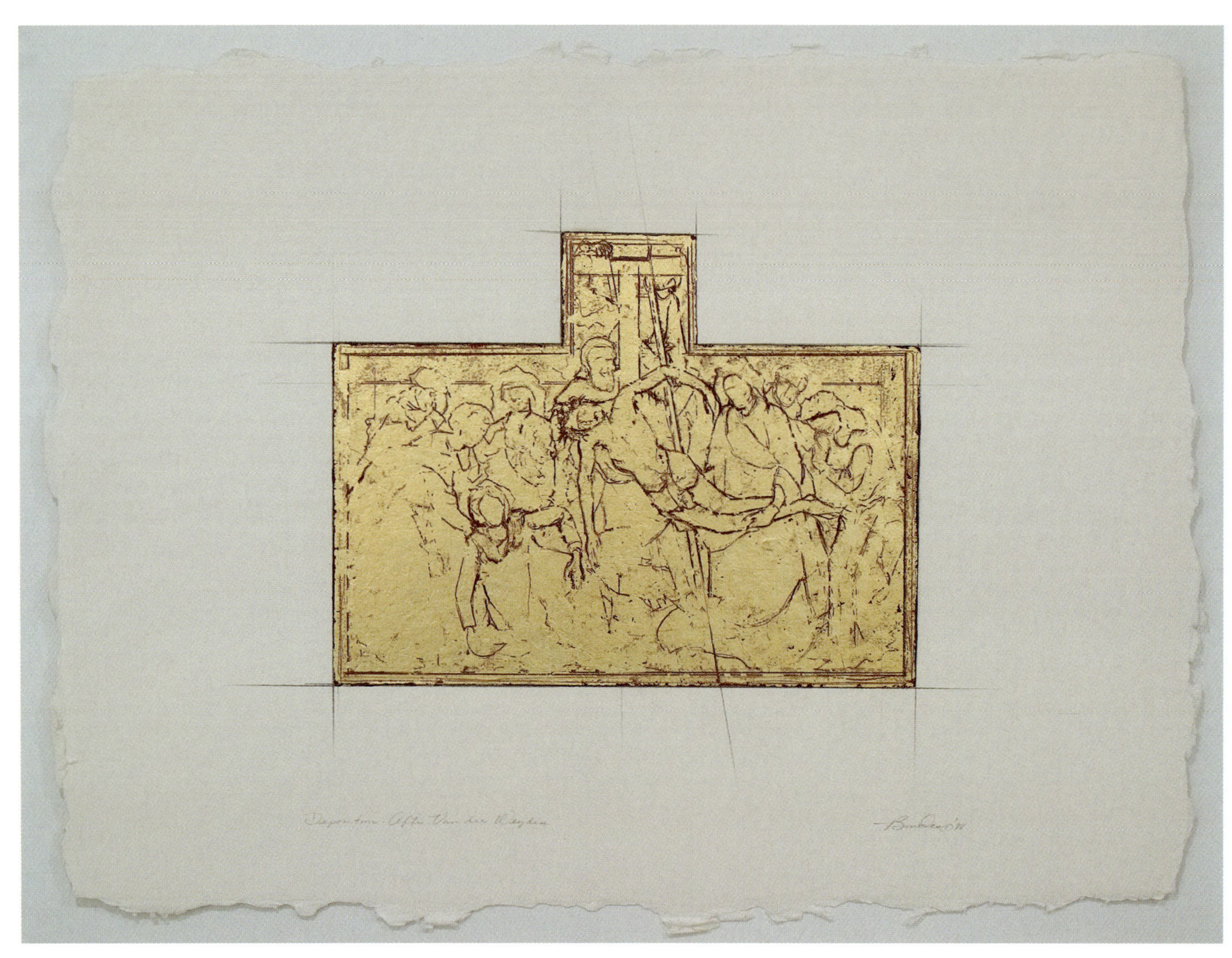

The Art of **Sandra Bowden**

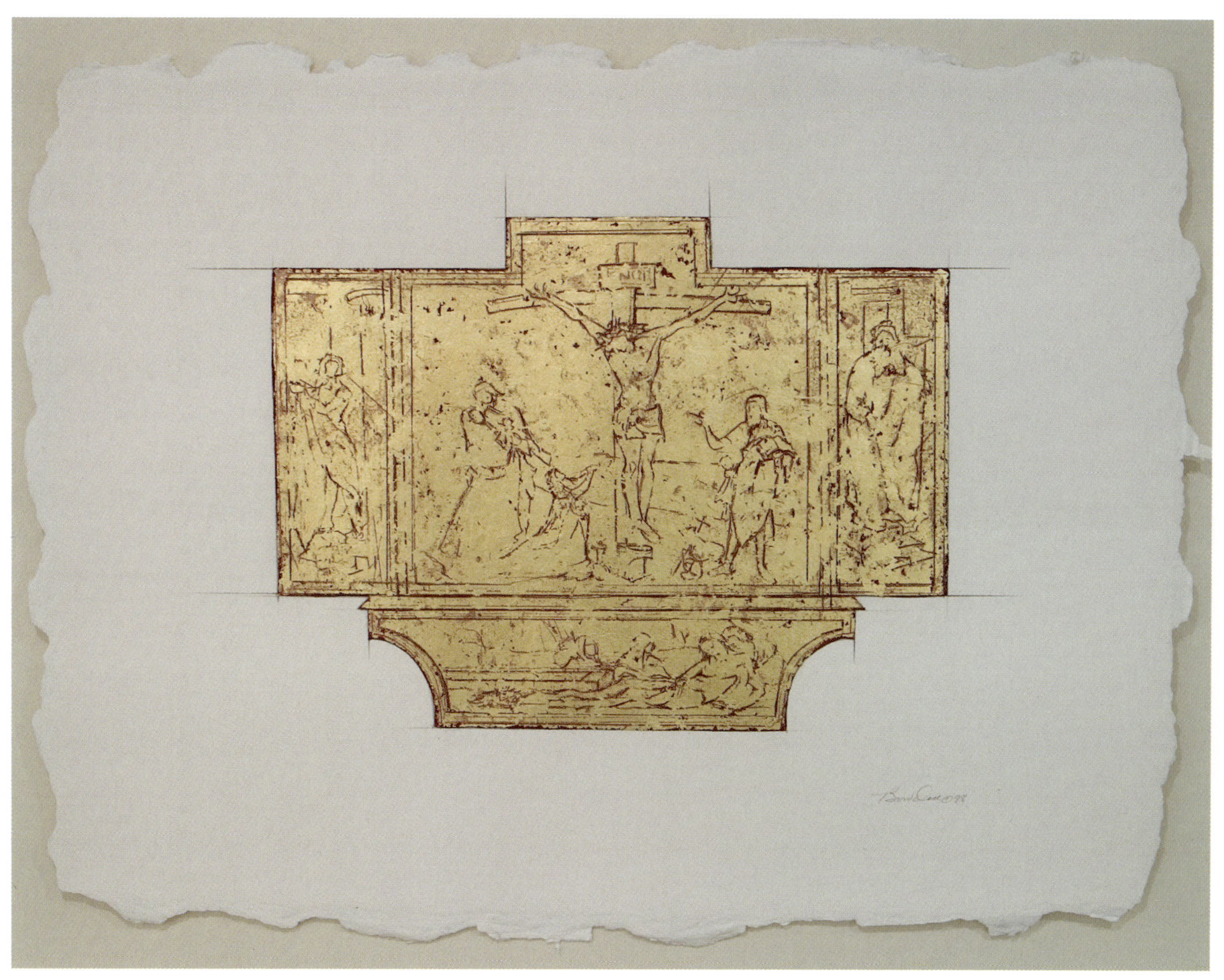

FIGURE 91
(OPPOSITE)
DEPOSITION AFTER
ROGIER VAN DER
WEYDEN (1399–64)
Mixed media
drawing with
22-carat gold leaf
1998
16 x 21

FIGURE 92
ISENHEIM
ALTARPIECE AFTER
MATTHIAS
GRÜNEWALD
(1475–1528)
Mixed media
drawing with
22-carat gold leaf
1997
16 x 12

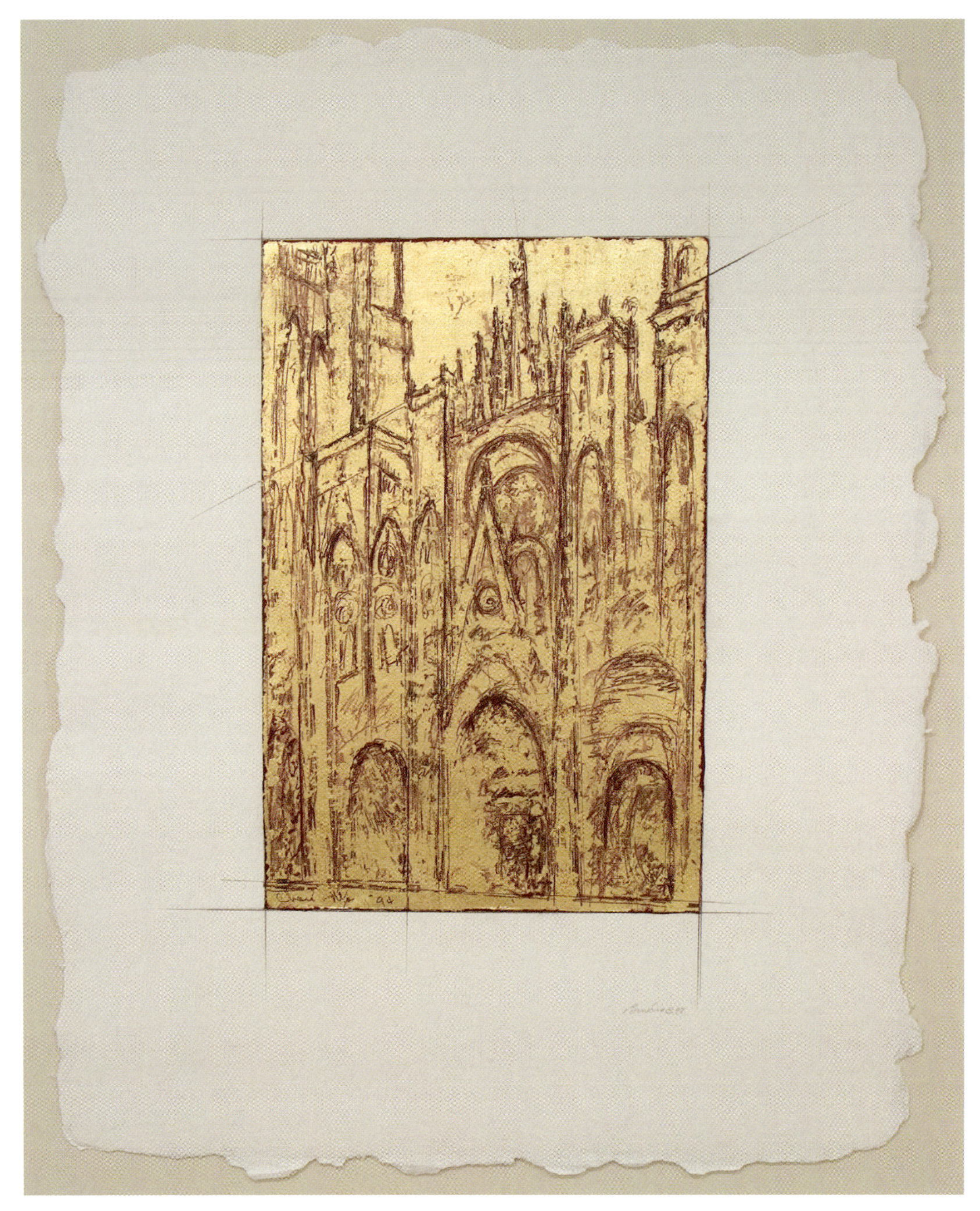

The Art of **Sandra Bowden**

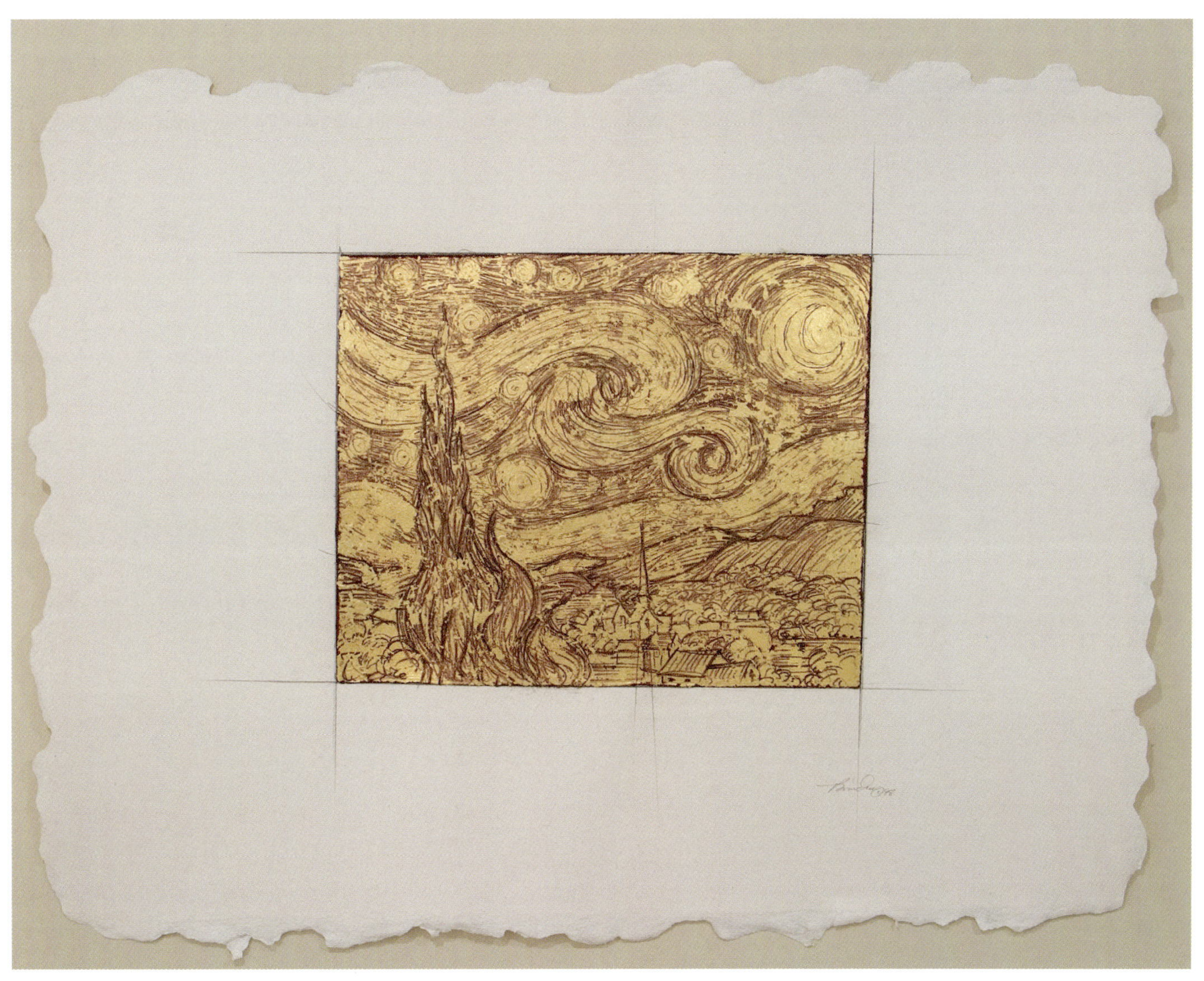

FIGURE 93
ROUEN CATHEDRAL
AFTER CLAUDE
MONET (1840–1926)
Mixed media
drawing with
22-carat gold leaf
1998
21 x 16

FIGURE 94
STARRY NIGHT
AFTER VINCENT VAN
GOGH (1853–90)
Mixed media
drawing with
22-carat gold leaf
1998
16 x 21

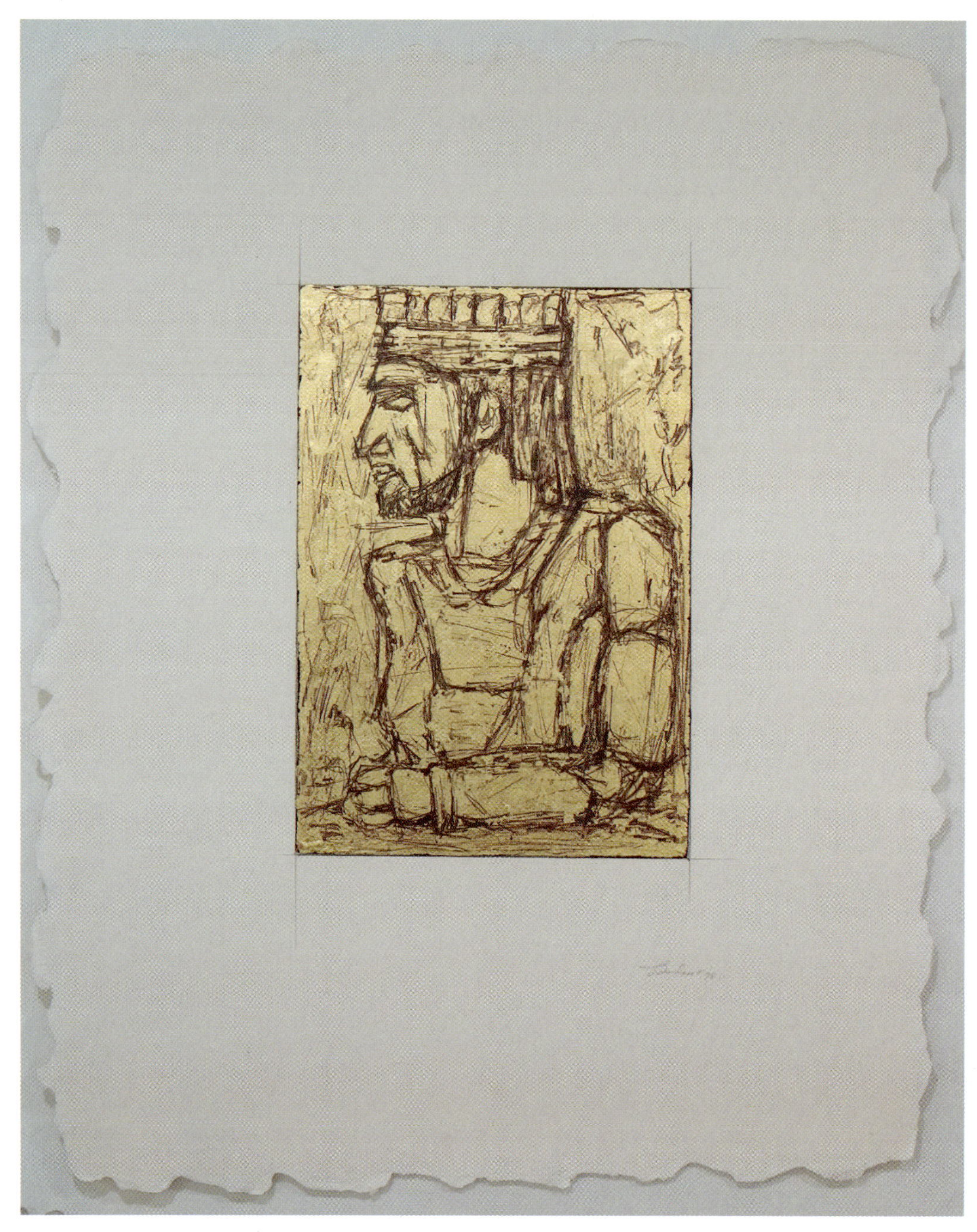

The Art of **Sandra Bowden**

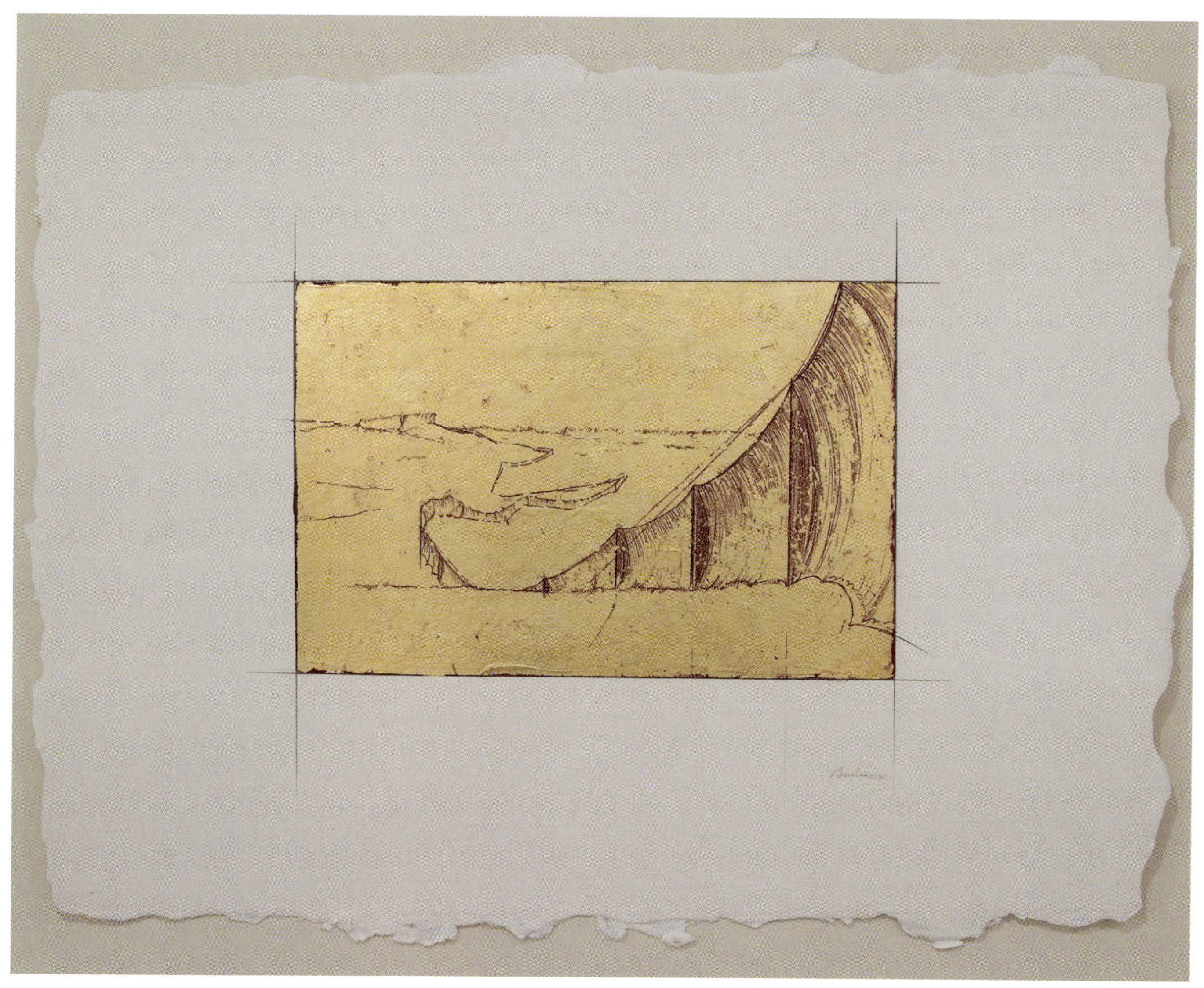

FIGURE 95
(OPPOSITE)
**THE OLD KING AFTER
GEORGES ROUAULT
(1871–1958)**
Mixed media
drawing with
22-carat gold leaf
1998
21 x 16

FIGURE 96
**RUNNING FENCE
AFTER CHRISTO
(B. 1935) AND
JEANNE-CLAUDE
(B.1935)**
Mixed media
drawing with
22-carat gold leaf
1998
16 x 21

Collage

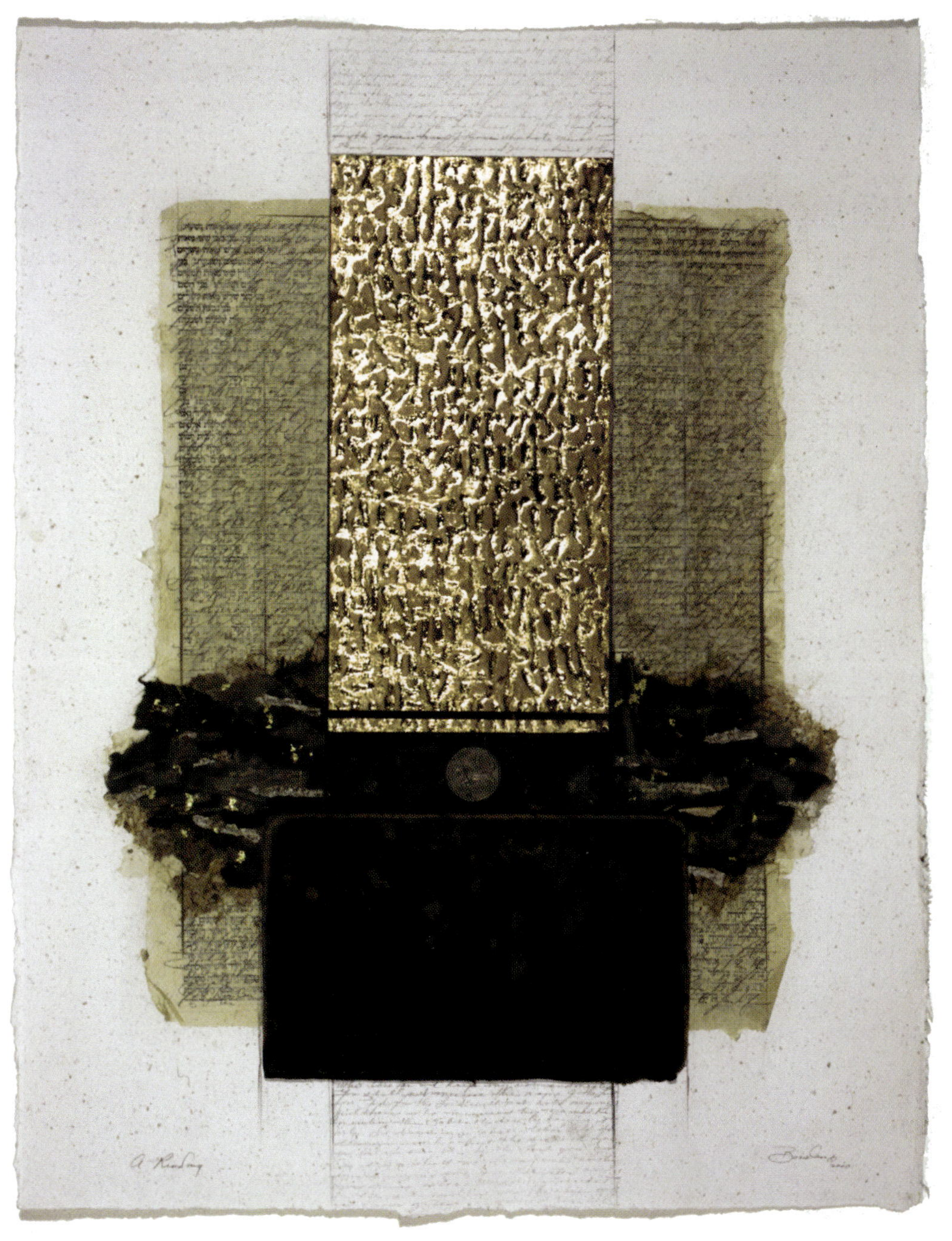

FIGURE 97
A READING
Collage mixed media
2000
26 x 20

Collages

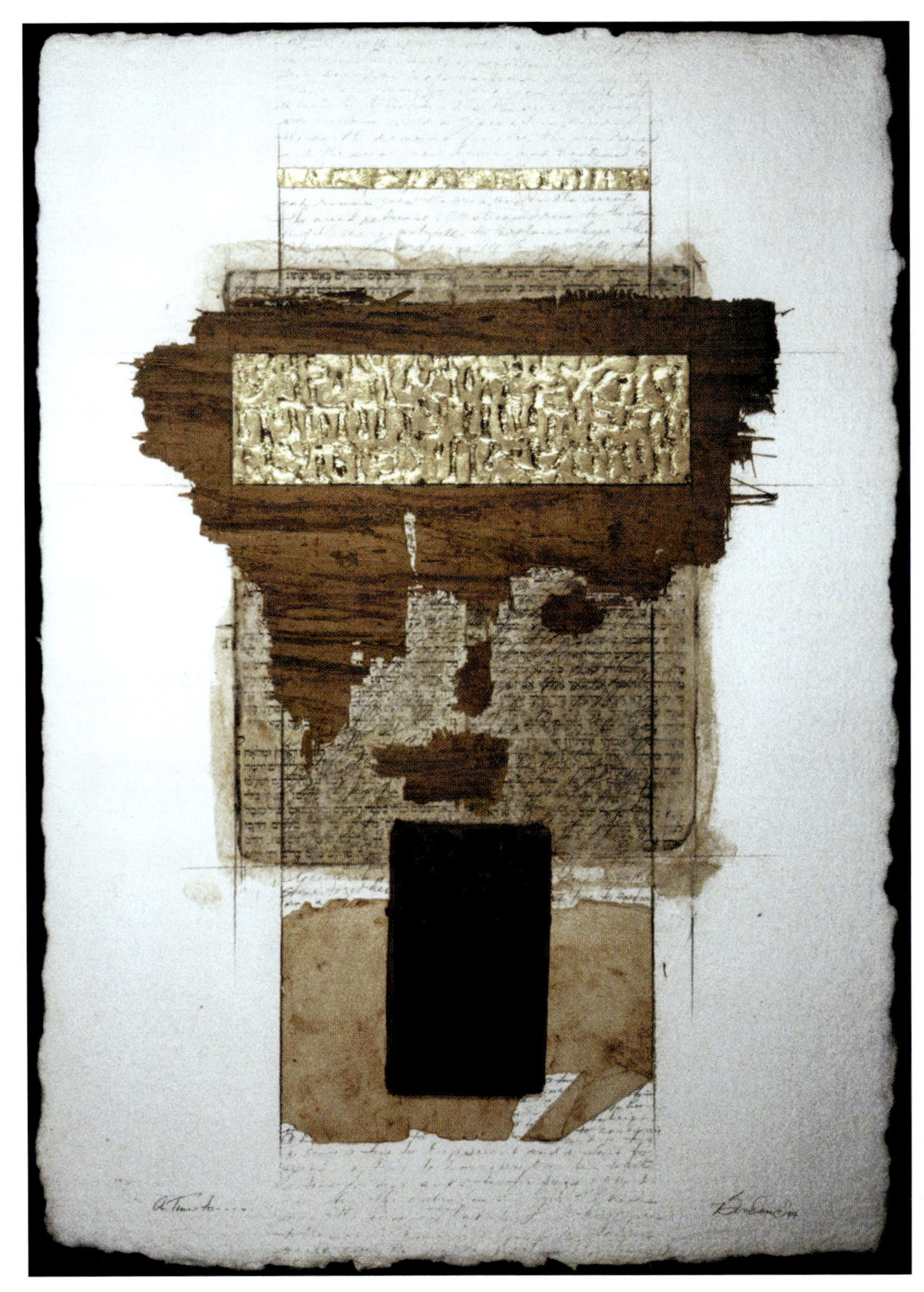

     The Art of **Sandra Bowden**

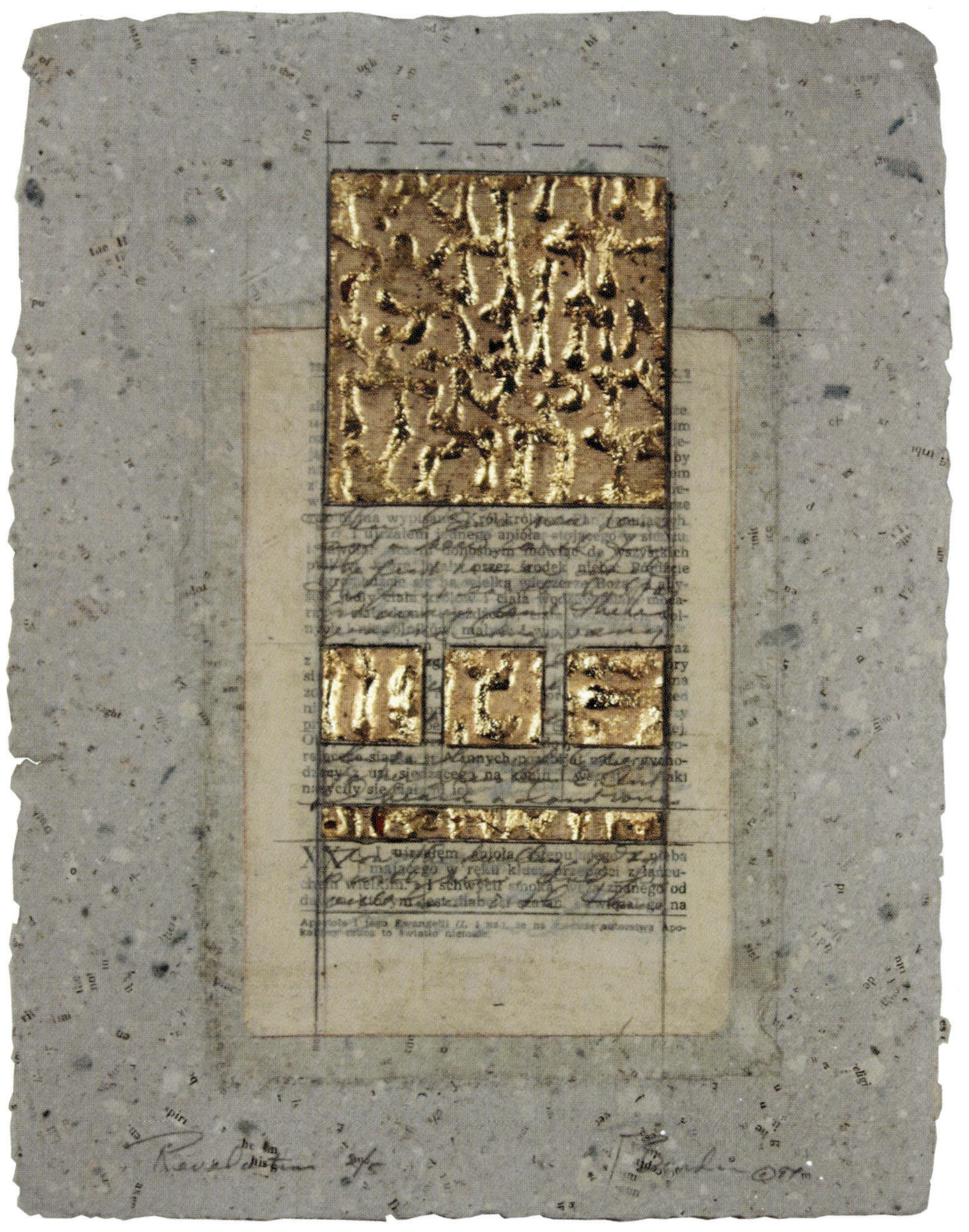

FIGURE 98
(OPPOSITE)
A TIME TO . . .
Collage mixed media
1999
21 x 15

FIGURE 99
REVELATIONS
Collage mixed media
1997
11 x 8 1/2

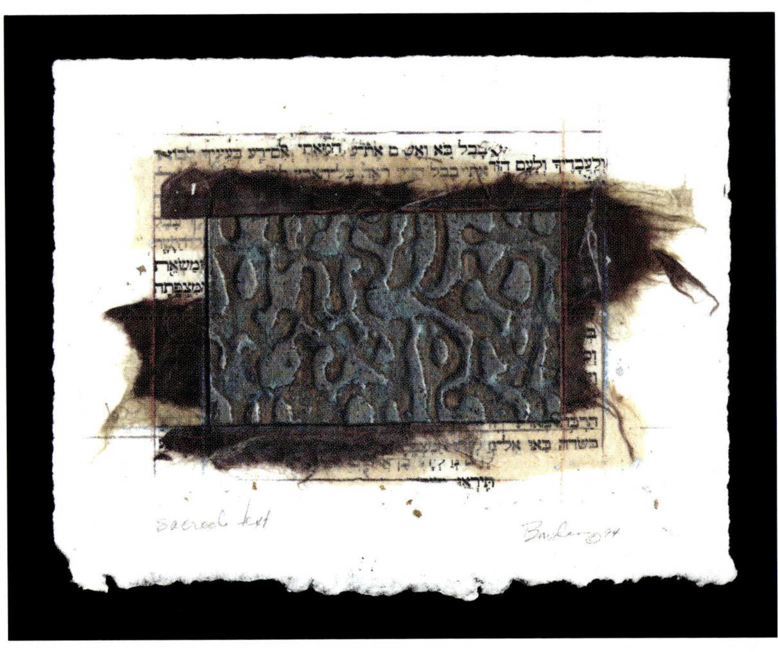

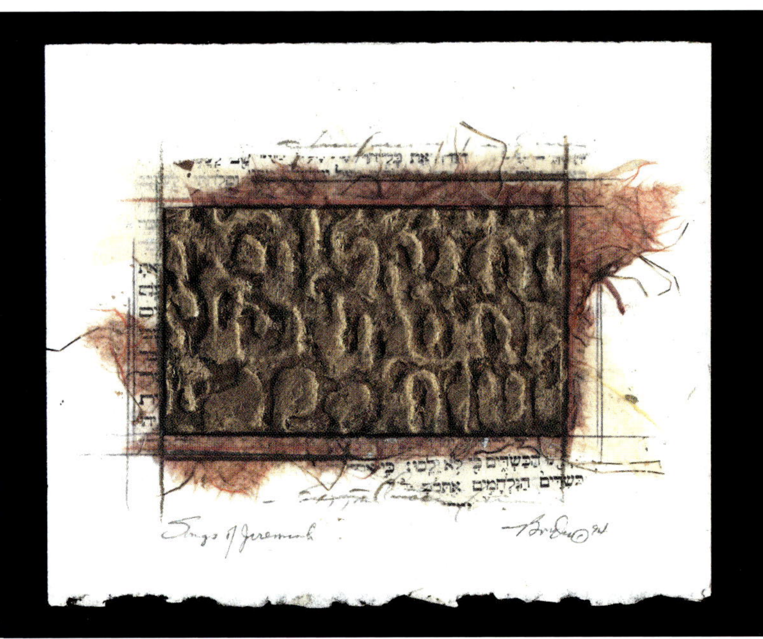

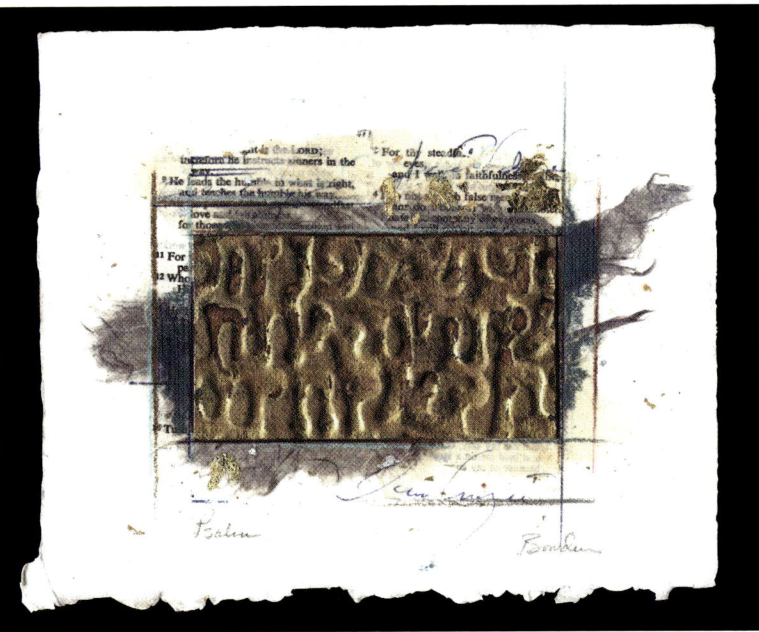

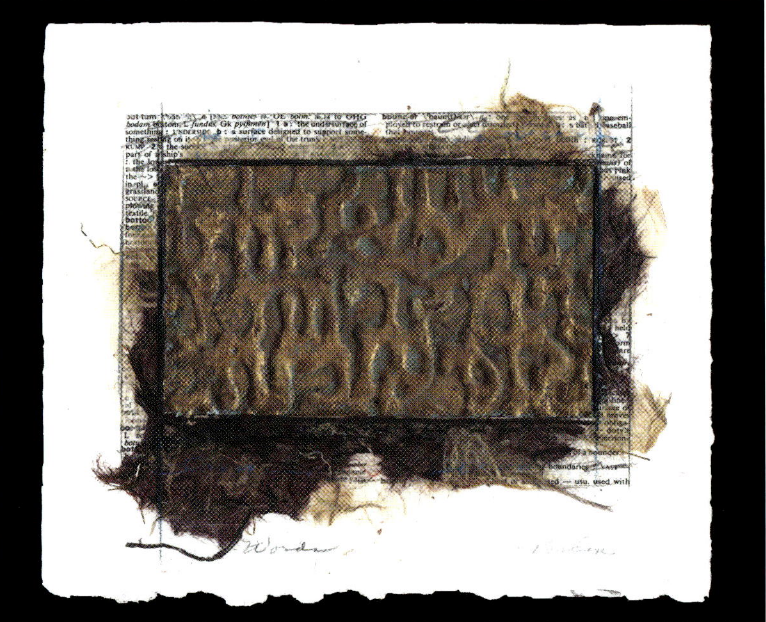

The Art of **Sandra Bowden**

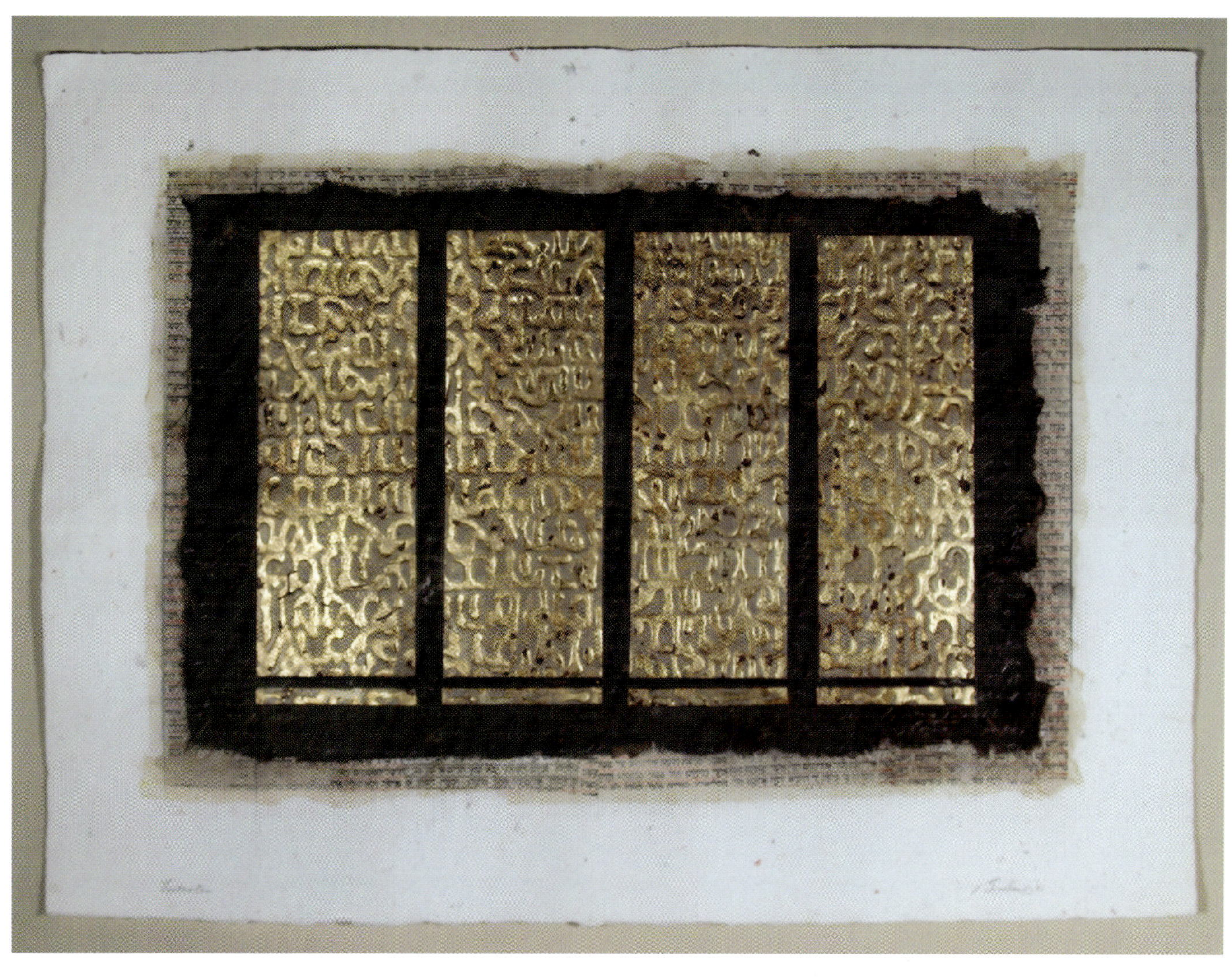

FIGURE 100
(TOP to BOTTOM
and LEFT to RIGHT)
**SACRED TEXT,
SONG OF JEREMIAH,
PSALM** and **WORDS**
Collage mixed media
1994 (**WORDS** 1995)
6 1/2 x 7 1/2

FIGURE 101
FOOTNOTES
Collage mixed media
1995
18 x 24

Collages

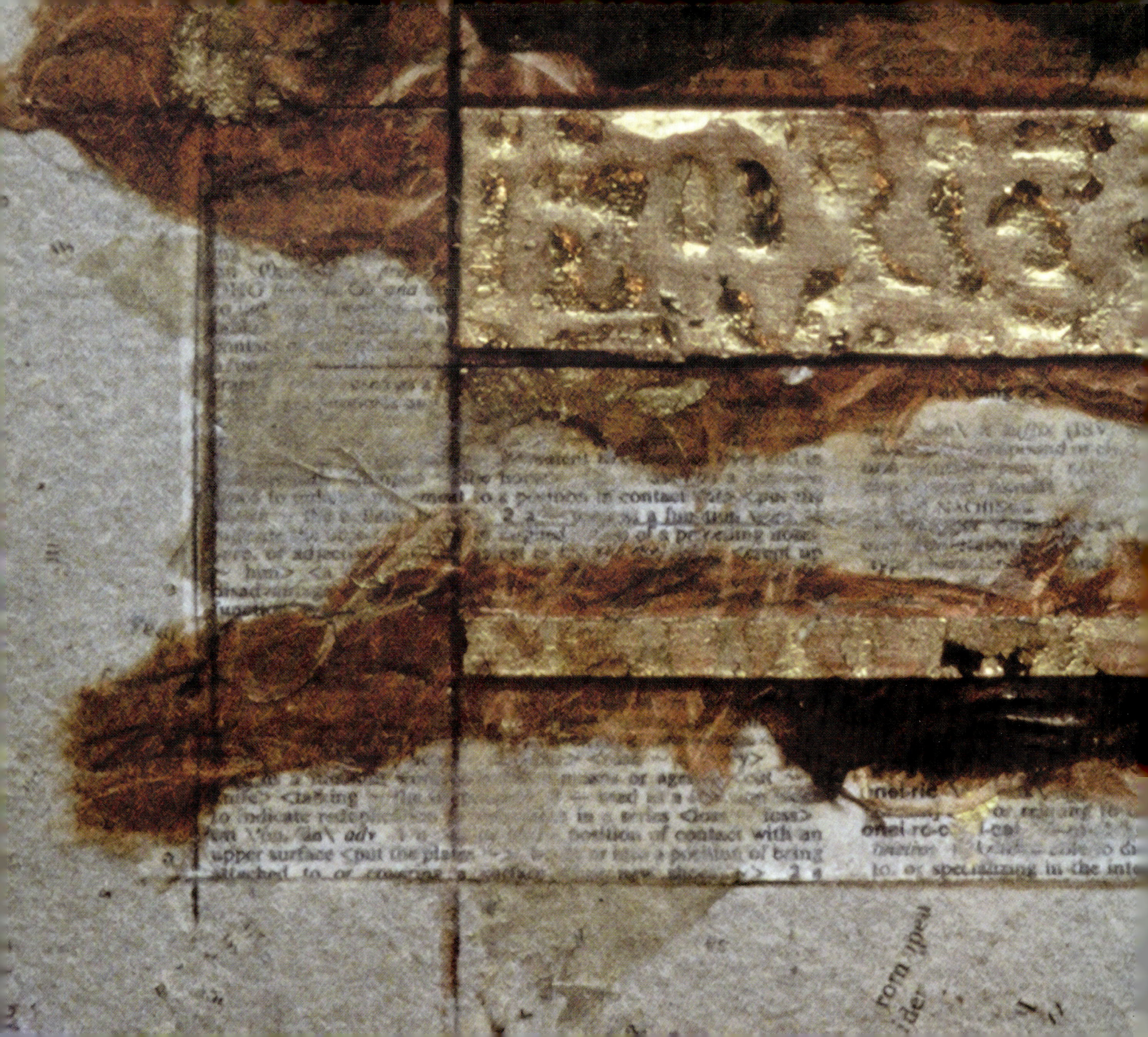

When Sandra Bowden launched her *Collage* series in 1994, back surgery had left her unable to produce paintings or etchings. Anxious to keep working, Bowden experimented with applying fragments of previously created Hebrew-text collagraphs to handmade paper. This led Bowden to a decade of new work in collage, including *Passage* (Figure 106), *Meanings* (Figure 102), *In the Beginning* (Figure 107) and *Logos* (Figure 105). These collages unite text and image in ways that stretch our reading of each.

Incorporating pages from the Bible, in various languages, dictionaries, musical scores, letters, pages from a diary, handwritten passages, fragments from her own collagraphs of Hebrew texts, and the leather covers of books found in a Paris flea market, Bowden's collages are more complex than they first appear. To mine the depths of her constructions, we need to understand the origins and nature of the collage technique, as well as how it has been used by contemporary artists.

Compared to some of the materials that Bowden uses, like the pages from a nineteenth-century Bible, and themes, like the Genesis creation narrative, that she engages in her art, collage itself is a recently conceived mode of imagemaking. "Collage," from the French word *coller,* which means "to glue," did not become a part of Western art until the early decades of the twentieth century, when Georges Braque and Pablo Picasso began pasting fragments of current newspapers, musical scores of popular songs, advertisements, and commercial wallpaper to the surfaces of their canvases.

Braque's and Picasso's collages combined drawing, painting, and pasting; these represented a new strategy of imagemaking through the accumulation of material rather than the rendering of illusion. In his 1958 *Art News* article "The Pasted-Paper Revolution," later revised as an essay entitled "Collage," Clement Greenberg wrote, "Collage was a major turning point in the evolution of Cubism, and therefore a major turning point in the whole evolution of modernist art of this century."[1] It could be argued that collage was the most important innovation in the visual arts between the camera and the computer. However, the camera and the computer are outside technologies applied to the visual arts, while collage grew directly out of the artist's method of contending with the problem of how to represent the modern world.

Collage was a decisive moment between Analytic and Synthetic Cubism. If we are to understand how later artists, including Bowden, have used collage, it is important to distinguish Analytic from Synthetic Cubism and situate collage between them. Analytic Cubism was primarily concerned with the deconstruction of the visual language by which three-dimensional forms are represented by two-dimensional forms. Analyzing how these forms break down into planes, Braque and Picasso explored the expressive potential of manipulating these planes, pushing them to a breaking point where they no longer read as representational. However, Picasso and Braque

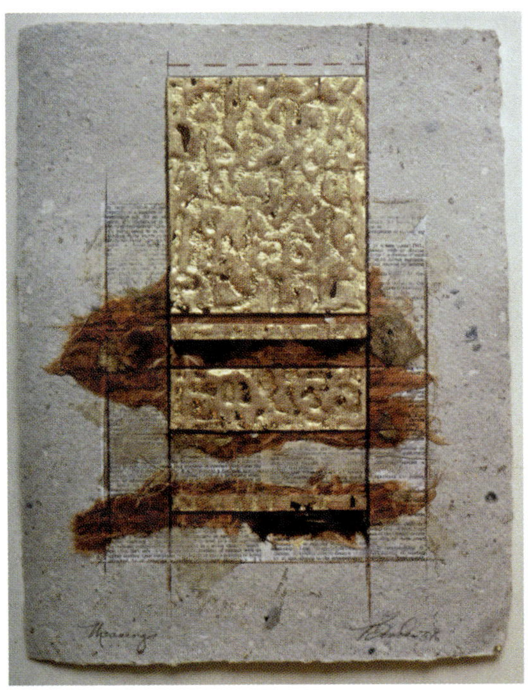

were committed to painting as representation and feared that any further deconstruction would end in abstraction. (Since the purpose of Analytic Cubism was to explore and manipulate how two-dimensional forms represent three-dimensional forms, abstraction was not an end they sought.) Braque and Picasso found that pasting commercial wallpaper, bits of newspaper, or sheet music to the canvas could further assert the literal two-dimensionality of their paintings without losing the representation of three-dimensional forms. Collage both solved certain pictorial problems created by Analytic Cubism and expanded the communicative potential of painting. Collage set the stage for Synthetic Cubism by suggesting new ways that imagery could be constructed out of a synthesis of parts into a whole.

Picasso's use of collage as a constructive strategy is evident in *Guitar, Sheet Music, and Glass* (Figure 103). This still-life could be read as a guitar, glass, page of music and newspaper lying on a table, seen from above. To deliberately and creatively subvert our reading of the image, Picasso has, on the one hand, arranged these bare minimum of forms such that if any one of these were removed, it would no longer suggest a guitar; however, on the other hand, he has given the viewer just enough visual information so that we immediately recognize these elements as a musical instrument.

Guitar, Sheet Music, and Glass simultaneously employs several types of languages, including French text, a musical score, painted imitation wood grain, drawing, printing, and, of course, collage. For someone who has never seen the Roman alphabet, the letters L-e-J-o-u are abstract forms that create no meaning. For someone who reads French, "Le Jou" is perhaps recognizable as a fragment of "Le Journal," which both means newspaper and is the masthead of a particular newspaper. In addition to the newspaper text, *Guitar, Sheet Music, and Glass* also contains a charcoal drawing, in an Analytical Cubist style, of a glass; a painting, in a more traditional or illusionistic style, of wood grain; and a sheet of music. Each of these sections demands to be read in its own separate language and poses questions about how the work as a whole should be read.

Like Picasso's *Guitar, Sheet Music, and Glass,* many of Sandra Bowden's collages combine both text and image. In *Meanings,* pages from a dictionary are collaged beneath a layer of tissue paper and pieces of Hebrew texts. The underlying surface of the work is handmade paper that contains fragments of a Bible commentary. This work straddles the divide between the image, as something to be read, and the text, as something to be viewed. Bowden describes one of the compulsions behind her work, saying, "I have always been interested in the powerful mystery of language and words. Written language is a pictorial system of shapes that we call letters, grouped together they form words, which have in turn enabled us to share complex ideas across barriers of time."[2]

None of *Meanings's* textual and visual layers are meant to be read with ease. Like Picasso's use of the fragment "Le Jou," the text elements in *Meanings* require the viewer to read beyond what is given, to search out its context and to piece its meaning together. In her collages, Bowden explores the boundaries of the communicative potential of the texts and imagery of the scriptures. By intentionally veiling the texts with translucent Japanese paper, or even other inscriptions, she compounds the possible readings of the work. Bowden states, "I am interested in that fleeting moment when we catch a glimpse of the truth, or momentarily grasp an association. This glimpse is enough to open a conversation if we are willing to be sensitive and attentive."[3]

Perhaps the contemporary artist who has most explored and pushed the boundaries of the collage technique is Robert Rauschenberg. In a work entitled *Rebus*, Rauschenberg combines posters, comics, a reproduction of Botticelli's *Birth of Venus*, images of athletes running, and more. A rebus is a puzzle in which images represent words, and Rauschenberg's presents the viewer with a visual puzzle that is unsolvable.

Collage, by its very nature, is an additive process. The fragments of Picasso's and Bowden's collages add up to multiple readings of the whole which compound rather than negate each other. However, as Rauschenberg constructs his image, he deconstructs its meaning. In *Rebus*, each additional fragment complicates rather than compounds our reading of the whole; in fact, as each new element undermines whatever meaning the previous combinations had suggested, *Rebus* becomes more and more difficult to read. If *Guitar, Sheet Music, and Glass* were an image of a still-life, Rauschenberg's *Rebus*, in which disparate things collide with nothing to give it order, is an image of postmodernism.

Postmodernism is not a unified discourse; like Rauschenberg's *Rebus*, it means different things to different people. However, there are three aspects of postmodernism evidenced in *Rebus*: questions of authorship, creative origi-

nality, and context that lead to meaning. The first of these issues has to do with the acknowledgment of authorship, that of the artist and ultimately God's authorship. In his essay "The Death of the Author," Roland Barthes argues that the author's creative intentions are unknowable and thus irrelevant. This leaves the reader to create her own meaning from the text, which for Barthes is the only certain thing. Barthes goes as far as to suggest that it is not the author who writes the text but the text that creates the author. He writes, "We know now that a text is not a line of words releasing a single 'theological' meaning (the message of the Author-God) but a multi-dimensional space in which a variety of writings, none of them original, blend and clash. The text is a tissue of quotations drawn from innumerable centers of culture."[4] Barthes's "death of the author" is the natural dead end of the path that began with Friedrich Nietzsche's pronouncement of God's demise. Barthes's philosophy is, nevertheless, still based on the truth that every author and creator is working in the image of the Author and Creator. He also writes, "to refuse to fix meaning is, in the end, to refuse God and his hypostases . . . ."[5] Although Barthes disputes the very existence of God, he has the intellectual honesty to explore the consequences of atheism's understanding of human creativity, writing that the author/creator's "only power is to mix writings, to counter the ones with others, in such a way never to rest on any one of them."[6]

The restlessness of postmodernism is evident in *Rebus*. As its title suggests, Rauschenberg's work leaves all construction of meaning to the viewer. He insists that the viewer, who brings her

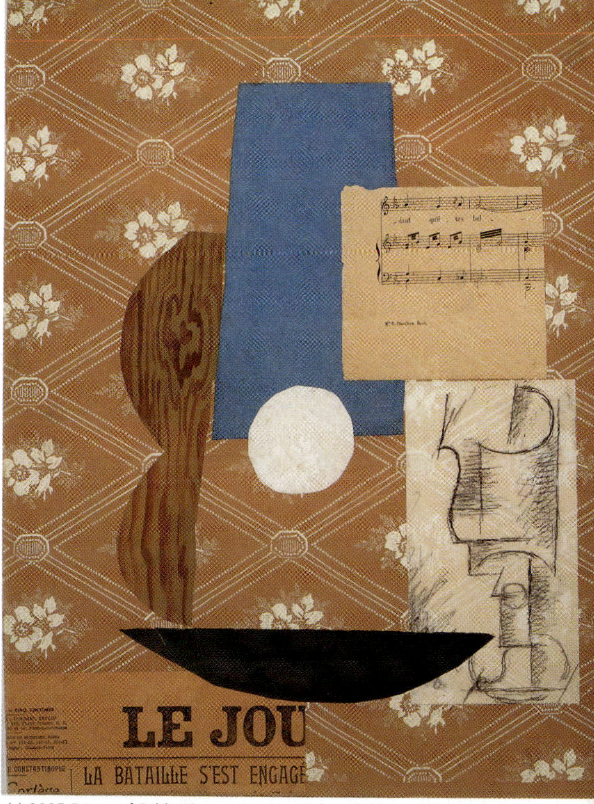

FIGURE 102
(OPPOSITE and PREVIOUS)
MEANINGS
Collage mixed media
1996
11 x 8 1/2

FIGURE 103
Pablo Picasso
GUITAR, SHEET MUSIC, AND GLASS
Collage and charcoal
on board
1912
18 7/8 x 14 3/4
Collection of the McNay Art Museum. Bequest of Marion Koogier McNay

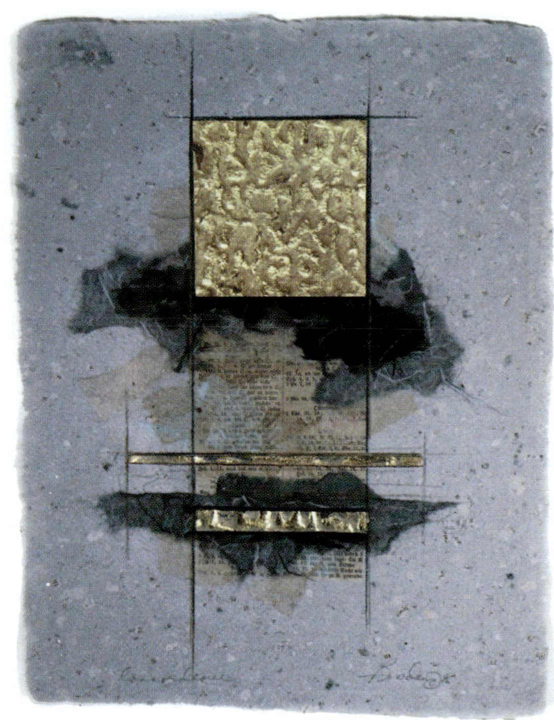

own set of ideas and experiences to the work, is the inventor of any interpretation. Rauschenberg's abdication of the construction of meaning to the viewer exemplifies a postmodern concept of creativity.

Although Bowden's art does not force her own reading on viewers, she does begin a conversation among the elements of her collage that the viewer can pick up and continue in the viewer's imagination.

In some of her works, Bowden sets up this conversation through the juxtaposition of similar substances or historically related texts. *Concordance* (Figure 104) layers pages from a concordance on a sheet of paper with pieces of a mid-nineteenth-century concordance ground into it. What these two concordances have in common, other than being used by Bowden in the same work, is their connection to the Bible.

The Bible, which Bowden holds to be the revealed word of God, is the ever-present foundation of her art. In addition to a page from a nineteenth-century concordance, *Concordance* includes a gilded text of ancient scripture that has become a signature motif of Bowden's work. These fragments of ancient languages are unreadable to most viewers, but they are not meaningless. Though they seem unintelligible, like a secret language or even speaking in tongues, the text was created for the express purpose of communication. In a 2001 interview, Bowden declares, "I believe we were created with a need to communicate which is manifested in the impulse to create."[7]

Bowden's commitment to authorship and creative originality sets her apart from many contemporary artists for whom art is locked in a paralyzing cycle of signifiers and a never-ending deconstruction of originality and truth in which parody is the only option. Jacques Derrida, in *The Origins of the Work of Art,* articulates this cycle. He writes, "The work of art stems from the artist, so they say. But what is the artist? The one who produces works of art? The origin of the artist is the work of art, the origin of the work of art is the artist, and neither is without the other."[8] The limitations of Derrida's argument become plain enough once they are applied outside the laboratory of literary theory, but he makes an important point that unless there is something or someone whose existence does not depend on anything or anyone, all origins are false since they depend on something else whose origin, in turn, depends on another. In such a world, parody and imitation are the only honest strategies.

If there is no God, then there is no point to human creativity and what we are left with is profound doubt regarding the potential of the artist to do anything original or meaningful. Much of contemporary collage, assemblage, and appropriation follows Derrida's "endless circle of allusion."

While the human artist cannot create *ex nihilo,* she has more than parody as her only option. Bowden's works, especially her collages, are significant in their appropriation of sources without parody. When Bowden uses a source, she borrows from its existing function and meaning the significance that this element has accumulated over the course of its history and, at the same time, adds to its history. In her careful and calculated use of sources, particularly sources that are old or otherwise remote from the present moment in

 The Art of **Sandra Bowden**

which she is working, Bowden rejuvenates them with contemporary significance.

Bowden's collage *In the Beginning* (Figure 107) explores the Genesis creation narrative in three languages. Bowden began with pages from a late-nineteenth-century Dutch Bible; over this she inscribed an English translation of this text; finally, she completed the work with the Genesis narrative in Hebrew divided into three parts. The work combines the printed page, handwritten lines, and the sculptured forms of the gilded texts. *In the Beginning* asserts that the foundation of Bowden's creative work is God's creative work and, in its incorporation of the artist's handwriting, is even so bold as to suggest that she has an active part in participating in the ongoing unfolding of the grand narrative of God's sanctification of His creation. In a 2001 interview, Bowden states, "Art is an extension of [the Genesis] Creation."[9] She also suggests that the narrative element of Christianity has been important to its presence in the visual arts over the past two thousand years, noting that "the narratives and characters of the Bible carry meaning which can be applied to every generation anew.... Herein lies the challenge for contemporary artists."[10]

One of the challenges that contemporary artists have faced is postmodernism's mistrust of all grand narratives. For many postmodern artists, the fragment has replaced the narrative as the central focus of the work of art. Since postmodernism has emerged out of the fragmentation of modernism, which itself was a utopian metanarrative, it is only natural that the fragment would be an important motif.

Composed of fragments torn from their con-

texts, Rauschenberg's *Rebus* is based on an absolute belief that there are no absolutes. This cardinal dogma of postmodernism is the foundation of the visual language that Rauschenberg employs to entice the viewer into his beautiful but perplexing web of disorder.

A key difference between Picasso's and Rauschenberg's collages is that the former's work combines various elements to create a representational image while the latter's collage does not. While Bowden's collages are closer to Rauschenberg's in that sense, she also returns collage to constructive purposes, as Picasso had used it, building an image out of disparate, and sometimes unrelated, elements. However, Picasso had depended on the creation of a representational image to hold the fragments of his collage together. Bowden assembles her work without falling back on the convention of the image as a window.

Bowden's collages are held together, conceptually and visually, by the word. Her engagement with texts is acknowledgment of the difficulty we have in using words and language to communicate meaning. This slippage of

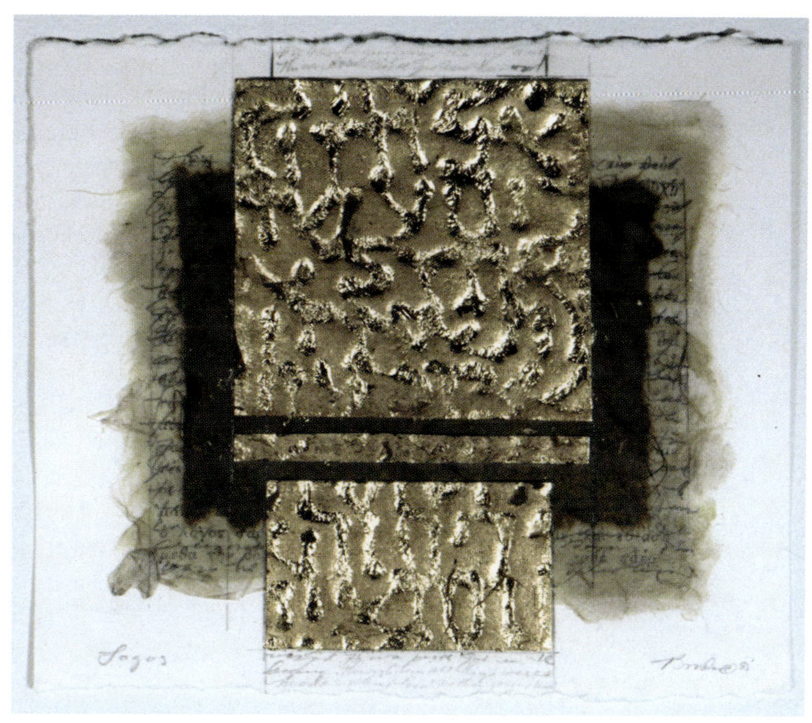

FIGURE 104
(OPPOSITE)
CONCORDANCE
Collage mixed media
1996
11 x 8 1/2

FIGURE 105
LOGOS
Collage mixed media
1995
6 x 8 1/2

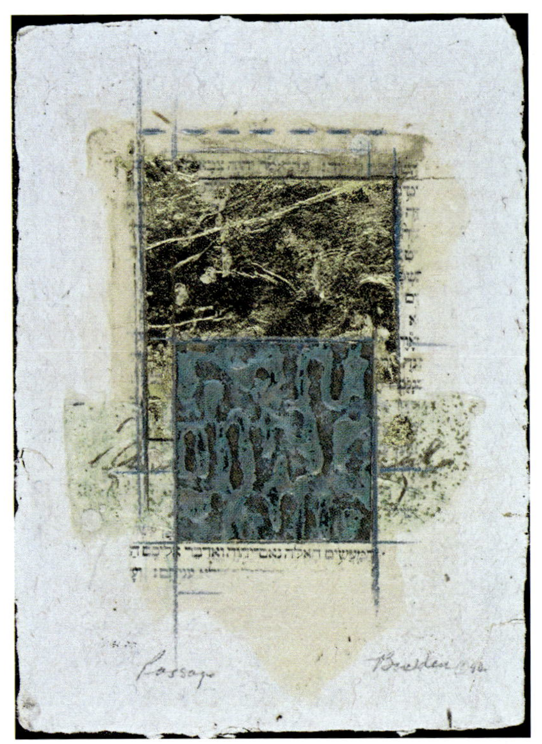

language is one of the consequences of our fallen condition. At the same time, she affirms the fact that we have to use words, despite the fact that all words are inadequate for the expression. Language's limitations are most apparent when we begin to talk about God and His divine mysteries. We often experience difficulty in finding any way of addressing God intelligibly, or speaking about God correctly. It is only through His grace that meaningful communication is possible at all. The greatest evidence of this grace is the word recorded in the scriptures and the Word made flesh. The Bible consists of words given by God; this affirms the usefulness of language. Thus Bowden can use text to address the viewer and God.

In *Logos* (Figure 105), a page from a Greek Bible of John 1:1 ("In the beginning was the Word, and the Word was with God, and the Word was God") is veiled by the same text, here written in English, a layer of tissue paper, and finally the Hebrew text of Genesis 1:1 ("In the beginning God created the heavens and the earth"). *Logos* visually establishes an interconnectedness between the creation through the word of God described in Genesis and Christ as the Word. The evangelist writes, in John 1:14, "And the Word became flesh and lived among us, and we beheld His glory…." In *Beholding the Glory: Incarnation through the Arts,* Malcolm Guite writes, "It may be that language itself, and the very possibility of communication through words, bears witness to the primal act of communication in the incarnation of the eternal Word: every effort to incarnate our own thoughts in the web of language in underwritten by God's expression of his Word in Christ."[11]

In the Incarnation, language became form. The mystery of Genesis 1:1 and John 1:1 stretches the adequacy of language to its breaking point. The word described in John 1:1 is a living image of the Word described in Genesis 1:1. Using that as her model, Bowden employs the text as an image of unfolding mystery. This mystery of the living word is foundational to Bowden's art; she takes a text, penetrates its interpretation, explores it visually, and presents it to the viewer as a complex and living entity.

Bowden's art incorporates many disparate fragments in such a way as to suggest a perception of these parts as precious remnants of a whole. These fragments of ancient texts bring the past into the present moment, keeping this history alive and reinvigorating it by establishing connections between it and the contemporary world. These fragments always retain contact with and point toward the whole. Indeed, one could read Bowden's work as anticipating a future reconciliation of the parts, a moment when the past and the present will dissolve into eternity.

While giving us a glimpse into certain mysteries of how God works the past and present together, Bowden's work, like *Was the Word* (Figure 1) create palimpsests, a text or manuscript that has been written or printed on more than once, in which one or more of these layers has been partially or entirely obscured. The tension of these texts suspended over one another gives Bowden's collages a visual dynamism. The texts move in and out of legibility as if they were engaged in a dance or game of hide-and-seek. However, in Bowden's work the promise "seek and you shall find" is satisfied time and time again. The mood of confident expectation represented in Bowden's work is similar to that expressed by the Apostle Paul in 1 Corinthians 13:9–12: "For our knowledge is imperfect and our prophecy is imperfect; but when the perfect comes, the imperfect will pass away.... For now we see in a mirror dimly, but then face to face. Now I know in part; then I shall understand fully, even as I have been fully understood." Bowden's works offer the viewer partial understanding, a glimpse of awe, with the promise of a full revelation in the future.

As much as any Christian working in the visual arts, Bowden takes the questions of the authorship, origins, and meaning of the work of art head on. She finds insights into these through her creative use of the Biblical texts. These are both the conceptual and visual foundation of her art. In their use of word and image, Bowden's collages help the viewer imagine them as intertwined in new ways and engage them as living in the present moment.

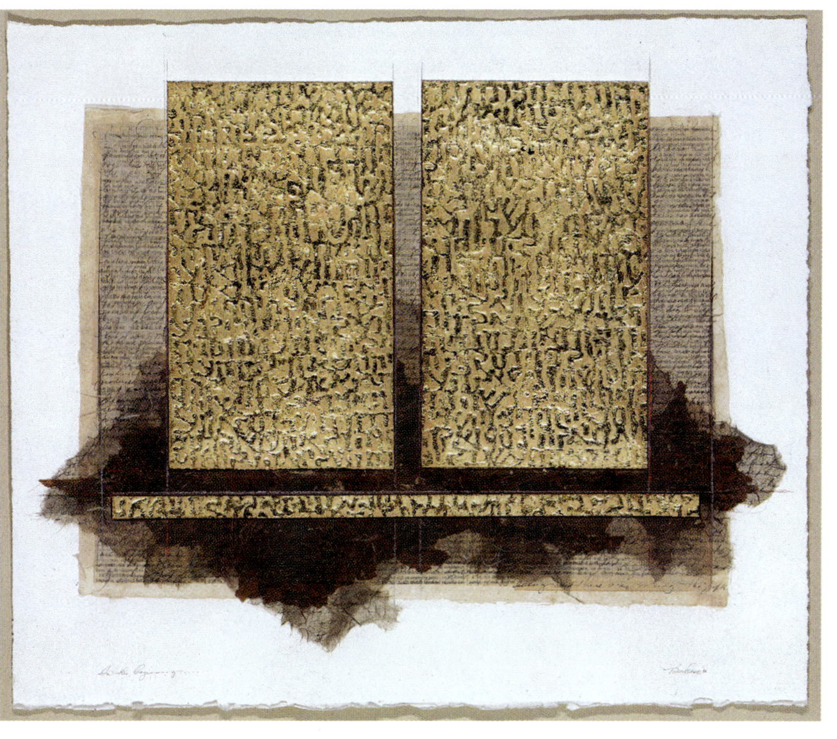

1   Cement Greenberg. "Collage" in *Art and Culture: Critical Essays.* (Boston: Beacon Press.1961), p.70

2   Sandra Bowden in *Objects of Grace: Conversations on Faith and Art.* James Romaine ed. (Baltimore: Square Halo Books, 2002), p.15.

3   Ibid. p.16.

4   Roland Barthes. "The Death of the Author" in *Image-Music-Text.* Stephen Heath trans. (New York: Noonday Press, 1978), p.146.

5   Ibid. p.147.

6   Ibid. p.146.

7   Bowden in *Objects of Grace.* p.11.

8   Jacques Derrida. *The Origins of the Work of Art.* p.31–2.

9   Bowden in *Objects of Grace.* p.11.

10 Bowden in *Objects of Grace.* p.13.

11 Malcolm Guite. "Through Literature: Christ and the Redemption of Language" in *Beholding the Glory: Incarnation through the Arts.* Jeremy Begbie ed. (Grand Rapids, MI: Baker Book House, 2000). p. 32.

FIGURE 106
(OPPOSITE)
PASSAGE
Collage
mixed media
1994
8 x 6

FIGURE 107
IN THE BEGINNING
Collage mixed media
1995
20 x 26

Illuminations

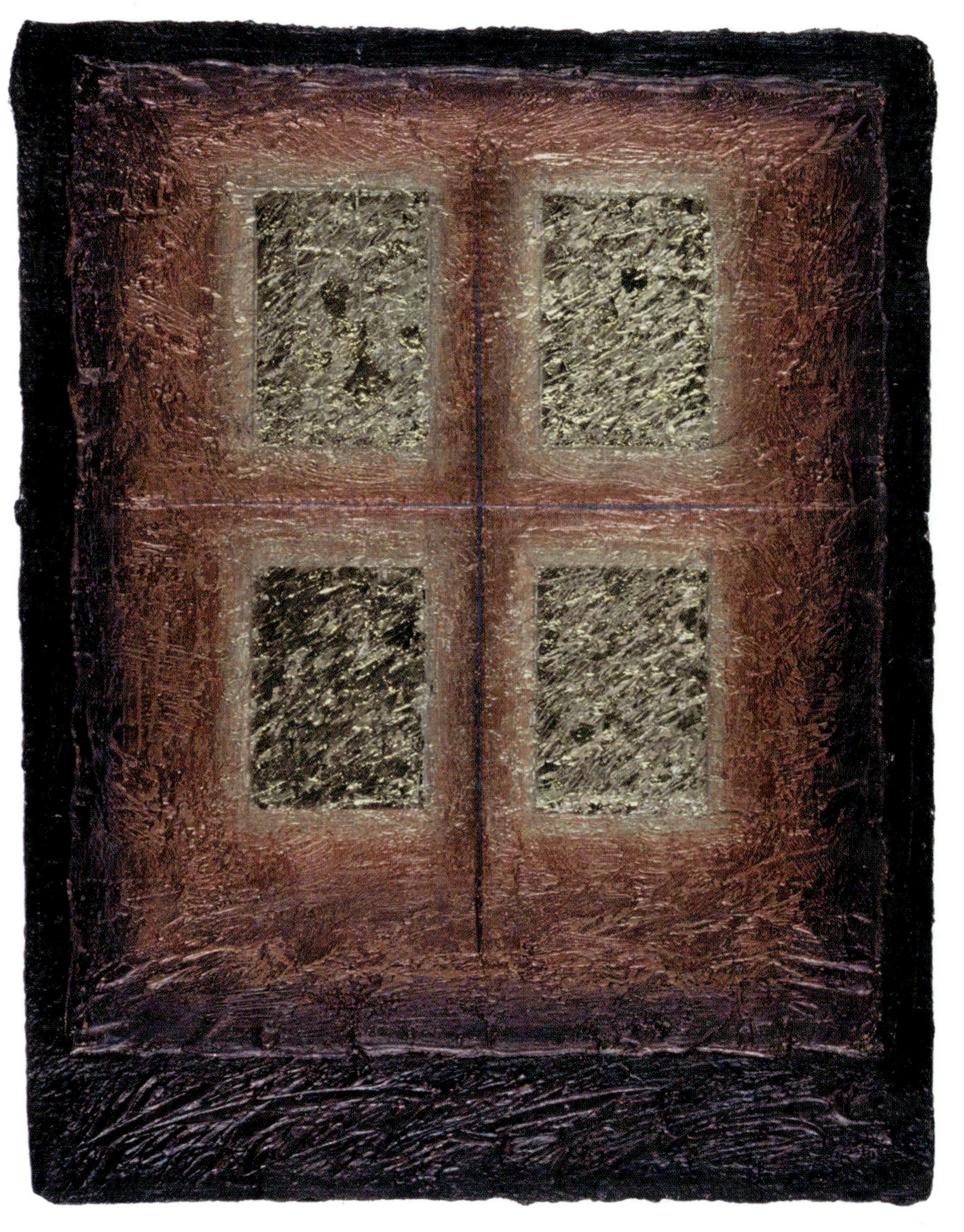

FIGURE 108
ILLUMINATION XXV
Acrylic mixed media
1993
26 x 20

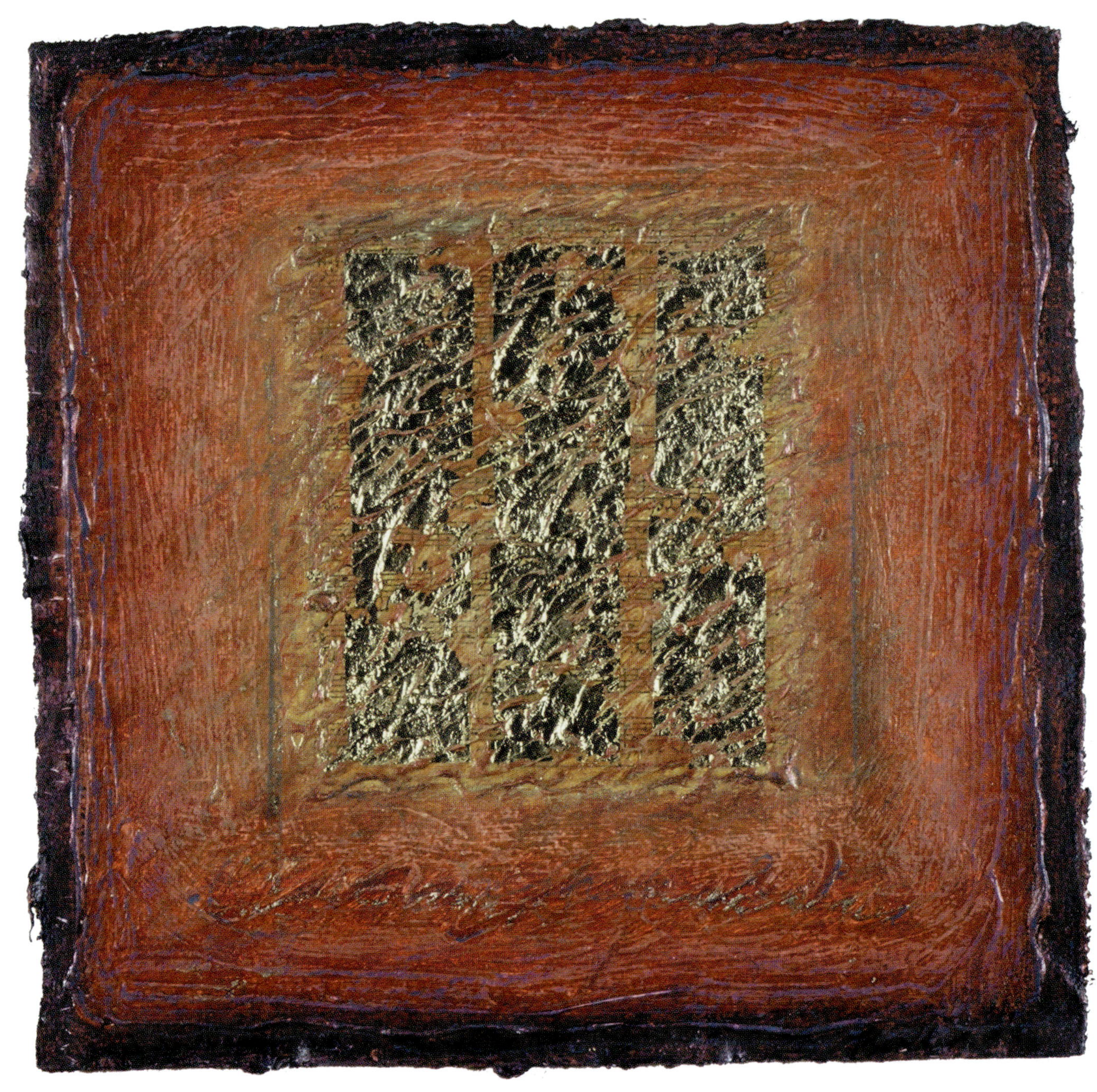

130   The Art of **Sandra Bowden**

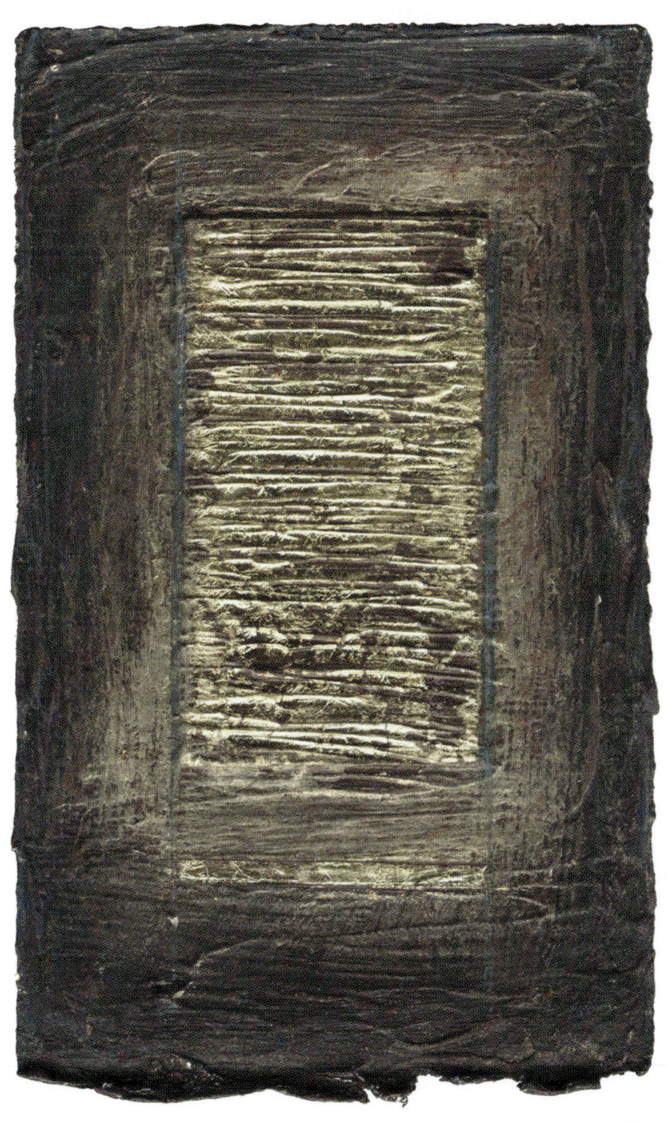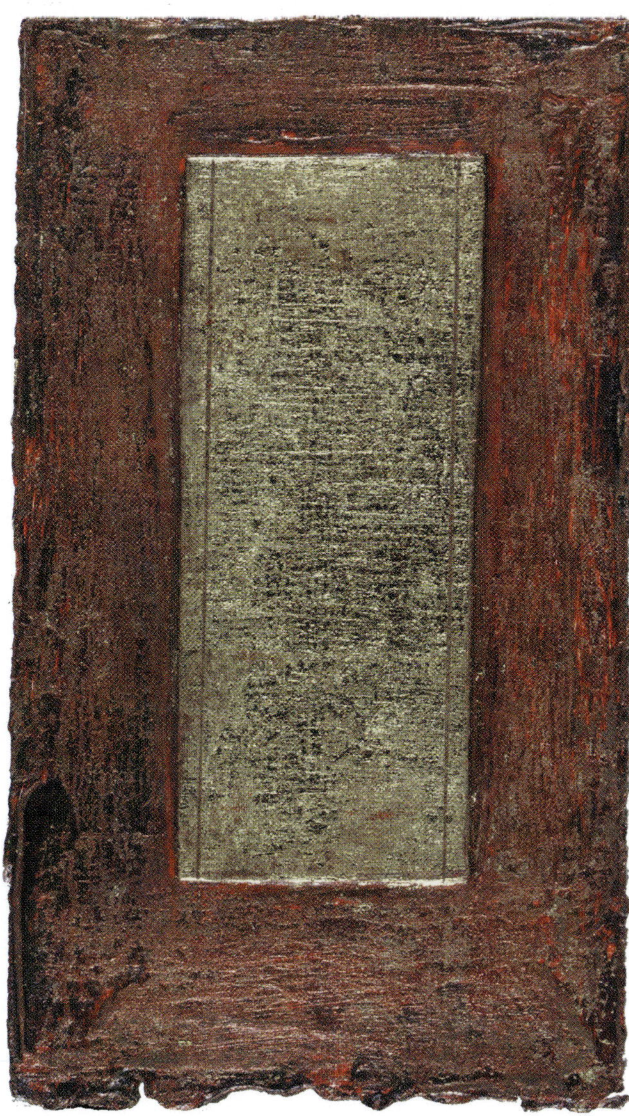

FIGURE 109
(OPPOSITE)
ILLUMINATION XVI
Acrylic mixed media
1990
10 x 10

FIGURE 110
(LEFT)
CODE II
Acrylic mixed media
1993
6 1/2 x 3 1/2

FIGURE 111
(RIGHT)
PAGE
Acrylic mixed media
1993
6 1/2 x 3 1/2

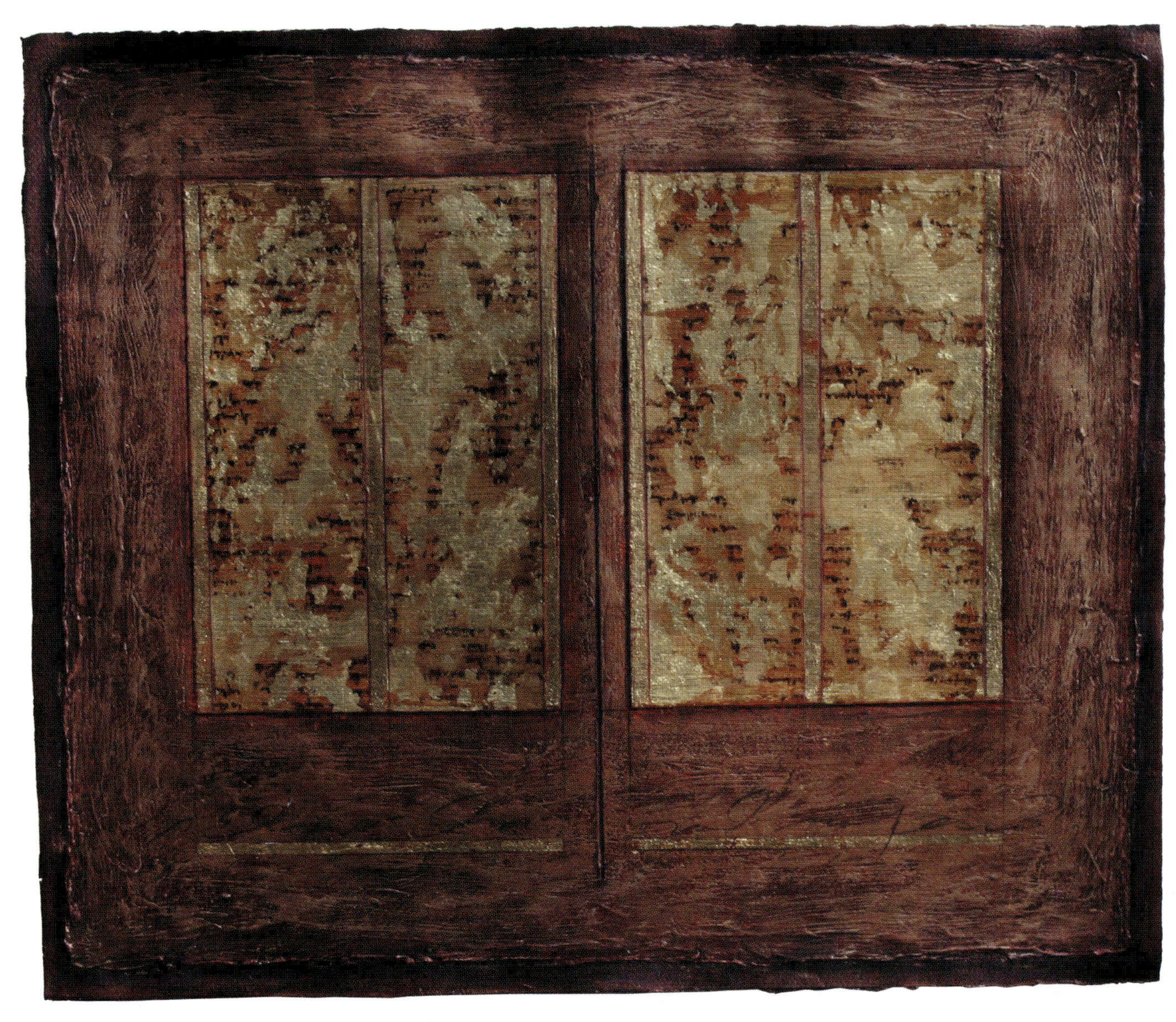

The Art of **Sandra Bowden**

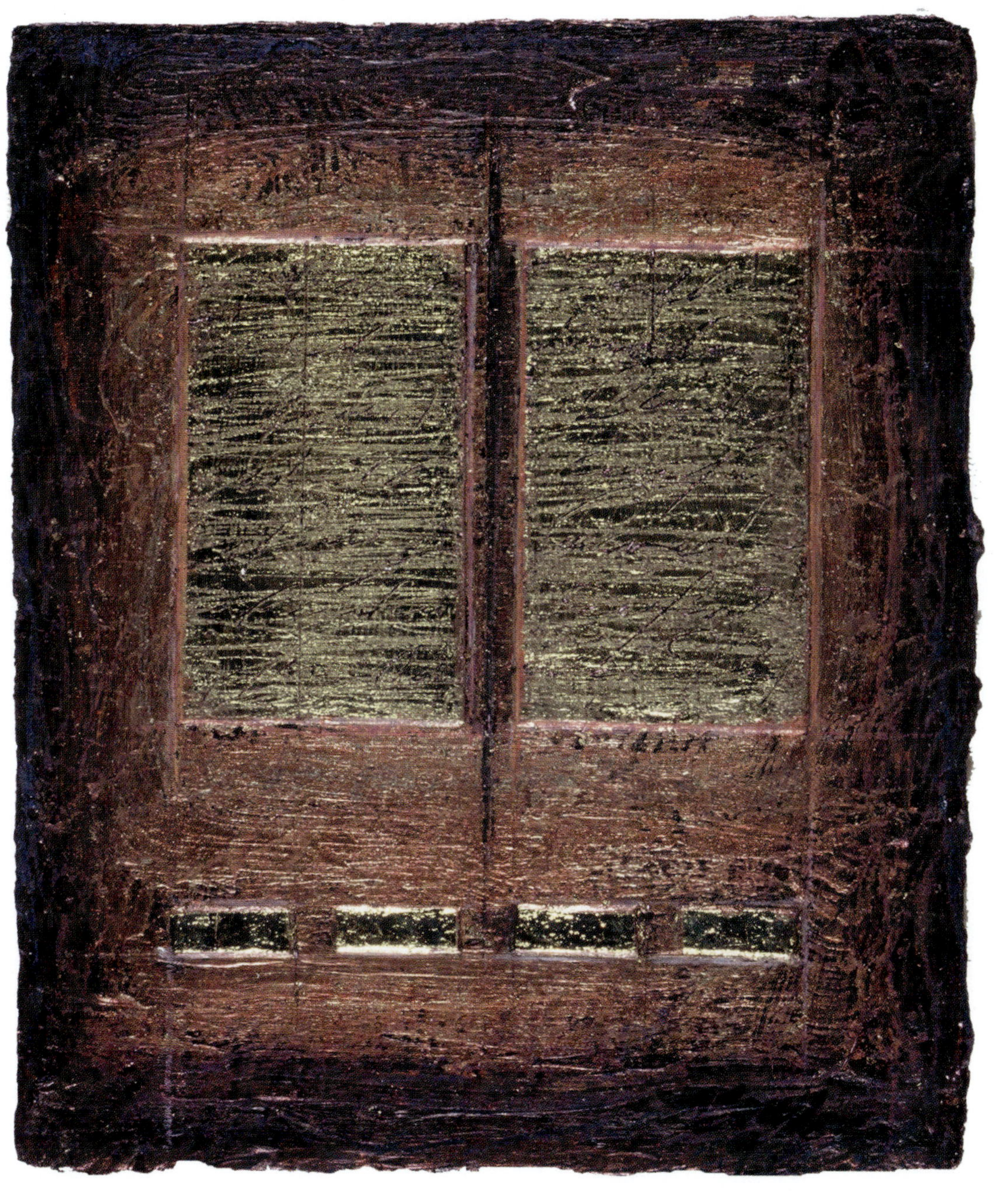

FIGURE 112
(OPPOSITE)
RECORD
Acrylic mixed media
1993
28 x 30

FIGURE 113
TEXT
Acrylic mixed media
1993
7 1/2 x 6 1/2

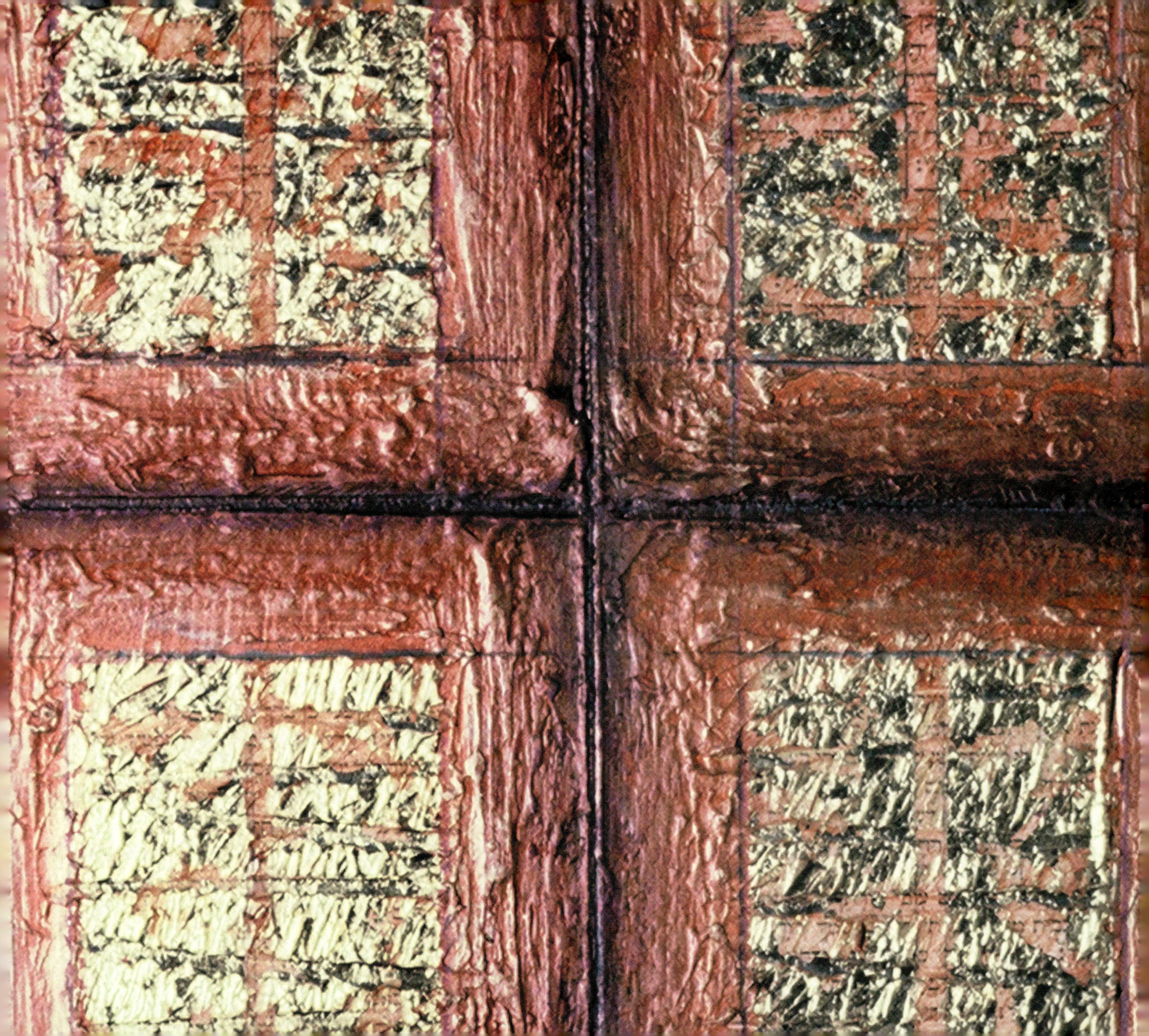

ENA GIURESCU HELLER

Medieval manuscripts tend to be more than a source of information and knowledge; they are also feasts for the eyes. Printed on expensive vellum or parchment, and handwritten with exquisite calligraphy, they are also often lavishly illuminated, embellished with decorated and sometimes figurative initials, rich borders and narrative images. The verb "to illuminate," which comes from the Latin *illuminare,* means to decorate with gold, silver and brilliant colors, as well as elaborate designs or miniature pictures. The level of decoration (including the choice of materials, such as gold leaf and expensive color pigments) increased a manuscript's worth and importance, and hence its chances of survival through the ages. The many manuscripts that have withstood the test of time teach us about the world that created and used them, about medieval faith, art and literacy. And over time, they have served as rich sources of inspiration for many artists working in different times, styles, and media.

Sandra Bowden's *Illuminations,* whose titles indicate the origins of the creative process that gave them form, are a case in point. The series developed after the artist's first trip to Europe in 1986 and her exposure to medieval manuscripts and paintings. These works are, according to the artist, "reverent responses to the extravagant beauty of these medieval manuscripts."[1] Most of the works in the series, which numbers over seventy, were done in the early 1990s in a mixed-media technique involving acrylic paints and gold and silver leaf. While they clearly pay homage to their medieval sources of inspiration, Bowden's *Illuminations* create a new and distinctive pictorial language. Different worlds are expressed through it: medieval illuminations and ancient scriptural text, contemporary pictorial technique and traditional symbolism.

The pictorial references of the *Illuminations* anchor them firmly in the world of precious ancient books. *Illumination XVII* (Figure 115), for instance, displays three vertical rectangles aligned in a horizontal composition. The work allows multiple readings. The divided compositional field may suggest a familiar format for full-page illustrations in medieval manuscripts. At the same time, the three vertical fields may be read as three different pages of an ancient manuscript that has only partly withstood the test of time: mere traces of writing and gilding

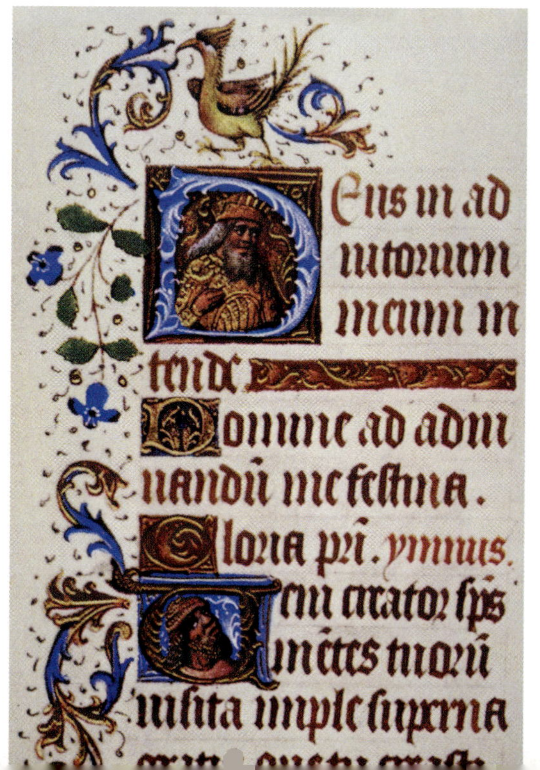

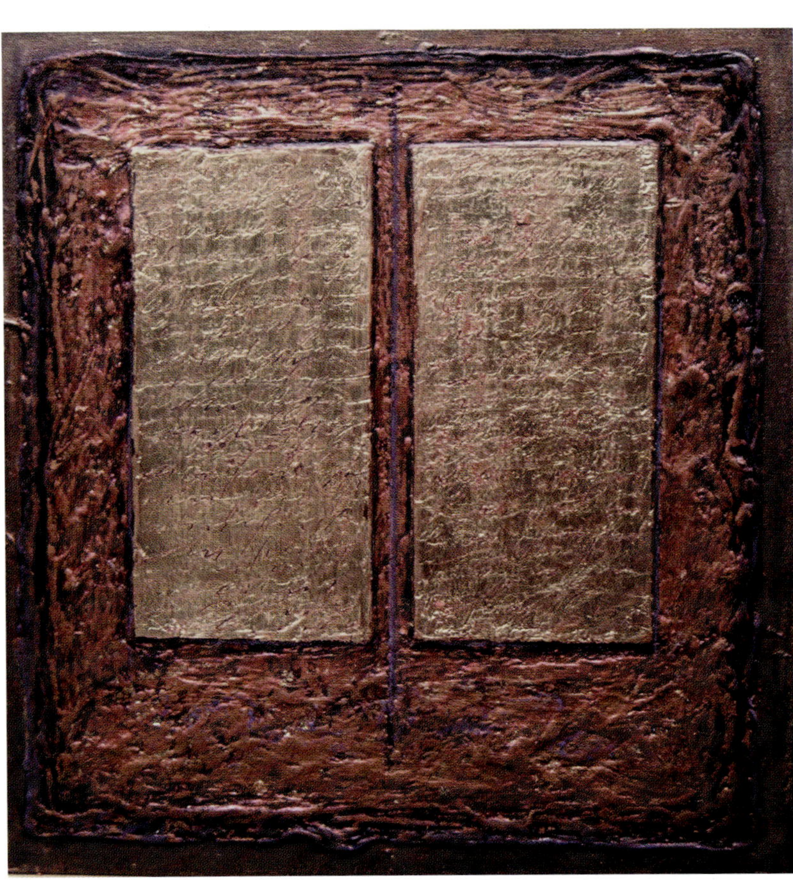

are now visible. The horizontal lines across their surface remind us of the ruling of a manuscript.[2] Yet another reading may be that they are three closed books, with richly decorated covers. Either way, they make us think of a time when books were rare and precious, painstakingly written by hand and expensively decorated. The background is a rich, textured maroon with inflections of gold, orange and yellow; it is a multilayered surface that contributes to the overall three-dimensionality of the work. The rich, layered texture which gives the work a distinctive tactility and three-dimensionality is typical of the entire *Illuminations*. The background acts as a frame within which the three rectangles can be read as compositions-within-the-composition, or perhaps windows onto the world they so well emulate: the world of precious medieval images. They are rare, expensive, and extraordinarily tactile. The tactility harks back not only to manuscript illuminations, but also to other aspects of the medieval pictorial world, including icons, bejeweled reliquaries and other liturgical objects.

Bowden's *Illuminations* relate strongly to their medieval predecessors. The connection is not only a matter of inspiration and artistic response. It is also present in the very approach of the artist, her relationship with materials, symbols, and composition. The medievalism of Bowden's *Illuminations* is apparent in three major areas: the use of symbolism, the aesthetic of proportions, and the attempt to capture the essence of things, both to synthesize and integrate.

Scholars of the Middle Ages have often noted the medieval tendency to understand the world in terms of symbol and allegory.[3] To the medieval mind, things were not always what they appeared to be—or rather not *only* what they appeared to be: they also stood for something higher, harder to depict, and harder still to explain. They symbolized values and concepts, most often of a religious nature, that guided people's lives but were often difficult to grasp or understand. An example is the lion. A lion painted on the pages of a medieval manuscript or carved onto the columns of a church signified so much more than the animal known for his majesty and might. The lion was recognized as a symbol of Christian watchfulness, since according to medieval bestiaries, lions always slept with their eyes open. He symbolized Christ's sacrifice for the redemption of mankind: legends spoke of lion cubs being born dead and revived only on the third day by their father's roaring, a rather transparent comparison to the biblical story of Christ's crucifixion and resurrection on the third day. Since the Gospel of Mark is the book of the New Testament that most fully dwells upon the

     The Art of **Sandra Bowden**

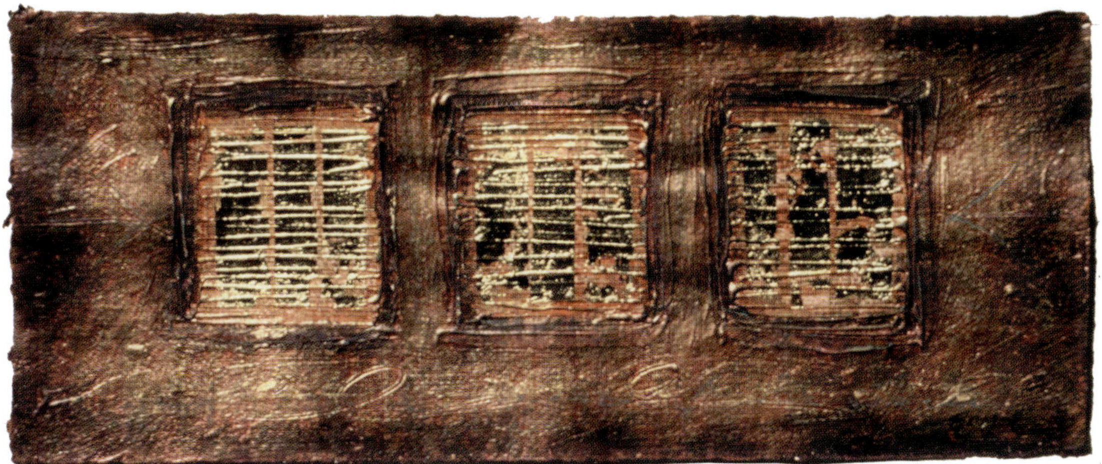

Resurrection, the lion also became a symbol for the evangelist Mark.[4] The meaning of the image, then, needs to be decoded, and its various levels discovered gradually.

The same is true of interpreting the *Illuminations.* Bowden's medievalism, like her technique, is layered. The works reveal themselves one layer of meaning at a time, uncovering a world rich in mystery, hidden truths, symbol and allegory. Take, for instance, *Hidden Worlds III* (Figure 116). Interwoven rectangular shapes superimposed on a maroon background create the composition. An almost-central square covered in gold leaf commands our attention, made more prominent by four elongated rectangles aligned directly below it, as if creating a pedestal of sorts. The relief of these rectangular shapes enhances the three-dimensionality of the composition, also visible in the texture of the background, whose thick impasto paint creates a dynamic presence. The gold leaf on the central square is partially peeled back, revealing patches of color akin to the background. Partly superimposed on the square are two circles of different sizes, whose contour seems to dissipate under the surrounding background. The circles also contain areas of purple—suggestions of continents on the surface of the globe. The reading of the piece starts with the circles and the gold leaf, and the surface shapes that resemble continents; continues with the layered rectangles behind (or underneath) the circles, partially hidden (or revealed) by the thick, painterly background; and concludes with the reading of the symbolism inherent in the composition and every one of its elements. The gold leaf brings forth the world of medieval painting where sacred figures and events are depicted against a gold background—a higher world that cannot be described by details of topography and landscape. The deep, rich maroon background is reminiscent of the purple-dyed parchment used for special courtly manuscripts in both the Byzantine and Carolingian Empires.

Another thoroughly medieval element of the

FIGURE 114
(OPPOSITE)
AND THERE WAS LIGHT
Acrylic mixed media
1992
18 x 17

FIGURE 115
ILLUMINATION XVII
Acrylic mixed media
1990
10 x 20

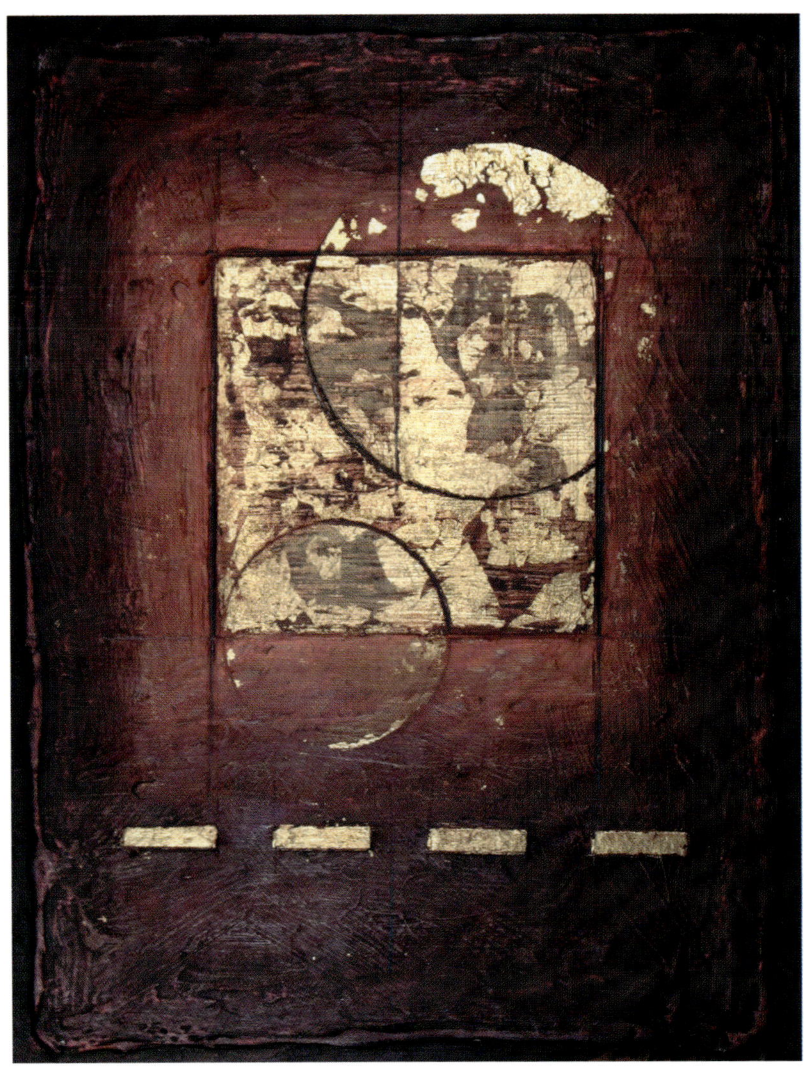

Illuminations is its aesthetic of proportion. In the Middle Ages, beauty was often thought of in terms of a formal, almost mathematical concept of unity in variety.[5] Rigorous geometrical frameworks of straight lines creating rectangles and squares, sometimes independent, other times superimposed, define Bowden's compositions. The relationship between these shapes, as well as between them and the overall work, regulates the composition. Proportion, geometry, and hierarchy define beauty—and at the same time reveal the hidden beauty of symbolism. *Illumination VI* (Figure 117) is divided into quarters by a visibly three-dimensional purple line; a grid of vertical and horizontal lines in turn subdivides the quarters. The background is dark maroon, almost black, around the edges and comprises gradually lighter shades of purple and red as it gets closer to the inner rectangles; inside the four smaller rectangles the light red, thick impasto lines are mingled with reflective gold, reminiscent of a source of light.

A strong work of abstract art, the composition can be interpreted in terms of geometrical relationships, correspondences of line and color, tactility of paint. Yet seen through the filter of medievalism (and from the perspective of the artist's *oeuvre*), the abstract form reveals specific meaning. The purple divider can be read as a cross, the symbol of Christianity, while the four rectangles suggest the Gospels of the New Testament. The composition reminds one not only of richly colored and gilt pages of manuscripts, but also of their covers, made of precious metals and adorned with glistening stones, prominently displaying the cross.

Last but definitely not least, the medievalism of the *Illuminations* is revealed through the artist's attempt to synthesize and integrate. The medieval view of the world focused on the essence of things and emphasized unity and integration, secured primarily through faith.[6] Bowden's works also attempt to uncover the essence. Their abstract character indicates a desire to strip forms of anything superfluous, to reduce them to their essential symbolism. Geometric forms, textured layers of paint, shimmering gold leaf, they all bring forth Bowden's elemental search for meaning.

A fundamental component of this meaning, and hence of the symbolism of the series, lies in the presence—sometimes obvious, often partly or almost totally obscured—of text within the compositions. Words have always played an important role in Sandra Bowden's art. Their

pervasiveness has been linked to the artist's religious upbringing, indicating the Protestant
preference for words over images.[7] Yet I would
argue that, at least in the *Illuminations,* it is not
necessarily a matter of choice. The text does not
replace the image, but rather it becomes
image. For the most part, textual insertions
(mostly from Scriptures, but also from
Gregorian chants and other early sources)
are so obscured by other compositional elements that they are not legible and, in many
instances, barely visible. The latter is true of the
text of a Hebrew psalm in *Code I* (Figure 119)
buried beneath thick layers of paint and gold,
as well as the Gregorian chant imbedded in the
broken columns of gold leafing in *Illumination
VI.* Since the words cannot be read, they become
yet another abstract element of the composition—beautiful in themselves, yet symbolic of
greater truths. However, the choice of textual
passages is hardly accidental. Take, for instance,
Illumination XVII, whose layers of gold obscure
fragments of Psalm 100, "A Hymn of Praise:"

Sing to the Lord, all the world!
Worship the Lord with joy; come before
him with happy songs! Acknowledge
that the Lord is God. He made us, and we
belong to him; we are his people, we are
his flock. Enter the Temple gates with
thanksgiving; go into its courts with
praise. Give thanks to him and praise
him. The Lord is good; his love is eternal
and his faithfulness lasts forever.[8]

The usage of this particular psalm, whose
presence Bowden chooses to reveal in her
description of the piece, is certainly deliberate
for an artist whose art openly celebrates the joy
and mystery of God.

Moreover, since the texts incorporated in
the compositions are mostly from the Bible,
their presence, even if hinted at rather than
spelled out, further links these works with the

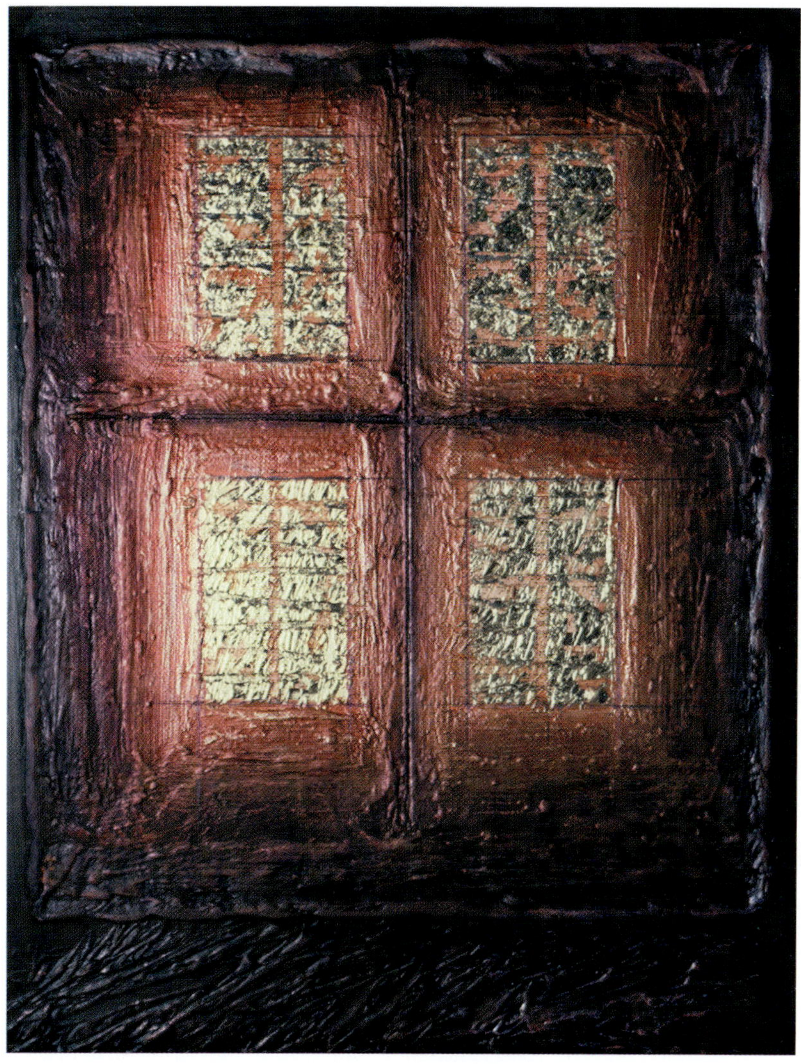

FIGURE 116
(OPPOSITE)
HIDDEN WORLDS III
Acrylic and gold leaf
1993
16 x 12

FIGURE 117
ILLUMINATION VI
Acrylic mixed media
1990
26 x 20

universe of the medieval manuscripts which inspired the artist in the first place.[9] Similar to other works from the series, *Code,* with its central partially gilt panel surrounded by a wide textured frame, invites multiple interpretations. One suggests a common page composition in a manuscript, with wide decorative borders and a central field reserved for narrative images or canon tables. Another may imagine the book cover rather than one of its pages: its heavy, leathery three-dimensionality invites comparison with the covers of medieval liturgical books, decorated with precious materials and jewels, as evidenced in a fifteenth-century *Armenian Gospels,* in the collection of the American Bible Society Library (Figure 118). Yet another may see a framed pictorial composition, an icon or altarpiece that would have played an equally important role in medieval private devotion. *Code,* as well as other works from the series, demonstrates that Bowden's medievalism extends beyond the world of illuminated manuscripts, while her pictorial vocabulary (expertly combining medieval and modern, universal and personal) is entirely her own.

The presence of a Gregorian chant in *Illumination VI* points to yet another medieval concept, that of artistic integration.[10] Indeed, in the medieval period the arts of architecture, painting, sculpture, music, and theater contributed to a total aesthetic experience best embodied in the grandiose Gothic cathedrals. I am reminded of a similar integration when I try to analyze the *Illuminations* in the context of Sandra Bowden's *oeuvre* to date. It is very hard—if at all possible—to completely separate the various stages of Bowden's career. Their rich symbolism, their layered compositions, their deeply felt message is consistent. The process of uncovering meaning, discovering hidden layers, is constant. And the methods of expression are sometimes similar or else stem from a common heritage. Bowden's medievalism, for instance, is not restricted to her *Illuminations.* The early *Texts,* for example, already embodied the rich texture of medieval manuscript illuminations, embellished with gold leaf and elaborate calligraphy. Many other works, both earlier and later than the *Illuminations,* combine text and image, symbol and word. A case in point is *Law and Gospel* (Figure 59) which has been rightly characterized as a combination of the artist's Hebraism and medievalism.[11] The work also points to the continuity between the calligraphic tradition of the Hebrew Scripture and the art of medieval illuminations. Another constant in Bowden's art is the search for—and gradual revelation of—hidden truth. According to the artist herself, ". . . [T]hat's the mystery I've spent a lifetime hunting for in my art—that veiled kind of expression which doesn't explain itself right away."[12] It is in this mysterious depth of the works (both figuratively, in terms of

The Art of **Sandra Bowden**

multiple layers of symbolism, and literally, in terms of the rich, layered texture of the canvas) that the strength and undeniable appeal of the *Illuminations* lies.

1   "Conversation with Sandra Bowden," in: *Objects of Grace: Conversations on Creativity and Faith,* James Romaine, ed. (Baltimore: Square Halo Books, 2002). p.20.

2   Before the text of a manuscript was copied, the scribe would rule the sheets. Sometimes vertical lines were required, too, to indicate the columns of text.

3   Umberto Eco, *Art and Beauty in the Middle Ages,* trans. by Hugh Bredin. (New Haven and London: Yale University Press, 1986). p. 52.

4   The lion illustrates the point that, to the medieval mind, animals, as well as plants, objects, etc., were a means of gaining perspective on Christian theology and a fertile source of information that could be used for religious instruction. See J.L. Schrader, "A Medieval Bestiary," *The Metropolitan Museum of Art Bulletin* (Summer 1986).

5   Eco, p.29.

6   Ibid., p.118.

7   "The Word Became Art" by Karen Mulder in *Christianity Today* (February 9, 1998).

8   *Good News Bible (Today's English Version)*, American Bible Society, 1976.

9   Although Bibles and other ecclesiastical books were not the only books produced in the Middle Ages, they constituted by far a majority.

10 See Virginia Chieffo Raguin, Kathryn Brush, and Peter Draper, eds. *Artistic Integration in Gothic Buildings.* (Toronto: University of Toronto Press, 1995).

11 Gene Edward Veith, "Sandra Bowden: A Christian Artist Steeped in Hebraic Aesthetics," in *Christianity and the Arts* (Winter 1999), p.22.

12 Mulder, "The Word Became Art."

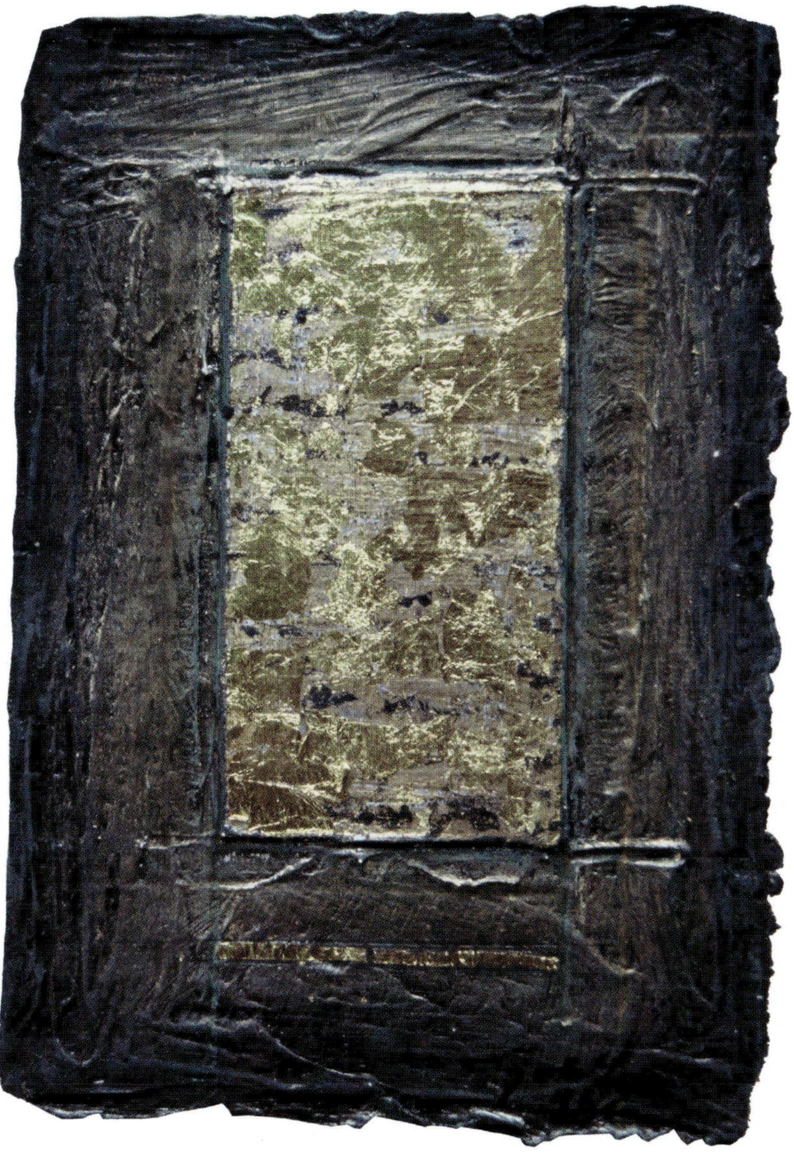

FIGURE 118
(OPPOSITE)
**15TH-CENTURY
ILLUSTRATED
MANUSCRIPT**
The Gospels/
Armenian Orthodox
*from the Collection of the
American Bible Society*

FIGURE 119
CODE I
Acrylic mixed media
1993
6 1/2 x 4 1/2

Artist's Books

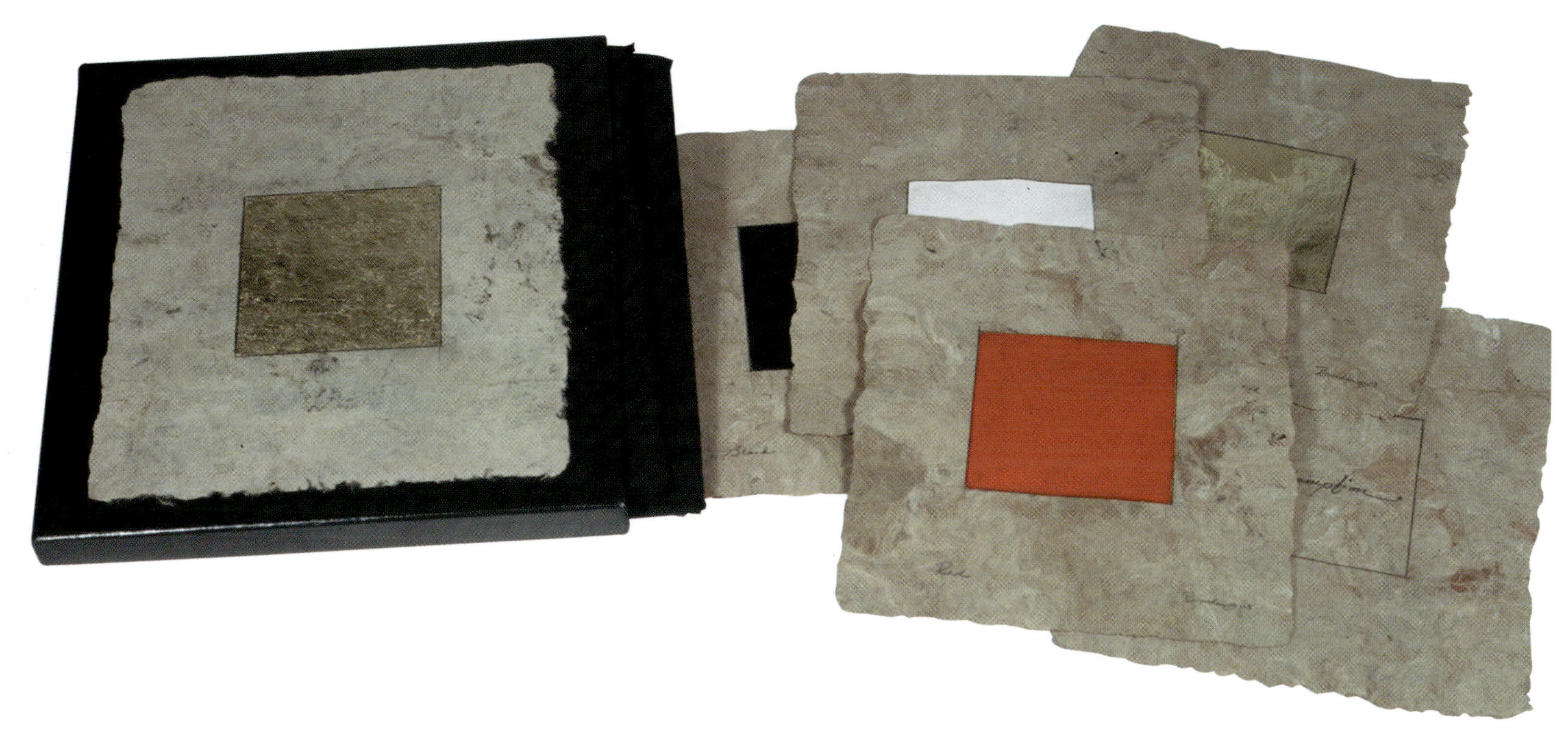

FIGURE 120
REDEMPTION BOOK
Mixed media
2004
9 3/4 x 9 x 3/4

Artist's Books

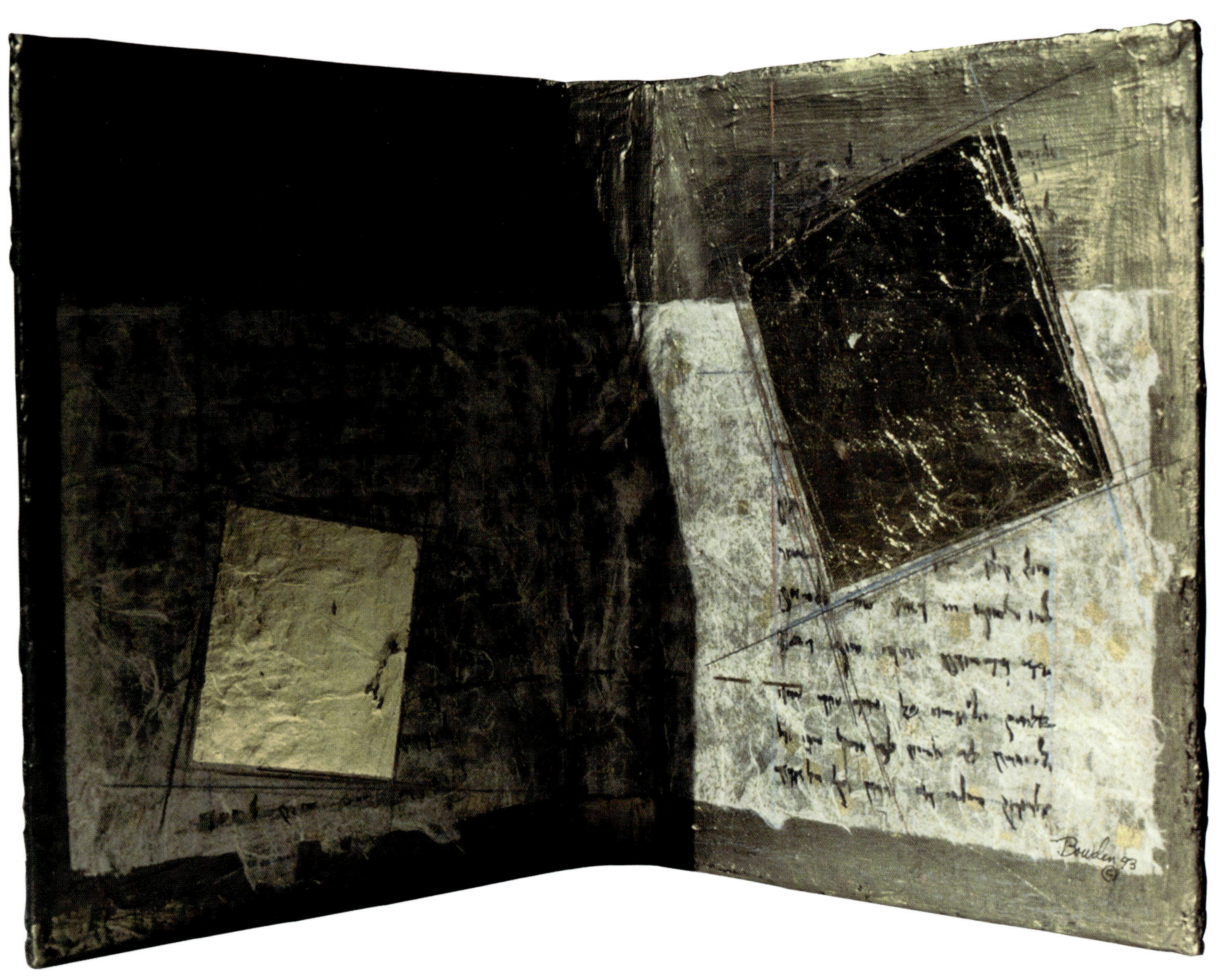

     The Art of **Sandra Bowden**

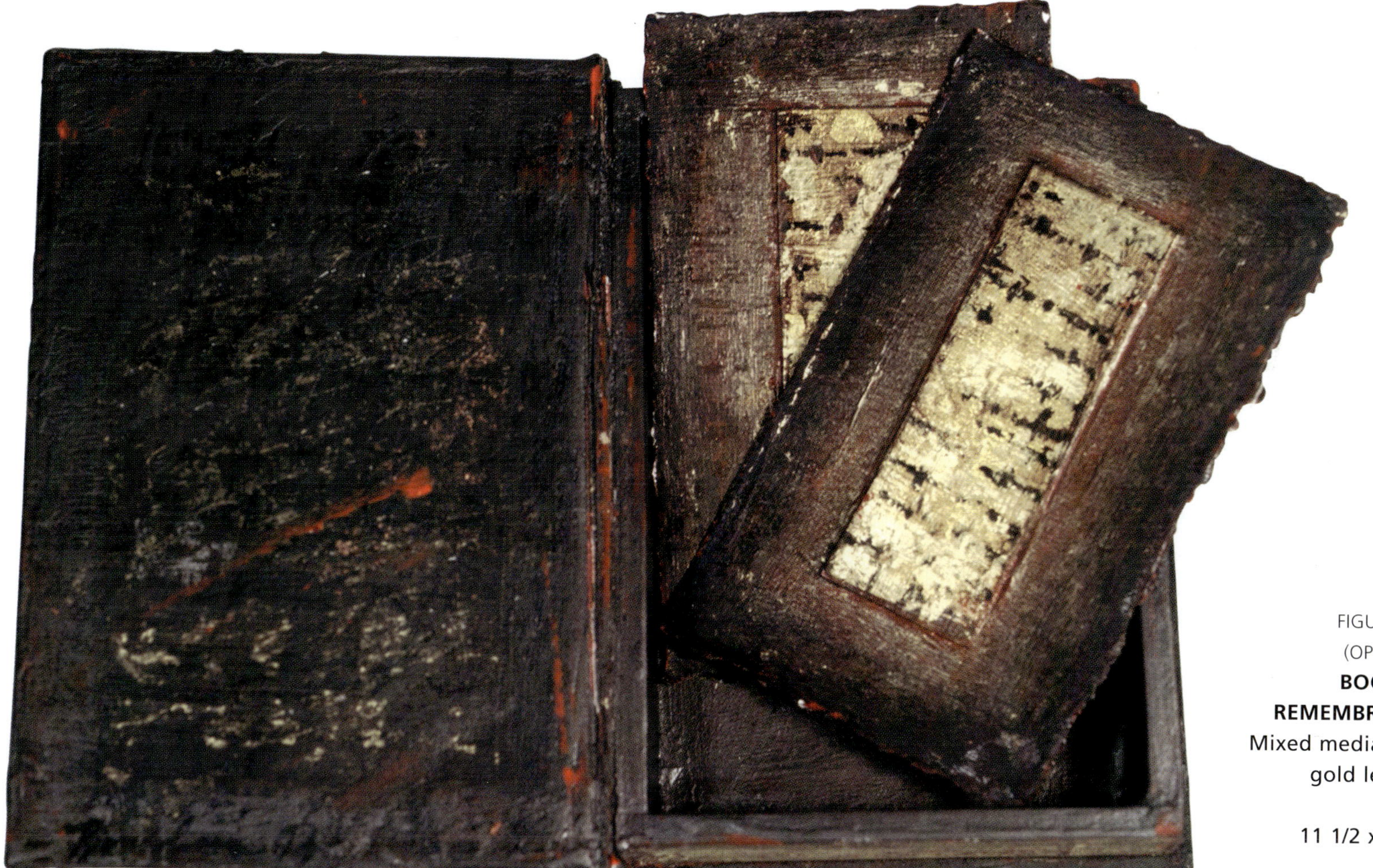

FIGURE 121
(OPPOSITE)
**BOOK OF
REMEMBRANCE**
Mixed media with
gold leafing
1993
11 1/2 x 9 x 2

FIGURE 122
BOOK FOR THE LAW
Acrylic mixed media
1993
6 1/2 x 4 1/2 x 1

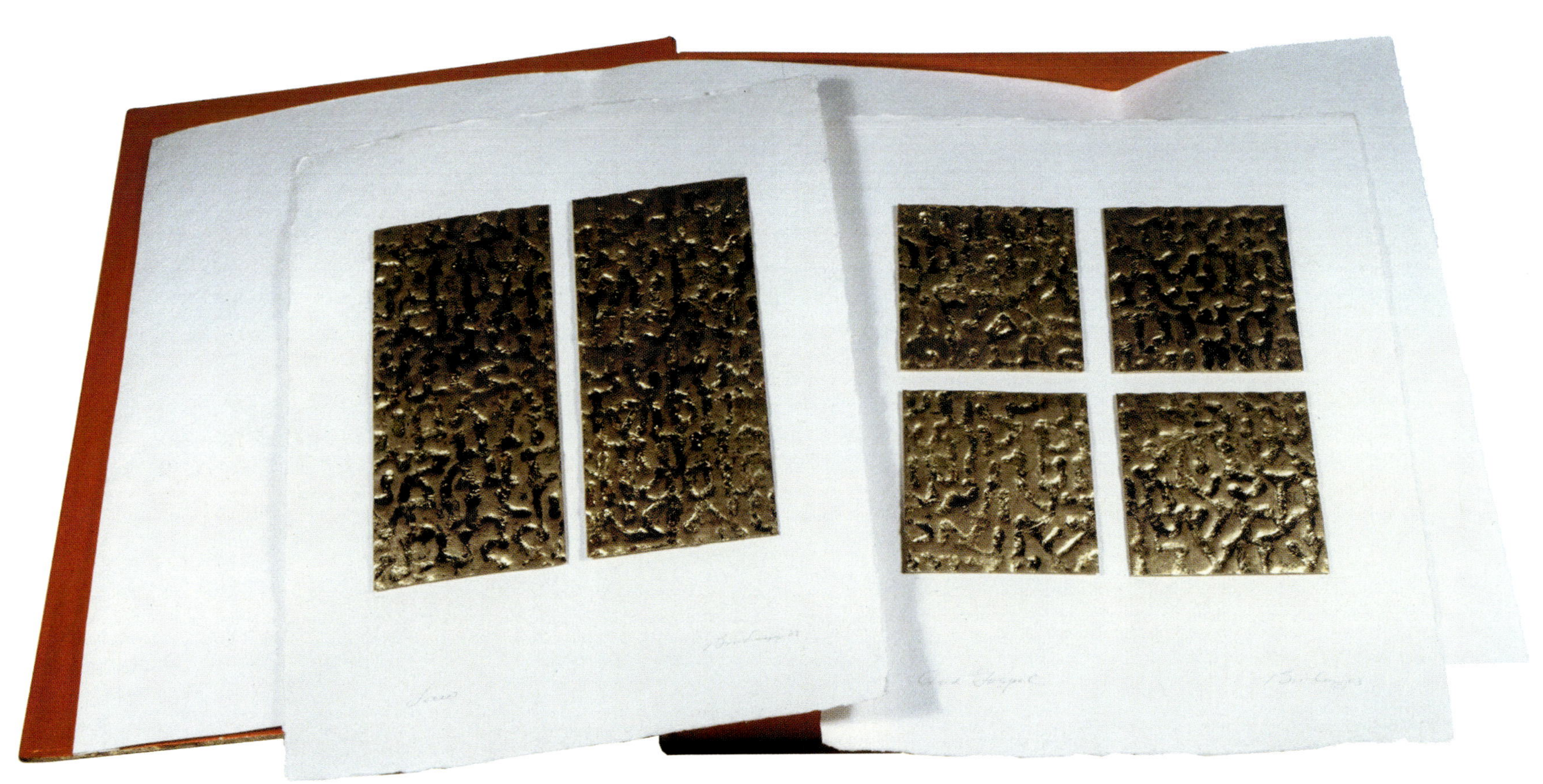

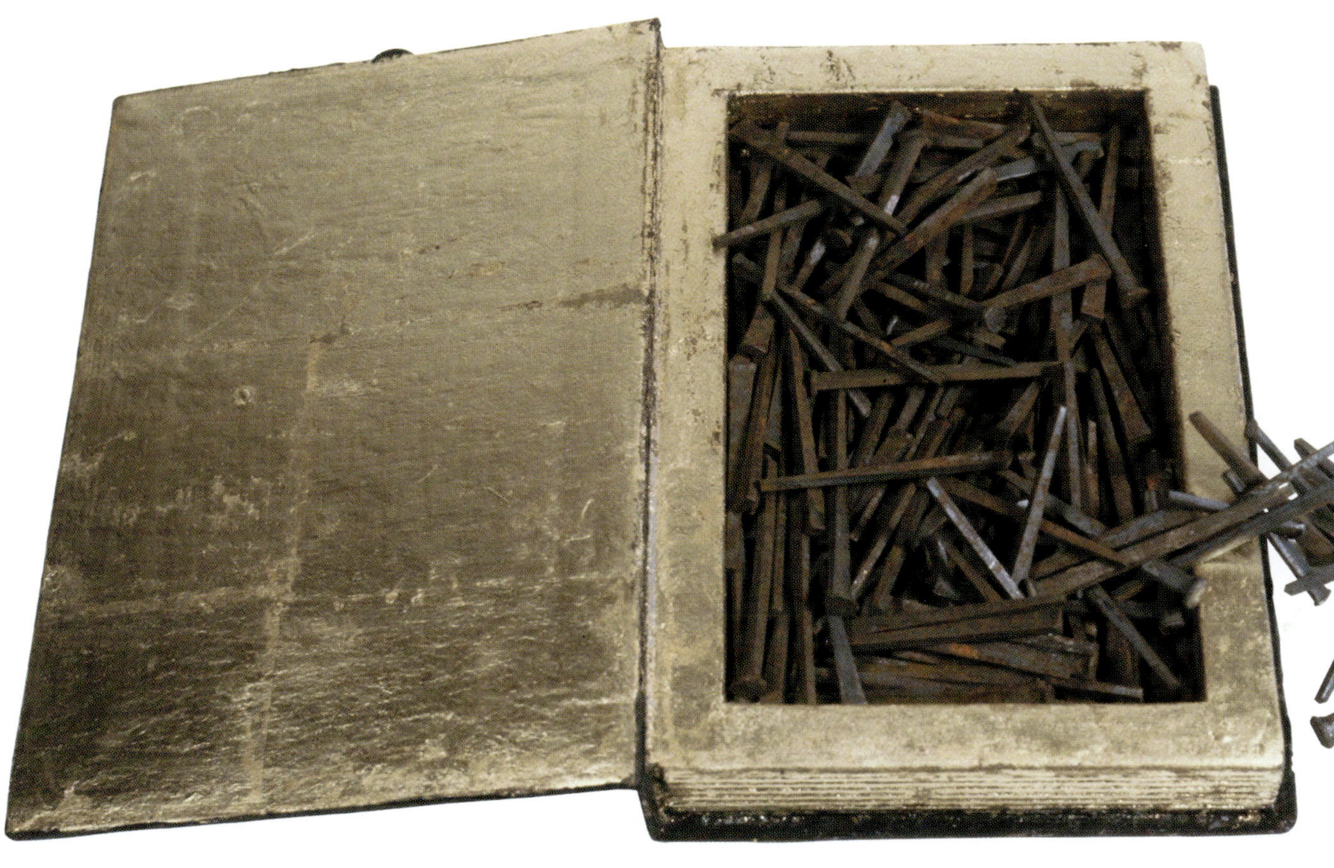

FIGURE 123
(OPPOSITE)
**BOOK FOR THE
LAW AND GOSPEL**
Mixed media
2003
13 x 9 1/2 x 2

FIGURE 124
BOOK OF NAILS
Mixed media acrylic
2003
9 x 6 x 1 1/4

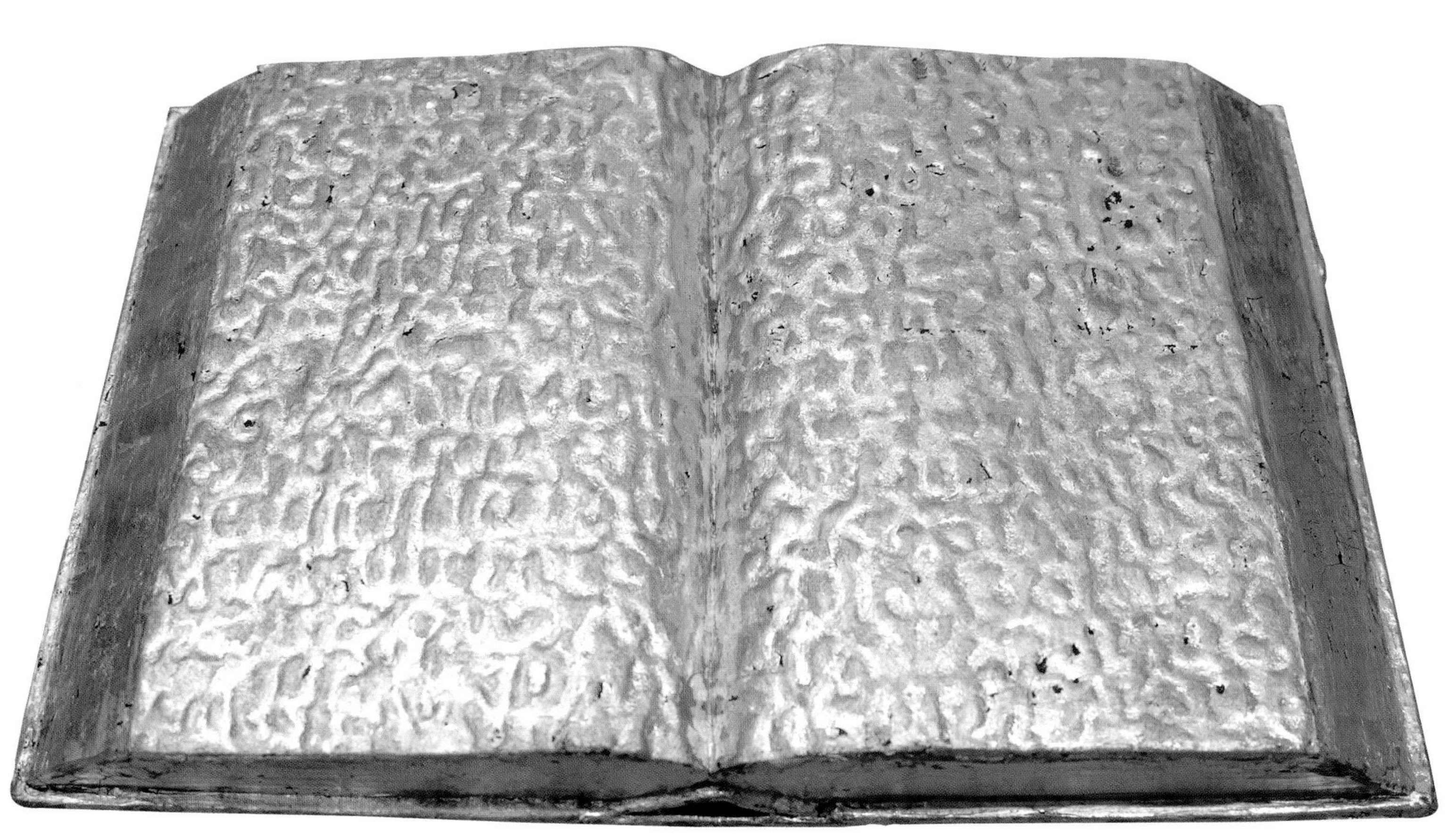

The Art of **Sandra Bowden**

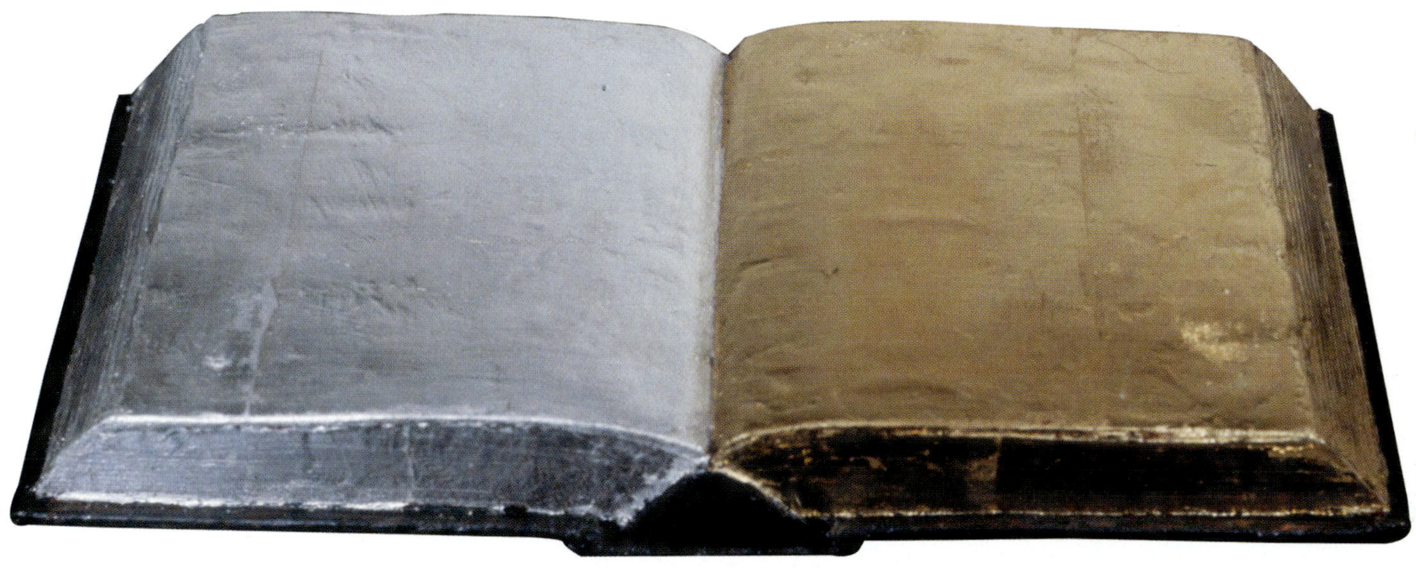

Artist's Books

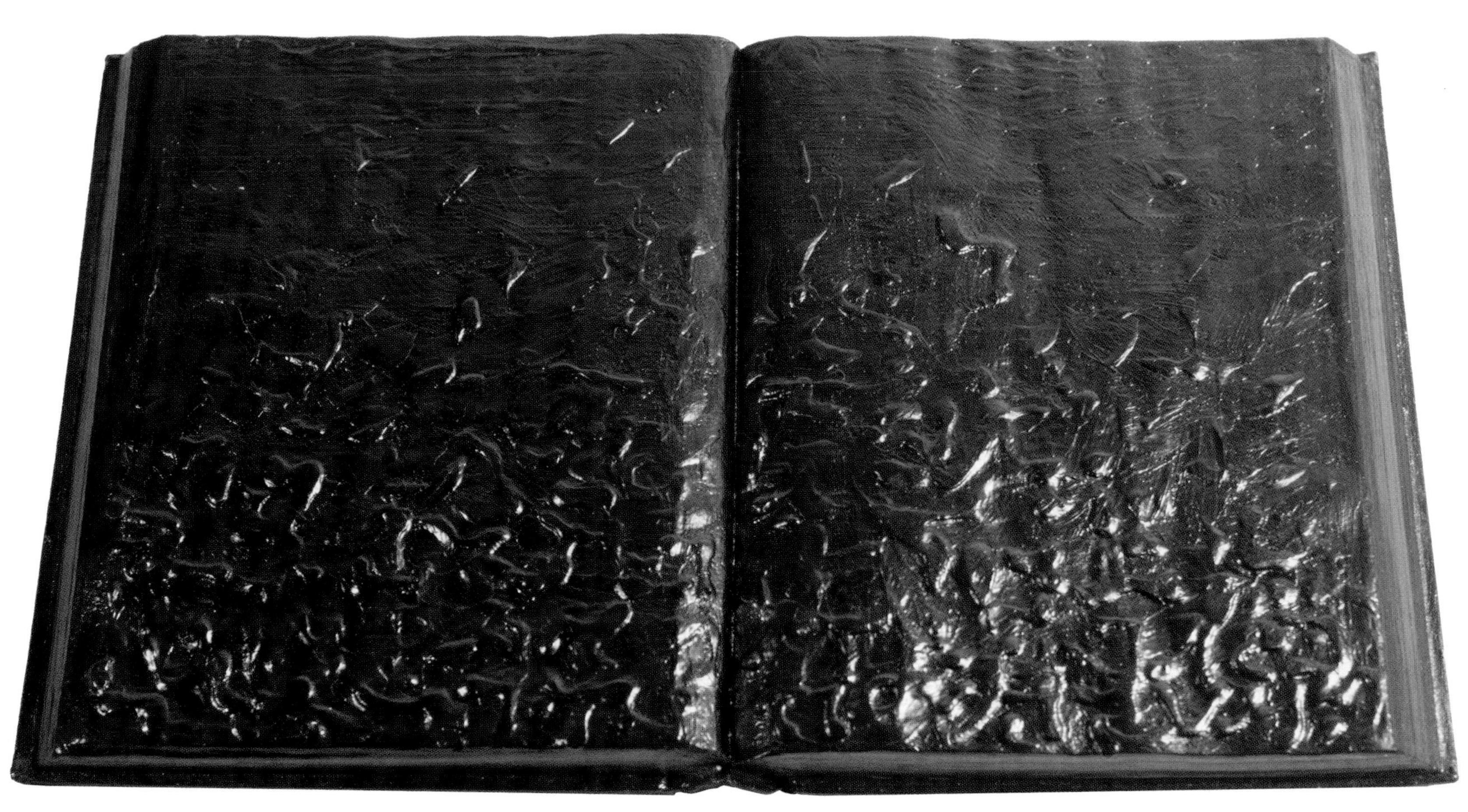

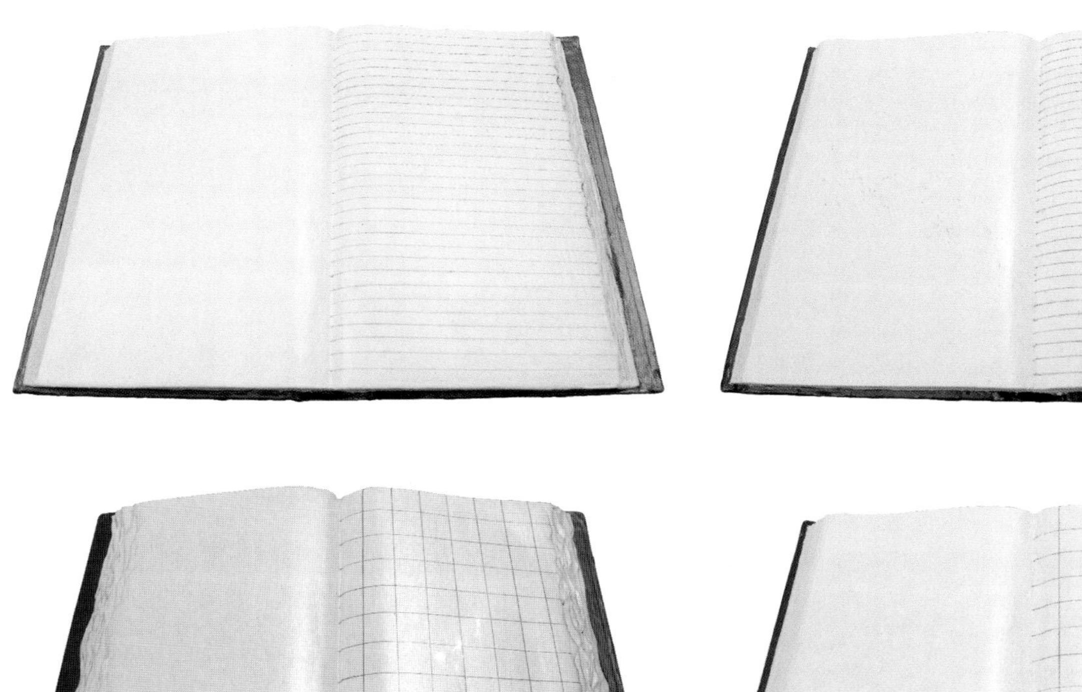

FIGURE 127
(OPPOSITE)
ABYSS
Acrylic mixed media
2003
9 1/2 x 15 x 1 1/2

FIGURE 128
LIBRO I–IV
(LEFT to RIGHT,
TOP to BOTTOM)
Mixed media
with gold leaf
2005
9 1/2 x 13 1/2 x 1 each

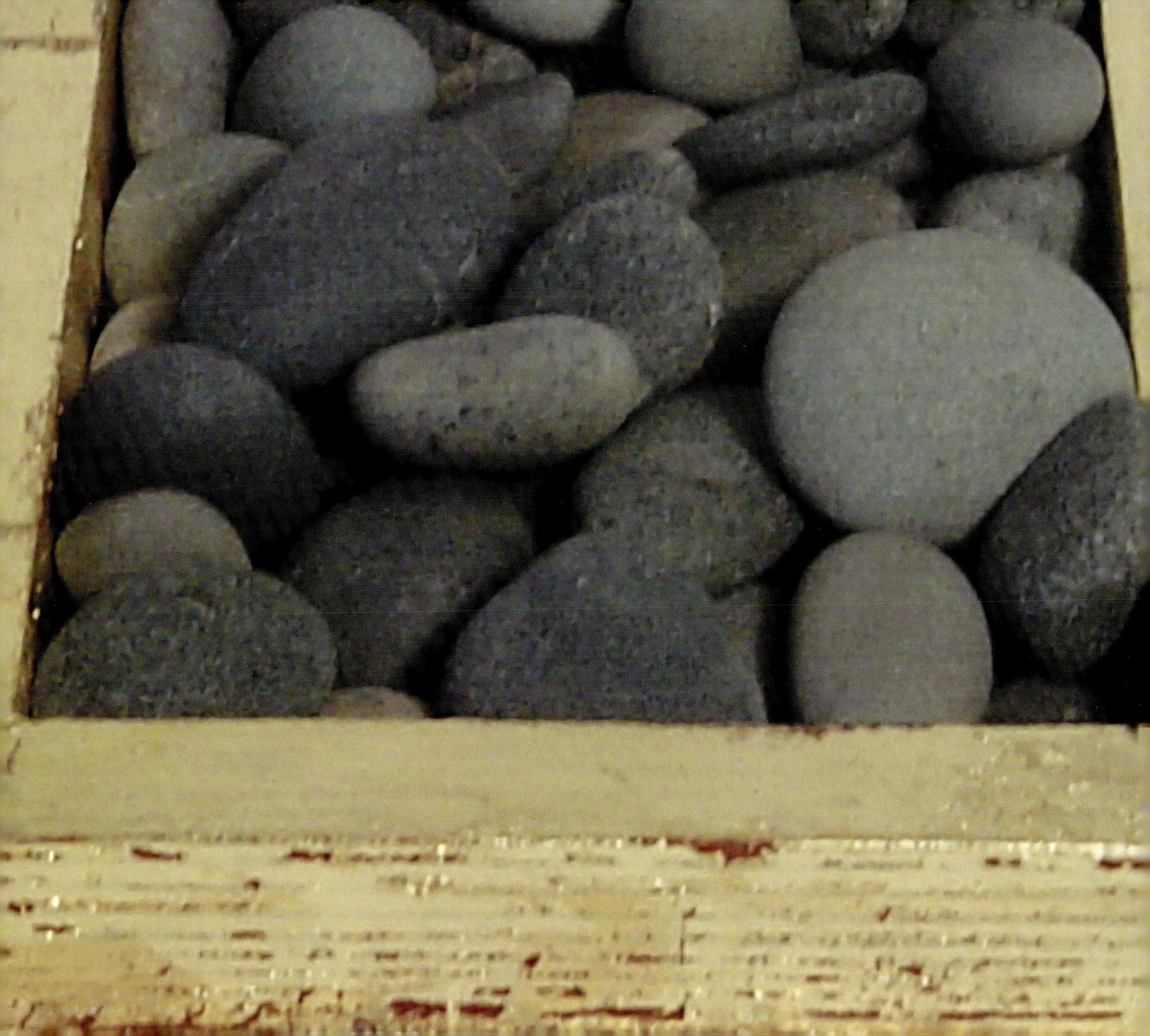

TERRANCE E. DEMPSEY, S.J.

Ireland's greatest treasure isn't a magnificent sculpture or canvas painting, a monument or grand building; it is a weathered book, a book with a history as torturous as that of the Irish people. It survived half a millennium of atrocities from the Vikings to Cromwell. This treasure is the Book of Kells (Figure 130), referred to in the Annals of Ulster as "the chief relic of the western world."[1] It is a book of the four gospels, used by the monastic community that was transplanted from Iona to Kells in the ninth century. The artists of the book integrated image and design with text to create a volume of unparalleled beauty. That this twelve-hundred-year-old book has survived at all is something of a miracle, and it survived largely because people fought to protect it. As an artistic celebration of God and the word of God, the book was their culture's prayerful engagement with the divine.

The first great books of any civilization are almost always linked to faith. The very preciousness of the materials reflects the importance attached to the texts. The neo-Darwinian anthropologist Ellen Dissanayake has talked about the universal impulse in people to "make special" those things that matter to them, and so quite naturally in religious cultures, the liturgies, ceremonies, and rites of passage are all made special by taking the ordinary and transforming it—through chant, movement, recitations, sacred objects, and ritual attire.[2] The "making special" sets this event apart from the mundane. It underscores the realities in life that are most important and gives meaning to all the other aspects of our lives. So too with the manuscripts, often a major component of ritual and ceremony, embellishment of the texts and of their covers reflects a desire to underscore the importance of the sacred texts that are being read, prayed over, and chanted.

Christianity has had a particularly distinguished history of illuminated manuscripts that bring together image and text, a history that was strongest from the late ninth to the fifteenth centuries and thereafter diminished. There are many reasons for the decline: the invention of the printing press, the Protestant Reformation, changing political and societal situations, and the sheer time and expense involved in creating these one-of-a-kind books containing scripture, the prayers of the hours, and music. Yet these works, although small in scale, are still revered as some of the greatest achievements in art history.

In Western art, with some exceptions, the use of extensive text with image has been chiefly the domain of the manuscript. When text was used in the large-scale works of art of the medieval period (frescoes, mosaics, panel paintings, stained glass, and sculpture), it was spare and used chiefly to identify the subject being visually depicted. In the Renaissance and for four centuries thereafter, large-scale works of art were almost totally devoid of text. Since the first decade of the twentieth century, however, many major artists have been incorporating texts into their paintings and collages. Most texts have a fragmented and disjointed sensibility about them when juxtaposed with image, as exemplified in the Cubist works of Pablo Picasso and Georges Braque; the Dadaist works of Marcel Duchamp, Francis Picabia and Kurt Schwitters; the Surrealist works of Joan Miro, René Magritte, and Max Ernst; and the more contemporary work of Jasper Johns and Robert Rauschenberg.

Another related phenomenon occurred in modern art—the creation of the artist's book. Almost all of the notable Western artists of the twentieth century have designed books that combine their images either with texts of well-known writers or to a lesser degree with their own writings. The texts have been literary, musical, political, art theoretical, philosophical and, even, religious.[3] One is reminded of Georges Rouault's landmark album of aquatint etchings *Miserère* (finished in 1927 but not published until 1948), and Ben Shahn's *Alphabet of Creation* (1954) as well as his *Ecclesiastes* and *Haggadah,* both published in 1967.

More recently, a new generation of artists has expressed interest in the power of the book and the illuminated manuscript to express their own faith experiences. Sandra Bowden is one such artist whose entire artistic *oeuvre* refers, directly or indirectly, to manuscripts, and she approaches her art as a practicing Christian. Her work, however, is not based on easy nostalgia or sentiment. Bowden reveals her keen understanding of the major artists of the twentieth century and she hearkens back to the work of Byzantine, medieval, and Renaissance artists. Bowden's *Artist's Books* merge tradition with the contemporary.

The presence of the handmade object is important for Bowden. First, it does not have a mass-produced feel. And second, with the loving care put into the creation of the books and illuminated pages, Bowden shows respect for the tradition that began with creation when God fashioned the first human from dust of the ground.

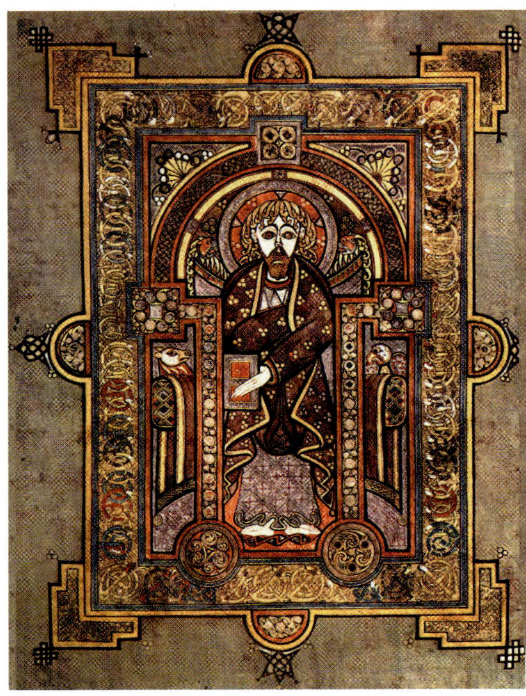

This essay began with a reference to the Book of Kells, and I return to that book because it is particularly relevant to the discussion of Bowden's work. In 1007, the Book of Kells and its elaborate cover were stolen and only the book was retrieved.[4] This cover, now missing, was a way to protect the manuscript, but more importantly, by means of embellishment, to draw attention to the fact that it contained the word of God. It must have been comprised of precious metals and stones, likely the reason for its disappearance. The book and its cover functioned as an ensemble, and there is some sense of melancholy in the knowledge that part of the history of the Book of Kells involved human greed and perhaps iconoclasm that caused the separation. Also, despite its extravagantly ornate designs, there is a weathered quality about the manuscript. Its

common with Kells. Like the Kells manuscript, Bowden's rich, complex designs at times have a weathered quality. This is especially true of her series of book covers. The finish of these covers is not highly polished or refined. There are gouges, furrows, and creases throughout. The covers themselves are thick and the surfaces uneven as the paint has been generously applied and, in some cases, allowed to congeal. The reflective gold leafing on top of these surfaces only emphasizes the weathered appearance of the covers.

history has not been a gentle one, and it plainly reveals that aspect of its history—water and dirt damaged it, pages were ripped from it, and holes were burned into it.

Bowden's creation of text and containers for the text bears something in

In her *Advent Book* (Figure 131). Bowden has created not only a book cover, but a portable triptych as well. The exterior of the book is comprised of small gold-leafed squares arranged in a grid eleven high and eight across. The squares are reminiscent of tesserae, the small

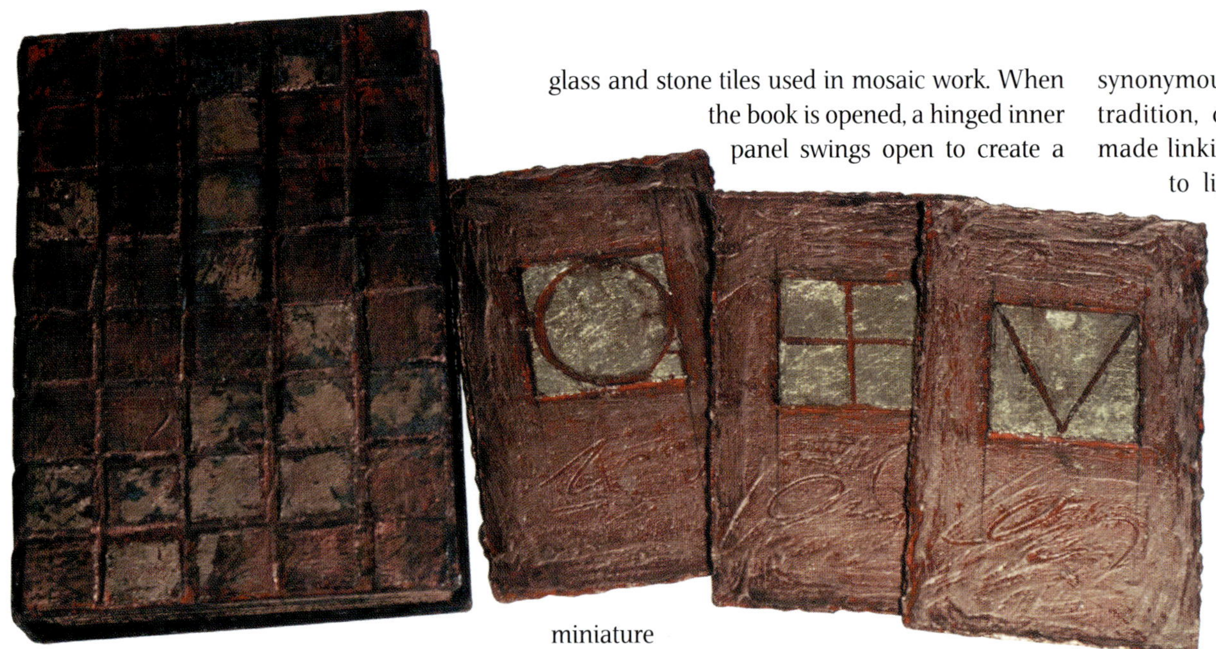

glass and stone tiles used in mosaic work. When the book is opened, a hinged inner panel swings open to create a miniature triptych. Appropriately named, the *Advent Book* is, in effect, a book that opens to reveal golden light, the light that has come into the world, as Jesus states: "I have come into the world as a light, so that no one who believes in me should stay in darkness."[5]

As we shall see, gold plays an important role in Bowden's work, and in this area she is linked to a long tradition. Gold has been an intrinsic part of the great religious manuscripts, and rightfully so. In almost every culture, gold, when available, has been used in the context of the divine. With its dazzling reflective powers and light, non-alloyed gold does not tarnish or rust. When burnished, it achieves a mirror-like glow resembling the light of the sun. No wonder that it seems to be a precious metal often employed as a material agent able to point to God. Gold with its association to light is important theologically. In many religious traditions, light is synonymous with the divine. In the Christian tradition, countless scriptural references are made linking God the Father and God the Son to light, and in some branches of the Christian Orthodox tradition, the theology of mystical light became codified in a movement called Hesychasm, which taught that followers could experience the divine light of God. Devoid of its mercenary associations, gold has a particularly powerful way of linking us with the divine. It was the metal of choice for the majority of Christian manuscript illuminators. It is the metal of choice for Sandra Bowden in her work.

Like the tesserae of Byzantine mosaics, the squares of gold leaf Bowden employs are not uniform in smoothness or shape. As a result, they do not form a perfectly even surface. Although they are in a grid arrangement on the *Advent Book,* Bowden has tipped the squares in slightly different positions so that the ensemble of gold squares catches light in a variety of ways, creating a shimmering effect. Similarly, the gold leafing on the book's interior reveals the creases and folds of the supporting panel surface that are characteristic of all of Bowden's books.

Of all the books designed by Bowden, the *Book of Remembrance* (Figure 121), at least its exterior, most closely resembles the *Advent Book.* The exterior of the cover contains the same arrangement of gold squares that occur in the *Advent Book,* eight across and eleven down. There are differences in this cover, however. Different purities of gold leaf have been used on the front cover, thus creating a pattern of lighter

The Art of **Sandra Bowden**

gold mingled with the darker gold. When opened, the book cover reveals no pages but only the suggestion of a letter or note glued to the interior panels of the cover, with two squares of gold leaf placed askew over the letter. The text, written in a beautifully calligraphed but totally imaginary language, suggests a record of those moments in our lives that have shaped us, moved us, changed us, those moments in our lives that to which we attach special importance, as Ellen Dissanayake might say, and that are protected and treasured in this glorious gold book cover.

The primary purpose of a book cover, no matter how embellished or simple it is, is to protect what it contains. In that case, it can often function like a reliquary or a shrine, protecting something of great significance inside. In her *Book for the Law* (Figure 122), Bowden has fashioned two small gold-leafed panels with the suggestion of ancient Hebrew text. Might these refer to the Decalogue? If so, she has created a miniature Ark of the Covenant into which these commandments of the Lord are to be placed. Unlike the biblical Ark, this book is quite intimate in scale, suggesting a portability that makes it easier for us to carry these commandments with us into the various aspects of our daily lives.

Her *Icon Book* (Figure 27), also small in scale, contains two images of the Madonna and Child from the Eastern Orthodox tradition, one of which is perhaps the most famous icon of this subject, the twelfth-century *Virgin of Vladimir.* Like the *Book for the Law,* this is also portable. It could easily fit into a suitcoat pocket or in a purse. It is not a flawless image but, like the original, it is missing paint in many areas. One is reminded of other great icons whose surfaces have been damaged

over the centuries but that nonetheless retain their power. Indeed, their power is enhanced because of the losses they have experienced. One such icon is *Christ the Pantocrator* (or "All Sovereign Ruler") by the fifteenth-century Russian painter Andre Rublev. Rublev's remarkable icon of Jesus stares at us with a gaze that cuts right through us. The area of paint missing from the upper right side of the icon, encroaching onto the forehead of Jesus, does not diminish the power of the icon. Rather, like the crucified Christ, it bears witness to a history not devoid of suffering—and yet like the resurrected Christ, the image triumphs over all adversity but nonetheless continues to bear the physical signs of its own suffering.

Similarly, both in the original *Virgin of Vladimir* as well as in Bowden's version of that icon, the areas of missing paint reveal an icon not isolated from the course of human history. Both the *Virgin of Vladimir* and the *Madonna and Child* icon on the exterior of the book cover are of the type of Eastern Orthodox Madonna called the *Eleousa,* or the "Tender Madonna." This type of Madonna is identified by the cheek of Mary touching the cheek of her son Jesus. In the Eastern Orthodox icon tradition in which images are often severe and aloof, this Madonna conveys

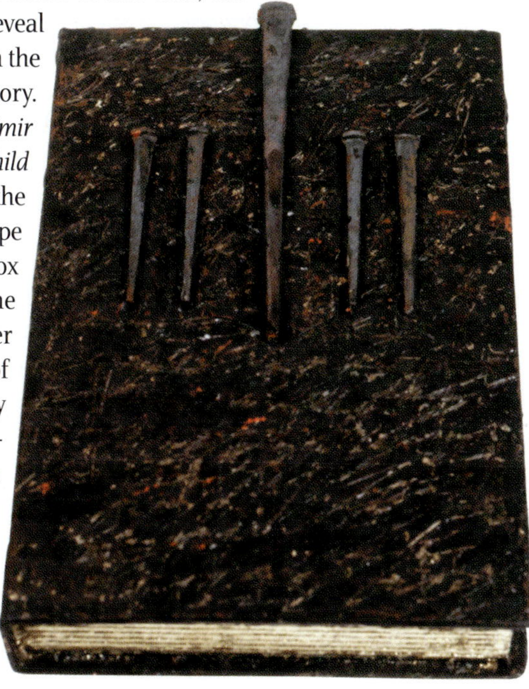

unconditional love without becoming sentimental. Here is the Virgin Mother of God showing tenderness for her son, pointing the way to Him for us, and reflecting on the premonitions she must have about the suffering He will later experience. It is Simeon's prediction, "And a sword will pierce your own soul," interiorized.[6]

In the *Trinity Book* (Figure 132), Bowden continues the book-as-case motif, and within this book cover case are three panels, each one with an undercoating of gesso and modeling paste that is covered with gold leafing. Each of the panels bears a different symbol representing one of the persons of the Holy Trinity. The first panel, containing a circle within a square, points to God the Father. Traditionally, the circle is symbolic of the eternal as there is no beginning or end. Bowden inscribes this circle within a square, traditionally symbolic of those matters related to earth—the four cardinal directions and the four seasons. It is the divine fully at home in the temporal ("God saw all that he had made, and it was good").[7] The second panel contains a cross within a square, symbolic of the redemptive sacrifice of Christ for all humanity on the Cross ("Now if we died with Christ, we believe that we will also live with him").[8] The third panel has an inverted triangle within a square. In addition to its obvious Trinitarian allusions, this inverted triangle can also refer to the descent of the Holy Spirit among us, a funneling shape pouring into us the spirit of God ("But you will receive power when the Holy Spirit comes on you; and you will be my witnesses . . . to all the ends of the earth").[9]

Many of Bowden's *Artist's Books* open to reveal some treasure inside, be it a triptych of gold, sacred remembrances, an image of the Law, a pic-

ture of the compassionate Mother of God, or a representation of the Trinity. However, *Closed Book* (Figure 133) denies us physical access to its interior but remains shut, like a miniature Holy of Holies. We do not know what it contains, or if it contains anything. Yet, in light of the other books created by Bowden, we can safely conclude that this sheds light on the faith experience. Indeed, it is a faith experience to trust that the contents refer to God. Bowden deprives us of the certainty that we as Americans so desperately seek. Instead, we are confronted with something that does not disclose its contents. It is something we cannot access. It frustrates us, dismays us, and perhaps even angers us. Paradoxically, this sealed book can become the doorway through which we fully enter into the faith experience where certainty is replaced by trust.

Two of Bowden's more recent books, *Book of Nails* (Figure 124, 134) and *Even the Stones* (Figure 135), continue the "book as container or vessel" theme found in *Book of the Law, Icon Book,* and *Trinity Book.* In *Book of Nails,* Bowden has fashioned a dark textured cover of blacks, browns, and flecks of rust, with five nails arranged, candelabra-like, with one long rusting nail in the center flanked on either side by pairs of shorter, rusting nails. The five nails reference the five wounds of Jesus on the cross. The edges of this book/box (where the pages should be) are leafed in gold, but upon opening the book the viewer sees a hollowed-out volume whose interior is filled with square old floor nails. These nails convey mixed signals—with the decisions we make in our lives, we may be complicit in causing Christ's suffering and by extension the suffering of others, while on the other hand, with the surprises that life offers each one of us, we may be companions in his cru-cifixion. The reverberations of Calvary are still very much with us.

Even the Stones is a surprising work. Unlike the brutality immediately suggested in *Book of Nails, Even the Stones* is beautiful, almost seductive and sensual. This book/vessel contains smooth, oval-shaped, gray stones, pleasant to the eye as well as to the hand. Its meanings are complex and even contradictory. The title refers to Luke 19:40, in which the Pharisees urge Jesus to rebuke his enthusiastic followers as he is making his tri-umphal entry into Jerusalem. In response, he tells the Pharisees that his followers will not be denied this moment, for even if they remain silent, the stones would cry out. In this sense, the stones become means for witnessing to the pres-ence of the Son of God among humanity. Elsewhere in Scripture, stones serve a similar metaphorical purpose. In the Book of Habakkuk (2:11), the Lord condemns the violence and greed of the Babylonians by indicating that even the stones and the beams of their homes (acquired through plundering) cry out against their atroci-ties. In both these passages, one affirming the glory of Christ and the other witnessing to the depravity of humanity, the stones testify to the depth of God's involvement in our lives. Nevertheless, there are many other scriptural meanings ascribed to stones: as markers, as sym-bols of solidity and permanence, and still others that link them to darker realities. The devil's first temptation of Jesus in the desert was his urging Jesus to turn stones into bread (Matthew 4:3). Stones can be weapons as well. As a means of triumphing over oppression, David slew Goliath with a stone (I Samuel 17:49), and as a vehicle for cruelty, jealousy, and judg-mentalism, the people were quick to want to stone the woman caught in adultery (John 8:7) and Christ himself (John 8:59). Bowden understands the com-plex theological meanings of these

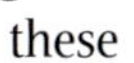
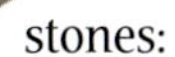

stones:
as objects that can affirm the goodness and glory of God and as objects that can

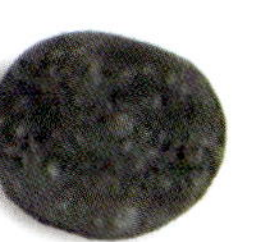

reveal the realities of sin and violence.

An extraordinary book is *Abyss* (Figure 127), a title inspired by the first two verses of Genesis: " In the beginning, when God created the heavens and the earth, the earth was a formless wasteland, and darkness covered the abyss, while a mighty wind swept over the waters."[10] What is remarkable about Bowden's book is the effect that she has achieved in conveying the sense of the abyss or the deep and God's eventual shaping of creation. The book is open with all the unseen pages glued together. Raised Hebrew text covers the open two pages of the book and over that text the artist has applied numerous layers of glossy pearl-black paint. The effect is that the open book becomes expansive and suggests a borderless, churning, inky sea. The waves and all the turbulence are caused by the word of God.

Ironically, this book suggests a vastness far beyond its physical dimensions. It brings to mind the painting by the nineteenth-century German artist Casper David Friedrich entitled *Monk by the Sea.* Art historian Robert Rosenblum has written with great sensitivity about the Friedrich painting:

> Friedrich had painted several boats on the sea, one extending above the horizon, but . . . then, in what must have been an act of artistic courage and personal compulsion, he removed them, leaving the monk on the brink of an abyss unprecedented in the history of painting, but one that would have such disquieting progeny as Turner's own "pictures of nothing" and the boundless voids of Barnett Newman.
>
> . . . Friedrich's painting suddenly corresponds to an experience familiar to the spectator in the modern world, an experience in which the individual is pitted against, or confronted by the overwhelming, incomprehensible immensity of the universe.[11]

Bowden's book suggests that same feeling of looking into the dark and churning abyss. Through her book, the artist asks us to have courage to confront darkness head-on. Our experience of the abyss results in our being challenged at the deepest level to face our demons, the cruelty of the world, the terror of the void, and the realization of our own mortality. It is the Dark Night of the Soul, a centuries-old tradition of Christian mysticism in which the metaphor of darkness signifies our faith encounter with the unfathomability of God. It is Rudolf Otto's Mysterium Tremendum, once again experiential, in which we are made aware of our own creaturehood in the face of an all powerful reality.[12] *Abyss* is the work done by someone who has a mature vision of life. Like Rembrandt's later paintings, which frankly address personal flaws and imperfections and which go beneath the surface to address life's mysteries, disappointments, wonders, and terrors, *Abyss* touches on these same concerns. For Bowden, there is an expression of abiding faith, for beyond the void, the vast darkness, is the Word of God.

In the first three verses of Genesis there is a movement from darkness to light. Bowden has echoed this movement in four of her newest books, *Libro I–IV.* If *Abyss,* done in 2003, is about faith in the presence of incomprehensible darkness, then the books of the *Libro* series, done in 2005, have the joyous transformative power of God as light as their central focus. *Libro I–IV,* painted in iridescent pearl white, have a quiet glow about them. After the drama of Abyss, these

   The Art of **Sandra Bowden**

works invite us to experience God as Elijah experienced him while praying and waiting in the cave: "After the wind there was an earthquake, but the Lord was not in the earthquake. After the earthquake came a fire, but the Lord was not in the fire. After the fire came a gentle whisper."[13]

There is a whisper-like tranquility within the *Libro* series (Figure 128). In each book the left page is blank, revealing only its subtly glowing surface, and the right page has graphite lines drawn on the surface of the pearl-white pages. For *Libro I* and *Libro II*, there are parallel, horizontal lines similar to the lines on a writing tablet, as if awaiting God's Word to be written into our lives; for *Libro III* and *Libro IV*, the lines are arranged as grids suggesting the constancy of God, a constancy that provides the structure and foundation in our lives. Yet these parallel lines and grids do not create the sense of rigidity, for the deckled edges of the pages give a sense of animation to the book, and on the right pages of all the *Libro* volumes, these irregular edges grow in size and begin to move across the surfaces like a gentle washing flow of water or grace. Certainty and mystery coexist in a delicate harmony.

Sacred manuscripts are not just about beauty, but also about their power to communicate the word of God in both text and image. This potent combination of the aesthetic and the religious has fascinated people and inspired them to go to great lengths to preserve these objects. As with the Kells manuscript, Bowden's books bespeak a sense of struggle, perseverance, and protection of what is most important. Finally, however, they express a faith strong enough to withstand the most insurmountable adversities and vibrant enough to offer to others the life-giving presence of God.

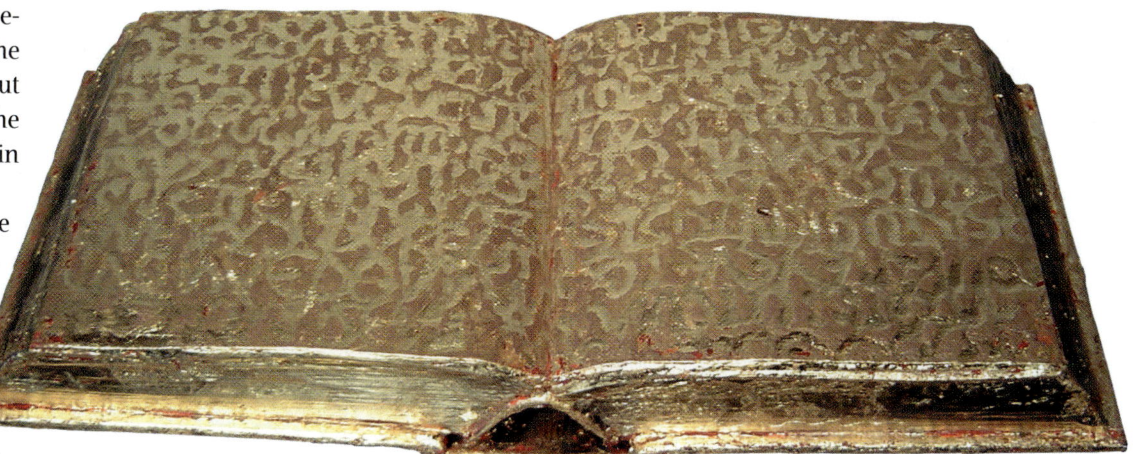

1 James Snyder, *Medieval Art: Painting, Sculpture, Architecture, 4th–14th Century*. (New York: Harry N. Abrams, Inc., 1988). pg. 186.

2 Ellen Dissanayke, *What is Art For?* (Seattle: University of Washington Press, 1988). pp. 74–106.

3 For a comprehensive view of modern artists' books, see: Riva Castleman, *A Century of Artists' Books* (New York: Museum of Modern Art and Harry N. Abrams, Inc., 1994).

4 Bernard Meehan, *The Book of Kells* (London: Thames and Hudson Ltd., 1994, p. 14).

5 John 12:46

6 Luke 2:35

7 Genesis 1:31

8 Romans 6:8

9 Acts 1:7

10 Genesis 1:1–2

11 Robert Rosenblum, *Modern Painting and the Northern Romantic Tradition* (New York: Harper and Row Publishers, 1975) pp. 13-14.

12 Rudolf Otto, *The Idea of the Holy,* trans. John W. Harvey (New York: Oxford University Press, 1923). p. 22.

FIGURE 136
RESURRECTION BOOK
Mixed media
2004
5 1/4 x 11 3/4 x 1 1/2

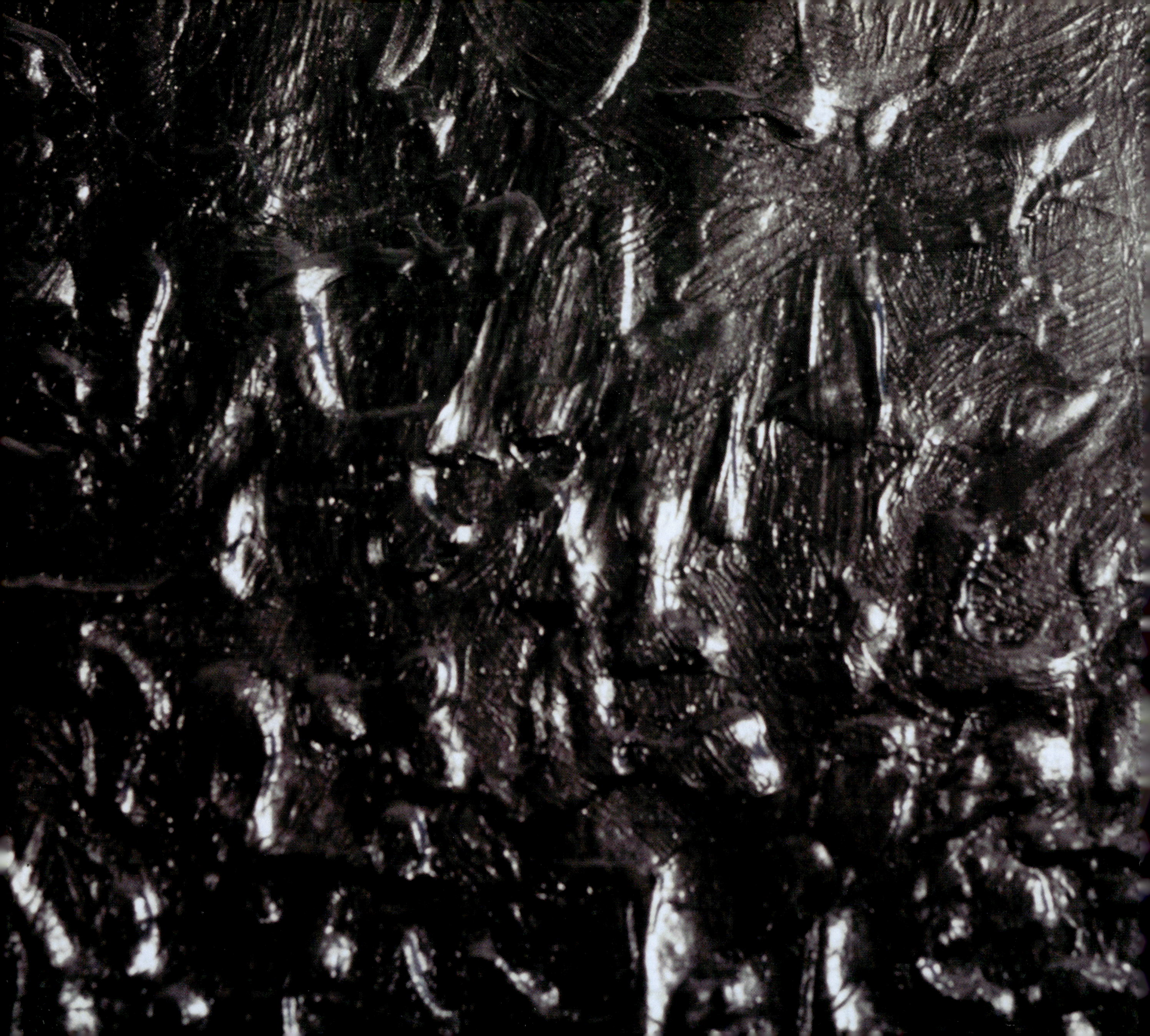

Early Explorations

Early Explorations was initiated because I was invited to participate in an art exhibit at the Beverly Baptist Church, in Beverly MA. One of the paintings in that show was *Ancient Writings*, a seminal piece which contained many of the elements of my life's future work: texture, collage, and text. I have often wondered whether I would have come to the place where my art and my faith intersected had it not been for this church-sponsored art show.

These pieces, for the most part, are very abstract, taking the original objects that inspired the piece in fragmented and reconstructed directions. I would find artifacts that offered intrigue, identify the fundamental visual structures, abstract them and rework the forms to construct textured surfaces that reflected these elemental components. Collage became the medium of choice and worked well to flesh out the ideas and insights that were brooding within me. This approach allowed the work to have rich surface texture that gave a tactile dimension to the art.

In these early years, the study of theology was a continuing interest. I was particularly drawn to the idea of origins or beginnings, so the Genesis story and how it related to writings and artifacts from other cultures became a focus. Cuneiform tablets captured my imagination—such as the Gilgamesh Epic—offering parallel, but different accounts of the flood and creation stories. In the early 1970s a few pieces with blocks of cuneiform approximations emerged in my work, a precursor of what was to come with Hebrew text. During this time I was also reading various scientific theories on Genesis and how scientists and theologians reconciled the account in Genesis to their respective fields.

By 1972 I had become interested in ancient languages. Thinking that I would not learn other more obscure languages from biblical times and since I had a interest in Old Testament studies, it seemed appropriate to learn Hebrew. I think I was searching for something mysterious and beautiful found in the language that would add depth to my work and spiritual journey.

The study of an ancient biblical language helped to interpret the text in new and fresh ways, adding subtle understanding and nuances of meaning. In pieces like *Origin* (1971) I am playing with forms that look like Hebrew text, but are only calligraphic impressions of the language. By the time of *In the Beginning* (1972), specific Hebrew passages had begun to find their way into the art.

ANCIENT WRITINGS
Oil collage, 1965, 26 x 16

This collage is a seminal piece that contains all the elements explored over more than forty years: collage, suggestions of calligraphic writing, limited color palate, and textured surfaces—all characteristics of what was to follow.

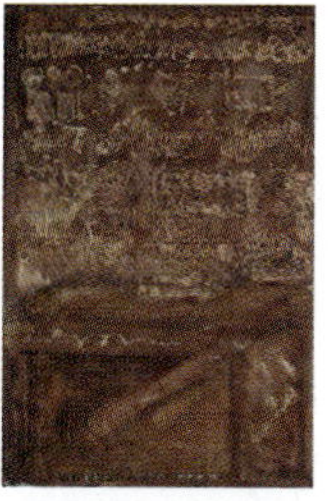

DELUGE
Oil collage, 1971, 20 x 20

The Gilgamesh Epic and the biblical flood story come together in this piece. Corduroy fabric fills the sky to suggest torrents of rain descending on a boat form that floats in the blue open surface of the canvas. A facsimile of cuneiform writing forms a pillar beneath the ark.

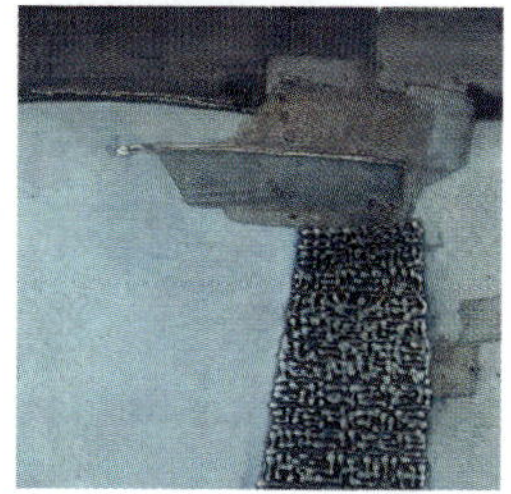

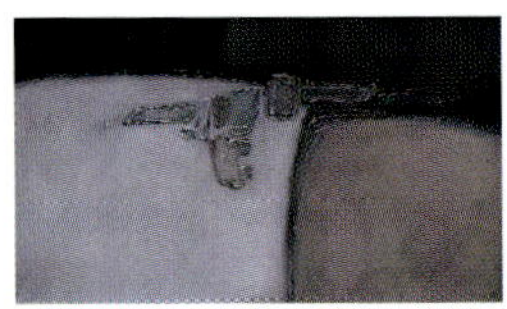

DESERT DIG

Oil collage, 1969, 36 x 60

In this early collaged painting I give tribute to paleontologists who have uncovered bones of dinosaurs in the desert, unlocking mysteries to the past.

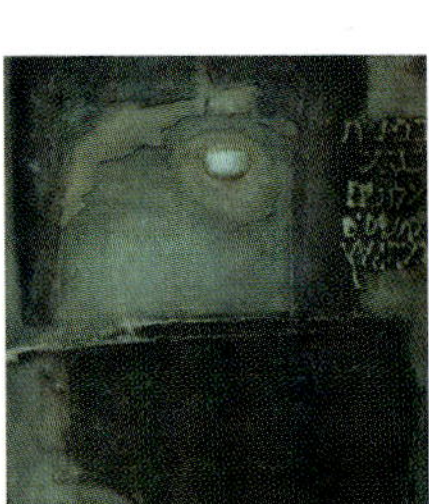

EMPTY TOMB

Oil collage, 1970, 48 x 36

The idea for this large abstracted painting came from an ancient Israeli tomb with a round stone positioned to open and close the entrance.

FOUND PIECES

Oil collage, 1971, 12 x 12 x 24 inch box
on pedestal with cap

Archaeologists sort through mounds of fragments, study their meanings and then reconstruct the past, many times giving us insight into the present. To reference ancient steles, (vertical stone columns found at border sites between countries), *Found Pieces* is a sculpture constructed of four collaged panels (side 1 is shown here) inserted between two segments of a black pedestal.

IN THE BEGINNING

Oil collage, 1972, 18 x 16

Early Hebrew thought conceived of the heavens as an arch suspended in the sky from which hung all the heavenly bodies. To the left of this abstracted arch the first line from the book of Genesis is written in raised Hebrew text, "In the beginning God created," below which is a spread of formless earth.

MOABITE STONE

Oil collage, 1970, 48 x 36

This monochromatic painting from early in my career celebrates the famous Moabite Stone and how its discovery unlocked clues to an ancient language.

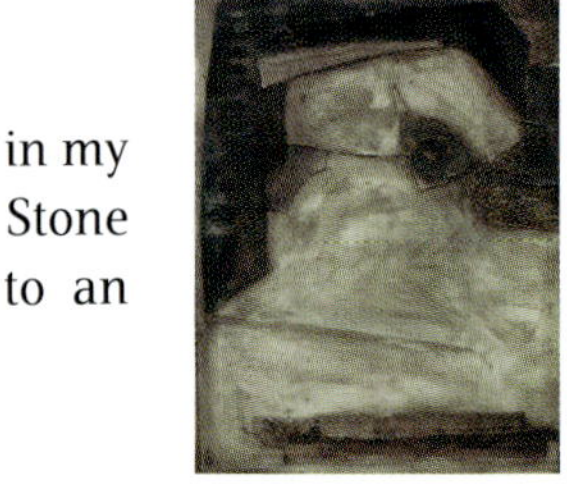
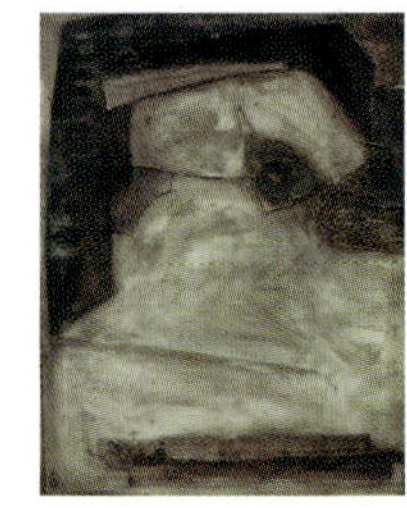

ORIGIN

Oil collage, 1971, 36 x 24

"Darkness was over the surface of the deep, And the spirit of God was hovering over the waters." Genesis 1:2

This collage was the first in my paintings that incorporated suggestions of ancient Hebrew. The forms of *Origin* show seeds of an approach that I would revisit throughout my career.

UNEARTHED

Oil collage, 1971, 20 x 20

Unearthed explores the probing, digging, sifting through the rubble, unearthing what has been hidden—the work of the archaeologist to unearth secrets to what has been buried from sight, only then to be discovered and interpreted.

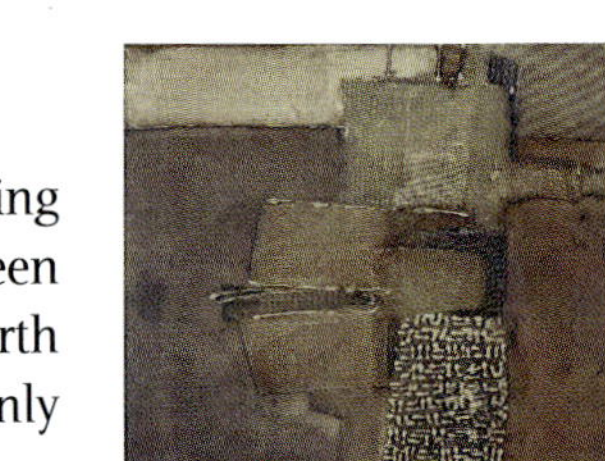
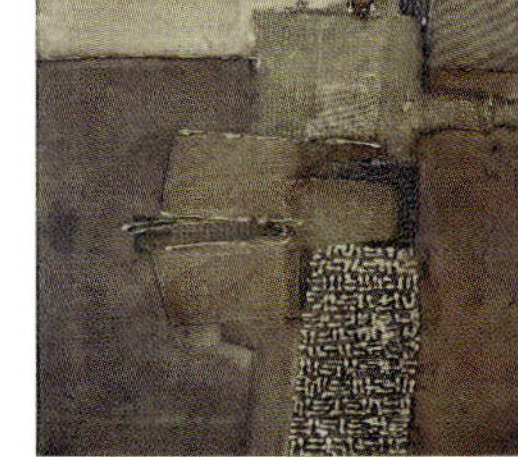

Geological Forms

As part of my quest into the past and how it relates to issues of faith and biblical scholarship, I studied geology at SUNY-Albany in the early 1980s and was fascinated with plate tectonics and explorations of earth's early architecture. A passage from Psalm 85 was particularly important to my search, "Truth will spring from the earth, and righteousness comes down from the heavens." I was looking for a way to understand where we find truth—how the natural world reveals and offers back some of its secrets. Although the tension between rational thought and spiritual life has been a subject of debate, I never found the scientific method to undermind my faith, but rather enlarge my view of creation and the Creator.

Over the progression of ten years (1972 to 1982), one can see the metamorphosis from a very abstract interpretation of created forms to a more recognizable landscape. Within the earth's strata I embedded layers of text, words buried between the levels of rock, resonating with the history of human culture.

By the late 1970s I was using blocks of Hebrew text that would become a signature element in my work for the next thirty or more years. This text includes specific Hebrew passages written carefully, but with spaces between words and lines eliminated, thereby creating a kind of text block that is not easily read. It is not important to me that the viewer can read the passage, but that the essential meaning and spiritual essence is conveyed in the work. In pieces like *Heavens Declare the Glory of God* entire sections of the landscape are filled with text. This approach reinforced the idea that *word* and *world* are joined in a kind of visual song.

AND ALL DEEP PLACES

Collagraph, 1978, 23 x 11 1/2

Buried in strata below the surface of the earth is the text from Psalms 135:1–4 which includes, "You covered the earth, and all the deep places with a garment, the waters stood above the mountains."

CAST FORTH

Collagraph, 1980, 22 1/4 x 12

This collagraph was inspired by my geological studies and fascination with origins. A celestial body is suspended in space and heavily textured fabrics create the strata below the surface of the earth.

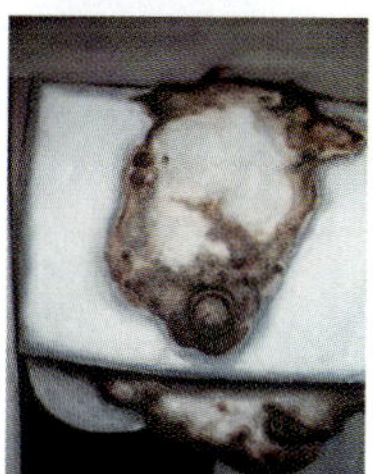

EARTH WAS WITHOUT FORM AND VOID

Oil Collage, 1972, 40 x 26

This piece conceives of creation as chaotic and convulsive sequences of events in which amoebic forms of matter take shape, floating in the vast expanse and suspended by great power.

HEAVENS DECLARE THE GLORY OF GOD

Collagraph, 1981, 23 x 12

The Psalmist tells us that by their very presence the heavens communicate an inaudible speech and offer universal praise. The sky section in this collagraph includes all of Psalm 19 in Hebrew, its overall pattern suggesting movement in the heavens.

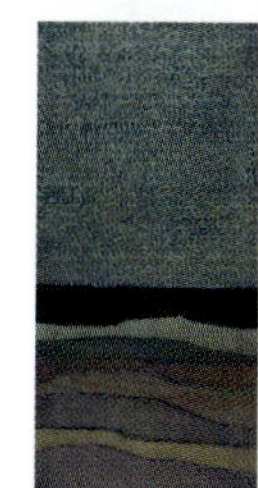

HURLED FORTH

Collagraph, 1981,15 7/8 x 20 3/4

Masses of matter are suspended in space only to be hurled forth by the Creator, giving birth to planets, stars and heavenly bodies. Sand, old buttons, and other textural elements were adhered to masonite to create the plate from which this image was printed.

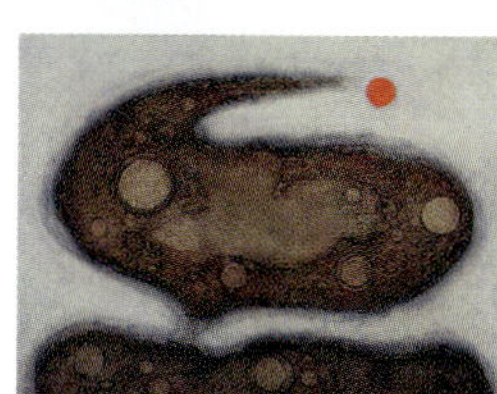

INNER GORGE

Collagraph, 1987, 30 x 22

Time, water and air carve a deep gorge within the canyon walls only to reveal secrets hidden beneath the surface of the earth.

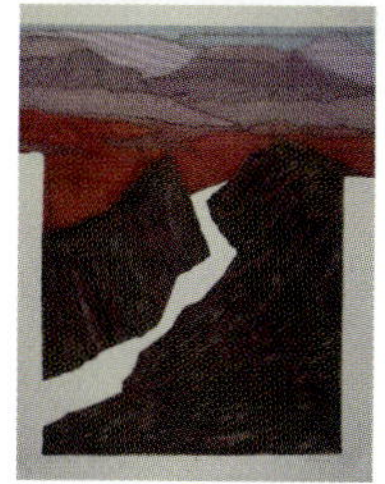

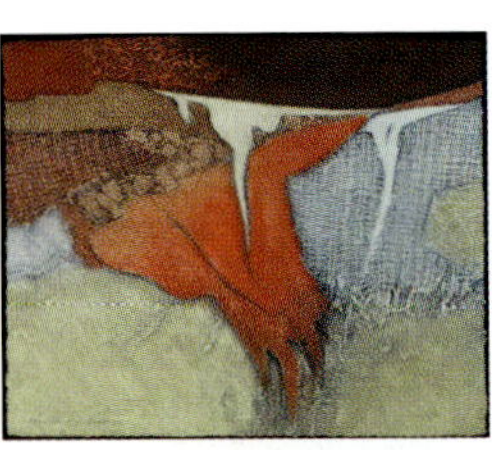

LAVA FLOW
Collagraph, 1981, 20 x 26
The earth convulses as lava flows from its depths creating new geological forms.

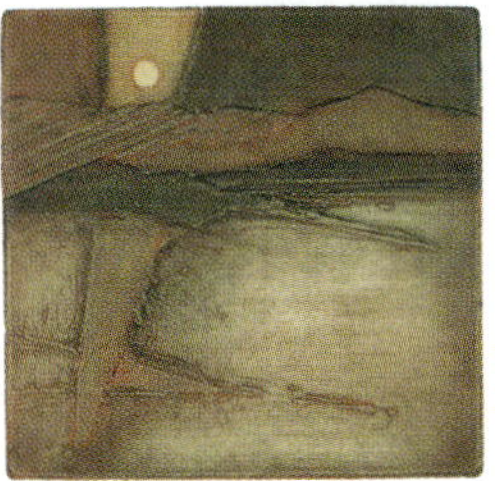

MOON RISING
Collagraph, 1980, 16 x 16
Just over the horizon of the night landscape a moon quietly comes into view.

Archaeological Findings

Biblical archaeology strongly influenced my work for many years. In the early 1980s I studied biblical archaeology at SUNY-Albany, and the *Tel Suite* was a direct result of that course and trips to Israel. I have come to think of myself as a perpetual student, but not a scholar. Rather than write a paper on the research and findings, my way of responding is to create a series of pieces that document my investigations.

I am particularly interested in how the archaeologist digs through many layers of earth, uncovers strata of centuries, then draws interesting and meaningful conclusions from the fragments. Many of my works include references to archaeological finds, tel sites (ancient archaeological mounds), and specific artifacts, combining images and overlapping ideas to suggest connection and continuity.

The *Tel Suite* and others in this series were created using a twentieth-century printing technique called *collagraph*. A collagraph is an intaglio printing process, which uses a collaged plate built up with a great variety of materials (strips of fabric, thread, aluminum foils, plants, marble dust, acrylic modeling paste) that are glued onto the surface of Masonite or cardboard. The surface is then painted or inked and run through an etching press at several thousand pounds of pressure, thereby transferring the paint and the texture to the surface of the paper. In order to create another print in an edition, the process is completely repeated.

The *Walls* assemblages included in this section are a more abstract response to the beautiful walled cities of antiquity. The subtle tones reflect the nuanced colors of the night as the dim light allows gradations of value too limited for the human eye to differentiate. Quiet shadows are cast from the raised squares applied to the richly surfaced background paper.

FORTRESS FINDS
Collagraph, 1983, 30 x 22
This collagraph depicts an ancient desert fortress, perhaps Masada. Numerous archeological artifacts are buried within the site. The central rectangle contains a text from Psalms similar to those found in a synagogue at Masada.

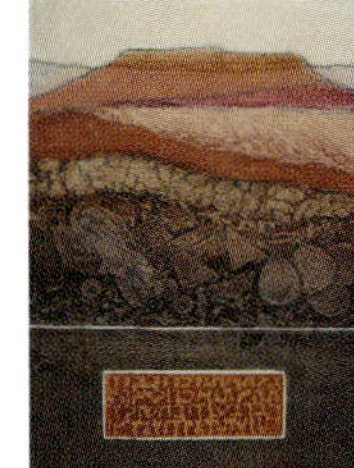

MASADA II
Collagraph, 1984, 30 x 22
This collagraph contains a present day view of Masada looking east toward the Dead Sea. For three years Masada was a literal fortress for the Jewish Zealots fleeing Roman rule in 70 AD. Projecting from the tel itself is the Roman ramp constructed to capture the defense. In the foreground, layered beneath the fortress are suggestions of various important archaeological artifacts

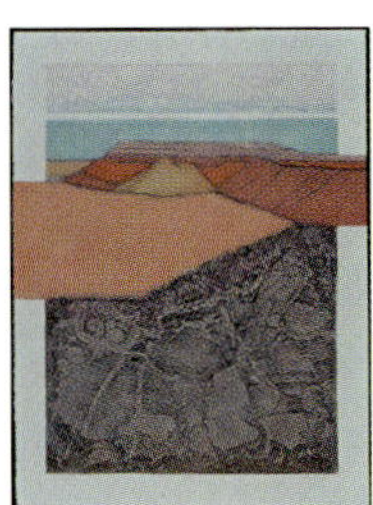

from this site; a straw basket, ostraca, scroll fragments, a sandal and stones that the Jews used to defend themselves.

Tel Suite

The Israelite *Tel Suite* is a collection of four intaglio collagraphs depicting important archaeological sites relating to biblical Israel. A tel is a mound covering the site of some ancient settlement, generally consisting of many layers of rubble and artifacts left by succeeding civilizations. Strata accentuated by horizontal lines divide the picture into three levels, forming a cross section of archeological time. In the Israelite *Tel Suite,* I bring together earth and time, incorporating the present landscape of each site, some finds embedded in a strata, and, centered in each piece, a significant specific object relating to the tels history. Each is a limited edition of one hundred with fifteen artist's proofs, printed on Arches Buff, 100% rag paper.

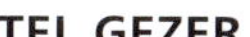

TEL GEZER
Collagraph, 1983, 30 x 22

Gezer was an important Canaanite city strategically located between Egypt and Assyria during biblical times. The city was included in the dowry King Solomon received from one of his wives. Excavations uncovered a boundary inscription that identified the city's name. Burial sites were found which included pottery, plates and jars, even though this custom was forbidden by the Torah. Centered within the collagraph, the Gezer Calendar, which dates to about 950 BC, is an agricultural calendar listing the months of harvest, in gathering and planting.

TEL HAZOR
Collagraph, 1983, 30 x 22

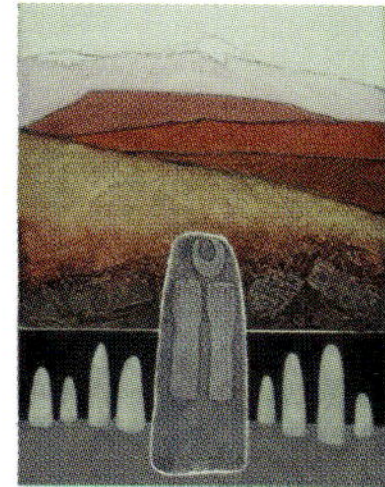

Hazor was a large Canaanite and Israelite city in Northern Galilee near Mount Hermon. The Bible refers to Hazor in the time of Joshua's battles. A Canaanite sanctuary was found in the lower city of Hazor that contained a number of basalt pillars, one with two hands raised toward a divine lunar symbol of a crescent moon and circle.

TEL LACHISH
Collagraph, 1983, 30 x 22

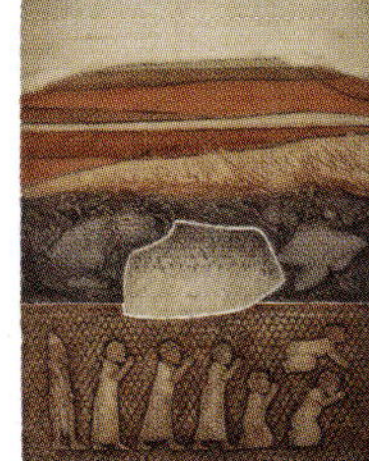

Lachish was a prominent Israelite city southwest of Jerusalem. Its significant finds include ostraca of great interest for linguistic research of ancient Hebrew because it is written in a cursive script, the most developed form of Paleo-Hebrew. The lower section of the print is a portion of a mural found at Nineveh depicting the Israelites being marched into captivity by King Sennacherib.

TEL MEGIDDO
Collagraph, 1983, 30 x 22

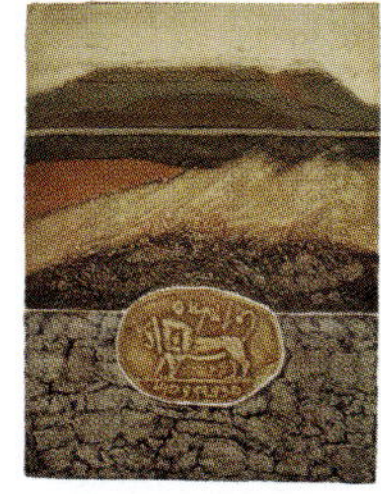

Megiddo was an ancient tel in the lush Jezreel Valley of upper Israel which has been excavated, uncovering twenty or more layers of civilization. James Mitchener's book *The Source* was inspired from the finds at this site. The most famous artifact from this tel is this lion seal, with the Hebrew inscription, "Belonging to Shema, servant of Jeroboam." The stonewall is a section of the Solomonic gate of the Israelite city.

THREE PROPHETS: ISAIAH, JEREMIAH, EZEKIEL

Collagraph, 1986, Three 26 x 20 panels

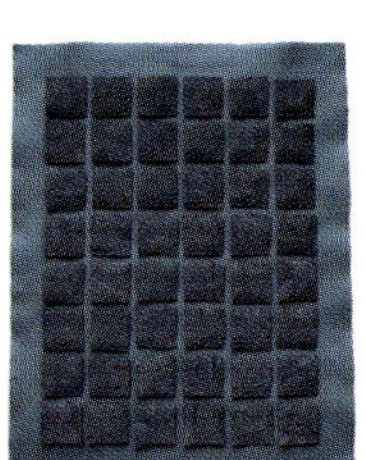

This triptych alludes through the use of color to three Old Testament prophets and their relationship to the cities they inhabited by focusing on their walls. Raised from the surface of the dark paper are small segments of ancient biblical walls: Isaiah's wall of the golden city of Jerusalem (shown); Jeremiah, the weeping prophet's wall of Jerusalem on fire; and Ezekiel's wall of Babylon with the intense ceramic blue which adorned its city's entrance.

MIDNIGHT WALL

Collagraph assemblage, 1986, 30 x 22

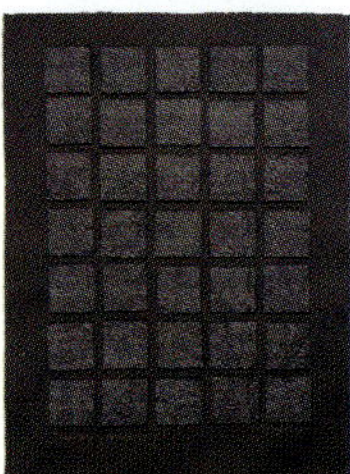

This piece is part of a series on ancient walls of biblical cities. The individual segments of the print are raised so as to cast shadows, suggesting the midnight atmospheric colors of a walled city.

NIGHT WALL

Collagraph assemblage, 1986, 26 x 20

In this collage assemblage the darkness of the night's blue stone panels cast their shadow against a black background of heavily textured paper.

WALLS OF STONE

Collagraph assemblage, 1986, 30 x 22

Walls of Stone reflects the beauty of one stone layered upon another as it builds the ancient city wall.

Texts

From the early 1970s the biblical text itself dominated my iconography. In these early pieces I used the written word as image, veiling the text by creating an overall pattern from the compacted writing and using a script similar to that of the Dead Sea Scrolls. The precise text is embedded in the block, but is nearly impossible to decipher—hiding, yet revealing.

Many times an embossed white border with more Hebrew or Greek lettering frames an interior panel of images or ancient script. This concept is taken from the Jewish *Midrash*, which is based on a Hebrew word meaning "interpretation" or "exegesis." *Midrash* can take the form of Hebrew commentary where the main text discussed is in the center of the page, surrounded by scripture that sheds light on the passage, with additional commentaries from other great thinkers. *He Spake and It Was Done* alludes to the biblical proposition that creation itself was accomplished by the power of the word of God, who spoke the universe into existence. The center section contains the first chapter of Genesis and is surrounded with a passage from Psalms that comments on creation. The idea of *Midrash* is that David and Moses are in conversation. This insight contains the very essence of my work—a conversation across time.

The first pure text piece, *In the Beginning* was a painting done in 1973, and later translated into a collagraph (1978). Since that time the text block has had a recurring presence in my work, even in the most recent artist's books, *Aureola I & II*. Artists have a way of recycling ideas over the years, using them again with new insights and imagination.

I have come to understand that language, the text, the Bible, are not meant to totally unveil the mysteries of God. When this happens, dogma, systematic theology and judgmental attitudes surface, and they destroy the very beauty and meaning of the Word. Language when used with poetry and imagination can be the instrument that takes us deeper into those mysteries.

BY THE WORD OF THE LORD WERE THE HEAVENS MADE

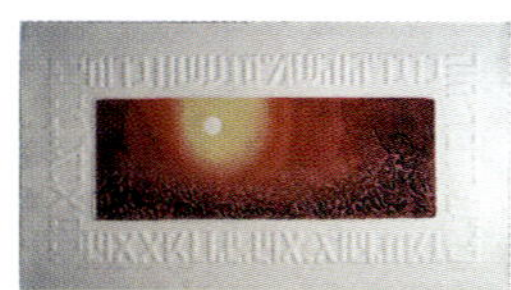

Collagraph with embossing, 1980, 18 x 30
The embossed Hebrew text from Psalm 33, "By the word of the Lord were the heavens made . . . . He commanded and it stood fast," surrounds the inner collagraph of another Hebrew passage from the creation story in Genesis 1, "In the beginning God created." These two texts record the exchange or conversation between Moses and David as they discuss the creation of the world.

GOD CREATED

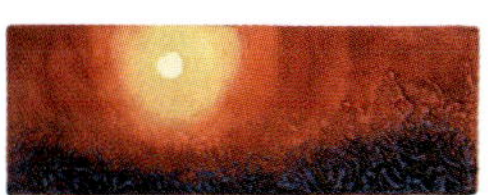

Collagraph, 1980, 7 3/4 x 21
God Created includes the creation story, written in Hebrew, but distorted by the heat and power of creation as expressed in the first chapter of Genesis, "The spirit of God moved upon the face of the deep."

HE SPAKE AND IT WAS DONE

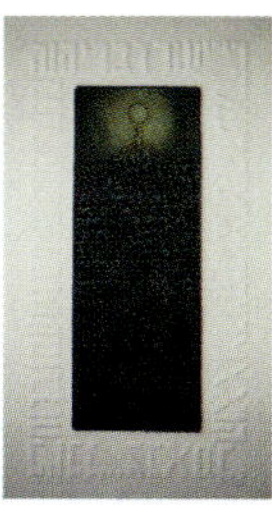

Collagraph with embossing, 1979, 30 x 18
A Hebrew commentary traditionally has the main text written in the center of the page, surrounded by other scripture that sheds light on the passage and commentaries by other great thinkers. This Jewish concept perceives of the various writers in conversation with one another. The central pas-sage of this print is the Genesis story that begins with "In the beginning God created." This text is surrounded with the words of David addressing creation, "by the word of the Lord were the heavens made . . .. He commanded and it stood fast, He spake and it was done" (Psalm 33). The ancients considered David and Moses in conversation.

IN THE BEGINNING

Collagraph, 1978, 21 x 8
The first chapter of Genesis written in a Dead Sea Scroll script becomes both the text and image of this collagraph. Two Hebrew words from the first verse of Genesis, "God created," rise from the center of the first line of text to form a celestial body.

IN THE BEGINNING WAS THE WORD

Collagraph and embossing, 1982, 30 x 18
This piece portrays an exchange between the Old and New Testaments. The Hebrew text, "In the beginning God created," begins the first chapter of Genesis and is the central focus of this print. A Greek embossing surrounds the Hebrew with "In the beginning was the Word . . . the Word became flesh and dwelt among us" (John 1:1, 14).

LAW AND GOSPEL

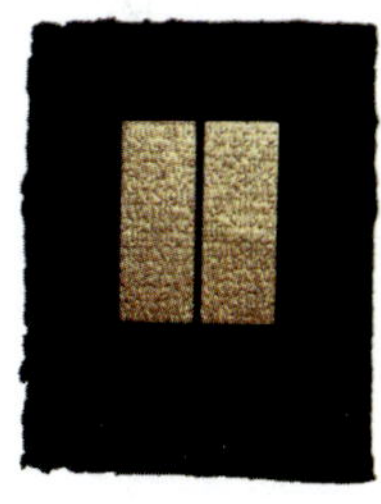

Collagraph mixed media (white background), 1994, Two 18 x 14 panels
Collagraph mixed media (black background), 1994, Two 26 x 18 panels (*Law* shown)
The Gospel builds upon the Law, their relation-ship deeply intertwined. With one additional horizontal cut, the tablets of the Law become four quadrants, suggesting a cross. Jesus said he came to fulfill the Law. When we have finished an item on our list of things to do, we put a line

through it, marking it done. This is what I was thinking as I took the Law, marked it done with a horizontal line, only to see a cross appear.

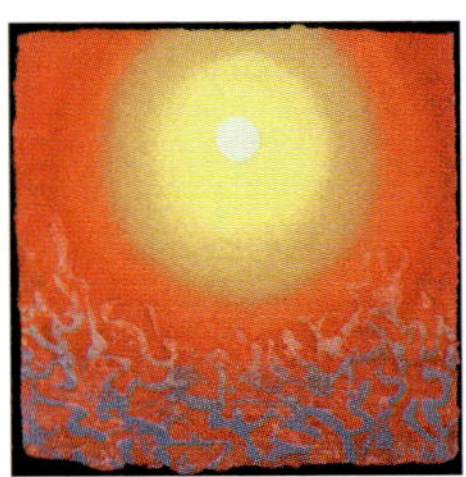

LIGHT
Collagraph, 1982, 10 x 10
In order to convey the power of creation, perceived as heat and light, the text of Genesis creation story has been highly distorted to reflect that movement.

Colors

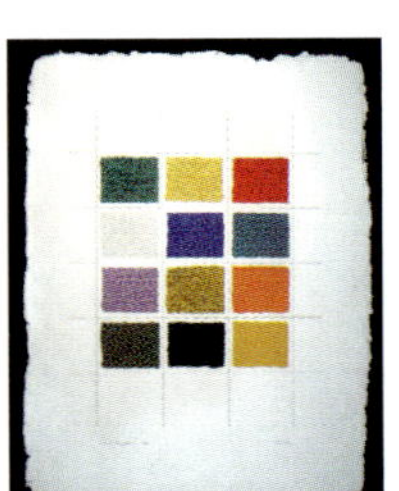

AARON'S BREASTPLATE
Collagraph assemblage, 1983, 40 x 30
The Scriptures have many allusions to garments. Exodus describes Aaron's priestly garments in elaborate detail, one translation reading that they were "for beauty and for glory." He wore a breastplate inset with twelve stones inscribed with the names of the twelve tribes of Israel. In this piece, not only are the names inscribed in the Hebrew, but the Genesis text that recounts the story of Jacob blessing his twelve sons is written into the individual collagraphs attached to the background paper. The breastplate was worn as Aaron entered the Holy of Holies, symbolically carrying the nation of Israel into the presence of God. For Christians it is also a symbol of Christ, the High Priest, who ushers His people into the presence of God.

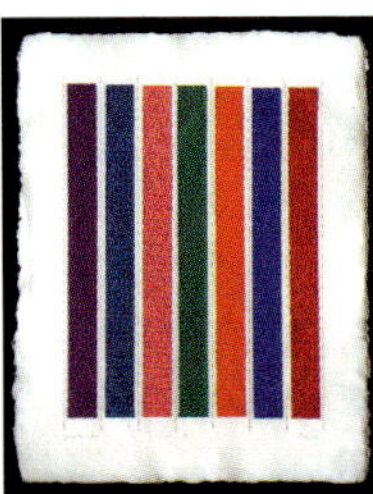

JOSEPH'S COAT
Collagraph, 1984, 40 x 30
The mere mention of Joseph's coat has for centuries suggested a garment of brightly colored stripes, even though a better translation might be a "highly embellished garment." Therefore, *Joseph's Coat*, one in a series of three Old Testament Color Images, has vertical bands of bright colored Hebrew text, containing the narrative of Joseph and his brothers. Graphite vertical lines drawn onto heavy white paper provide a setting for the color panels.

PROMISE
Collagraph assemblage, 1983, 40 x 30
The rainbow has been a symbol of hope for centuries, giving evidence in technicolor of God's eternal promises. The story of Noah was first written in ancient Hebrew on a plate, segmented and painted the colors of the rainbow, then individually attached to the background paper and set within horizontal graphic lines.

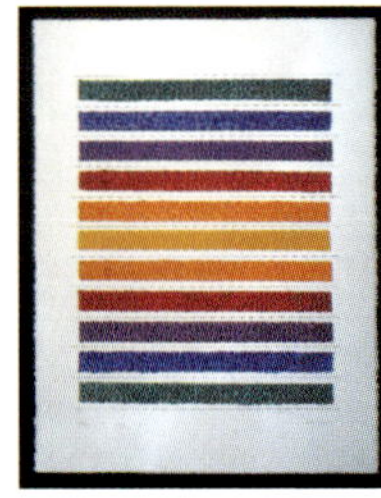

TEN COMMANDMENTS
Collagraph mixed media (two separate editions, one on white and one on black paper), 30 x 22, 2003
The *Ten Commandments* were constructed of ten gilded collagraph sheaves floating above the surface of the paper. The entire Decalogue was written on a Masonite plate, printed on an etching press in a sienna color on a heavy paper, then gilded and surfaced with iridescent craypas to give a luminous quality to the image.

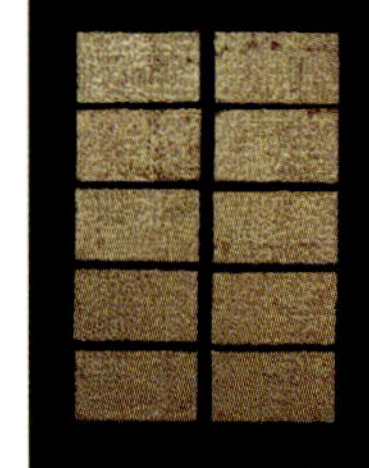

TWELVE TRIBES
Collagraph assemblage, 1987, 19 x 13
This small black assemblage contains twelve separately applied collagraphs that represent the twelve stones on Aaron's breastplate.

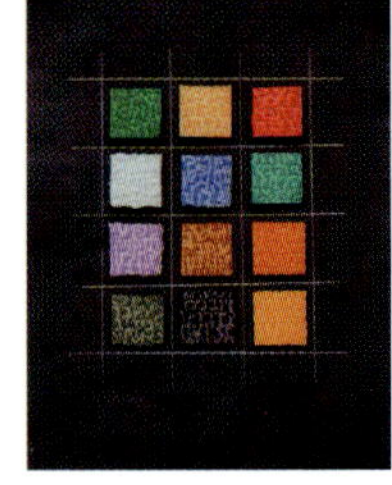

Crucifixions

The crucifixion is central to Christianity, a crossroad of history. Its power has compelled artists for centuries to contemplate its meaning. It is my hope that these crucifixion pieces add to that conversation and build upon what has been voiced in previous generations.

How is it that a crucifixion finds its way into the body of work by an artist whose entire *oeuvre* is dedicated to text and words? My theology informs my understanding of word. The New Testament Book of John portrays Christ as the "Word made Flesh," providing the link to understanding the mystery of the Word as Image.

For me one of the most powerful crucifixion images in all of art history has been Grünewald's *Isenheim Altarpiece,* even though there are other images that have carried weight in my work. This piece heavily influenced my collage oil crucifixion paintings of the early 1970s. Each crucifixion painting included a dimensional crown of thorns created by embedding old floor nails into gesso and modeling paste.

The encounter during my 1997 trip to Italy with the crucifixes that hung above the altars of early Italian churches made a lasting impression. These magnificently beautiful structures prompted an entire body of work. In these pieces I have very carefully used the exact proportions of the cross form, transferring it to paper, painting a burnt sienna underlayment, then gilding the surface, finally adding line to suggest the Body of Christ and the delicate patterns in these crucifixes. My purpose in doing this series was to cast these early and beautifully shaped crosses as a kind of contemporary icon, because in fact, they had their roots in early icons.

The story of the conversion of St. Francis of Assisi in front of a cross-shaped icon that hung above the altar in Assisi moved me deeply. In response to this experience St. Francis wrote:

All Highest, Glorious God, cast your light into the darkness of my heart. Give me right faith, firm hope, perfect charity, and profound humility, with wisdom and perception. O Lord, so that I may do what is truly Your most holy will. Amen.

Coming from a religious tradition where only the spoken or written word was recognized to be a means of grace, I was struck by the power of the image to reveal God—a very reassuring confirmation for a visual artist.

CRUCIFIXION
Oil collage, 1972, 40 x 48

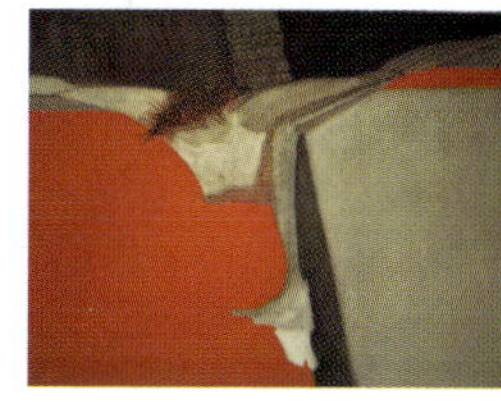

Painted in 1972, this is one of my first artistic encounters with painting the crucifixion. The crown of thorns was made of old floor nails embedded into modeling paste, allowing the texture and raised surface to contrast the intense red flat areas. A cavity in the torso was used as a way of expressing the theology of Christ emptying Himself. We have a saying in English, "I am starved. I can feel my stomach touching my backbone." This seemed a fittingly descriptive way of visualizing this 'kenosis' or Christ's emptying of Himself.

CRUCIFIXION WITH CROSS OF MAITREDE DE SAN FRANCESCO [AFTER UNKNOWN ARTIST?] Acrylic mixed media, 1992, 24 x 18

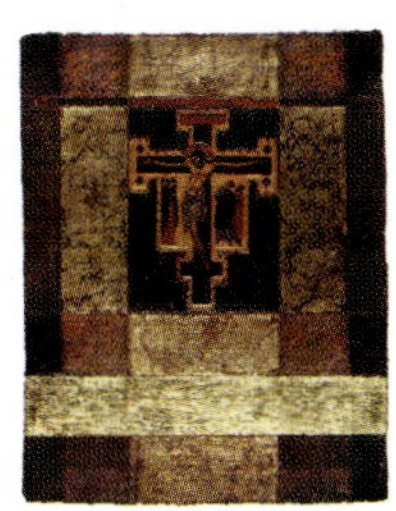

A thirteenth-century crucifixion by Italian painter Maitrede de San Francisco is the centerpiece for this rich mixed-media painting. Many layers of gold and variegated leafing have been worked into the surface and rubbed away, with other layers of paint, crayon, and pencil added again.

HEAD OF CHRIST
Oil collage, 1976, 30 x 36
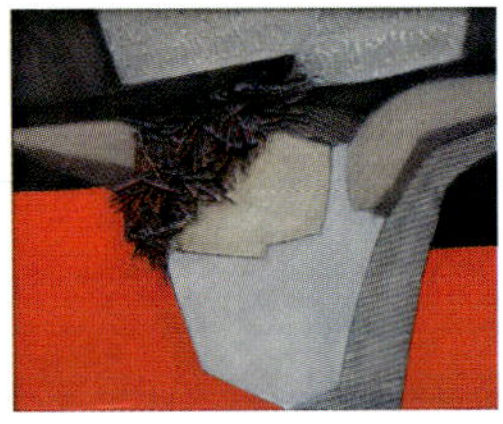
Old floor nails, embedded onto the surface of the canvas, create the crown of thorns placed on the head of Christ and give strong textural interest to this close encounter with the crucified Christ.

HE WAS WOUNDED FOR OUR TRANSGRESSIONS
Collagraph mixed media, 1992, 30 x 22
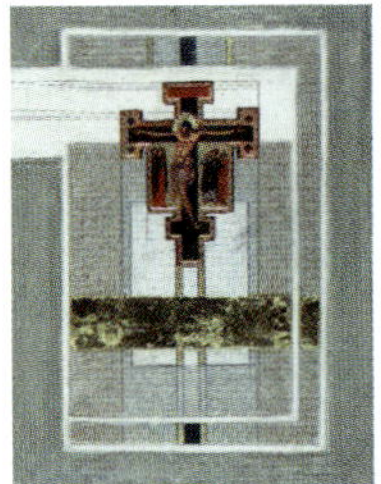
A reworked photo of a fourteenth-century crucifixion by Italian painter Maitrede de San Francesco is the centerpiece for this mixed-media collagraph. The entire text of Isaiah 53 has been handwritten on the print's surface surrounding the crucifixion image. Beneath the cross is a facsimile of the *Sanctus*, from Benjamin Britten's *War Requiem*, written for the rededication of Coventry Cathedral. These various elements give associations that invite the viewer to contemplate the Holy.

IT IS FINISHED
Oil collage (shown) and drawing, 1976, 48 x 36
Collagraph with acrylic painting, 1980, 16 3/4 x 23
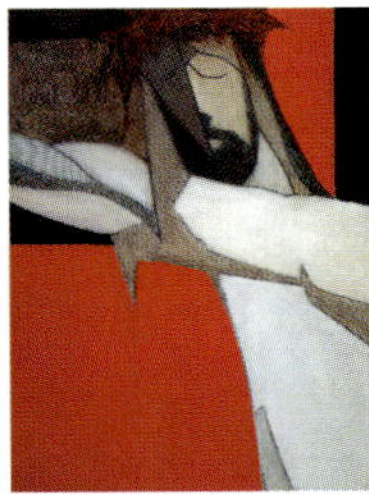
The crucifixion event has compelled artists for centuries to contemplate its meaning. The inscription above Christ's head reads, "Jesus of Nazareth, King of the Jews," written in Hebrew, Greek and Latin. Layers of fabric and other materials provide the surface texture. The crown of thorns has been constructed using old floor nails. The abstracted

forms speak to the brokenness Christ endured as a means to restore humanity to wholeness. Contained within the torso is a large arrow shape, thrusting itself into a flat broad area of red.

IT IS FINISHED II
Oil collage and drawing, 1976, 48 x 36
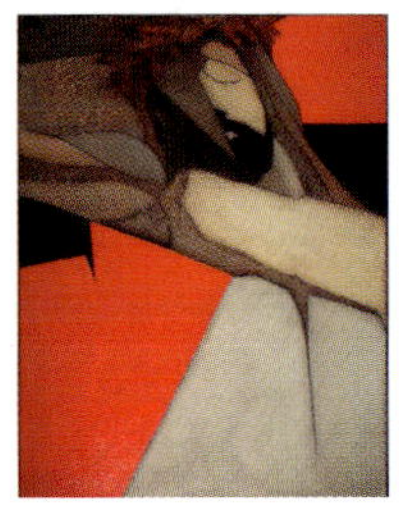
This version of the Crucifixion has the arrow thrusting from the large red expanse into the side of the body, causing a kind of kickback motion in the torso. The Hebrew, Greek and Latin text, "Jesus of Nazareth, King of the Jews," was placed above the head of Christ by Pilate. Scholars tell us that the order of the texts would have probably been Latin, Greek and then Hebrew to accommodate the political powers, but Scripture listed the text in an order that flowed from the historical sequence of God's presence among his people.

JESUS OF NAZARETH
Oil collage, 1976, 48 x 48
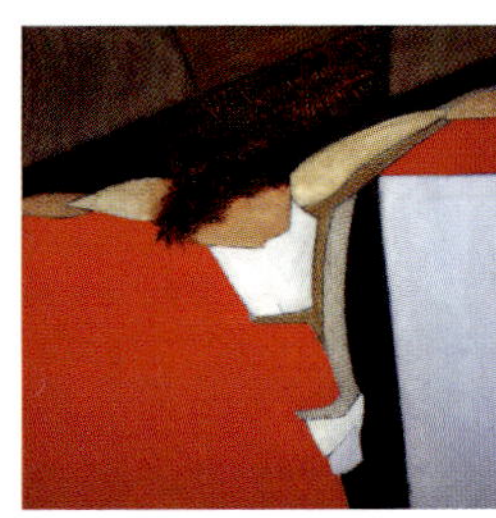
Another crucifixion image from this series, entitled *Jesus of Nazareth*, uses an angular working of the forms and positions the viewer slightly above the dead Christ. The sign is prominently placed above the head of Jesus, and the hollowed-out abdomen area creates a strong tension in the silhouette of the corpus against the intense red background. Antique floor nails were built up to form the crown of thorns creating further visual tension in the piece.

LAST SUPPER
Oil collage, 1976, 40 x 60
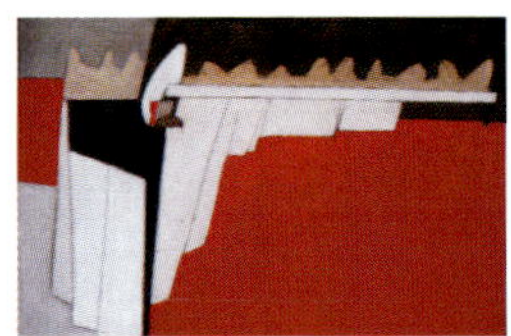
Leonardo da Vinci's *Last Supper* has influenced Western art history's interpretation of the meal shared with His disciples before His crucifixion.

This early painting demonstrates that influence, as it places the thirteen figures seated at a long table with Christ holding the chalice as he offers his friends bread and wine, His Body and His Blood.

PSALM XXIII

Acrylic mixed media, 1988, 26 x 18
Collagraph mixed media, 1990, 30 x 22
The Shepherd Psalm has been a cherished image for Christians throughout the centuries. This piece incorporates the Hebrew text from Psalm 23, the title page of Leonard Bernstein's *Psalm XXIII*, written for the Chichester Cathedral in England, and an early Christian sculpture of the Good Shepherd with the lost sheep.

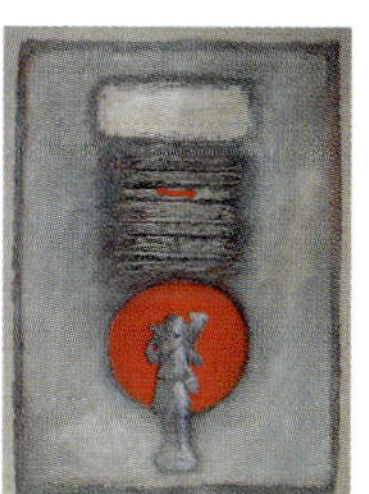

SANCTUS

Acrylic mixed media, 1988, 36 x 26
The *Sanctus* from Benjamin Britten's *War Requiem*, written for the dedication of Coventry Cathedral, and a twelfth-century German crucifixion form a kind of antiphon within this work which is a companion to Psalm XXIII.

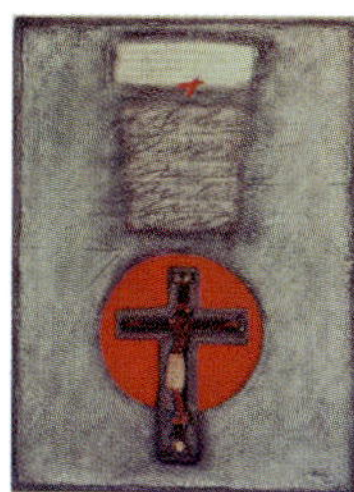

SANCTUS

Collagraph mixed media, 1990, 30 x 22
This mixed media acrylic painting incorporates several collaged elements: the *Sanctus* from Benjamin Britten's *War Requiem*, written for the dedication of Coventry Cathedral; the text from Revelation 4, "Holy, Holy, Holy, is the Lord God Almighty;" and a twelfth century German crucifixion.

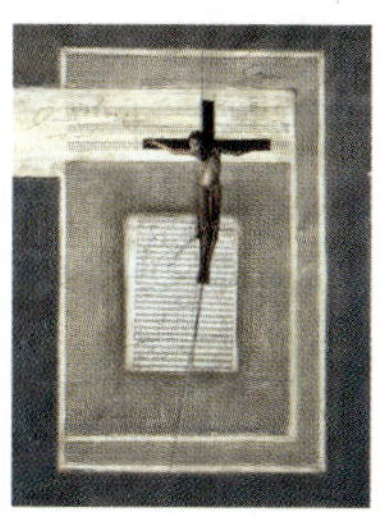

SEVEN LAST WORDS

Collagraph mixed media, 1990, 20 x 20
Seven Last Words was commissioned by the choir of St. Sophia Greek Orthodox Church in Albany, New York. It includes a Greek icon of the crucifixion, Christ the Pantokrator from the Hagia Sophia in Istanbul, the seven last words of Jesus written in Greek and surrounding the cross form, and a musical score entitled *Crucifixion*, written by their choirmaster and used in the Good Friday service of St. Sophia for over twenty-five years.

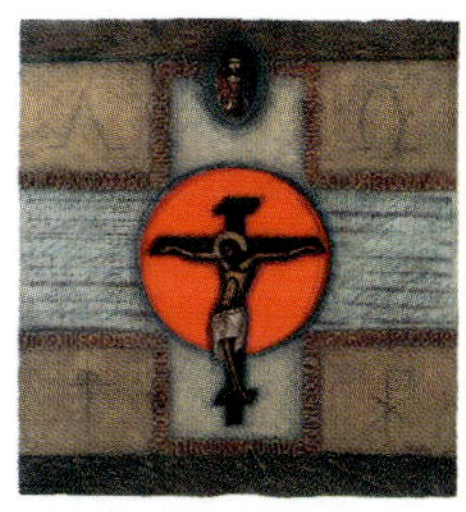

Illuminations

Scribes and illuminators have preserved the written word with devotion, love and care. Over the centuries many different approaches were devised to record and embellish important text. Many manuscripts were elaborately decorated with painted elements, gilded surfaces and great imagination. Their beauty inspired my *Illuminations*.

In 1990 I was invited to participate in an exhibition at Emma Willard School in Troy, NY, entitled *4 x 12 x 12*, a show that restricted the size of each piece. In reflecting on the illuminations and stunning medieval paintings that I had seen in my trips to Europe, I launched a new series. I can remember the excitement of creating the first few illumination pieces for this show, discovering how to transform the paper into a luminescent surface reminiscent of ancient and medieval illuminations.

Various early Gregorian chant facsimiles, Bible pages, or other documents are barely visible beneath the layers of glazes. I have used iridescent paint and oil crayons, as well as a variety of gold, silver and multicolored foils, to give these pieces a surface richness.

Perhaps the works most directly reflective of the medieval manuscripts are the small acrylic paintings that have panels or columns, sometimes surfaced with suggestions of writing, other times left blank. They not only remind us of ancient scrolls or illuminations, but their deeply textured surfaces recall the appearance of stone, blending several of my interests into the work.

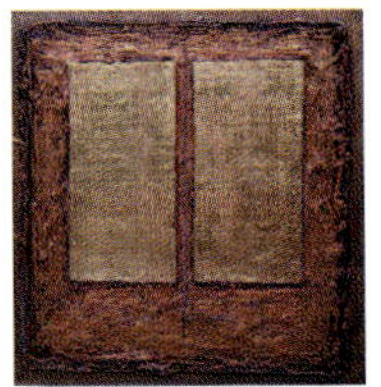

AND THERE WAS LIGHT
Acrylic mixed media, 1992, 18 x 17
The words from first chapter of Genesis, "And there was light," are inscribed into the surface of the gold leafing, as if onto an illuminated page. Light and word become connected.

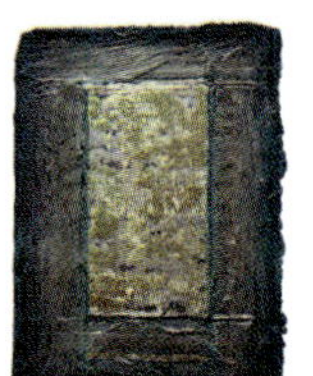

CODE I
Acrylic mixed media, 1993, 6 1/2 x 3 1/2
Gold leafing and layered text hint of medieval manuscripts and illuminations. Suggestions of a Hebrew psalm text are barely visible beneath the layers of gold, inviting contemplation of the Holy.

CODE II
Acrylic mixed media, 1993, 6 1/2 x 3 1/2
Horizontal striations of thick impasto, metallic acrylic paint, oil crayons and pencil were used to create the richly surfaced painting that brings to mind a written manuscript.

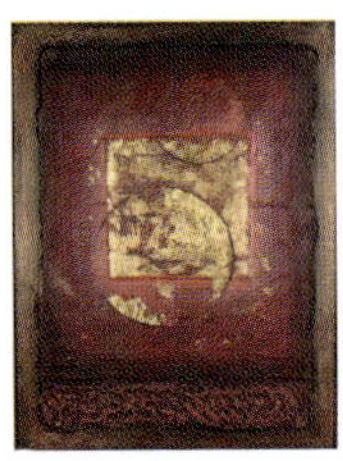

HIDDEN WORLDS I, II (shown), III
Acrylic and gold leaf, 1993, 16 x 12
Circles suggesting the earth and inscriptions etched on the surface of the painting hint to worlds only imperfectly revealed—seen in part.

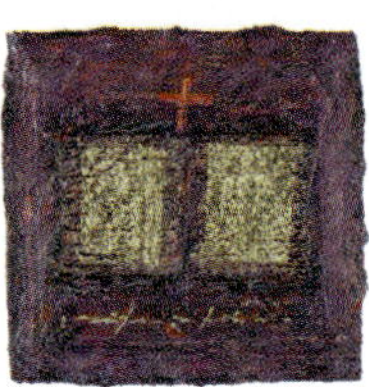

ILLUMINATION III
Acrylic mixed media, 1990, 10 x 10
Throughout the centuries scribes and calligraphers have used numerous artistic approaches to record the Word. *Illuminations* respond to the beautiful medieval illuminations.

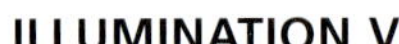

ILLUMINATION VI
Acrylic mixed media, 1990, 26 x 20
A Gregorian chant is barely visible through the broken columns of gold leafing.

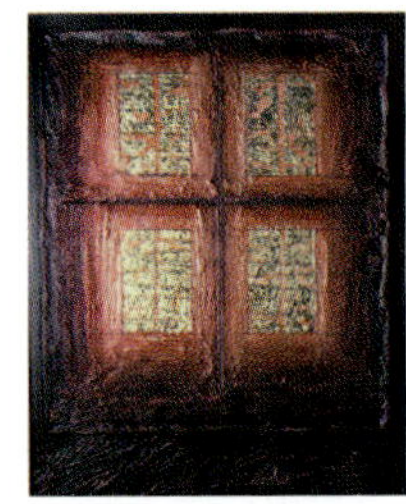

ILLUMINATION XVI
Acrylic mixed media, 1990, 10 x 10
An early score by Michael Praetorius is set beneath the transparent impasto layers of acrylic medium and strips of gold leaf. Metallic acrylic paint, oil crayons and colored pencil were used to create the richly surfaced painting.

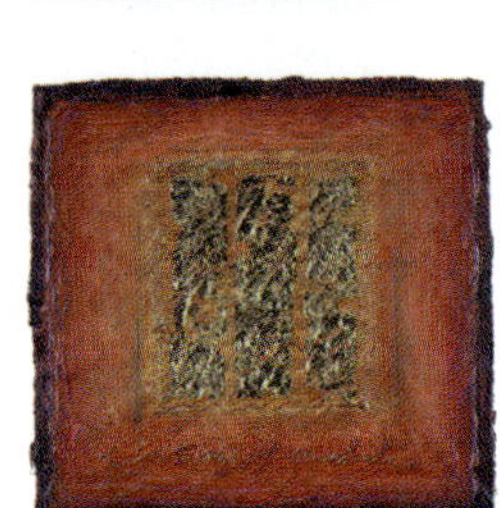

ILLUMINATION XVII
Acrylic mixed media, 1990, 10 x 20
Fragments of Psalm 100 are just visible beneath the layers of gold in each of the three page segments. Gold leafing and layered text hint of medieval manuscripts and illuminations.

ILLUMINATION XXV
Acrylic mixed media, 1993, 26 x 20
Gold leafing and layered text hint of Medieval manuscripts and illuminations. A Hebrew psalm text is hidden beneath the layers of gold in the four quadrants of this cross formation in its visual tribute to medieval book covers.

PAGE
Acrylic mixed media, 1993, 6 1/2 x 4
A simple gold leafed page with suggestions of column guides fills the frame of this small work—awaiting thoughtful inscriptions.

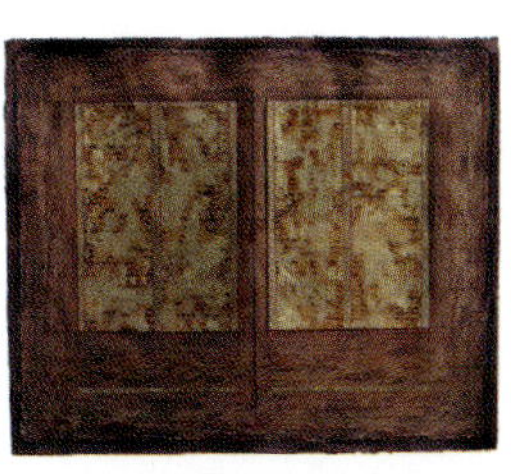

RECORD

Acrylic mixed media, 1993, 28 x 30

Only suggestions of words remain to be deciphered from this ancient record. The richly surfaced painting gives tribute to the long and revered tradition of writing the Scriptures in delicate and beautiful script to preserve its Holy Word.

TEXT

Acrylic mixed media, 1993, 7 1/2 x 6 1/2

Two columns with gilding and incised calligraphic notations are set parallel to each other on a background of rich maroons and violets.

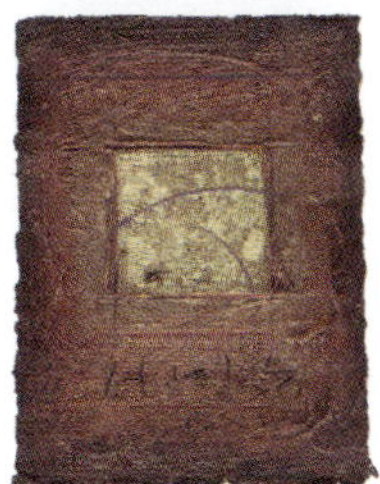

TITLE I

Acrylic mixed media, 1993, 6 1/2 x 4 1/2

Deep colors of iridescent paint have been applied to this little painting which contains a square gold leafed central plate intercepted by an arc.

Music Notations

Knowing that I was interested in manuscripts and ancient languages, a friend gave me several facsimiles of musical scores of the masters. They immediately caught my imagination and I gathered others, only to amass nearly 500 copies. Soon I could recognize various composers' "handwriting" as a kind of language or alphabet. Music is a unique written language that transcends barriers of tongue and time, allowing an orchestra with musicians from all over the world to make harmony via the written score.

More than any other source in Western history, the Scriptures have inspired musicians to compose literally thousands of sacred compositions. In this series, copies of the masters' facsimiles have been juxtaposed onto the picture, along with archaeological artifacts, images from art history and imaginary musical scoring, thus creating another setting for the Word as Image.

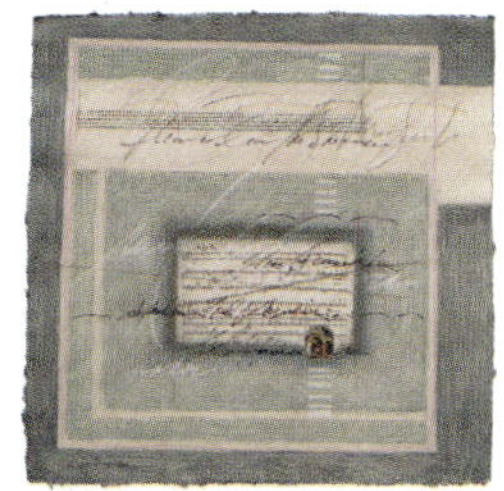

CRADLE SONG

Collagraph mixed media, 1988, 20 x 20

The familiar lullaby of Johannes Brahms, *Lullaby and Good Night,* can easily be read from the facsimile centered on this collagraph. The nativity scene is from a Renaissance painting in the chapel of Santa Maria Novella in Florence.

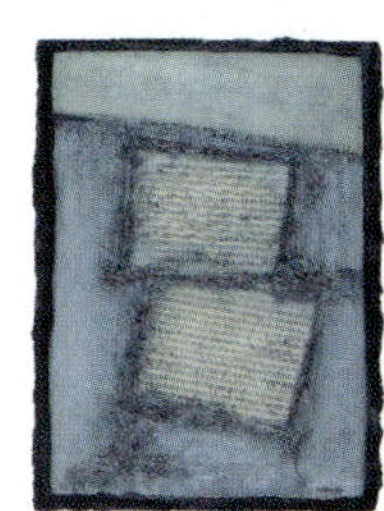

SONATA

Oil Collage, 1987, 30 x 22

Two pages of a piano sonata of Ludwig van Beethoven are layered onto the surface of this collagraph mixed-media print. Beethoven's scores contained many frantically scratched out and reworked portions. The surface graphic work reflects the character of his original manuscripts.

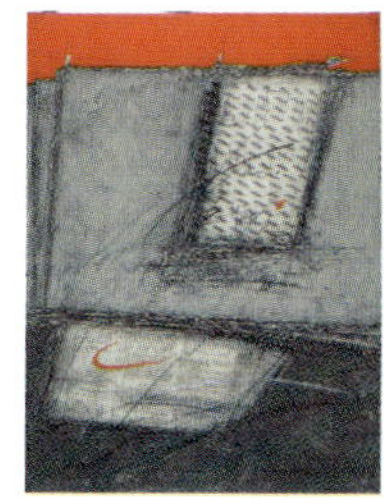

HOLY, HOLY, HOLY (SANCTUS)

Collagraph mixed media, 1990, 30 x 22

The Greek passage from Revelations 4, "Holy, Holy, Holy, is the Lord, God Almighty who was and who is and who is to come," and Benjamin Britten's *Sanctus* exchange voices in this visual antiphon.

Collages

Collages developed while I was recovering from back surgery in 1994. Unable to work in the studio, either painting or using the etching press, I had to find another way to be productive. I began by cutting portions of old collagraphs, reassembling them into new formats on interesting handmade papers. I had become a collector of fine handmade papers and they gave great impetus to the project. *Passage* was the first piece created in this series. This small work became the catalyst for another ten years of exploration.

During this time I had assumed the presidency of Christians in the Visual Arts and had limited time in the studio. Working in collage allowed me the opportunity to continue creating when studio time was limited because of other obligations.

Pages from Bibles written in various languages, dictionaries, and musical scores were collaged to the papers' surface, then layers of Japanese rice papers or other richly textured paper were added. Friends and acquaintances offered Bibles, used hymnals, old books and musical manuscripts for my collection. John Rutter, the English choral composer, sent me copies of some of his scores. Bibles arrived from Cambodia and the Orient, and several people gave me their old Swedish or German Bibles—all for the cause.

Most pieces contain sections of Hebrew text that were initially created as a collagraph, gilded, then finished with a final application of iridescent craypas to give added luminescence to the surface.

There are always connections between the elements included in my work; choosing texts that dialogue with one another, then adding other materials that extend the conversation. To add rich visual interest, in a few of the pieces I have used covers of old leather books that I found in the Paris flea market. Antique coins, letters, pages from diaries or scrapbooks and book title pages have also been applied at various times.

When I reflect on my many years of being an artist, it is evident that collage has consistently been the medium that helps to express the things that intrigued my imagination. The fascination of combining disparate elements, joining them together to give a coherent statement, has offered endless hours of pleasure and enjoyment to my life in the studio.

A READING
Collage mixed media, 2000,
26 x 20

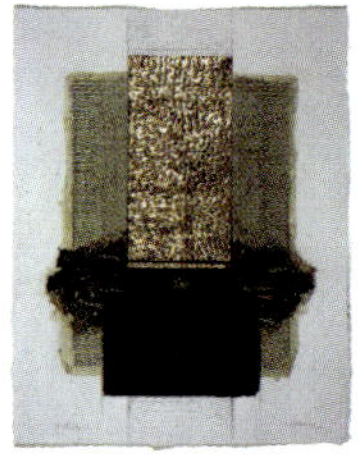

Buried beneath the layers of oriental papers and handwritten passage of the Law are pages from a Hebrew Bible. They contain the story of Ezra reading the Law to the Israelites after their return to Jerusalem from captivity in Babylon. Attached to the surface of the collage is a Jewish coin with the Lion of Judah and a leather cover from an old book with a Star of David scratched into its surface. The central panel of gilded Hebrew text is a portion of the Decalogue. All these elements bring together a conversation that demonstrates the centrality of the Law to the Jewish people.

A TIME TO . . .
Collage mixed media, 1999, 21 x 15

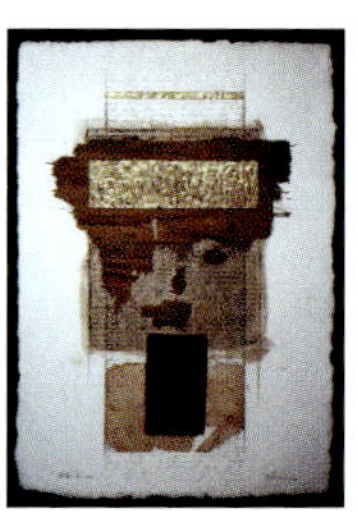

"There is a time for everything, and a season for every activity under the heaven: a time to be born and a time to die, a time to . . .." This passage from Ecclesiastes is nearly hidden beneath layers of Japanese rice papers with the Ten Commandments handwritten in English above all the collage materials. A small segment of gilded Hebrew text floats above the dark bark paper, reminiscent of ancient scrolls. A timeworn leather Bible cover recalls the cherished place such a book had for its owners.

CONCORDANCE

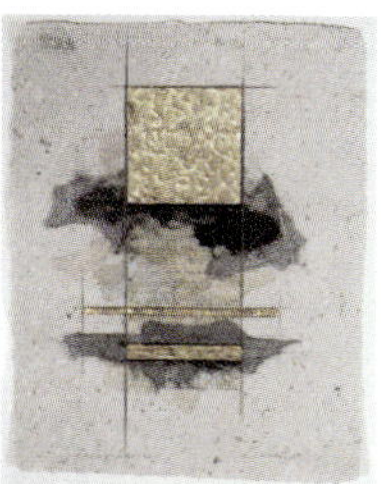

Collage mixed media, 1996, 11 x 8 1/2
A page from an old concordance was adhered to a handmade paper that contains fragments from a mid-nineteenth-century Bible commentary.

CORANTO

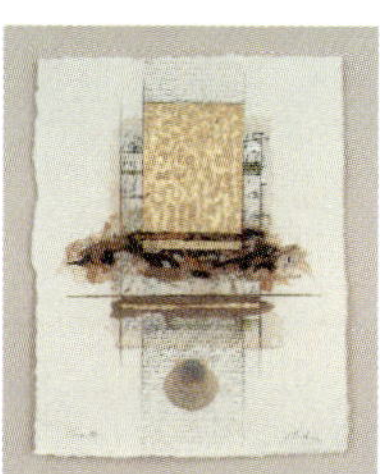

Collage mixed media with gold leafing, 2001, 14 x 11
An early sheet of lute music entitled *Coranto 85* is veiled behind layers of Japanese rice papers. Three panels of gilded Hebrew text are aligned in the middle of the collage resting on top of darker paper fragments. A scallop shell is mounted above the handwritten English text from the sixteenth and seventeenth chapters of Psalms.

FOOTNOTES

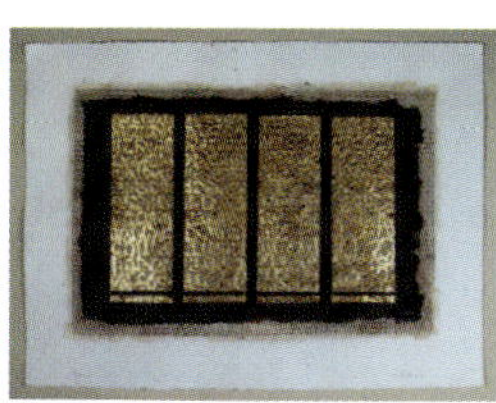

Collage mixed media, 1995, 18 x 24
Four columns of gilded Hebrew text are spread across a heavy rice paper that is superimposed over pages from a Hebrew Bible. Footnotes, or small strips of text, rest beneath each column.

HEAR, O ISRAEL

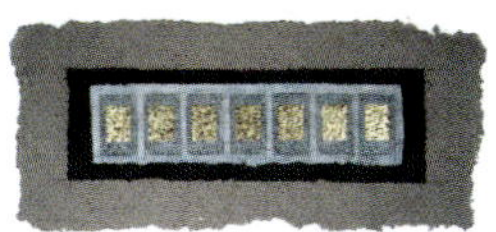

Collage mixed media, 2001, 16 x 33
Deuteronomy 6: 4–9 contains a beloved portion of the Torah known as the Shema, which translated from the Hebrew is, "Hear, O Israel." This passage is posted on the doorways of every Jewish home as an affirmation and a declaration of faith in one God. This collage is constructed on banana paper, and seven gilded Hebrew panels with portions of the Ten Commandments float above a white vellum section that has been built up with transferred portions of the Deuteronomy text. The same passage has been inscribed in English over this transfer. Surrounding the central panels are the words "Hear, O Israel," repeatedly written to echo the words of Moses.

IN THE BEGINNING

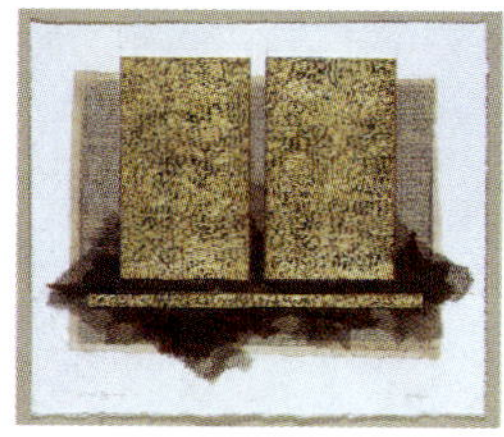

Collage mixed media, 1995, 20 x 26
Beneath the coats of papers are pages from a late-nineteenth-century Dutch Bible that includes the story of creation. Inscribed on the surface is a modern English translation of that text, and the center panels are portions from the Genesis story in a Hebrew gilded text.

LOGOS

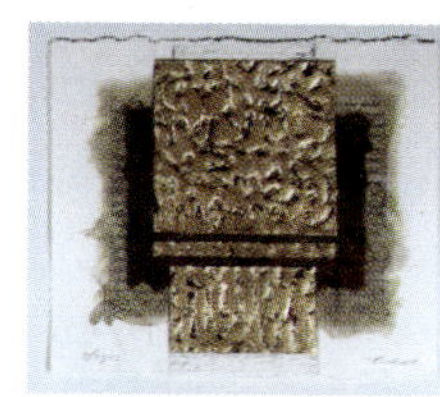

Collage mixed media, 1995, 6 x 8 1/2
A page from an old Greek Bible is layered into this collage, with gilded Hebrew panels centered on the piece.

MEANINGS

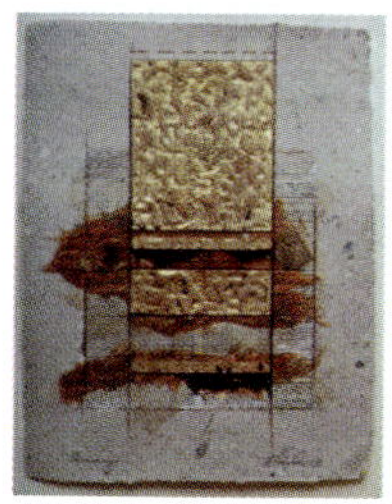

Collage mixed media, 1996, 11 x 8 1/2
Pages from an old English dictionary are layered beneath the collaged surface. The central panels have a portion of the Ten Commandments made by gilding a collagraph of the text. The background paper is handmade and contains fragments from a mid-nineteenth-century Bible commentary. These fragments were embedded into the paper as it was made.

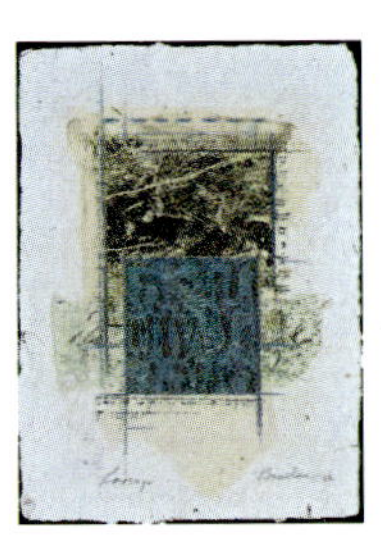

PASSAGE

Collage mixed media, 1994, 8 x 6
This exploratory work was the first in my *Collage* series. Elements combined in this collage include a passage from the book of Numbers, rich oriental papers and a portion of the Ten Commandments.

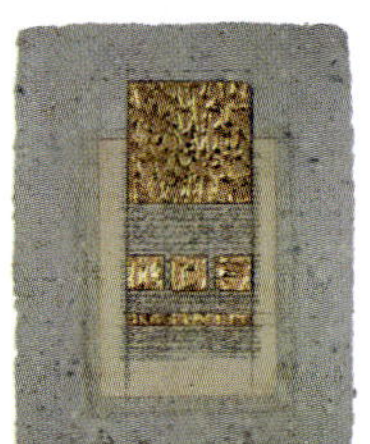

PSALM

Collage mixed media, 1994, 6 1/2 x 7 1/2
Barely visible behind the layers of rice papers is a psalm from a King James Bible. A portion of another Old Testament text is gilded and mounted on the top surface of the collage.

PSALM 150

Collage mixed media, 1996, 11 x 8 1/2
An eloquent expression of joy, Psalm 150 is celebrated in a French hymn from 1568. The gold center panel contains Hebrew calligraphy from the Psalms.

REVELATIONS

Collage mixed media,1997, 11 x 8 1/2
From an old Polish Bible, a page from the Book of Revelation has been adhered to an intriguing handmade paper that contains bits of Bible commentaries dating to the mid-1800s.

SACRED TEXT

Collage mixed media, 1994, 6 1/2 x 7 1/2
A page from the Torah has been layered beneath rice papers and collagraph sections of Hebrew text were surfaced with iridescent craypas.

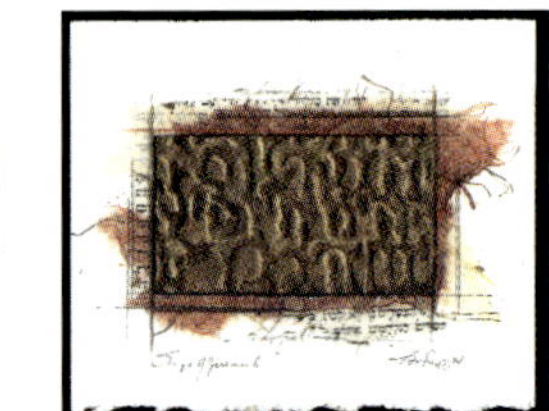

SONG OF JEREMIAH

Collage mixed media, 1994, 6 1/2 x 7 1/2
A passage from the book of Jeremiah is buried beneath the layers of rice paper and overlaid with a collagraph of gilded Hebrew text.

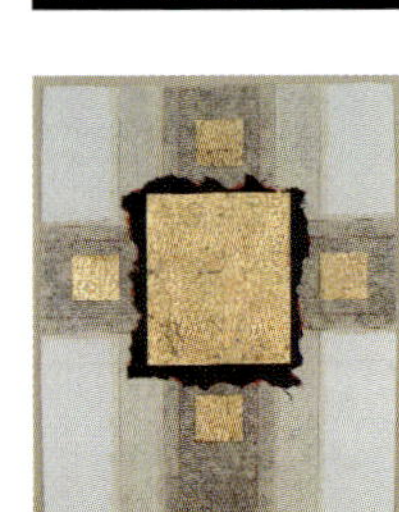

WAS THE WORD

Collage mixed media, 1996, 30 x 22
Pages from a Greek New Testament are visible beneath the many layers of Japanese rice papers. The final gold-leafed Hebrew text gives interest and contrast to the other text elements as it creates the central cross form. Handwritten portions from the first chapter of the Gospel of Saint John are inscribed to the surface of portions of the work.

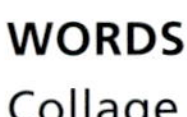

WORDS

Collage mixed media, 1995, 6 1/2 x 7 1/2
A page from an old dictionary lies beneath the layers of rice papers.

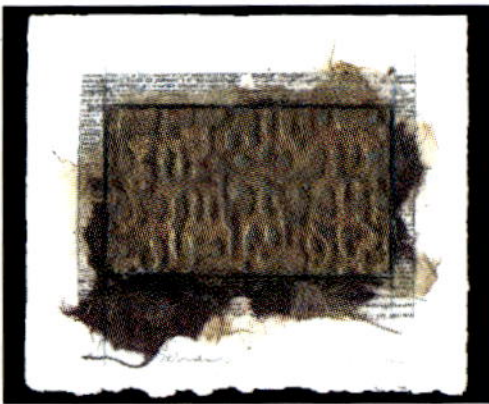

Art History Interpretations

There are many ways to study the great works of art that have illuminated the minds and hearts of many generations: taking a course, reading art books, visiting museums. My love affair with the history of Western art is the result of personal face-to-face encounters with the works in museums, churches and galleries all over Europe and the United States. Their beauty and intrigue have beckoned me to study and meditate on their images and in turn inspired this series of work. Two things have propelled my interest in the great works of art from our Western culture. In 1980, with only the weakest background in art history, I started traveling to Europe and the Middle East, and found that I wanted to have a better understanding and grasp of the unfolding history of the art that had led to the twentieth-century art that I knew. Also, my involvement in Christians in the Visual Arts (CIVA) put me in a place where a solid knowledge of art was a vital necessity. Being around other artists who knew and loved the great works of art only fueled my interest.

However, even with many excursions to Europe, it was not until the 1997 CIVA trip to Italy that this encounter with art history surfaced in my work. We were all encouraged to create a piece of art in response to the trip. I had been overwhelmed with the beauty of the large crosses that hung over the altars of many of the Medieval and Renaissance churches. With the few supplies that I had in my room, I invented a new kind of paper-polychromed drawing. The old saying that "necessity is the mother of invention" certainly proved true in this case. This one piece prompted several years of work that explored the canon of Western art history.

The direct result of this first piece was a traveling exhibition, *Art History 101: Icons of Western Art,* that celebrates the history of art from a little different perspective. Each work is a delicate translation in line and gold, recreating it as an "icon" from the canon of Western Art. Arranged chronologically the chosen paintings and sculptures span nearly 2500 years and represent some of the most beloved works in Western civilization.

Each historical piece is carefully reproduced in silhouette form, painted on Twinrocker May Linen, a feather-deckled handmade paper. A layer of iridescent craypas is added to the painted area and thin sheets of 22-carat German gold leaf are then applied to the surface. Finally, the original image is suggestively drawn using pencil, stylus, etching points, or anything that will incise the somewhat soft layers of gold. Lines extend through and beyond the frame of the piece, giving an almost architectural setting for the work.

ANNUNCIATION AFTER FRA ANGELICO

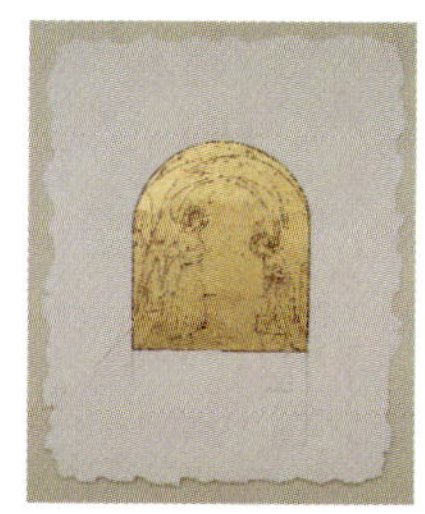

(1387–1455) Mixed media drawing with 22-carat gold leaf, 1997, 21 x 16
Opposite each bed in the cells of the Cloister of San Marco in Florence, Fra Angelico painted a fresco with a scene from the life of Christ that was to be a focus for each monk's contemplation. This tender portrayal of the annunciation is one of Fra Angelico's most loved works.

ANNUNCIATION AFTER SIMONE MARTINI

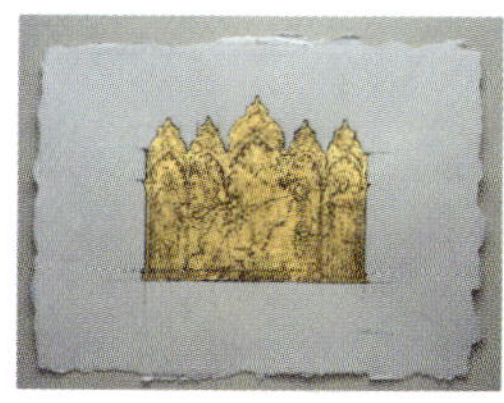

(C. 1284–1344) Mixed media drawing with 22-carat gold leaf, 1997, 16 x 21
The figures of Simone Martini, an influential late Gothic artist of the Sienese school, have a stunning fluidity. They sweep across the scene, dazzlingly beautiful, like some mystical inhabitants both of our world and of heaven. His sense of drama is remarkably present in *The Annunciation,* now in the Uffizi Gallery in Florence. We see Mary shrinking, almost aghast at the solemnity of being asked be the bearer of God's Son, yet even at this moment, Mary moves with the familiar elegance of Martini's figures.

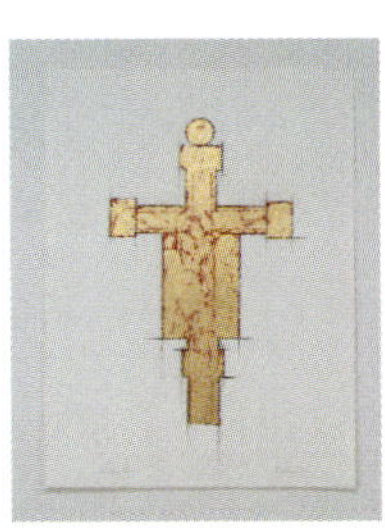

AREZZO CROSS

Mixed media drawing with 22-carat gold leaf, 1997, 14 x 11

This drawing was the first in my *Art History Interpretations* and was a response to the many powerful crucifixes that hung above the altars of the churches in Arezzo, Italy.

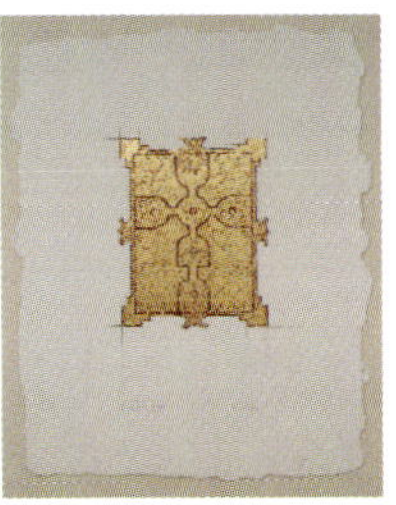

CROSS PAGE FROM LINDISFARNE GOSPELS AFTER UNKNOWN ARTIST (C. 700 A.D.)

Mixed media drawing with 22-carat gold leaf, 1998, 21 x 16

Between 600-800 A.D. Irish Christians founded monasteries that became seats of learning and the arts. Their artistic expression combined the intricate patterns of from ancient Celtic interlaced with early Christian geometric and decorative embellishments. A manuscript containing the Word of God was seen as a sacred object whose visual beauty reflected the importance of its content.

One of the finest of these manuscripts is the *Lindisfarne Gospels. The Cross Page* is an imaginative creation of breathtaking complexity. The miniaturists, working with a jeweler's precision, created a delicate page of astonishing beauty.

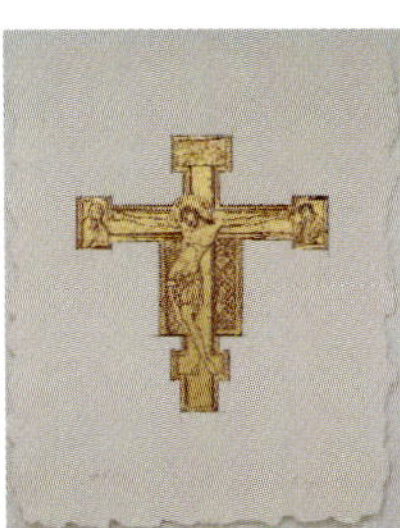

CRUCIFIX AFTER CIMABUE (1240–1302)

Mixed media drawing with 22-carat gold leaf, 1997, 21 x 16

The elegantly long and graceful corpus on this cross from the Basilica of Santa Croce in Florence demonstrates the influence of the Byzantine icon painting. Cimabue's *oeuvre* represented a step forward in the evolution of medieval art as he succeeded in introducing a number of novel elements into the solemn and static Byzantine art.

These innovations included more human expressions and form.

This crucifix was included in the traveling exhibition, *Art History 101: Icons of Western Art*, which celebrated important works from the canon of Western art by echoing their form with gold leaf and sufficient line to reveal the identity of their sources.

CRUCIFIX AFTER GIOTTO DI BONDONE

(1266–1337) Mixed media drawing with 22-carat gold leaf, 1997, 21 x 16

This powerful crucifix, painted around 1300, is attributed to Giotto and graces the Basilica of Santa Maria Novella in Florence. Giotto breathed fresh life into painting and his pieces demonstrate a new physical awareness of the figure.

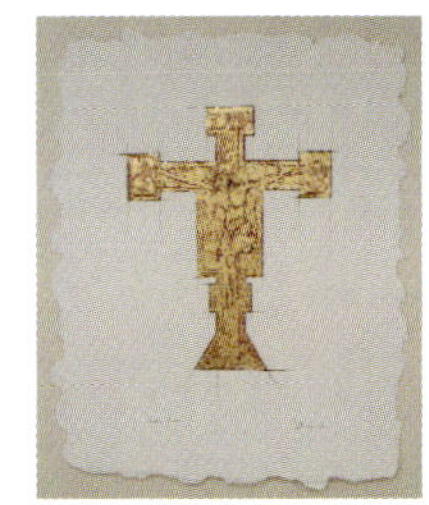

CRUCIFIX AFTER THE MASTER OF THE BLUE CRUCIFIX (13TH CENTURY)

Mixed media drawing with 22-carat gold leaf, 1997, 21 x 16

Because of its brilliant blue lapis color, one of Assisi's treasures is a crucifix known only as created by the Master of the Blue Crucifix. The corpus is elongated and shows the strong influence of the Byzantine tradition.

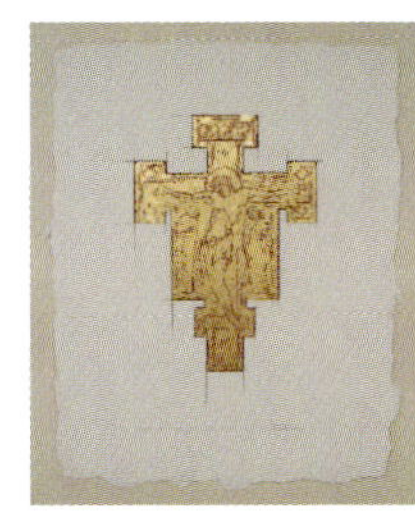

DEPOSITION AFTER ROGIER VAN DER WEYDEN

(1399–64) Mixed media drawing with 22-carat gold leaf, 1998, 16 x 21

Rogier van der Weyden was a master of expressing human emotion. No artist has infused the deposition with more pathos than van der Weyden. The holy mourners spread across the surface of the painting lamenting, the event as Christ falls from the cross physically dead, and Mary, his mother, drops to the ground emotionally exhausted.

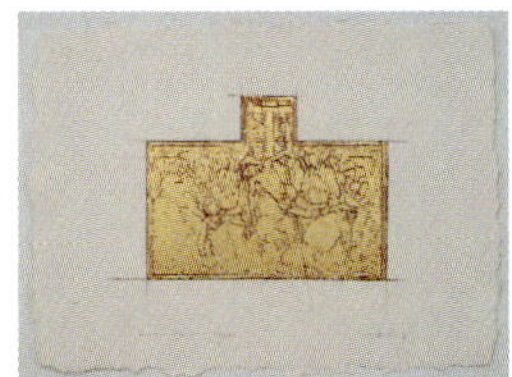

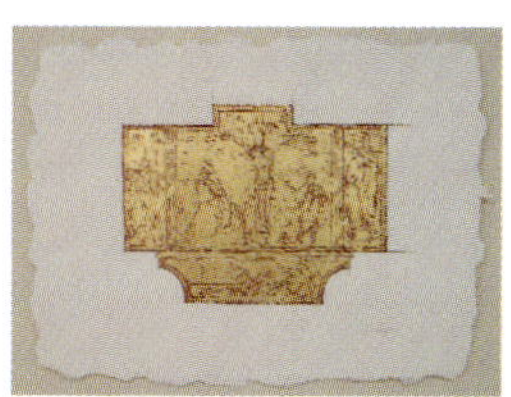

ISENHEIM ALTARPIECE AFTER MATTHIAS GRÜNEWALD (1475–1528) Mixed media drawing with 22-carat gold leaf, 1997, 16 x 12
Grünewald, one of the most important artists of the early-sixteenth-century Renaissance in the North, painted this crucifixion with a startling power of expression, interpreting the event with deep psychological insight. The central panel of the altarpiece is a powerful and compelling work; John the Baptist points to the sore-infested body of Christ saying, "He must increase, but I must decrease." At the foot of the cross, John holds Mary, the mother of Jesus, and Mary Magdalene kneels in repentance before the cross. The predella panel portrays Christ being laid to rest in a sarcophagus.

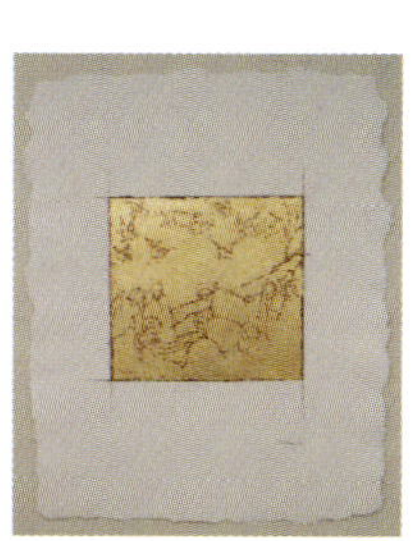

LAMENTATION AFTER GIOTTO DI BONDONE (1266–1337) Mixed media drawing with 22-carat gold leaf, 1997, 21 x 16
Giotto's art was highly innovative, and he may be considered a progenitor of the art revolution that led to the Italian Renaissance. The *Lamentation* (or *Pietà*) is a fresco in his series illustrating the Life of Christ in the early-fourteenth-century Scrovegni (or Arena) Chapel in Padua. He treated religious subjects with a new spirit, infusing them with a freshness that conveyed insightful human emotional content.

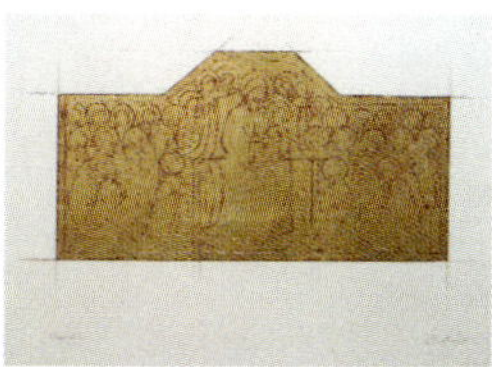

MAESTÀ AFTER DUCCIO DI BUONINSEGNA (ACTIVE 1308–1311) Mixed media drawing with 22-carat gold leaf, 1998, 16 x 21
Maestà (majesty) is the central panel of the altarpiece for the Siena Cathedral. It shows the Mother and Child enthroned and surrounded by angels and saints. Duccio was influenced by the Byzantine tradition, but also demonstrates his insight and use of perspective as evidenced in the drawing of the throne and accentuated with the lines extending beyond the image in my drawing. I was particularly taken with the halos that surround each person forming a cloud of circles surrounding the Madonna and Christ Child.

NAME THE CITY, CHURCH AND ARTIST Mixed media drawing with 22-carat gold leaf, 1997, Four 18 x 14 gilded crosses with an accordion book measuring 12 x 54

Large painted wooden crucifixes hung above the altars of thirteenth and fourteenth century Italian churches. Some were as high as eighteen feet. In their similarity each has its own characteristically different form. This suite of four crosses is a response to their beauty and power.

Name the City, Church and Artist was originally in the 1997 CIVA conference exhibition in Montreal with the theme of *City, Art and Faith*. It was designed to ask the viewer to identify each cross. The answers to the puzzle were found in the accompanying book.

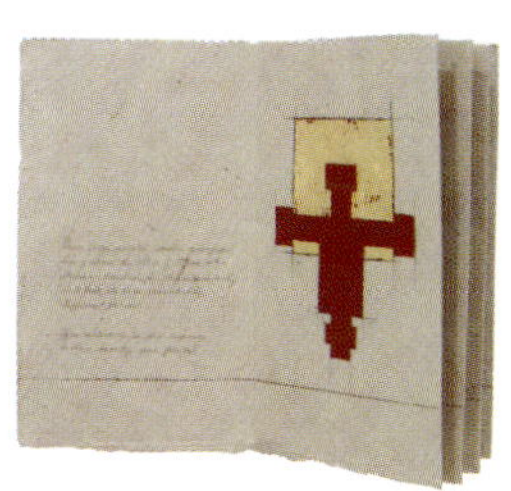

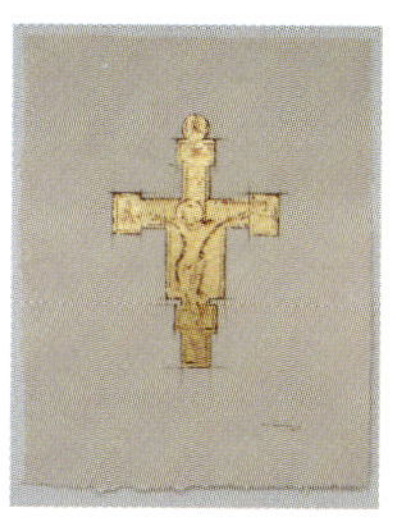

NIKE OF SAMOTHRACE AFTER A HELLENISTIC SCULPTURE (C. 300 B.C.) Mixed media drawing with 22-carat gold leaf, 1998, 21 x 16
The famous *Nike of Samothrace*, or *Winged Victory*, considered one of the best examples of Hellenistic Greek sculpture, portrays the goddess of victory at the moment she lands atop the prow of a ship, with her wings spread and her garments gracefully clinging to her form. Today she celebrates beauty and symbolizes the ideal of perfection.

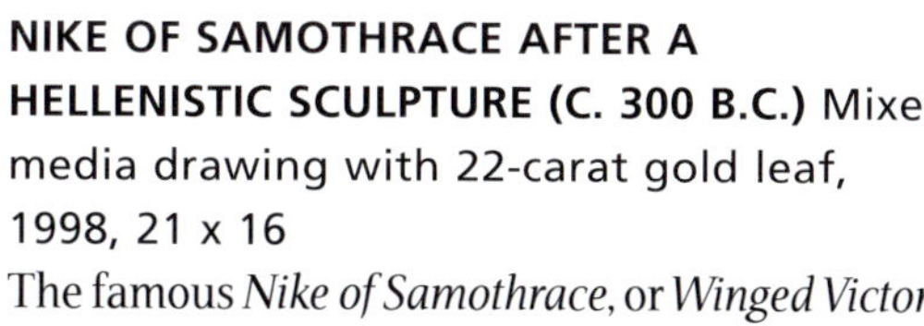

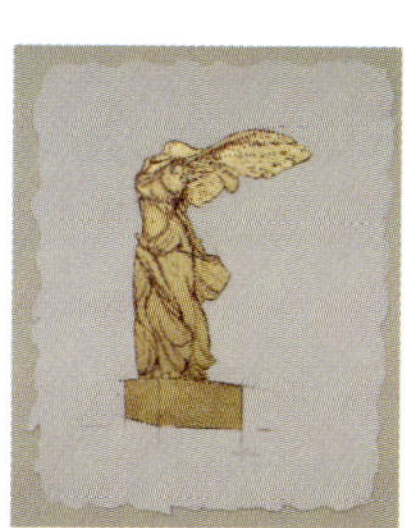

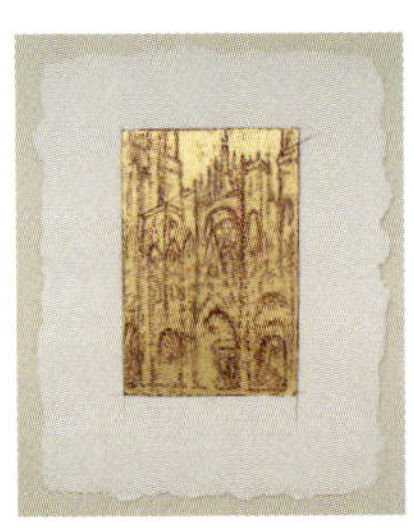

ROUEN CATHEDRAL AFTER CLAUDE MONET (1840–1926) Mixed media drawing with 22-carat gold leaf, 1998, 21 x 16

One of the most impressive of Monet's series was devoted to Rouen Cathedral's west portal. Like most of the Impressionists, Monet's interest does not rest in the subject or architectural elements of the cathedral, but with the light as it bounces off the façade and casts deep, shifting shadows.

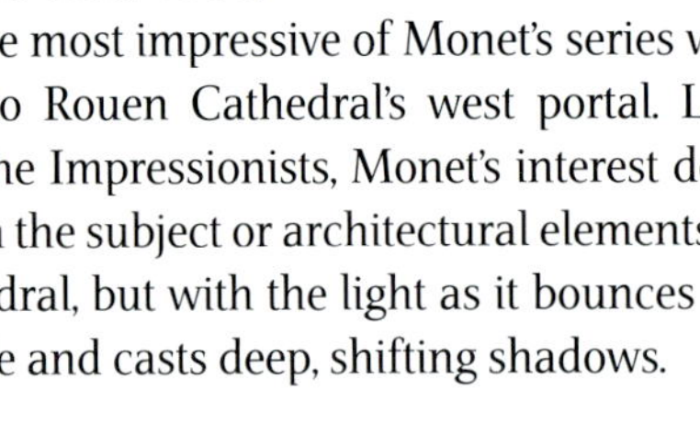

RUNNING FENCE AFTER CHRISTO (B. 1935) AND JEANNE-CLAUDE (B.1935) Mixed media drawing with 22-carat gold leaf, 1998, 16 x 21

Christo's *Running Fence* was an enormous conceptual art project, erected for two weeks in September 1976 in California's Sonoma and Marin counties. The fence was a fabric barrier, twenty-four miles long and eighteen feet high.

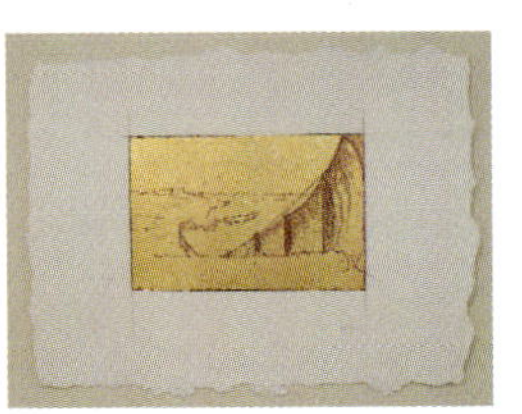

STARRY NIGHT AFTER VINCENT VAN GOGH (1853–90) Mixed media drawing with 22-carat gold leaf, 1998, 16 x 21

Starry Night is instantly recognizable because of van Gogh's unique style and emotional impact. It is filled with symbolism that reflects his profound spiritual beliefs.

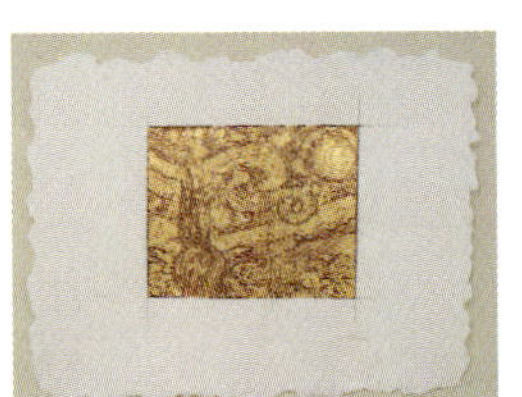

THE GOOD SHEPHERD (3RD CENTURY A.D.) Mixed media drawing with 22-carat gold leaf, 1997, 21 x 16

The shepherd figure was used in pre-Christian times but came to be a beloved symbol of both David and of Christ the Good Shepherd. Many have survived, but this one from the Vatican Museum is unique in that it is nearly life size. Its size and the absence of any of David's attributes, such as a lyre, identify it as Christ.

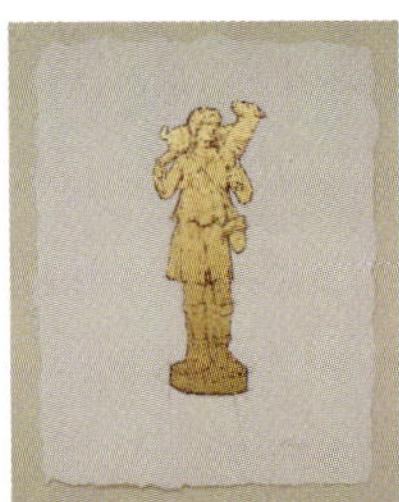

THE OLD KING AFTER GEORGES ROUAULT (1871–1958) Mixed media drawing with 22-carat gold leaf, 1998, 21 x 16

Rouault was unique among modern artists of the early twentieth century, finding inspiration from his Catholic faith. His work identifies with both the suffering of Christ and human suffering. His art invites us to join in that suffering and to gain wisdom from it, as the emotional content of *The Old King* (1916–36), who is in mourning, suggests.

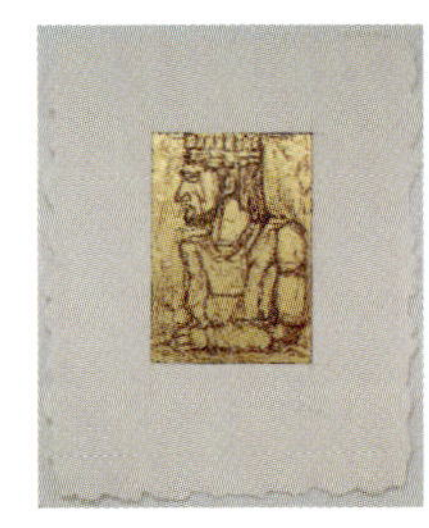

TRINITY AFTER ANDREI RUBLEV (C. 1360–1430) Mixed media drawing with 22-carat gold leaf, 1998, 21 x 16

The *Trinity Icon* was painted by Andrei Rublev, the most famous of Russian icon painters. Within Christian iconography, the three angels who appeared to Abraham in the Old Testament story have become representative of the three persons of the Trinity.

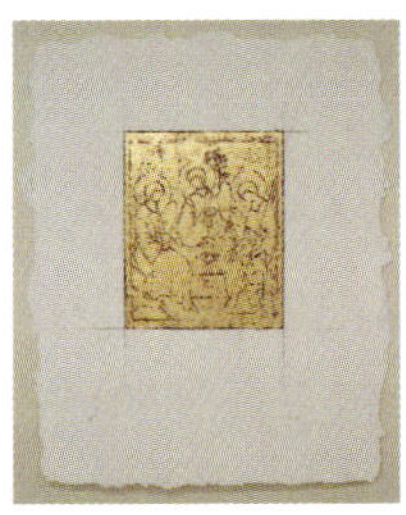

Artist's Books

A natural progression for one who was interested in the contribution language has made to humankind would be to eventually use the book itself as a format for expression. I discovered some book-boxes and imagined transforming them into a painting surface.

The dimensional book-boxes that were the first in this series built upon the painting techniques of the earlier illuminations. Sometimes the book cover became the surface upon which to paint and inscribe imaginary text. In other cases small paintings with line-work, script or images were placed as contents in the book. *Book of Nails* (2004) contains a cluster of old floor nails from the same keg that was used to create the crown of thorns for the crucifixion pieces. It is evidence again how materials and ideas recycle, giving birth to new, but related insights.

My most recent works use actual books that have been screwed open and finished to display a variety of surfaces which include the familiar raised Hebrew and Greek texts, Braille, or graphic elements carefully incised onto the luminescent painted books. The back of each artist book contains calligraphic writing etched into the gilded surface of the covers.

The fascination of the book as the vehicle for my art and a container for the Word has only grown over the years, and points my compass to the future.

ABYSS

Acrylic mixed media, 2003 , 9 1/2 x 15 x 1 1/2
"And the spirit of God moved upon the abyss." This text from Genesis 1 is distorted as it swells and moves over the "face of the deep." The pages from an actual book were glued together and then surfaced with a pearled black paint, suggesting the deep, the unknown, the abyss—a mystery to unfold.

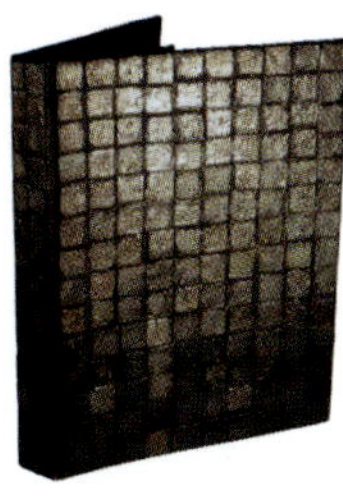

ADVENT BOOK

Acrylic mixed media, 1992, 15 x 11 1/2 x 2
The exterior of *Advent Book* is comprised of small painted and gold-leafed squares arranged in a grid. When the book is opened, a hinged inner panel swings open to create a miniature triptych. Appropriately named, *Advent Book* is, in effect, a book that opens to reveal light, the light that Jesus referred to when He said, "I have come into the world as a light, so that no one who believes in me should stay in darkness." Light comes, fills our

world, then floods our inner spaces with reflections of that light.

AUREOLA I (shown) & II

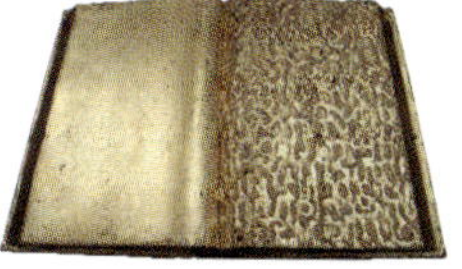

Mixed media, 2004, 11 1/2 x 9 1/2 x 1
Aureola is an enveloping radiance or halo—a fitting title for these two books that are covered with 22-carat gold leafing. The heavily textured surface of the Hebrew on one page of the open book adds dimension and texture to reflect the light of the text.

BOOK FOR THE LAW

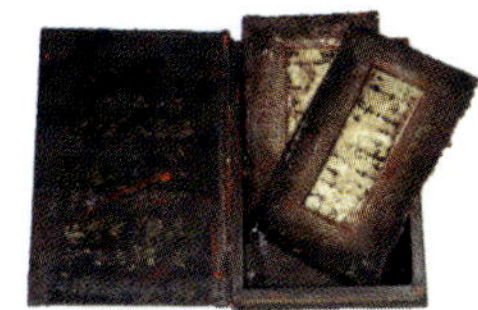

Acrylic mixed media, 1993, 6 1/2 x 4 1/2 x 1
Book for the Law contains two small gilded mini-paintings with fragments of ancient Hebrew script referencing the Decalogue. This three-dimensional book-box has been textured using gesso and modeling paste, then richly surfaced with layers of gold leafing. The book creates a kind of Ark of the Covenant; although small in comparison, its intimate scale creates a portability that makes it easier for us to carry these commandments with us into the various aspects of our daily lives.

BOOK FOR THE LAW AND GOSPEL

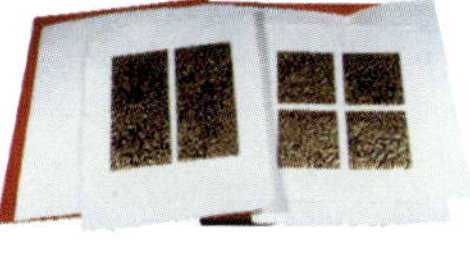

Mixed media artist book, 2003, 13 x 9 1/2 x 2
A collagraph print that contains the text of the Ten Commandments entirely covers the case of *Book for the Law and Gospel*. The collagraph was printed a deep sienna ink, then a layer of 22-carat gold was applied to its surface. The inside of the book-box has been painted in cadmium red and holds a folder. Inside the white paper casing rests two collagraph prints; one titled *Law* and the second *Gospel*. Like the cover, these prints were created by gilding collagraph prints.

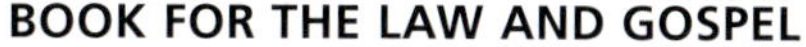

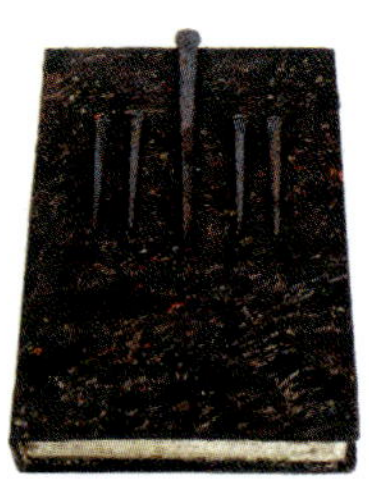

BOOK OF NAILS

Mixed media acrylic, 2003, 9 x 6 x 1 1/4

A mound of old rusted nails set in a book-box lined with precious gold seems an unlikely combination, setting in place vivid contrasts; polished and tarnished, good and evil, eternal and that which decays. Another obvious connection would be that the piece references the container from which the soldiers pulled the spikes to nail Jesus to the cross. The cover has one large antique floor nail and four smaller ones that again allude to the crucifixion.

BOOK OF REMEMBRANCE

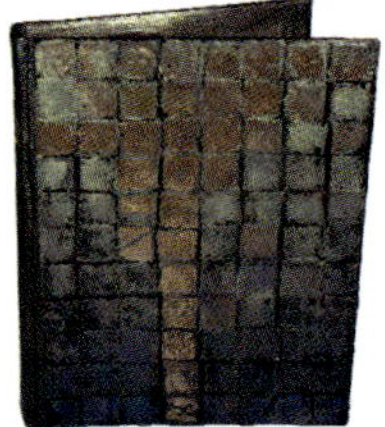

Mixed media with gold leafing, 1993, 11 1/2 x 9 x 2

Different purities of gold leaf have been applied to the mosaic pattern of the cover of *Book of Remembrance*, thus creating a pattern of lighter gold mingled with darker gilding. The central panel reverses the sequence of colors, bringing a stream of light into the darker top section. When opened, the book cover reveals no pages, but only the suggestion of a letter or note glued to the interior panels of the cover, with two squares of gold leaf placed askew over the letter. The text, written in a beautifully calligraphed but totally imaginary language, suggests a record of those special moments in our lives that have shaped us, moved us, changed us, those moments in our lives to which we attach special importance.

CLOSED BOOK

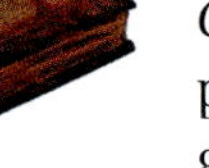

Acrylic mixed media, 1993, 8 1/2 x 5 1/2 x 1

Closed Book, with its heavily textured surface, is painted with acrylic paints and embellished with gold and copper leaf. This book denies us physi-

cal access to its interior but remains shut, like a miniature Holy of Holies. We do not know what it contains, or if it contains anything. It is a faith experience to trust that the contents refer to God.

EVEN THE STONES

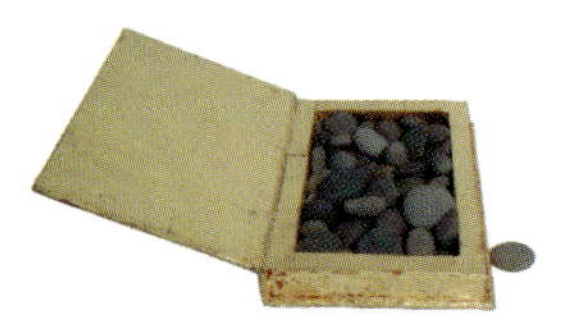

Mixed media, 2004, 9 x 6 x 1 1/4

Matthew quotes Jesus as saying that from "even the stones" he can raise up those who will praise Him. The naturally polished stones were found on the beach near my home and inspired this artist's book.

ICON BOOK

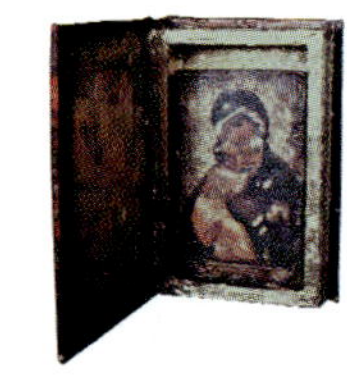

Mixed media with gold leaf, 1993, 4 1/2 x 3 x 3/4

Icon Book, small in scale, contains two images of the Madonna and Child from the Eastern Orthodox traditions. An icon of the *Virgin of Vladimir,* Russia's most beloved icon, is cradled inside the container. The cover which is encrusted with layers of gold leaf and roughly etched surface, evidences the use of a timeworn and precious object of meditation. *Icon Book* carries with it a paradox; the book now represents the Word, which has been very important to my work, The Word Incarnate, the Child. The vehicle of the book, as a vessel of revelation, now holds Mary, the vessel of the Christ Child's revelation to the world.

LIBRO I, II, III (shown) & IV

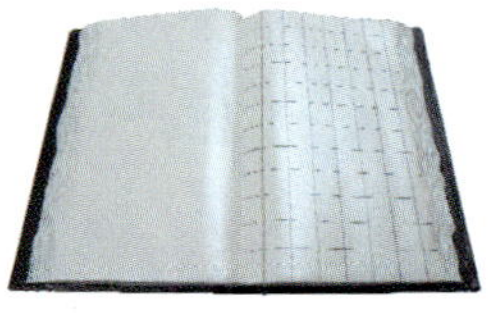

Mixed media with gold leaf, 2005, 9 1/2 x 13 1/2 x 1 each

By questioning the certainty of truth, postmodernism has used language theory in an attempt to deconstruct the very foundations of Western culture. Two elements in these artist's books reconstruct a vision of order and certainty; the physical book represents learning and knowledge and the lines and grids suggest a sense of order, a world with foundations cohesively held together.

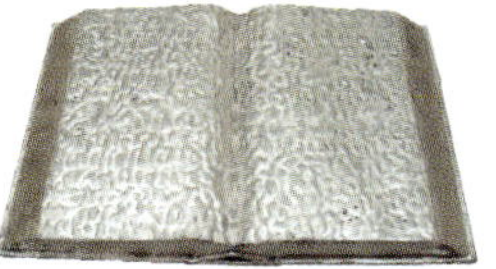

LIKE REFINED SILVER
Mixed media with silver leaf, 2004,
7 x 11 x 1/ 1/8
This silver-coated artist's book appears on the back cover of *Faith and Vision: Twenty-five Years of Christians in the Visual Arts,* a book celebrating CIVA's silver anniversary. The face of the work contains the Hebrew passages from Psalm 12 which read, "The word of the Lord is flawless, like refined silver."

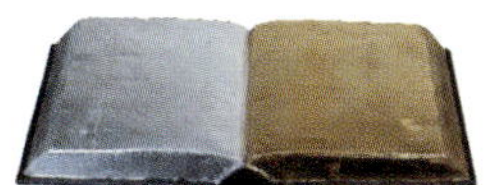

NEITHER SILVER NOR GOLD
Mixed media with silver and gold leaf, 2004, 5 1/4 x 11 1/2 x 1 1/2
The Bible links silver and gold literally dozens of times, usually alluding to the futility of their worth in relation to eternal values. This artist's book, originally a thick, but small volume, is permanently fixed in an open position to create a kind of painted sculpture. An intense red underlayment of color is applied, and then half was gilded with 22-carat gold leaf, while pure silver covers the other portion.

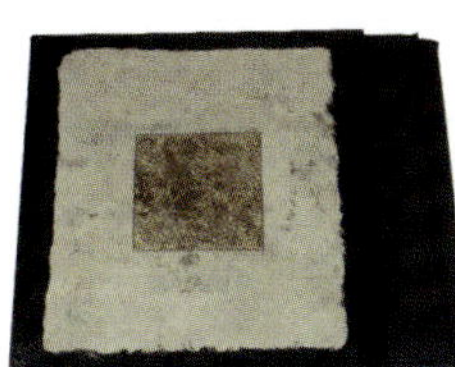

REDEMPTION BOOK
Mixed media, 2004, 9 3/4 x 9 x 3/4
In the fifteenth and sixteenth centuries it was not uncommon to have mediation books without words. This artist's book titled *Redemption Book* echoes the same intention as these early illustrated sacred volumes.

Inside the interior casing are six sheets of bark paper which form the pages of this artist's book, each with a painted square: black, red, white and gold and a title page. Colors tell the unfolding story of redemption, from the black of sin to the non-tarnishing gold square representing eternity or heaven. All the pages are wrapped in a folder of roughly textured black handmade paper and then inserted into an iridescent black casing—hidden from sight, but waiting to be found and interpreted.

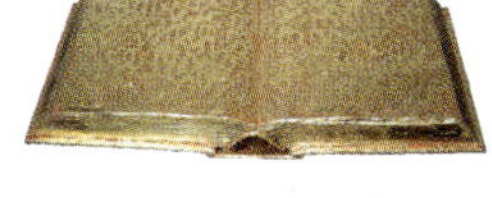

RESURRECTION BOOK
Mixed media, 2004, 5 1/4 x 11 3/4 x 1 1/2
The Greek text from Luke's account of the Resurrection has been applied to the top of this open book. The face of the book was underpainted in a deep bold red, covered with gold leaf, and then a final application of iridescent oil crayon added a subtle variation to the surface.

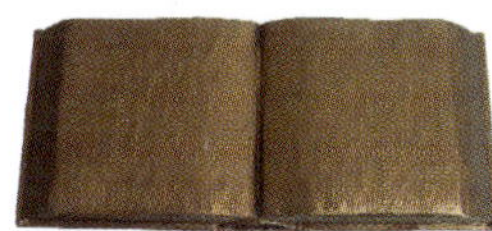

TOUCH AND SEE
Acrylic mixed media, 2004,
5 1/4 x 11 1/2 x 1 1/2
Seeing is not only with the eyes. Pages from a Braille Bible cover the surface of this antique bronze colored book.

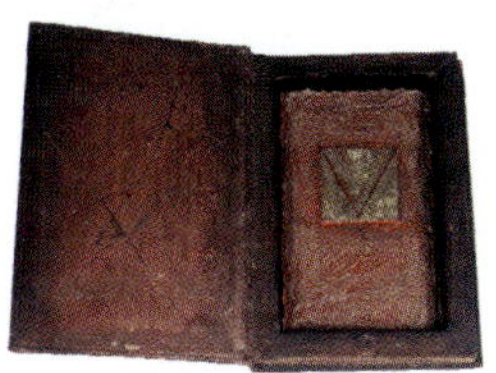

TRINITY BOOK
Acrylic mixed media, 1993, 9 x 6 x 1 1/4
Trinity Book contains three small gilded mini-paintings, each symbolically representing a person of the Trinity: the circle is a symbol of God; the cross form references Jesus; and a triangle shape points downward picturing the Holy Spirit as a descending dove. These pieces have been textured using gesso and modeling paste and richly surfaced with layers of gold and copper leafing.

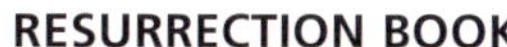

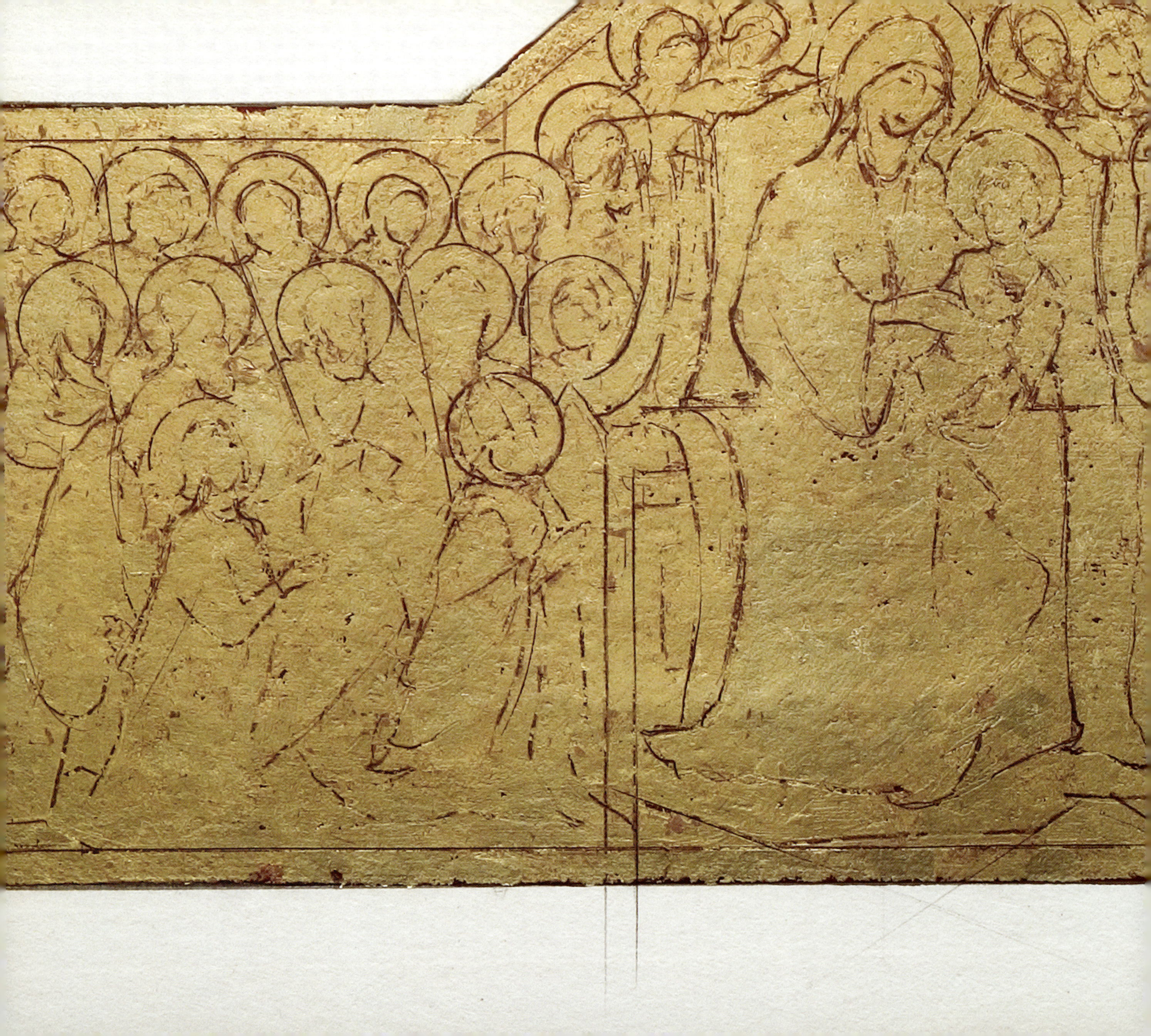

SOLO EXHIBITIONS

Icons & Logos: The Art of Sandra Bowden A forty-year retrospective, Gordon College, Wenham, MA, August–October 2005

Word as Image, University of Massachusetts at Dartmouth, Dartmouth, MA, July 2004

Illuminated Inscriptions, First Presbyterian Church, Portland, OR, April 2004

Songs for the Journey, Kyle Gallery, Falmouth, MA, 2003

Via Crucis: The Way of the Cross, Instituto San Lodovico, Orvieto, Italy, March 2002

Word as Image, Chowan College, Chowan, NC, February 2002

Art History 101: Icons of Western Art, Center for Christian Studies, Charlottesville, VA, March 2002

Art History 101: Icons of Western Art, Taylor University, Upland, IN, January 2001

Word as Image, Light of the Word Mission Gallery, Techny, IL, December 2000

Art History 101: Icons of Western Art, Houghton College, Houghton, NY, March 2000

Art History 101: Icons of Western Art, Saint Xavier University, Chicago, IL, January 2000

Art History 101: Icons of Western Art, Sterling College, Sterling, KS, September 1999

Word as Image, Nyack College, Nyack, NY, April 1999

Word as Image, United Theological Seminary, New Brighton, MN, March 1999

Word as Image, Mill River Gallery, Ellicott City, MD, January 1999

Art History 101: Icons of Western Art, Oklahoma Baptist University, Shawnee, OK, January 1999

Art History 101: Icons of Western Art, Roberts Wesleyan College, Rochester, NY, November 1998

Art History 101: Icons of Western Art, Union University, Jackson, TN, October 1998

Art History 101: Icons of Western Art, Wheaton College, Wheaton, IL, September 1998

Illuminations, Gallery W, Sacramento, CA, April 1998

Meditations Across Time, Visions Gallery, Albany, NY, May 1998

Word as Image, Meetinghouse Gallery, Andover Newton Seminary, Newton, MA, March 1997

Illuminations, Center Galleries, Albany, NY, December 1996

Word as Image, Bible Lands Museum, Jerusalem, Israel, May 1996

Word as Image, Cross View Lutheran Church, Edina, MN, May 1996

Word as Image, Evangel College, Springfield, MO, March 1995

Word as Image, United Theological Seminary, New Brighton, MN, September 1995

Word As Image, Foxhall Gallery, Washington, DC, November 1995

Word as Image, Kolbo, Boston, MA, November 1994

Chapel and Cultural Center, Troy, NY, 1991

Celebration Designs, Minneapolis, MN, 1990

Roberts Wesleyan College, Rochester, NY, 1990

Hillel, Rose Warner House, Cincinnati, OH, 1990

Houghton College, Houghton, NY, 1988

Concordia College, Seward, NB, 1986

Shoestring Gallery, Rochester, NY, 1986

Vanderbilt University, Nashville, TN, 1985

Wenniger Graphics, Boston, MA, 1985

Touchstone Gallery, Hendersonville, NC 1985

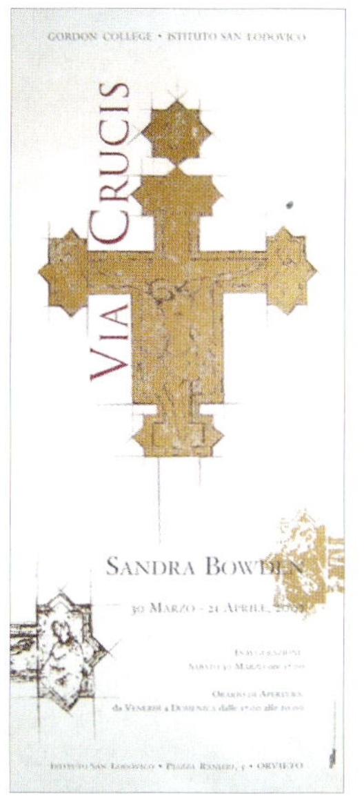

Monroe Community College, Monroe, MI, 1984

Western Theological Seminary, Holland, MI, 1984

Reflections of Creation, Interiors Gallery, Saratoga, NY, 1984

Center Galleries, Albany, NY, 1983

Ethel Putterman Gallery, Orleans, MA, 1983

The Earth Is The Lord's, Teays Valley School for the Arts, Charleston, WV, 1983

Barrington College, Barrington, RI, 1983

Regis College, Weston, MA, 1983

Asbury College, Wilmore, KY, 1983

Biblical Textures, Kolbo, Boston, MA, 1982

Text and Textures, Kolbo, Boston, MA, 1981

Creation, Ethel Putterman Gallery, Orleans, MA, 1981

Celebrating Old Testament Creation Themes, The Meetinghouse, Philadelphia, PA, 1980

Gallery 3, Roanoke, VA, 1980

Kolbo, Brookline, MA, 1979

Celebrating Old Testament Creation Themes, Arthur's 2005, New Orleans, LA, 1979

Ethel Putterman Gallery, Orleans MA, 1976

Houghton College, Houghton, NY, 1976

Private Gallery, Kensington, MD, 1975

Patmos Gallery, Toronto, Ontario, 1973

State University of New York at Cobleskill, Cobleskill, NY, 1970

Gordon College, Wenham, MA, 1966

Group Exhibitions and Awards

The Next Generation: Contemporary Expressions of Faith, Museum of Biblical Art, New York, NY, August–November 2005

Spirituality & Religion in a Modern World, Union Street Gallery, Chicago Heights, IL, March 2005

Narrative in Contemporaray Art, Foxhall Gallery, Washington DC, March 2005

Sacred Arts Exhibit, First United Methodist Church, Evanston, IL, November 2004

22nd Annual Christian Art Festival Exhibition, Cross View Lutheran Church, Edina, MN, May 2004

Fourth Annual Festival of Christian Art, First Prize for *Redemption Book*, Woodbury Lutheran Church, Woodbury, MN, March 2004

Printmakers of Cape Cod (juried show), Cape Museum of Fine Art, Brewster, MA, March 2004

Gifts of the Spirit 2003, Juror's Award for *Chronicled*, First Presbyterian Church, Portland, OR, November 2003

The Blood of the Lamb, Timer-Warner Gallery, Lynn, MA, November 2003

Works of Faith, First Presbyterian Church, Portland, OR, September 2003

Under Cover: Book Arts, St. Louis Arts Guild, St. Louis, MO, September 2003

21st Annual Christian Art Festival Exhibition, Festival Award for *Was the Word*, Cross View Lutheran Church, Edina, MN, May 2003

17th Ecclesiastical Art Exhibit, Historic Trinity Church, Detroit, MI, May, 2003

41st Annual Christian Art Show, Honorable Mention for *Crucifix after the Master of the Blue Crucifix*, Ascension Lutheran Church, East Lansing, MI, April 2003

Saint John's Religious Art Festival, Saint John's Lutheran Church, Sacramento, CA, April 2003

Festival of Christian Art, Woodbury Lutheran Church, Woodbury, MN, February 2003

Bread Upon the Waters, CIVA Traveling Show, January 2003–August 2006

Visions VII, Cathedral Basilica of the Assumption, Covington, KY, January 2003

Cross Country III, Weaver Gallery at Bethel College, Mishawaka, IN, January 2003

Small Works Show, Foxhall Gallery, Washington

DC, December 2002

A New Light: Advent, Christmas and Epiphany, ECVA online exhibition, December 2002

Contemporary Works of Faith, Liturgical Art Guild, Columbus, OH, October 2002

Festival of Christian Art, First Prize Award for 2-D Art, Woodbury Lutheran Church, Woodbury, MN, 2002

Inner Visions, Visions Gallery, Albany, NY, September 2002

Wanderings: Journeys Toward Home, Genema Gallery, Atlanta, GA, June 2002

VI Annual Sacred Art Exhibition, Best of Show Award for *Hagaddah*, Golden Isles Arts and Humanities Association, Brunswick, GA, May 2002

Out of Darkness into Light, Episcopal Church and the Visual Arts online exhibition January 2002

Collector's Items: Biblical Art and Private Devotion, The Gallery at the American Bible Society, New York, NY, January 2002

Visions VII, Cathedral Basilica of the Assumption, Covington, KY, September 2001

One Festival, Purchase Award for *Chronicled*, One Summer Festival, Memphis, TN, 2001

19th Annual Christian Art Festival, First Prize for *Psalm of Thanks*, Cross View Lutheran Church, Edina, MN, May 2001

A Presence Seen, CIVA Biennial Conference Exhibition, University of Dallas, Dallas, TX, June 2001

Like a Prayer: A Jewish and Christian Presence in Contemporary Art, Tryon Center for Visual Art, Charlotte, NC, December 2000

Faces of December, University of Massachusetts at Dartmouth, MA, December 2000

Anno Domini: Jesus through the Centuries, Provincial Museum of Alberta, Edmonton, Canada, October 2000

Visions VI, Cathedral Basilica of the Assumption, Covington, KY, September 2000

Abstraction: The Power of Memory, Christians in Visual Arts (3-year traveling show), September 2000

Fourth Annual National Sacred Art Exhibition, Golden Isles Arts and Humanities Association, Coastal Georgia Community College, Brunswick, GA, July 2000

The Word as Art: Contemporary Renderings, The Gallery at the American Bible Society, New York, NY, July 2000

Sacred Arts Festival, Archdiocese of Los Angeles, Pasadena Convention Center, Pasadena, CA, June 2000

Where All Are Welcome, Honorable Mention for *Hear the Word*, Trinity Presbyterian Church, Denton, TX, June 2000

Ecclesiastical Art Exhibit, Historic Trinity Church, Detroit, MI, May 2000

All Cape Cod Show, Creative Arts Center, Chatham, MA, May 2000

18th Annual Christian Art Show, Ascension Lutheran Church, East Lansing, MI, April 2000

Spirit Infused, Salisbury State University, Salisbury, MD, March 2000

Spirit, Hand and Vision, First Presbyterian Gallery, Fort Wayne, MI, February 2000

Drawn to Christ: Cross Country II, Bethel College, Mishawaka, IN, January 2000

Gifts of the Spirit, First Presbyterian Church, Portland, OR, December 1999

Images for Advent, Episcopal Cathedral, Boston, MA, November 1999

Women of Vision, Foxhall Gallery, Washington DC, November 1999

Visions V, Juror's Award for *Prayer*, Cathedral Basilica of the Assumption, Covington, KY, September 1999

Passion of Christ: Sorrows of Mary, El Santuario

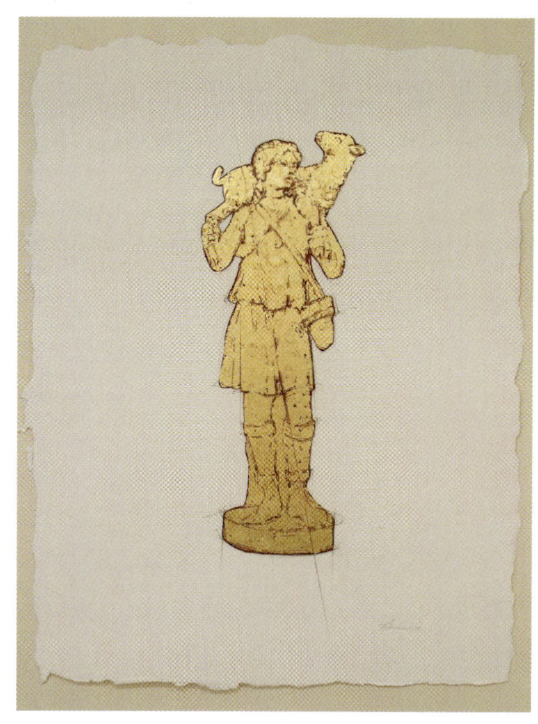

FIGURE 137
THE GOOD SHEPHERD (3RD CENTURY A.D.)
Mixed media drawing with 22-carat gold leaf
1997
21 x 16

de Nuestra Senora de Guadalupe, Santa Fe, NM, July 1999

Images of Mary, The Mariological Society of America, Award for *Annunciation after Fra Angelico*, Marian Library, University of Dayton, Dayton, OH, 1999

Third Annual National Sacred Art Exhibition, Golden Isles Arts & Humanities Association, Brunswick, GA, July 1999

20/20 Vision, CIVA Conference Exhibition, Mequon, WI, June 1999

Behold the Wood of the Cross, Georgetown University, Washington DC, Spring 1999

17th Annual Christian Art Festival, Cross View Lutheran Church, Edina, MN, April 1999

Passion and Suffering, Christian Fine Arts Association, Littleton, CO, March 1999

15th Ecclesiastical Art Exhibit, Historic Trinity Church, Detroit, MI, March 1999

Threads that Bind, Fourth Presbyterian Church, Chicago, IL, March 1999

Four Seasons Photography, Kirkland Art Center, Clinton, NY, March 1999

Nativity, Biblical Arts Center, Dallas, TX, December 1998

The Artist as Collector, Messiah College, Grantham, PA, October 1998

Italian Influences: A Contemporary View, Foxhall Gallery, Washington DC, October 1998

Jubilee 2000, Art & Cultural Center, Fallbrook, CA, September 1998

Third Annual National Sacred Art Exhibition, Golden Isles Arts & Humanities Association, Brunswick, GA, July 1998

Inner Visions, Visions Gallery, Albany, NY, Summer 1998

15th Anniversary Show, Douglas Gallery, Minneapolis, MN, May 1998

16th Annual Cross View Christian Art Festival, Second Prize for *Crucifix after the Master of the Blue Crucifix*, Cross View Lutheran Church, Edina, MN, May 1998

12th Ecclesiastical Exhibit, Historic Trinity Lutheran Church, Detroit, MI, May 1998

Paper Plus: An Invitational, Arts Center Gallery, Saratoga, NY, May 1998

Creations '98, Liturgical Arts Guild, Columbus, OH, May 1998

The Virgin Mary in Art, Juror's Award for *Annunciation after Fra Angelico*, International Schoenstatt Center, Waukesha, WI, May 1998

Works of Faith, Juror's Award for *Law and Gospel*, First Presbyterian Church, Portland, OR, March 1998

26th Annual Art Show, Daylesford Abbey, Paoli, PA, March 1998

Paper in Particular, Columbia College, Columbia, MO, March 1998

Arte Sagrado, Concordia University Austin, TX, March 1998

Sacred Arts XVIII, Honorable Mention for *Crucifix after the Master of the Blue Crucifix*, Billy Graham Center Museum, Wheaton, IL, February 1998

CIVA Italy, Gordon College, Wenham, MA, January 1998

Cross Country I, Bethel College, Mishawaka, IN, January 1998

Earth, Sea and Sky, Ashwell Gallery, Beverly, MA, January 1998

Works of Faith, First Presbyterian Church, Portland, OR, December 1997

Works on Paper VII, Shepherd College, Shepherdstown, WV, October 1997

Art Rageous, Cornerstone Festival, Chicago, IL, July 1997

Sacred Art Show, Golden Isles Arts & Humanities Association, Brunswick, GA, July 1997

Artists Books, Oculus Gallery, Seattle, WA, June 1997

Vital Intersections: City, Art & Faith, CIVA

Conference, Montreal, Canada, June 1997

15th Annual Christian Art Festival, Cross View Lutheran Church, Edina, MN, April 1997

Things to Think on, Merrick Free Art Gallery, New Brighton, PA, April 1997

Contemporary Works of Faith '97, Schumacher Gallery, Columbus, OH, March 1997

Arte Segrado, Concordia University, Austin, TX, March 1997

Second Annual Small Works Exhibition, The Art Place Gallery, Chicago, IL, March 1997

Songs of Ascent, Aughinbaugh Art Gallery, Messiah College, Grantham, PA, March–April 1997

Sacred Arts XVII, Billy Graham Center Museum, Wheaton, IL, March–May 1997

Amazing Art in Small Frames, Juror's Award for *Logos*, Madison Avenue Art Gallery, Germantown, TN, December 1996

Icon Influences, Visions Gallery, Albany, NY, December 1996

Reflections of Faith IV, Concordia College, Ann Arbor, MI, December 1996

Creation: Contemporary Christian Art and Artists, Purchase Award for *Law and Gospel*, Rall Gallery, Doane College, Crete, NE, November 1996

The Word in Worship, Washington Theological Union, Washington, DC, October 1996

Words & Images, Calvin College Center Art Gallery, Grand Rapids, MI

National Christian Fine Arts Exhibit, Purchase Award for *And There Was Light*, First United Methodist Church, Farmington, NM, 1996

Jewish Arts Fest of Dallas, JCC of Dallas TX, August 1996

Inner Visions, Visions Gallery, Albany, NY, July 1996

10th Ecclesiastical Art Exhibit, Historic Trinity Church, Detroit, MI, May 1996

Liturgical & Sacred Art Exhibition, Springfield Arts Association, Springfield, OH, May 1996

XV Celebration of Art, Park Synagogue, Cleveland Heights, OH, May 1996

Behold the Lamb: Life of Christ, Biblical Arts Center, Dallas, TX, March 1996

Arte Sagrado, Juror's Commendation for *Holy, Holy, Holy*, Concordia College, Austin, TX, March 1996

The Passover & Passed Over, First Prize for *Book of Remembrance*, Ashwell Gallery, Beverly, MA, March 1996

Sacred Arts XV, Third Prize for *Law and Gospel*, Billy Graham Center Museum,

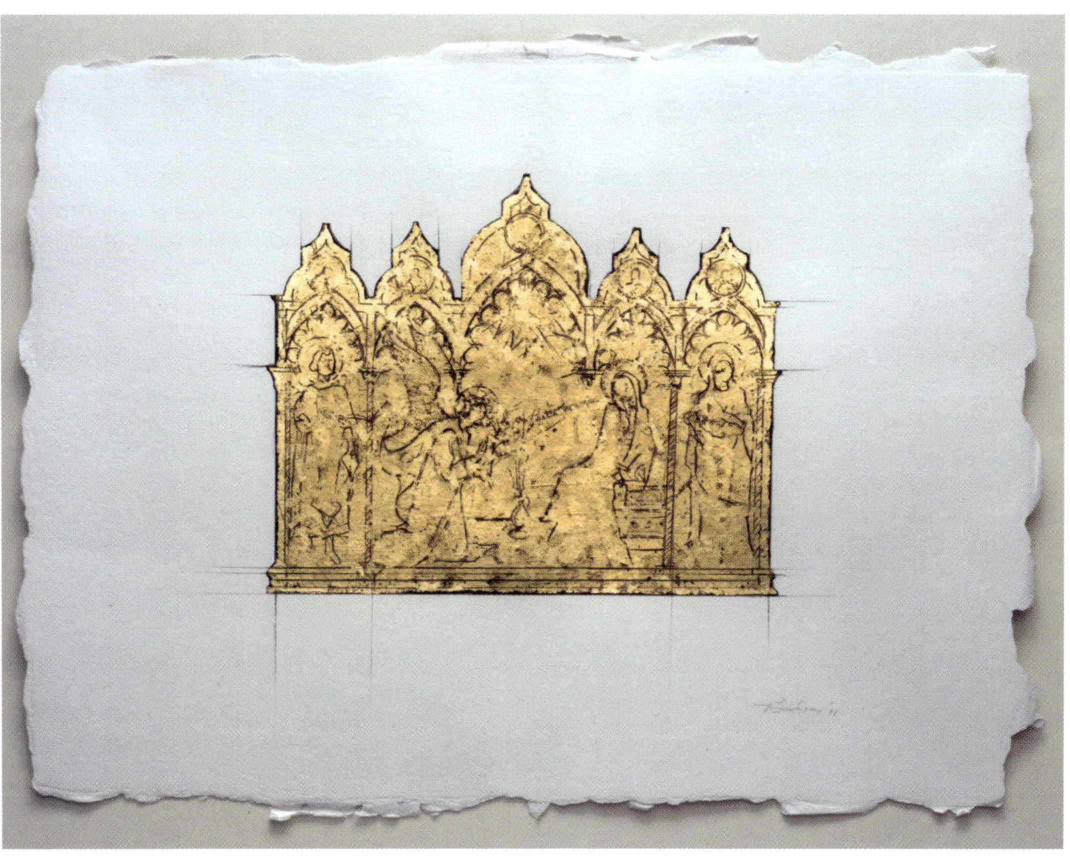

FIGURE 138

ANNUNCIATION AFTER SIMONE MARTINI (C. 1284–1344)
Mixed media drawing with 22-carat gold leaf
1997
16 x 21

Wheaton, IL, March–May 1995

Contemporary Works of Faith, Purchase Prize for *These Are the Words,* The Schumacher Gallery, Capital University, Columbus, OH, March 1995

9th Annual Ecclesiastical Art Exhibit, Historic Trinity Church, Detroit, MI, May 1995

A Testament of Art, Hampshire College, Amherst, MA, October 1994

National Christian Fine Arts Exhibit, Choice Award, Farmington, NM, 1994

Cosmos and Creation, Queens College, Cambridge, England, July 1994

Reflections of Faith, Kreft Center for the Arts, Ann Arbor, MI, 1993

13th Biennial Contemporary Works of Faith, Liturgical Art Guild of Ohio, Schumacher Gallery, Columbus, OH, 1993

Small Wonders, Foxhall Gallery, Washington DC, 1993

Cross View Christian Art Festival, Second Prize, Cross View Lutheran Church, Edina, MN, 1992

The Cross—a Contemporary Image, ELCA Churchwide Center, Chicago, IL, 1991

Forms and Fibers, Ann Grey Gallery, Saratoga, NY, 1991

Summer Stock, The Rice Gallery, Albany Institute of History and Art, Albany, NY, 1991

Uncommon Threads, Niskayuna Art Gallery, Niskayuna, NY, 1991

UNO, Newman Center, New Orleans, LA, 1991

12th Biennial Contemporary Works of Faith, Liturgical Guild of Ohio, Schumacher Gallery, Columbus, OH, 1991

Works on Paper, CIVA Traveling Exhibit 1991 through 1992

Sacred Arts XI, Honorable Mention for *Sanctus*, Billy Graham Center Museum, Wheaton, IL, 1990

Art for Faith's Sake, Purchase Award for *Illumination*, Visions Gallery, Albany, NY, 1990

4 x 12 x 12, Emma Willard School, Troy, NY, 1990

8th Annual Christian Art Festival, Honorable Mention for *Sanctus*, Cross View Lutheran Church, Edina, MN, 1990

Sacred Art 200, General Assembly of the Presbyterian Church, Philadelphia, PA, 1989

Art for Faith's Sake, Visions Gallery, Albany, NY, 1989

Sacred Arts X, Billy Graham Center Museum, Wheaton, IL, 1989

7th Annual Christian Art Festival, Honorable Mention for *Sanctus*, Cross View Lutheran Church, Edina, MN, 1989

Visions of Christ's Coming, Visions Gallery, Albany, NY, December 1989

Christian Imagery in Contemporary Art, Albany Institute of Art, Albany, NY, 1988

Images of the Holy Land, William Spoelhof Gallery, Calvin College, Grand Rapids, MI, 1987

Sacred Arts V, Billy Graham Center Museum, Wheaton, IL, 1985

Ryan Johnson Gallery, Fairfax, CA, 1983

Monroe Community College, Monroe, MI, 1983

Text and Texture, Seraphim Gallery, New York, NY, 1983

Einladung zur Vernissage, SB=Rahmen Gallery, Munich, Germany 1982

Elca London Gallery, Montreal, Canada 1980

Two on Paper, Towne Gallery, Lenox, MA, 1980

Wenniger Graphics, Boston, MA, 1979

Art of the Spirit, Falls Church, CT, 1979

Artists of the Mohawk-Hudson Region, Albany Institute of History and Art, Albany, NY, 1969–1978

22nd Anniversary Exhibition of Painting and Sculpture, Berkshire Art Museum, Pittsfield, MA, 1973

Munson-William Proctor Institute, Utica, NY, 1973

College of Saint Rose, Albany, NY, 1972

Saratoga Performing Arts Center, Saratoga, NY, 1970

COLLECTIONS

Jewish Institute of Religion Museum, Hebrew Union College, New York, NY

American Bible Society, New York, NY

Vatican Museum of Contemporary Religious Art

Haifa Museum of Modern Art, Haifa, Israel

Bancohio National Bank, Cleveland, OH

Shaave Cedek Synagogue, Montreal, Canada

General Electric Corporation, Selkirk, NY

Messiah College, Grantham, PA

Concordia Seminary, Minneapolis, MN

Billy Graham Center Museum, Wheaton, IL

Holiday Inn International, Memphis, TN

Temple Gates of Heaven, Schenectady, NY

Taylor University, Upland, IN

Waldorf College, Forest City, IA

Union University, Jackson, TN

Evangelical Lutheran Church of American, Chicago, IL

Roberts Wesleyan College, Rochester, NH

Calvin College, Grand Rapids, MI

International Business Machines

Concordia University, Mequon, WI

Western Theological Seminary, Holland, MI

Key Bank, Albany, NY

Roanoke College, Roanoke, VA

Saave Cedek Synagogue, Montreal, Canada

Judaic Heritage Society, New York, NY

Calvin College, Grand Rapids, MI

Monroe Community College, Monroe, MI

United Theological Seminary, New Brighton, MN

Zion Lutheran Church, Schenectady, NY

Albany Catholic Diocese, Albany, NH

Houghton College, Houghton, NY

Gordon College, Wenham, MA

Evangelic College, Springfield, MO

Temple Beth-El, Glens Falls, NY

Museum of Contemporary Religious Art (MOCRA), St. Louis, MO

Museum of Biblical Art (MOBIA), New York, NY

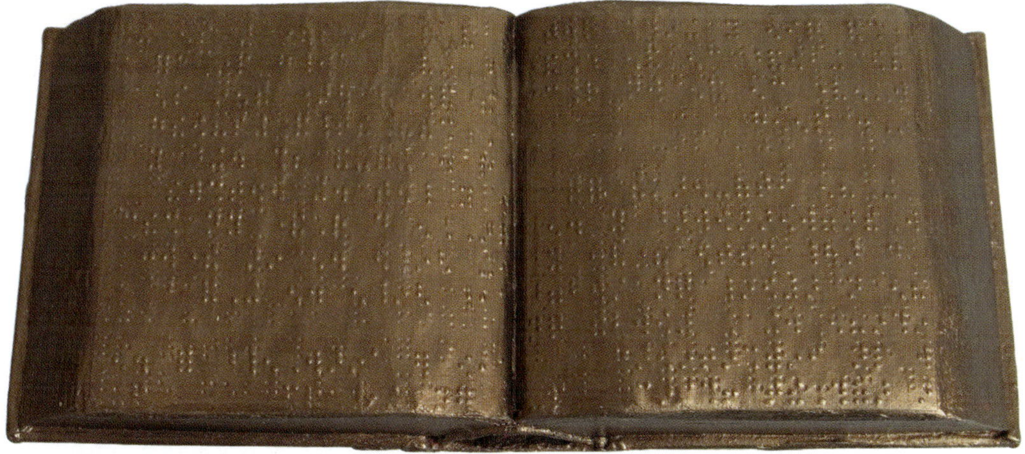

COMMISSIONS

Church of the Holy Cross, Warrensburg, NY, stations of the cross and altar frontals, 1993

St. Paul's Episcopal Church, Albany, NY, frontal and chasuble, 1993

Good Samaritan Nursing Home, Albany, NY, season of pentecost paraments, 1992

Knesseth Israel Synagogue, Gloversville, NY, stained glass windows, ark, and menorah, 1991

Saint Sophia Greek Orthodox Church, Albany, NY, painting, 1990

Episcopal Diocese of Albany, NY, bishop's chasuble, 1990

Albany Catholic Diocese, Albany, NY, bishop's chasuble, 1989

TOUCH AND SEE
Acrylic mixed media
2004
5 1/4 x 11 1/2 x 1 1/2

Selected Bibliography

The Art of Sandra Bowden, Square Halo Books, 2005

Saint Xavier (university magazine), cover art using *Ancient Road to Masada*, Winter 2005

God's Friends, "Visual Artists and the Spiritual Life: A Conversation," several reproductions November 2004

Memories, Hopes and Conversations: Appreciative Inquiry and Congregational Change, cover art using *Meanings*, The Alban Institute, 2004

Reluctant Partners: Art and Religion in Dialogue, The Gallery at the American Bible Society, reproduction of *It Is Finished*, 2004

The Memories of God, Fortress Press, cover art using *Gezer,* 2004

Why Jesus Died, cover image using *It Is Finished*, Fortress Press, 2004

A-PLUS Art/Antiques/Design, three page feature article on Sandra Bowden's art and collection, April 2004

Behold: Arts for the Church Year, three reproductions and center section poster, February-March 2004

Record, American Bible Society magazine, cover art using *It Is Finished,* Spring 2003.

Under Cover: Book Arts, St. Louis Arts Guild, St. Louis, MO, reproduction of one piece in catalog, September 2003

Behold: Arts for the Church Year, Wood Lake Books, BC, Canada, *Law and Gospel* center section of book September 2003

Morning of Prayer, 74th General Convention of ECUSA, cover art using *He Was Wounded for Our Transgressions,* August 2003

episcopallife: Convention Daily, cover art using *He Was Wounded for Our Trangressions,* July 30, 2003

Objects of Grace, Square Halo Books, chapter on Bowden with several images, 2002

2001 Calendar, Aid Association for Lutherans, *It Is Finished* reproduced for August

WORLD, "The Good, the True, the Beautiful", by Hannah Eagleson, reproduction and commentary, July 14, 2001

The Episcopal Times, "Chatham Artist Encourages Visual Arts in Christian Church Life", by Eileen Pittenger, article with reproductions, Summer 2001

The Word as Art: Contemporary Renderings, The Gallery at the American Bible Society, New York, NY, catalog reproduction of *It Is Finished,* July 2000

New York Daily News, "Spread the Word: Gallery is a Blessing" by Mila Andre, *It Is Finished* with commentary, July 28, 2000

Like a Prayer: A Jewish and Christian Presence in Contemporary Art, Tryon Center for Visual Art, Charlotte NC, commentary and reproduction of *Trinity Book,* December 2000

It Was Good: Making Art to the Glory of God, Square Halo Books, image and preface written by Bowden, October 2000

Worship Leader, cover reproduction of *Tel Hazor,* May/June 2000

Our Christian Heritage in Art, Bob Jones University Press, reproduction of *Revelations,* 1999

Chicago Tribune, "Judeo-Christian Dialogue Moves into World of Art," by Patrick T. Reardon, review of *Threads that Bind* and reproductions, March 30, 1999

Christianity and the Arts, "Christian Artist Steeped in Hebraic Aesthetics," by Gene Edward Veith, article with reproduction, Winter 1999

Beyond the Essene Hypothesis, Eerdman's Publishing Co., cover art using *Inner Gorge,* 1998

Christianity Today, "The Word Became Art," article written by Karen Mulder on Bowden's art with two reproductions, February 1998

Christianity and the Arts, "Things Visible & Invisible," reproduction of *It Is Finished,* 1998

Mosaics, Evangelical Church of America, video magazine, interview and segment, December 1997

Good Friday Bulletin Cover for ELCA, *It Is Finished,* 1,000,000 copies, April 1998

Studies in Ancient Yahwistic Poetry, Eerdman's Publishing Co., cover art using *Lachish,* 1997

Fortress Press Catalogue, cover art using *It Is Finished,* 1995

Artists Showcase, Biblical Archaeology Review, Holy Writings reproduction, July/August 1995

Crucifixion of Jesus, Fortress Press, *It Is Finished,* cover art 1995

Epiphany, "Interview with Sandra Bowden" by Liu David, 1995

ARTS Journal, "Word as Image" essay by Cindi Beth Johnson, 1995

They Cried to the Lord, Fortress Press, cover art, 1994

Charisma and Authority in Israelite Society, Fortress Press, cover art using *Aaron's Breastplate,* 1994

Long Ago God Spoke, Fortress Press, cover art using *Light from Darkness,* 1994

Today's Liturgy, cover art using *It Is Finished*, Lent, 1994

Biblical Israel: A People's History, Fortress Press, cover art using *Lachish,* 1993

State of the Arts: Bezalel to Mapplethorpe, Crossway Books, essay on Bowden's art, 1991

Art for Faith's Sake, Evangelical Lutheran Church of American collection catalog, reproduction of *It Is Finished,* 1989

Outlook, Jewish Women's League, *Lachish* used for cover art 1988

The Jewish Calendar 5745, cover art using *Megiddo,* 1984-5

They Cried to the Lord, Fortress Press, cover art using *Hebrew Harpists,* 1984

Colorado Homes, photo of collagraph, February 1982

Jewish Yellow Pages, write up and reproduction of *He Spake,* 1980

The States-Item, Art Out of the Bible, article on Bowden's art, New Orleans, LA, 1979

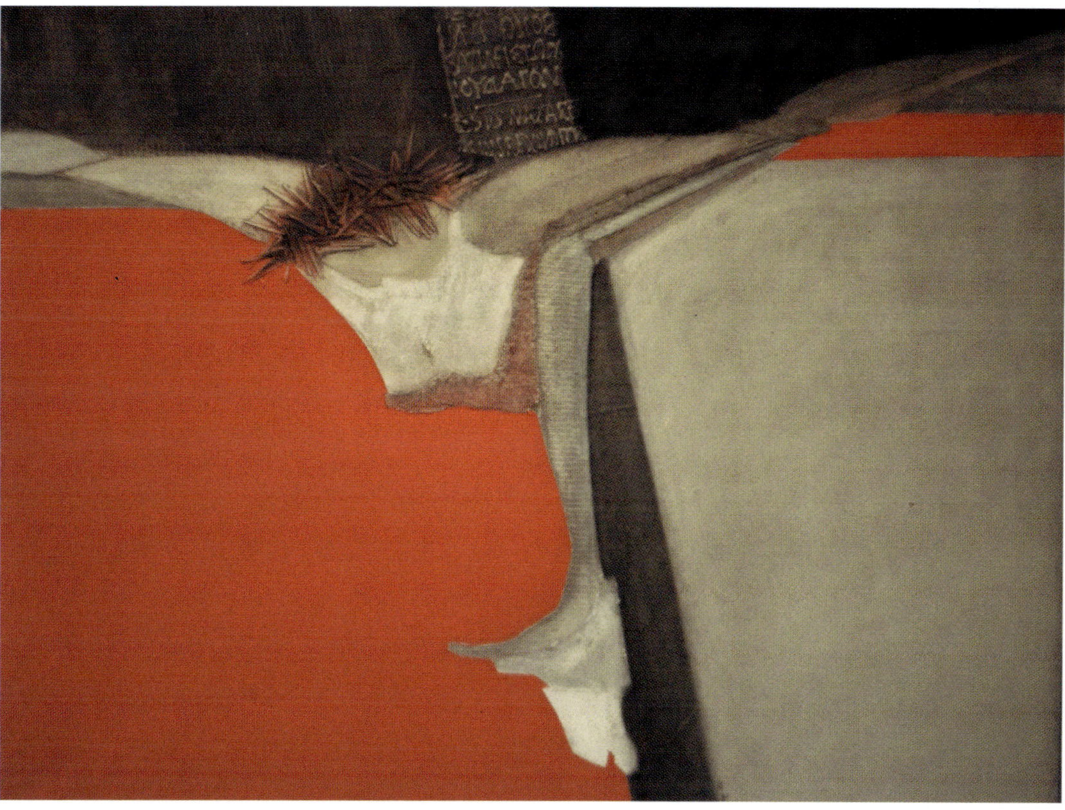

FIGURE 140
CRUCIFIXION
Oil collage
1972
40 x 48

Contributors

FR. TERRENCE E. DEMPSEY, S.J., is a Jesuit priest and the Founding Director of the Museum of Contemporary Religious Art (MOCRA) at Saint Louis University in St. Louis, Missouri. Fr. Dempsey holds a Master's in English and a Master's in art history from Saint Louis University; and a Master's of Divinity from the Jesuit School of Theology at Berkeley. In 1991, he received his doctorate in art history and religion at the Graduate Theological Union in Berkeley in conjunction with the University of California at Berkeley, while studying under the direction of Jane Daggett Dillenberger and John Dillenberger and Peter Selz. Fr. Dempsey is also the author of numerous articles and a frequent lecturer.

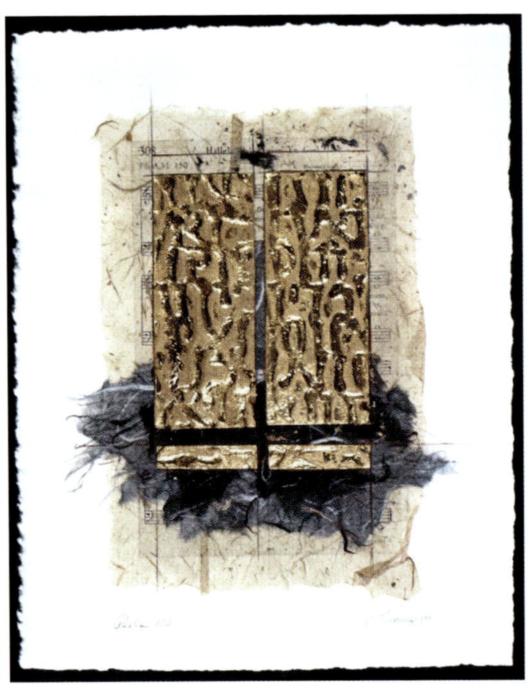

ENA GIURESCU HELLER is Executive Director, Museum of Biblical Art, New York City. She has a PhD in art history from the Institute of Fine Arts, New York University, with a specialty in medieval art and architecture. She has taught art history at the College of the Holy Cross and Manhattanville College, and was the founding director of the Gallery at the American Bible Society. She is contributing editor of the volume *Reluctant Partners: Art and Religion in Dialogue* (2004) and of the exhibition catalogue *Icons or Portraits? Images of Jesus and Mary from the Collection of Michael Hall* (2001), and a contributor to the forthcoming volume *Women's Space. Parish, Place and Gender in the Middle Ages* (2005).

BRUCE HERMAN is a painter who lives and works north of Boston. He is professor of art, chair of the department of art and gallery director at Gordon College. His paintings have been exhibited nationally and internationally. He has been the recipient of many grants and awards including Pew and Lilly Foundation grants and the Philip Guston Award from Boston University. His work is housed in several museum collections including the Vatican Museum of Modern Religious Art and the Armand Hammer Museum at UCLA.

EDWARD KNIPPERS is a distinguished artist with over 150 awards and exhibitions including: The Prize of Salzburg in printmaking from Oskar Kokoschka's School of Vision; *Setting the Stage,* Los Angeles County Museum of Art; *Spiritual Impact, The Paintings of Edward Knippers,* The Virginia Museum of Fine Arts; *Violence and Grace,* The University of Oklahoma Museum of Art; *The Naked Truth, Biblical Paintings by Edward Knippers,* Mill River Gallery. His work has been published in *Life, Christianity Today, The Critic, The Washington Post, Image, The Washington Times, New American Paintings, The Dallas Morning News, The Baltimore Sun, Christianity and the Arts, The Richmond News Leader,* and *The New Art Examiner.*

KAREN MULDER has, since 1981, taught internationally on modern and contemporary art as a faith expression, cofounding Christians in the Arts Networking, Inc. and serving on the boards of the Newington-Cropsey Cultural Study Center, the C.S. Lewis Foundation, and Christians in the Visual Arts, for which she organized conferences and seminar tracks.

The Art of **Sandra Bowden**

After teaching at Messiah College and Union University, she returned to academia as DuPont and Governors Fellow in Architectural History at the University of Virginia, writing a dissertation on postwar glass installations in Germany, continuing to contribute critiques to *American Arts Quarterly, Material Religions,* and various artists' monographs or book projects.

JAMES ROMAINE teaches art history at Bethel University's New York Center for Arts and Media Studies. He is a PhD candidate at the Graduate Center of the City University of New York, writing his dissertation on the art of Tim Rollins and K.O.S. He is a frequent lecturer on faith and the visual arts and has authored numerous articles, in the *Art Journal of the College Art Association, American Arts Quarterly,* and *Image: A Journal of the Arts and Religion,* and books, including *Objects of Grace: Conversations on Creativity and Faith.*

WAYNE ROOSA is professor of art history/department chair at Bethel University, St. Paul, Minnesota. His BFA and BA were earned at the University of Colorado, Boulder; his MA and PhD at Rutgers University in New Jersey. His catalogue essays on American painter Stuart Davis have been published internationally. He is an annual contributor to *Image* and has twice served as juror for the NEH Summer Grants, as well as for the Minnesota State Arts Board grants. He was an Andrew Mellon Research Fellow the Metropolitan Museum of Art in New York, and an NEH grant recipient for work on Stuart Davis.

JEAN BLOCH ROSENSAFT, Director of the Hebrew Union College-Jewish Institute of Religion Museum in New York, previously served as assistant director of education at The Jewish Museum in New York and coordinator of educational publications

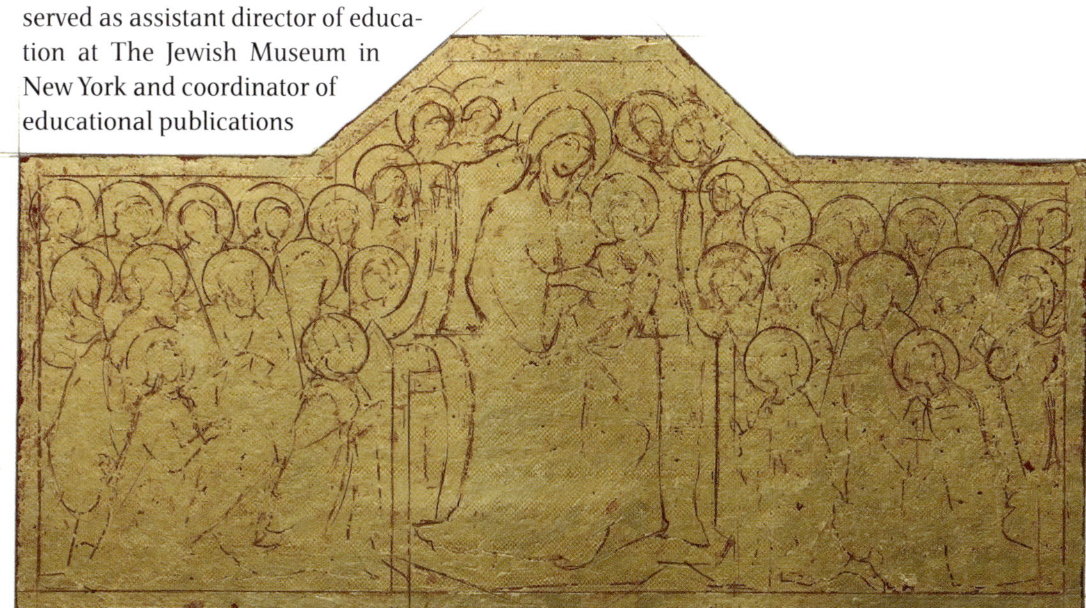

and school programs at The Museum of Modern Art in New York. A member of the United States Holocaust Memorial Museum's Collections and Acquisitions Committee, she is a past officer of the Council of American Jewish Museums. Among the exhibitions she has curated are *"Chagall and the Bible," "Justice in Jerusalem Revisited: The Eichmann Trial,"* and *"Rebirth After the Holocaust: The Bergen-Belsen Displaced Persons Camp, 1945–1950."*

FIGURE 142
MAESTÀ AFTER DUCCIO DI BUONINSEGNA (ACTIVE 1308–1311)
Mixed media drawing with 22-carat gold leaf
1998
16 x 21

Other Titles from Square Halo Books Featuring Sandra Bowden . . .

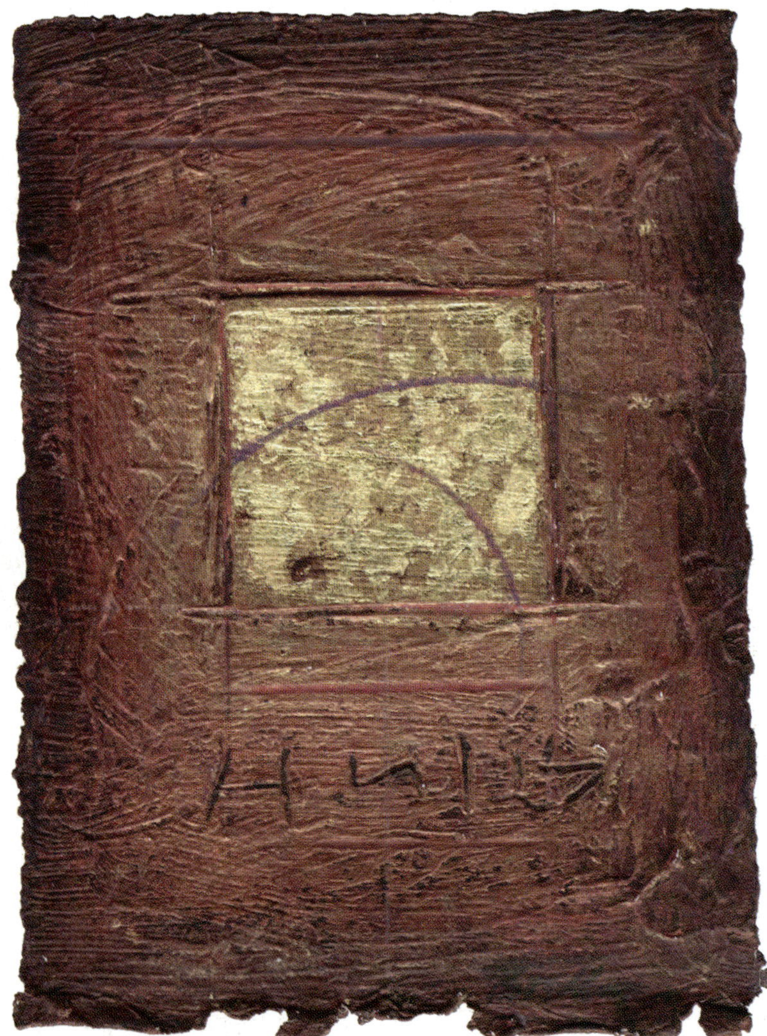

TITLE I Acrylic mixed media, 1993, 6 1/2 x 4 1/2

IT WAS GOOD: MAKING ART TO THE GLORY OF GOD

A collection of thirteen essays covering a wide range of topics focused on the practice of making art from a Christian worldview. "It will help you think Christianly about art, stimulate you to be creative for God's glory, introduce you to some artists who are seeking to glorify God in their work, and . . . cause you to stop and worship the One whose glory is beautiful beyond all imagining."

—*Critique*

OBJECTS OF GRACE: CONVERSATIONS ON CREATIVITY AND FAITH

"[A] colorful and concise collection of interviews and art from some of America's most intriguing Christian artists . . .. The sheer beauty of the design and production values of this book is itself a major achievement, one that gives hope both for the church and the larger culture."

—*Image: A Journal of the Arts & Religion*

FAITH + VISION: 25 YEARS OF CHRISTIANS IN THE VISUAL ARTS

"CIVA has been, for 25 years, a unique organization that has demonstrated that religion has not completely vanished from art with the advent of modernism. It has been a bridge between the worlds of art and religion, and a source of information, support, and nurturing for artists exploring the long tradition of Christian art and iconography.

The handsome volume is a well-deserved homage to this remarkable organization. I hope it will help not only understand the history of CIVA and its community of talented artists, but also inspire a wider, interfaith dialogue about the relationship between art and religion."

—*Ena Heller, Director of the Museum of Biblical Art* (MOBIA)

w w w . S q u a r e H a l o B o o k s . c o m